FIRE

WORKS BY ANAÏS NIN

FIRE

From *A JOURNAL OF LOVE*

The Unexpurgated Diary
of Anaïs Nin

1934–1937

With a Preface by Rupert Pole
and Biographical Notes and Annotations by
Gunther Stuhlmann

HARCOURT BRACE & COMPANY

New York   San Diego   London

Library of Congress Cataloging-in-Publication Data
Nin, Anaïs, 1903–1977.
[Diary of Anaïs Nin. 1934–1937. Selections]
Fire: from "A journal of love": the unexpurgated diary of Anaïs
Nin, 1934–1937/with a preface by Rupert Pole
and biographical notes and annotations by Gunther Stuhlmann.—1st ed.
p.   cm.
Includes index.
ISBN 0-15-100088-3
1. Nin, Anaïs, 1903–1977—Diaries. 2. Women authors,
American—20th century—Diaries.   I. Title.
PS3527.I865Z466   1995
818'.5203—dc20   94-41645

Designed by Lisa Peters
Printed in the United States of America
First edition
A B C D E

CONTENTS

PREFACE

Fire is the third volume of the "Journal of Love" series, following *Henry and June* and *Incest*.

From 1931, when she began her first love affair with Henry Miller, Anaïs Nin engaged in a lifelong search for the perfect love and confided this search to her diary. (The discipline of daily writing in her diary since 1914 had given Anaïs the uncanny ability to describe her deepest emotions at "white heat" immediately following an event.) She continued her diary—always written by hand—until her death in 1977. The 35,000 pages are now in the Special Collections Department of UCLA, where they are available to scholars.

In the 1920s, after John Erskine and others told Anaïs that her diary contained her best writing, she began to explore ways to publish the diary without hurting others. Later Henry Miller told her to publish "the whole thing—let it all hang out." Anaïs devised a number of plans to publish the diary: transforming the diary into fiction, doing it as a diary but with fictitious names, or making it a diary with both real and fictitious names. None of these satisfied Anaïs's need to protect her husband and others, however, and she turned to writing fiction.

Finally, in the mid-1950s, tired of receiving only underground recognition, she decided to publish the diary with real names and to edit out her personal life, her husband, and her lovers. The first edited diary, published in 1966, had no volume number: the cover simply said *The Diary of Anaïs Nin*, since no one, not even Anaïs, thought there would be a volume two. But after the overwhelming reception to "Diary One," Anaïs went on to edit and publish six more volumes, continuing to the very end of her life.

Much earlier, at the beginning of our relationship, Anaïs told me she did not want me to read the unedited diaries. I respected her wish. But in the early 1970s, when we were preparing the diaries to go to UCLA, Anaïs said, "It is now time for you to read the diaries. I want you to read them all."

I sat for five days and read the 35,000 pages.

"Do you judge me?" Anaïs asked.

"No. You had the courage to live out your dreams and to write about them. Someday this must be published."

"All right, this is your task. I want you to publish the diaries just as I wrote them."

The publication of "A Journal of Love," the unexpurgated diary of Anaïs Nin, began in 1986 with *Henry and June*. Nothing of importance has been deleted from the published volumes. The chronology follows exactly Anaïs's entries in her diary. The grammar and punctuation reflect Anaïs's "white heat" writing.

In *Fire*, the present volume, the setting moves back and forth between Europe and America. Anaïs continues her relationship with her husband, Hugh, and her love relationship with both Henry Miller and Dr. Otto Rank. The break with Rank is, however, inevitable, as is, perhaps, the search for the "man who would deliver me from all of them." And so appears Gonzalo Moré: "The tiger who dreams. A tiger without claws." Anaïs remains true to her philosophy of love. "I came back [to France] to live my own life—to find my self, but that is a dismal necessity compared to that of loving . . . loving comes first . . . loving, losing, yielding."

Anaïs's reality cannot be described in facts, as Anaïs has herself best said: "I live in a sort of furnace of affections, loves, desires, inventions, creations, activities, and reveries. I cannot describe my life in facts because the ecstasy does not lie in the facts, in what happens or what I do, but in what is aroused in me and what is created out of all this. . . . I mean I live a very physical and metaphysical reality together. . . .

"It is true that because of my doubts and anxieties *I only believe in fire*. It is true that when I wrote the word *fire* on this volume I did not know what I know today, that all I have written about June, who only believed in the fire, is true about me. That this is the story of my incendiary neurosis! *I only believe in fire*.

"Life. Fire. Being myself on fire I set others on fire. Never death. Fire and life. *Le jeux*."

As I noted in my preface to *Incest*, when the "Journal of Love" series of Anaïs Nin's unexpurgated diaries is complete, we will have an extraordinary lifetime record of the emotional growth of a creative artist, a writer with the technique to describe her deepest emotions and the courage to give this to the world.

—Rupert Pole
Executor, The Anaïs Nin Trust

Los Angeles
January 1995

N O T E

The text of *Fire* is taken from diary books forty-eight through fifty-two, as numbered by Anaïs Nin. Diary forty-eight is untitled, but titles for the other four are respectively: *Révolte, Drifting, Vive la Dynamite and Nanankepichu,* and *Fire.*

All translations of passages in French or Spanish were made by Jean L. Sherman. Lisa Guest has offered invaluable help in the preparation of the typescript.

DECEMBER 1934

*M*Y SHIP BROKE THE SPEED RECORD SAILING TO-
ward New York. It was night and not morn-
ing when I arrived—fittingly, for the night is now the beginning for
me and the root of all days. The band was playing, and the skyscrapers
were twinkling with a million eyes, seemingly standing on black air;
and a man was whispering: "Listen, honey, I love you, listen to me,
honey, I love you. Honey, you're marvelous. Isn't it grand, honey, to
arrive in New York while I make love to you. I'm mad about you,
honey. You won't do me wrong? You won't forget me, honey? I love
your hair, honey. Listen to me . . ."

"The music is too loud," I said. "I can only hear the music." But
I was looking for Otto Rank, for the *other,* looking at the lights, the
Babylonian city, the wharves, the people, and not "honey" but "dar-
ling," and eyes shining like patent leather, with a love taller than the

skyscrapers, a love inlaid with a million eyes and windows, and tongues.

His eyes. "Oh, darling!"

But it was a dream. We were wrapped in cotton, in silk threads, in webs, in moss, in fog, in the sea—flavor of distance to be annihilated.

My room. Which, he said, had been the Waiting Room. Laughter begins to flower and tinkle, like a box full of savings. We had been saving it, dime by dime, for use today. That was to be the texture, the perfume and the color of our alliance: humor and a long-saved laughter.

Very slowly, with hands, tongues, mouths, we unwrapped and untied ourselves, laying open gifts. Gave birth to each other again, as separate bodies who enjoy collision. Not the lovers of Paris, whose caresses could not become prolonged indefinitely into space, daily living, daily motions and actions.

I've found the one I can play with, play really, play the woman, play everything in my head or body with a blood rhythm. Not the play of ideas where the instinct rebels against realization. He says, "I have an idea." And he invents, creates, fantastically and magically— life. Every detail of life.

I am not alone, embroidering. He leaps, he directs, he realizes. He is more adept at realizing, more adroit in details; he can be the criminal and the detective, Huckleberry Finn and Tom Sawyer, Don Quixote, June, Louise, or Dr. Rank, analyzing in his strange way, which is generating his own self, born in our love.

New lovers. With all New York pointing to ascension, to exultation, to climax, to heightening. New York, the brilliant giant toy with such soft-oiled hinges. In our hands, in his nervous, quick hands. I have an idea, and in a new and sudden rhythm we began to swim: retorts, answers, response, interplay . . . my world, shared.

I knew of the sameness of feeling, but not of the sameness of thinking. The love of embroidery, of complexity, for the love of disentangling.

He read me from *Huckleberry Finn*. The freeing of the Negro, with the adventurous spirit emphasized. The claptrap of literature.

The additions, complications, circuitous manner. We found in there our "coat of arms," the game spirit, the creations and inventions.

One of the first things he took me to see was the "magic door" [at Pennsylvania Station]. All in metal, it opens just when your shadow touches it. He liked to see me glide up to it.

I have never known such a joy. I live continuously in fantasy, yet in human reality too. My instincts are at peace. No control, revolt, distaste, or conflict. And my imagination is free. I am myself. His faith in me gives me wings.

On the clearest, sunniest day, he took me to the Empire State Building.

To be aware of New York because it is our city and it matches our mood, and to be in complete possession of it, too. Not intimidated. Insolently allied, the complicity of New York favoring our pleasures and joys. Acoustics good for laughter.

The theater. It was deficient, and so he began to read all manner of things into it. I said to "write it." We rewrote the plays. We invented the play. And I mentioned my admiration of Ferdinand Bruckner. Coincidence. Someone in a Vienna paper had thought "Bruckner" was Rank's pen name. So I baptized Rank "the playwright."

We sit, equally breathless, before the curtain rising. Only now the magic world does not lie behind the curtain. It has spread into one vast symphony: our talks, our ideas, our love, his work, on all levels at once, as I always wished to live. Living in every cell. Unfolding a thousand new selves.

Broadway. Bath of electricity. The cellophane symphony. The transparent brilliance over all objects. This texture which is not real.

Breakfast in the dim hotel restaurant. I give him the essence of the day's news. That is, humorous juxtapositions by clipping phrases, unexpectedly arranged, giving a hilarious result. That I slip under his door while he is analyzing a patient. As soon as the patient leaves he reads it. He comes to my room, laughing.

With him, I have struck the area of humor, born of the shock of the trip. A trip is like throwing dice. The days are bright and shiny here. One feels new every day. The poetry of smooth motion, of all your desires being answered, of all your needs divined and immediately accomplished.

People I don't dare to look at too closely. They seem a bit deficient. They too are cellophane, a sort of perpetual Christmas morning. I don't know. I'm really in love with Him and with buildings, granite, electricity, 6,400 windows, *survoltage,* pressure, streets, and crowds. I don't listen to Americans. I play with Him in the city of tomorrow. A good acoustic for laughter!

In a letter to Rank I had said I didn't want to dance; that was acting for the world. I preferred acting all the roles for him.

We began playfully with "The Secretary." The secretary was not so good at first, because of the curse of her Father's severity and his: *"Tu n'as pas l'esprit scientifique."* So she trembled and shook and made errors born of her panic. But when he saw that she had headed a letter with the date of her sailing instead, he was only amused, even pleased. My mind was obviously on our own story. At his laughter, and tolerance, and tenderness, the secretary was surprised, moved, and magically affected. That is, she became a good secretary. The next day she was cool and applied briskly a certain gift for order and quick action under his dexterous guidance.

The secretary left her work at six. An hour later we were at the restaurant, exchanging the most amazing answers, retorts. It is like the marvelous talking one does with one's self, regretting never to attain the same brilliance publicly.

Ripples and ripples of humor and irony.

The theater.

Broadway. Creamy drinks. Harlem.

Sitting in dusky lights with Negroes unleashed.

Never imagined he could not dance. Never imagined Dr. Rank could have led such a serious life that he had never danced. But he is not Dr. Rank. He's a little man whose blood can throb insanely.

"Dance with me."

I make him forget his fear and his awkwardness. I just dance. At first he is stiff, he trips, is dislocated, lost. But at the end of that first dance he began to dance. Magical. And the joy it gave him. "A new

4

world—oh, my darling, an entirely new world you have taken me into."

His joy gave me joy. The first step of his dancing with all the meaning I give to dancing. All around us the Negroes wild, dancing wildly. And he sauntering, awkwardly, as if he were learning to walk. I didn't teach. I danced and he danced along with me. He was amazed at my gaiety. I did want to dance with the Negroes, freely and wildly, secretly, but this was so strange, my leading him into a dreamlike freedom of motion, after he had given me the freedom of motion to live. Giving back pleasure, music, and self-forgetting, for all that he gave me. No more thinking. No more thinking. I made him drunk.

Driving home. Radio in the taxi. More music. Laughter in his eyes. Gardenias in his buttonhole and on my fur collar. Gardenias, wild orchids, white Georgian violets, silver paper, and fake pearl-headed pins.

An orgiastic night. "Still dancing," he said; "love like a dance." Wild abandon.

He wakes at five in the morning, so aware; he is as excited as I was with Henry [Miller], unable to sleep for the wonder. He awakes passionate and brimming with ideas. I am more sleepy, more relaxed. A certain ultimate keenness has worn away. I enjoy lying back, swinging, lulled by happiness. It seems to me he is giving me the great, keen new love I gave Henry, the *active* love, the leaping, restless, wide-awake love in which I rest as Henry rested in mine. I dream, I sleep, I receive. He is awake, aware, full of activity, leadership, inspiration.

Harlem. He could not forget it. He was eager to return. He dreamed of it. Could hardly come to the end of his hard day's work.

He works in Room 905 [at the Adams hotel], where there is a salon and a bedroom. I have a room next door to his, which is like a sitting room.

Soon we talked about my need of another address. I did not want to have another, did not want to fragment myself again. No. But there was no other practical way. Again, I joked about the two toothbrushes. I resisted it. But all along I was thinking, If I have to have another room it will be at the Barbizon Plaza Hotel. I wanted to see the old place with new eyes, remember John [Erskine] to make certain that I had forgotten him. Rank helped me to decide, first by his natural decisiveness, then because he liked the idea of my being occasionally in another place that would be new for him, and away from his office and from Dr. Rank. He seeks to escape that role as much as I seek to escape being Mrs. Hugh Guiler.

We came together and chose the smallest room, as wide as the bed is long, with a tiny desk and bureau, all in russet brown, very much like the inside of a valise or a jewel box.

I moved, partially, away from Rank the Monday after my arrival. We decided he would help me with the details of my deceptive games, because he can be more accurate and more realistic, and because he says the woman in me always leaves a clue, wants to be discovered, mastered, wants to lose.

In this room I am now alone, in the evening. He had to go to a dinner and I did not want to go out with anybody else. I wanted my diary, because for the first time my most beautiful game of all has turned into tragedy. I mailed, by mistake, a letter for Hugh to Henry, and one for Henry to Hugh.* ("With a desire to let them know, to escape," Rank later said.) At the same hour that I received Henry's cable saying, "Anaïs be careful Hugh received first letter with check envelopes interchanged disregard Bremen letter OK now," Rank had made the following note between two analyses: "Telling to all, wanting all to know. Secret impossible."

All those days before, we had spent our time in our beautiful world. Gilbert and Sullivan plays, the American Ballet, a day in the hotel at Hartford. His letters, early in the morning (I only sleep in his bed on holidays), slipped under the door with a tiny frog.

---

* The letter to Henry Miller, dated November 26, 1934, was not, as he later complained, a "love letter," but a brief and somewhat neutral report of Anaïs Nin's activities. It contained two checks for a hundred francs each, one for Miller and one for the Hungarian photographer Brassaï, who had taken some photos of Nin in Paris before her departure. The letter, incidentally, served to reassure her husband, Hugh Guiler, about the nature of her relationship to Miller. See *A Literate Passion: Letters of Anaïs Nin and Henry Miller, 1932–1953*, edited and with an introduction by Gunther Stuhlmann (San Diego: Harcourt Brace Jovanovich, 1987), pp. 233–246.

Letters full of a frightening understanding of me. I lock them in a kind of niche in my desk, which has a little door. That's the castle. Later, he adds to it a tiny penguin, and a small candlestick he stole from the doll house at the Child Guidance Institute. (He wanted to bring me the whole house. He asked the startled directors for it!)

In the Gilbert and Sullivan play the soldier gets a cramp trying to play the role of a poet. I feel now that will never happen to me while I am with him.

I went out and sent him a miniature of a Japanese garden, with a little house and bridge. Our garden. As a pre-vision of seeing *The Mikado*. With an invitation from "Anita Aguilera"* to come to Room 703 at the Barbizon Plaza, at eleven, after his lecture. He sends a beautiful red plant, which is shedding its leaves tonight while the radio plays blues.

He came and entered into the playing spirit with his strange, divining love. Came telling, as always, of the magic he had been working during the day.

The night I saw the American Ballet performance: another surrender, another abdication. I cannot take to the stage, always because of a man. Single, not collective performances! I watched the dancing with delight and restlessness and despair. All art, all dancing, all imagining given to love, everything given to love, to love. She turned, turned like a disk, turned, and in the center of the stage, as if she could never stop. Other women touched her, embraced her; she went on turning. Wheel and earth, stars and cycles, turning, watch and wheels turning. A man embraced her and she ceased. At this I dissolved into an inexplicable sadness, which Rank felt without looking at me.

The next day I was asking him questions about his childhood. He suddenly gushed out endless stories. Then stopped to weep. "Nobody ever asked me this before. I have to listen to others all the time . . ." I heard about the mischievous and dreamy boy, Huckleberry Finn. His wife had only been able to take care of the *sick* boy, as Hugh

---

* A stage name Anaïs Nin used for some of her dance recitals in Paris.

took care of the sick child in me. But we were lonely. We had nobody to play with. The gay child, the inventive child, the spirited and wild child, was lonely.

That night, in the Hartford hotel room, we discovered definitely the twinship. He says I think as he does. I guess what he is going to say. I catch it so quickly, the feelings, emotions, all the same, the sense of ecstasy, the extravagance, the quickness, the seeing through, the attitude toward love, the selectivity, the imaginings, the created roles.

The more fantastically we play, the more real the love becomes. And he touches all things with the magic of meaning. Finding the meaning does not wither him as it does others. So he connects all that happens to us with his analysis, synthesizing, creating, interchanging, giving. On the train he writes his lectures. In the hotel room he wrote notes on "Life and Play." For this we disguised ourselves, he in my velvet kimono, I in his hat and cigar (the hat we discovered one night on Broadway, a Huckleberry Finn hat, and bought immediately), so that he could penetrate feminine psychology and feelings. I was at the typewriter and wrote my own ideas, with the red ribbon, in between.

JANUARY 3, 1935

THE UNCANNY SENSITIVITY AND INTUITION. I CAN hide nothing from him. He can read every nuance of my moods. He weeps easily, laughs. Oh, to be so alive, to be alive. I'm weeping and laughing. It's marvelous.

Life a dizzy whirling. Rank wooing me with understanding; with his imagination, which is infinite; with his intricate and dazzling mind; with Huck, the Huck who got lost in Dr. Rank—freckled, homely, tattered, clownish, rough hewn. Then Henry, awakening slowly to my trickeries, revealed by the mixed-up letters, and awakening to his passion for me, suffering, writing madly, cabling, and treating me as he treated June. I become June and then his love for me becomes like his love for June—passion. So the long mad letters come, and the cables. And Huck, Huck begins to suffer exactly as I suffered when I first loved Henry, when he was still full of June and I tried to spare him, as Henry did not spare me, spare him the confidences, etc. But Rank cannot be deceived. We talked, talked. He knows everything, except that my love for Henry is not quite dead, will not die. He knows everything, except that Henry's love letters move me. A mad life.

He awakens early, at six. He cannot sleep for the wonder, whereas the wonder makes me more and more human, more hungry, more sleepy, more natural. He awakens at six and comes to my room. I love that moment when he comes into my arms; it is Huck then, not Dr. Rank, a natural, spontaneous, impulsive, shiny-eyed Huck, with his everlasting "I have an idea." The brightness, the wakefulness I had for Henry, who was sleepy. Now I am heavy with sleep. I laugh at Huck's new pranks, at his ideas, but I fall asleep again. He is restless and alert. He takes a bath. He feels as I felt when I waited for Henry's awakening. He has figured out the sleep, too: "Child of nature. You belong to the night. I have to give you up to the night." A universe perpetually deepened and embellished. I thought really that it was his snoring that kept me awake, and that for the sake of sleep I had to run away and find another reason. I said I was so aware of him that I couldn't sleep. He feared it was his too-much love, his obsessional attentiveness, his overwhelming worship. We had one evening of misery. He felt I was withdrawing because he was loving too much. I had, it is true, found it strange and even frightening, this never being alone, after I had complained of loneliness. No loneliness ever, with that watchful, keen, uncanny knowing being there, all tentacles, all divination.

Cables: "Eternal love, Henry." *Letters:* "Anaïs. Cable me immediately that you are my woman, that you are not betraying me, that you will live with me, that we will be together. . . . I'm desperate.

Say something that will reassure me. . . ." *Cable to Henry:* "I am your woman always, Henry. We will soon be together. I am working for our freedom. Have faith in me."

Huck and I start a scrapbook, a riotously funny one. Huck gives me a little log house. I print on the door of it: Huck and Puck. Do Not Disturb. I give Huck new slippers and with what he wanted to spend on a new typewriter for me, I get him a radio-phonograph. Most of all, we give each other tricks. Tricks and countertricks. Cut out from newspapers, from the *New Yorker,* postcards from the aquarium. We invent, add, make puns and jokes. No end. Then suddenly we get acutely, profoundly serious. Then he is grateful, stutteringly grateful for the life I give him, the human life, the dancing, the enjoyment, the materialization, concretization, sensualization. From spectator and analyst to actor, full actor.

JANUARY 7, 1935

*H*ENRY ON THE SEA. COMING WITH WORDS OF great and eternal love. I radio him: "You have boarded the magic ship again."

I danced for Huck, spontaneously, in my Spanish costumes, and he was moved because he said I was his creation, dancing, and also that he was dancing in me.

Telephone calls. Flowers. Red roses. Courtship. Flattery. Adulation. Carnations. Henry is suffering, but he has become real. Our love has become real to him. I buy cigarettes, magazines, little things, clothes, for his room, 703 [at the Barbizon Plaza]. I prepare the room for him. I prepare to envelop him. In his last letter he begs me, "Be tender to me, be loving. I need you so much. I have given myself to you." This new love for me, for the Me who ran away, who forgot him, who was cruel: I want it. I have become June. He uses the same phrases, but they sound more sincere. Suffering. Real suffering. Real tears.

Hugh, too, is running after the *feu follet,* the will-o'-the-wisp. Obsessed, courting, wooing.

The core of my life is a tragic and deep situation which I cannot face. I cannot abandon Hugh. I cannot hurt Henry. I cannot hurt Huck. I belong to all of them. So I think of orchids. I send [my brother] Joaquin a cable because he is giving his concert in Havana tonight. I write Mother, who is in Mallorca.

Erskine telephoned one hour after he saw Joaquin and heard I was here. I did not telephone back. I wrote a note that I was going away. I pushed him off.

The core: Henry, my Henry. Mad, like Knut Hamsun, false, and full of literature, and lacking in understanding. Henry.

Huck, Huck, so true in his feelings, so deep in his feelings, so deep in his thoughts, laughing and weeping.

No tragedy. We don't want tragedy. If only I can continue with the lies, the illusions, oh, the lies to Hugh, and yet not all lies. When I received his red roses New Year's night, I hated them, and yet I was so moved. Moved. I kept one under my pillow. Unalterable ties. Indissoluble ties. I can only add, expand. I cannot break, dissolve, push away.

Orchids. My patient Miss X, the dancer. Outwitting the neurotic. Like a chess game. Huck coming in between his patients, always running. Our shopping day. Black tulle underwear and dancing slippers. Our talks. Our fairy tale. Our creations. Too beautiful, too fragile, he says. Too subtle. The twins. Impulsiveness, emotion. Abandon, absolutism. We give, give. I am given back all that I ever gave, by Huck. All. Given, enveloped, worshiped. "I worship you." But we are human for each other. He is Huck and I Puck—not gods.

He says I am so honest in my feelings. The lies are only in the head. The feelings are in the diary. I didn't even go into the lies much in the diary. It was the feeling that was important to me. There I never lie. I lie only for others.

Henry on the sea. I had to prepare his room. I had to take him again into my arms. I don't know why.

When Huck and I went away to New Haven, I got sick. As sick as when I abandoned my father to meet Henry in Avignon.

J A N U A R Y 2 6 , 1 9 3 5

*H*ENRY ARRIVING ON THE FOG-BOUND SHIP, DE-
layed, arriving slowly, a changed man, a trem-
bling man, but whole, determined, awake. He had been writing: "Fear, fear, what a prey I have been to fear. The great fear of losing you. The fear that I had not lived up to your image of me. That almost destroyed me. I was so nearly lost that I feared I would go mad."

As soon as I kiss him I know that I love him with a blind instinct beyond all reason, with all his defects. Yet he seems new, strong, different. Yes. And Rank, the analyst, interprets: "Changed because he lost you, only changed because he lost you, but nothing in your relationship can change. It is too late."

Too late for changes, too late perhaps for explanations and ideological webs, but the love goes on, the love goes on, blind to laws and warnings and even to wisdom and to fears. And whatever that love is, perhaps an illusion of a new love, I want it, I can't resist it, my whole being melts in one kiss, my knowledge melts, my fears melt, my blood dances, my legs open. Henry. His mouth. His hands. His wholeness, his awareness. He is full of me now, full of me, aware. I take him to the little room Rank and I chose and wanted to use for dancing. The radio was on. There were flowers, little gifts, books, magazines. It was small, warm, glowing. Henry was dazed, dazed, and yet all alive, alive with pain and jealousy, asking questions, kissing me. We got into bed. Everything as before, yet new. How he gets into my being by all the pores and cells, with his voice, his blue eyes, his skin, everything. An invasion. I read the letter he wrote me on board. He talked wildly about not wanting me to work anymore, wanting to protect me, wanting to marry me, wanting to take me definitely away from everybody. We wept with joy. "Oh, Anis, Anis, Anis,* I need you more than I ever needed a human being. I need you like life itself."

I was weeping, denying any treachery, weeping at a life I could not understand, for now that I had hurt Henry, run away from him, tortured him, he loved me so much more, loved me insanely, and I was being given more than June—his body, his soul, his creation. He hated his writing now, he hated all the sacrifices made for it, he hated having permitted me to be a whore for him, as he allowed June to be.

Yet, with all that, I had the courage to leave, to say I was staying with Hugh's family to calm Hugh's doubts and prevent him from coming. I left at midnight, wondering and fearing how it would feel to meet Huck, and if I would be torn and pulled as before.

I must have become accustomed to double feelings, double loves, double lives, for I met Huck without change of feeling, knowing anyway that my love for Huck was much less strong; but I could take his caresses, I could sleep in his bed, I could weep a little with compassion for Henry, I could act that it was nothing but compassion, I could be tender and unshaken; yet I was acting, I was acting, I wanted to be with Henry.

The next day I found Henry still broken, low voiced, hurt, happy, churned. He had noted down his awakening, weeping with a desire to dig himself a groove somewhere, with me. Hurt that I had left him alone for that night. Hurt, yet knowing he was saved by his strength to come, and had saved us. Lying on the bed we raved about the myths and legends, about Tristan and Isolde, about his struggle to reach me, his struggle through the fog. In Paris, he had suffered

* Henry Miller habitually mispronounced her name as "Anis."

agonies. Had not eaten or slept well since the mixed-up letters, spent all his food money on cables, indifferent to all, lonely, desperately jealous, realizing suddenly all the lies I had told, realizing the gratuitous lies, the unnecessary lies, like Hugh saying he would get me on the boat with him even if I were ill, and all the time I knew I was sailing alone. But by this I wanted Henry to know how difficult it was for me to leave him, how I was resisting, by getting sick, sailing away. He analyzed my face, my expressions, my appearance of profound sincerity. Henry has come changed, determined I will no longer make sacrifices for him, no longer go begging for him. Fighting for me. The room so small and warm, and he had brought over the Spanish shawl, the orange velvet bed cover, the orange coffee cups, symbols of Louveciennes and the studio. His tears, his sensibility, his shivering still from the violent shock I gave him, trembling still from the violent new birth. Had I finally given birth to Henry Miller as man?

I had said I was staying with the Guilers to quiet Henry. The next morning he was in despair again. He had in his hands five or six telephone messages. The telephone had been ringing constantly. Men. Men's voices. Calling repeatedly. Henry asking questions, overflowing with hatred of Rank. His voice enveloping me, flowing into me, his mouth so rich, his eyes so intense, his skin so tender. My love for him alone no lie, no lie, so outgoing, such a loss of the self, to the point of losing the happiness Huck gave me, losing and giving everything away, Huck too, to Henry, to blind love . . .

Jealousy and caresses, deeper caresses, greater and keener desire. Darkness, pain, perversity, tragedy, and more and more human love.

Loss of wisdom, of heroism, of secrecy. Human love. I grow more real to him as I become less and less good, more woman, more defective, more evil, more woman and more love, more desire, more pain and more joy.

Return to Huck. Huck, to whom I cannot lie because he is so much like me that he knows. He knows everything that is happening. He knows Huck will lose because he is too good. I see it as Huck being as noble as I was when Henry struggled with his love for June.

Noble, heroic, truthful—at the cost of his happiness—full of understanding and forgiveness.

I play tricks to see Henry. Small deceptions. Analyzing my first patient, writing letters for Huck, running errands, calling on Lucrezia Bori with Joaquin, seeing [Theodore] Dreiser twice and refusing to sleep with him, lying down with [George] Turner because Huck is next door, working, and I want to betray him there, on the couch we lie on, in the room he keeps for me, pulling down everything sacred, desecrating, cheapening, only because Huck can come in and see it, because it is Huck's room, and because when Huck comes in I have to act again, innocence and annoyance at being pursued by Turner. Forgetting it all instantly to rush to Dreiser, then to Henry at midnight; arriving late for Huck, who is weeping. Inventing weekends in the country because Huck wants his Saturday and Sunday, then really going on a weekend at the Perkinses', then inventing a night in the country for Huck in order to spend a whole night with Henry, returning with a valise in which I carry the nightgown given to me by Hugh and to be worn only for him, but which I wore for Henry, as well as the red Russian dress Huck gave me for his weekends, on which Henry spilled his glass of port while at a studio party where we met Emil [Schnellock's] friends. Intercepting my last letters to Henry, returned from Paris, because in them I tell him Hugh was coming to explain my not being free at night, then deciding to tell Huck that Hugh is coming over so that Huck will leave for his California tour and I may be with Henry for three weeks. Pretending I will join Huck in New Orleans to help him leave while knowing I won't; pretending Hugh is coming; pretending, pretending. Every day Henry discovers a new lie and his doubts are re-awakened, yet our caresses are so whole that I tell him I marvel at how he can doubt me; how can he imagine I would leave him and go to anybody else after such hours, such intermingling of blood and breath?—which is exactly what I do. My face never showing the lie, because my face shows my feelings and my feelings are a deep, earth-blind love for Henry.

The night Henry and I went out together he insisted on taking me home, which he never does. I showed too clearly the desire not to be taken home to the Guilers. As he had insisted so much, I had given him a false address on East Eighty-ninth Street. Now, while I tried to divert his attention from taking me home, I was forced to acknowledge I had lied about the number because I feared he would come up to the apartment in one of his mad moods and speak to the Guilers or insult them. "God damn you," said Henry. "You are incurable." And then his faith collapsed again, even though two hours before we had been lying in his bed, caressing each other deliriously.

Finally, after stopping off at Fifty-seventh Street, where I coaxed him to drink a soda, thinking he would let me go home alone, I let him walk with me to the bus stop on Fifth Avenue. But seeing the torment and doubt on his face, I said, "All right, come with me. I want you to come. That will reassure you." We got on the bus and while we talked I was thinking quickly that now I must find a house with two entrances. But as I had never been on East Eighty-ninth Street I wondered what I would find on the corner, perhaps a club or a private house, a Vanderbilt mansion. Yes, nearly this, for there was nothing there but a big empty lot on the right and private houses on the left. We walked along the snow-covered sidewalk in the icy cold night, talking sweetly about other things, Henry's voice so vulnerable, until I spied an apartment on the corner of Eighty-ninth Street and Madison Avenue where the Guilers might very well live. Henry kissed me good-night right there, a warm clinging kiss which moved me deeply. And then I made this unbelievable addition to the difficulties of the game. I said, "So that you will see I am telling the truth, the Guilers are on the sixth floor. When I get there I will turn on the light, on and off, once, as a signal that I am there. As [their daughter] Ethel sleeps there, I may not come to the window, but the light will tell you." And I left Henry standing there in front of the house. First of all the front door was locked and I had to ring for the doorman, whom I had not expected to see. Then when I asked him, "There is a door on Madison Avenue, isn't there?"—just to say something because he had asked "Where are you going?" very roughly—he answered, roughly again, "Where are you going? Whose apartment are you looking for?" Then I said, "Nobody's. I just came in here because there was a man following and annoying me. I thought

I might go through and slip out of the other entrance, and get a cab and go home."

"That door is locked for the night. You can't go through there."

"Well, then I'll stay here for a while, until that man goes."

And I sat down in the dark, red-carpeted hall, in a red plush chair, while the doorman paced up and down. Thinking of Henry waiting outside for that light signal, and of Huck waiting for me since midnight, waiting for me with peculiar anxiety because the night before I had not come home at all, had spent the night with Henry (telephoning Huck "from New Canaan" that the car was stuck in the snow, which he knew was not true, so that he could not sleep the rest of the night and I found him in the morning yellow with grief and anger). Sitting there, heart beating, head pounding, mind whirling. Got up and walked cautiously to the door and saw Henry was still waiting in the cold, looking at the window. Pain and laughter, a physical pain out of love for Henry, laughter from some secret demoniac source.

I said to the doorman, "That man is still there. Listen, I must get away somehow. You must do something for me." He called the elevator boy. The elevator boy took me down to the cellar, through a labyrinth of gray hallways. Another elevator boy joined us. I told them about the man following me. Up some stairs, and they unlocked the back garbage door. The garbage cans were lying around. One of the boys went out to get a taxi. I thanked them. They said it was a great pleasure and that New York was a hell of a place for ladies. I got into the taxi. I lay down on the seat so that Henry could not see me as we passed along Madison Avenue.

Huck was sobbing. I could think only of Henry, Henry standing out in the cold, waiting. His kiss. His mouth. Huck was sobbing. He looked pathetic, but I felt only Henry, Henry, cold and tormented. I wept. I said things to Huck, lulling things, terrible things, true things. "You are not the one who should weep. It is you I came to. I struggled to get to you. But I'm here. And Henry is standing outside, waiting in the cold. Why do you cry?"

Thinking, thinking, while the tears washed down my eyelash paint, How can I reach Henry, how can I reach Henry, what will he think, is he back in his room?

"Listen, Huck, above all I don't want Henry to know about you. I just want him to think it is a natural break. I don't want him to be tortured. If I am forced into that it will be like the time I came to you for help."

In a few moments I arouse his pity, especially when I refer to the past, when I came because I was caught between my Father and Henry; especially when I threaten to run away from both him and Henry.

So I won a moment's respite and permission to telephone Henry. I went to my room. Henry was back; he had waited twenty minutes. During the scene with Huck I had thought of what I would say to Henry to explain why the lights did not go on. "I made a mistake about the windows. When I got home, all the lights were on, Hugh's mother and Ethel were up. There were visitors, I could not even go to the window without attracting attention."

But Henry did not worry about the reason. He was full of gratitude for my having tried to reassure him, for my telephoning him, for *attempting* to signal with the lights, grateful and touched for I-don't-know-what, more for the love he felt. Anyway, after hearing his voice I was instantly calm. No tragedy. No discovery. Now I turned to consoling Huck. I began to amuse him; I even made him laugh at the story of the apartment house. I stood in the middle of my room, in my black-lace nightgown, telling the story and laughing, and Huck was marveling, wondering, and smiling.

But I could not bear his caress. I stifled his desire. We were both exhausted. Utterly exhausted.

To lie, to evade tragedy. I cannot be myself without causing tragedy. But tragedy is living. Huck said last night, "I have never lived so intensely, never." Laughing, crying; ecstasy, delirium, peace, exhaustion, passion, pain, joy, peace, illuminations, pain, human life. At six o'clock that morning, after the night I spent with Henry, when Huck knew I was with Henry, he made a note which, among other things, said that following one's instincts alone is human, that faithfulness in love is unnatural, that morality is man-made ideology, that self-denial, which is necessary to be good, is denial of the bad natural self out of self-protection, and thus the most selfish thing of all.

It was part of his all-night struggle against anger and jealousy. He wanted to run away, he wanted to forgive, he acted and felt all that I acted and felt over Henry's weaknesses.

Now I am at once June and Henry to Huck. I act, do, disturb, upset, create tragedy. I am natural, I deceive, I cheat, I am lazy, I tax his forgiveness. Yet he loves me for what I am. Now I am both June and Henry. And Huck is what I was anciently, when I acted heroically, wisely, superhumanly toward Henry. Today I am preeminently human. I weep, laugh; I make scenes. I fight. I lie. I defend myself. I do not try to be good. I give in to my love for Henry. I deceive Huck. I tell him I can't leave for California with him because Hugh is coming, while knowing that Hugh is not coming, and that I am preparing to live with Henry until Hugh comes. I borrow the ring I gave Huck, to have a similar one made for Henry, pretending I am having a seal made. I am always on the point of being discovered by a telephone message, by the mail Henry gets at the Barbizon, by my forgetting my brassiere at Henry's place, the one Huck gave me and knows and would miss, by unconscious slips of the tongue, by saying something about Huck having seen my broken hairbrush and because of this giving me a black lacquer set in a beautiful valise. Every other phrase a lie. To tranquilize Huck when I go out with Henry, to tranquilize Henry.

FEBRUARY 1, 1935

WITH HUCK THINGS GET SO SUBTLE, SO TENUOUS, so psychic that they are impossible to write. He is endowed with uncanny intuition, feels everything, and I have great pains to delude him. Sometimes I can elude his interpretations. As he does not know the truth, he gets lost in his explanations. For example, now he is preparing to leave for California. He wants me to meet him in New Orleans. We planned a few days' vacation there before Henry came. Now I don't want it. Huck buys me a beautiful valise, for New Orleans. He has "N.O." engraved on it. We play with it; he himself fills the black lacquer boxes with powder, cream, etc. All the time I know I am packing for Henry, to join Henry. But I say to Huck, "You see, I am packing for New Orleans. Playing with the idea that I am leaving with you." That makes him happy. I also tell him that until Hugh comes I will stay here in Room 906—but the very day he leaves I am moving in with Henry, into a double room somewhere. So the valise lies on the armchair, and Huck gets me underwear, things I am to wear only for him, but which I will wear for Henry.

Yesterday we had photographs taken. Mine were for Henry, because in Paris I had given all Henry's photos of me to Huck.

The time since I arrived has been so enormous, so fantastic, crowded, that I will never recapture it. Pursuit. I have been pursued as a woman as never before, constantly, by every man I see. I enjoyed it at first. Now it tires me. No rest anywhere. Henry's jealousy. Huck so possessive, intense, absorbing. Too much love, too much love! I am being stifled. I pick up my diary because I am being devoured, dismembered, by love. I love it and I dread it. No self—no freedom; everything, and all of me, outside, entangled, given.

Notes. Visit to Dreiser. Rocking chair in his bedroom. Talks of my "celery stalk" hands. Philosophy of materialism. No soul, belief. "Stay here for the night. You are so exquisitely formed. An individuality, yet unobtrusive." Light of Broadway in large window. "People come to take." He felt I came to give, but mistook nature of gift.

After scene with George Turner I felt the fear of pursuit. Turner and then Dreiser. Weary of being a woman. May be an obscure fear of what happens when you are an exciting woman that keeps you from becoming one. I felt hunted down that day.

Wonderful, Henry's love. "It is only ten in the morning and I am crazily in love." June is canceled out. He gives me the same kind of mad love. Wild and crazy with jealousy. Month of torture in Paris, not sleeping, not eating. Cable from Hugh addressed to Barbizon after I had said Hugh had forced me to stay with his family. Hard to explain. Henry says, "I need you more than any human being in the world. Like life itself. Tell me, tell me what has happened." Begging for the truth. Exactly the Henry he was with June. The wise love become passion because of pain. And I felt the danger, the perversity of it. Meeting the ship, arriving in the fog. Feeling that no matter how I love others, when Henry comes I feel a yearning and stirring of the womb as for none other. He had fought through obstacles to come to me. Knowing his passivity and helplessness, his struggle to come so as not to lose me was a great sign of love. Barbizon room prepared with radio on. The luxury of a new experience for Henry. Showing his torn coat to valet. Not knowing how to act. How this tied up, by contrast, with the night we went to see the "street of early sorrows" where he played as a boy. Night in Brooklyn. Snow. Red-brick house. Dutch village. Little houses and streets. His school. His window. His boy friends. The tin factory. Background of *Black Spring*. Everything in the early pages written in Louveciennes. Night so vivid, yet a dream. Street leading to the ferry down which he walked with "his hand in his mother's muff." At this I wept and laughed hysterically.

That night I had lied to Hugh in order to stay all night with Henry. All the time we linked this with Louveciennes, where the childhood came into life again in the heat of my interest, and became the poetry of *Black Spring*.

Letter to cousin Eduardo: About my life. Do you want to hear? *Surrealism* is not the word. It is dizzying and marvelous though very painful at times, but, my God—what an overflow of everything. Love, flowers, gifts, white violets, holes in my stockings, open pocketbook, patients, cables, telegrams, full mailboxes, pursuits, lies, narrow escapes, dramas, tears, flowers, phone calls, dramas, laughter, radio in the taxi while you ride, fever and ecstasy and liver trouble, sunbaths, early mornings, hard work, letters, correspondence, dictation. "Yes, this is Dr. Rank's assistant speaking; yes, he will be back in New York at the end of March. He is on a lecture tour. Yes. Who is calling?" I need a husband, a protector, a *barrage*. Too many people. I like life too much. Hundreds of people. Social star shining over me. People for breakfast, lunch, dinner, and bed. Never alone. But happy. Now I must go and order some Vichy. *Love.*

Moved February 2 to 28 E. 31st Street, Room 1202, with Henry, as "Mrs. Miller." Emil telephoned, asking for Mrs. Miller, and wrote Mrs. Miller a letter: "Dear Mrs. Miller—Are you quite happy in your new home? We are here to give you perfect service. Just pick up the receiver and say, 'husband.' The man who adores you. Guess who!"

Walk with Henry to Henry Street, Brooklyn, cellar where he lived with June and Jean.* It is now a chop suey place. Walk across Brooklyn Bridge, where he sat. Morbid and terrifying. Walk through Chinatown. Evenings with Henry's friends. Henry goes crazy as soon as a man gets near me and singles me out. Rants and raves in talk while watching me. Obsessed with me.

Long talk one night, after burlesque show. About having canalized all his desires to me. Only wants me. Wants to know if I feel the same absolute. Emotional night ending in an orgy. I say I have no other desires. But: "It was you who pushed me into life. Now that I am fully in it you are hurt because I am made love to. Before, I wanted nothing else but you. In Clichy, I was unhappy when I could not be alone with you." Everything reversed. Now I want people and Henry is not enough. Henry terribly passionate. Erection every night. Wears me out. I also have powerful orgasms, like never before, only comparable to nights in Clichy, where I thought I would go mad with joy.

Don't miss Huck at all. But Huck knows and writes me he knows I wouldn't have gone with him even if Hugh were not arriving. I pretend that Hugh is arriving Thursday. When Huck comes February

---

* The story of Henry Miller's *ménage à trois* with his wife June's friend "Jean Kronski," as she called her, appears in various of his works, including the abandoned novel *Crazy Cock*, originally entitled *Lovely Lesbians*.

21 (for my birthday) there will be a clash because he will find out Hugh didn't come.

Telephoning 2 East Eighty-sixth Street Sunday morning from Henry's room to find out if there are any telegrams from Huck which I must answer, knowing I will not be back to Room 906 before Monday morning. Girl answers: No. I say to Henry: "No telegrams (*soi-disant* on business matters). If there had been one I would have asked her to read it out to me and saved myself a trip."

Henry: "Read it out? Then there couldn't be any love in it! Or else this is one of those specially designed lies to make me believe there wasn't any love in the telegram." (Exactly!)

Talk in the dark with Huck started by my struggle with this idea, that "woman's notorious inadequacy in grasping ideas, abstractions, is only a semblance. It is merely a question of planes." I maintain the principle of our ideology is the same, only woman's is in miniature, a personified ideology directed into the symbol (man).

Huck had same problem as I had: not being human; that is, being too good. I was not human with Henry. For his creation I sacrificed myself, as Huck sacrificed himself for his analysis. When he saved people they were his creations. He was not permitted to be human, or even to love them. Write the tragic life of an analyst!

Evenings in 906. Dinner in the room with Huck. Radio. Black-lace nightgown. I danced for him. I read to him from my Father story manuscript.* He is concerned only with the meaning. A philosopher and not an artist. Talked about his childhood. Love of the theater. Going hungry to see a show in Vienna. Always affected because I inspire him to talk about his childhood. About himself. Grateful. Says he never met anybody with such an interest in human beings—such a feeling for them. Never found anyone he could talk to. I unleash a

---

* Anaïs Nin's Father story, much revised under different manuscript titles, including "The Double," eventually became the title story in *The Winter of Artifice* (three novellas), published by the Obelisk Press in Paris in 1939.

flow. Resuscitate whole personality by awakening both memories and potentialities.

After Henry came nightmares of a dismembered Hugh. A frequent dream. It is I the dismembered one. Hopeless duality. I must live with it.

Huck's dream of getting me away and alone. Remembers driving through Connecticut with joy. But I was sick. I did not want to be alone with him—jailed again, as by Hugh. But I did want Henry to jail me. Is real love possessive? I wanted Henry all alone in Louveciennes. I tried to be all things to Henry. Suffered from his interest in [Walter] Lowenfels and in so many people. Now I do the same for Huck. Now I love less possessively. Neither one. What does that mean?

FEBRUARY 13, 1935

*T*HE MORE I DISCOVER HOW MUCH I WILL BE FORgiven (my power), the more independence I feel. My desire now is to run away with Henry. I know both Huck and Hugh would forgive me. But I dread the tragedy of it all. To be myself is this, to be dual. And you can't be dual without tragedy. I live on a hundred planes at once. Created a subtle, strange world with Henry, then with Huck. Enriching both, capable of both loves and of creating and nourishing both. Desiring unity but incapable of it. Playing a million roles. What I am to George Turner. What I am as secretary. Love of luxury, flowers, all that is rich, expansive, free, colorful, lovely.

I carry a little key-holder with key of 703 (Barbizon Plaza, no more); key of 905, Huck's room; key of 906, my room at the Adams; and now 1202, where I live with Henry.

Moving in with Henry. Seeing Huck off February 2 at one. Weeping. Springlike day. Packing half an hour after Huck left. To pay rent for Henry's room, I have to borrow from money Huck left me to join him in New Orleans, knowing I will not go to New Orleans.

Henry's room cheerful, in business district where his father once had a tailor shop, and where I worked as a dress model in Jewish wholesale shops. Henry began to sing—for the first time since I left him, he said. Woke up singing. Was terribly tender and passionate. I prefer to hear him sing. "You have a terrible power in your hands, Anis." I can make him suffer as much as June did. He says, more than June. That in Paris he suffered more than with June and came closer to insanity. Had hallucinations and obsessions. Fever. Delirium. He loves me as much. But after the suffering inflicted by June he took refuge in creation. He did not give himself to me until now. He could not. He was a broken man. Now I know he belongs to me body and soul. Marvels at his own fixation on me. Deep sleep. Peace. Mrs. Miller. No "psychological center" office (my Room 906 at the Adams) until Monday. Doing my nails quietly, little things. No more pulling and tearing. Henry writing story of a murder in the *banlieu*. Thinking of Huck tenderly and without desire. Huck's soul in his deep eyes as the train rolled away. Absolute. But my feeling was one of freedom and of joy to be able to be with Henry. On the last night with Huck, saw the film *The Good Fairy*. He sees me everywhere and reads me into everything. Asked me to take up my Spanish dancing while he was away, but I can't.

Three days of violent bilious attacks, which Huck interpreted as withdrawal from life because Hugh was coming and because Huck was going away, but I knew sickness was due to conflict. Difficulty of returning to Huck and lovemaking after being with Henry. Sickness in Henry's room. He wanted to take care of me. How to get away? "Why not call up the Guilers," Henry said. "Tell them you are sick." I can only think of saying that Rank has the only medicine which stops the vomiting. Beg Henry to let me go. He brings me to the Adams. I pretend Rank is not there, and that I have to wait for him. Must have medicine.

But Huck knows. Says Henry is my neurosis, that I probably still love him. Return to him means return to neurosis, which is easier than health and happiness. But while he talks I know only that I love Henry wholly, body and soul, and only parts of other people. Huck is physically repulsive to me—I have to close my eyes. First blind passion gone. But Huck's need of me now makes me forget what I want. I am the giver of life and illusion.

Henry said he could not be unfaithful to me when I made him suffer—could not bring himself to do it for revenge. His night with Blaise Cendrars [in Paris] obsessed with thoughts of me. Henry's craziness when in love, like mine. Huck's too. Emotional, unbalanced in love. Need of creation to steady ourselves. Jealousy, in the three of us, like Proust. Huck's is as yet unavowed, as mine was before. Henry saying, "It is ten in the morning and I am crazily in love." Later: "I'm lovesick."

Another day. Went to a party at Sylvia Salmi's—Henry drunk like a sot. They all drink because they are stupid and empty. I wanted to leave Henry there and come away, but he wouldn't have it. He reeled off and followed me. We stood on the street corner and I screamed, "Go back there, stay there, drink all you want, be what you want, but let me out of it. I don't want that. I can't do it. It bores me. It's stupid. I just don't want to be there. I don't want to see you drunk."

Henry absolutely drunk. And I couldn't bear it—the ugliness of it. Reeling. Couldn't find the keyhole. Saying he was sorry all the time. Terribly sorry. He didn't want to go back there. He only wanted me. In the bathroom he fell into the bathtub. His breath was foul. I was terribly sad, like the time June was so ugly and smelly. Henry begging me to talk to him, not to be angry. "I'm so sorry, Anis, I'm so sorry. It's humiliating. I hate myself."

I wouldn't let him take me. I turned away, bewildered, not knowing what to do—what to feel. Sadness and pity, but not anger. Only knowing I can't do that. No pleasure. I hate them all, idiots; and empty, so empty. Black mood and loneliness. Craving Hugh and Huck, needing them, their goodness.

*H*ENRY AWOKE IN A GRAVE MOOD. WHEN I CAME home that evening he had made our first dinner at home. Had also begun to write. And yesterday he was off again in one of his finest poet moods, at his best, reeling off feverish *Black Spring* pages on the dream stuff—pouring out images.

Meanwhile, the afternoon after Henry's drunkenness, Erskine again telephoned me and came up to see me. A mellow John, graver, deeper, still full of that deceptive brilliancy and sensualism. Sensual voice.

I was unexpectedly unbalanced by his visit—highly nervous, legs giving way, ice cold hands, beating heart. Furious at myself. But I talked feverishly. He said that what had struck him deeply the night he saw me at the opera was the sadness of my eyes. He would believe me sad, unhappy. He insisted on it. Thought I was bluffing myself. He observed confusion and chaos, which I call living by one's emotions instead of one's mind. I made a drunken speech on my flow, on spilling out. He left saying he was very much worried about me. I wanted to laugh. I was full of mischief. I startled him, told him outright about my love affair with my Father, really startled and shocked him.

"Anyone who comes near you can feel the life force and the sex force in you."

Still so big. I felt the need to lean. When I heard he was going on a concert tour for a few days, I felt lost. He made me feel weak. But that's only feminine trickery, a feminine mood.

The truth is that I am full of ecstasy, full of continuous inner drunkenness. The violinist, who comes for help, stirs and interests me.

I am full of ideas for the "Alraune" stories,* full of obsessions (fire-engine emotions), full of emotions and a sense of wonder and adventure. Henry makes me as happy as he makes me unhappy. When we are shut in together and he writes poetry and we talk, I live only in today. I don't worry about duality. I write marvelous lies to Hugh and to Huck. I don't want Huck's physical presence—nor Hugh's. When I am with Henry I am at peace. He showers me with love. A continuous love. He gains in wisdom and in understanding. He leans delicately over my work, my ideas, my moods. I live in a climate, a physical climate. Huck is again the mind realm. I don't know. I don't know. I don't care.

The afternoon I saw John (who keeps saying, "If only you hadn't been Hugh's wife") carried me into a mood of deviltry again. Not love. Deviltry. When I met John's wife, Pauline, at the opera—a lonely, gray-haired, serious, deep-eyed woman—I was struck by the fear with which she looked at me. A fear women have of the prostitute, the whore, the actress, a great fear of the sexual power. Now that I don't want John, I know I can have him. So I elude him. Nothing has happened to him the last few years—he is rotting away in comfort and American superficiality. He lived with Helen, after Lilith, that is, for four years, and refused other women so as not to be torn asunder. I recognize the same old coward. I felt him unhinged and disturbed by our meeting, scared, and feeling that I was the strongest because I didn't care.

Cannot tell Henry because he would be jealous.

Richard Maynard telephones every day. The violinist plays at Town Hall tonight. After three talks with me, she played as "I never

---

* The figure of Alraune, inspired by a German film starring Brigitte Helm as the artificially created voracious sexual persona, served Anaïs Nin as a symbol in her efforts to capture the essential qualities of June Miller. Her "Alraune" manuscript eventually emerged in two different versions, as the "poetic" distillation in *The House of Incest* (Paris: Siana Editions, 1936) and as the realistic "human" novella "Djuna," which appeared only once, in the first edition of *The Winter of Artifice* (Paris: The Obelisk Press, 1939) and was omitted from all later revised editions. An excerpt, "Hans and Johanna," appeared in *Anaïs: An International Journal*, Volume 7, 1989 (Becket, Massachusetts).

played in my life before, thinking of you as a shadow and seeing your green ring flashing before me."

FEBRUARY 28, 1935

*P*OOR HUCK—LOST. HE LOST BECAUSE HE CANNOT be lied to. He lives too fast because of his mind. He refuses to permit the rhythm of delusions and the pain of life.

When he came back, I was at the station, very early. Misgivings. Would I be able to lie with him? Could I bear his kisses? But the old love made it all possible. We had such a full day, until midnight. Locked in the room together—talk, caresses, meals together, laughter. Huck *knew* I was lying—did not know how. I told him I had to lie to him because Henry had been very ill, even been operated. I *had* to stay with Henry, take care of him. But I told Huck I couldn't write about this as it would have worried him, ruined his trip. That pity for Henry was stronger than any love or happiness. What does it matter what I said? Huck *felt* the whole truth, knew he had lost, but he didn't show it—didn't *know* it all until I was gone. We seemed happy. We planned that I would spend half the week in Philadelphia with him—half in New York—planned horseback riding, a day of rest; planned for his work. We lay in the dark and talked as before, quibbling, jesting. I did not acknowledge to myself even what I now see so clearly in the diary—that I don't love Huck. Always Henry. No one but Henry. I thought I could continue to make Huck happy. But he, he had realized during his trip that I must belong to him, that he could not bear separation from me.

Everything was changed. I didn't want his kisses. The gifts he poured on me didn't make me happy, somehow. But, oh, the pity, the pity I feel now as I write, the pity which is the cause of my deceptions.

No one understands that. The pity which makes me write him a love letter, even today.

I left him at midnight. Knowing that if he did not accept my story of Henry's illness and need of me, then it would all be over, because I would never leave Henry. How terribly sure I was of my life with Henry—of its rightness, in spite of what I regret, terribly, that Huck gave me: absolute understanding, a fiery love, strength. All this I sacrificed to an absolute, and poor Huck himself—poor Huck. Yet he can say, like the others, that in two months I gave him more love and more happiness than he ever knew in all his life. I know what I gave: life, pain, ecstasy. I know what I took away; his faith, his faith in woman, in love, in his philosophy. Cannot balance. Never can balance. I don't know. He says now that I was very cruel, that I hurt everybody by trying *not* to hurt them, that I have wounded him where he is most sensitive. "I wrote a book on truth and reality; that is what you have most confused in me. I don't know anymore, now, what is truth or reality. What are you? A chaos. Why, how could you write me all those details of Hugh's arrival?"

"To make your trip possible."

All this, the bitter words, the ugly words, came at the end, after he left on Monday morning—left 906 without a word, taking away all his presents. I waited, wondering, not believing he would really go away, writing notes. Then he telegraphed the Adams (not me) he was returning. So on Wednesday morning I got up at five, a bitter cold morning, went out in the dark and snow to get to his room at six—an hour which had meaning for us (It was at six A.M. in Louveciennes that he woke up and came to my bed. It was at six he used to come into my bed at 906)—meaning just to kiss him into faith again, just as Henry kissed and laughed my own faith back when I suffered from doubts.

But Huck was angry, hard. He insisted on an exchange of rings, on giving me my valise, on not talking, not explaining. He said I had been, all through, terribly cruel; that he was glad he had broken away; that he had no regrets. At this, of course, I was angry, but I did not understand what he really felt until he said, "I can't live this way—not knowing, never knowing what is the truth, filled with doubts and uncertainties, insecurity."

"It's your head that makes you doubt. When you are with me you can't doubt, you don't doubt, because then you *feel* the truth" (still lying, why?).

"That's true," said Huck. "But will you be with me all the time? You saw how unbearable the trip was for me."

"No, I cannot live all the time with you."

He shook his head then, despairingly. Talked about an act of self-preservation. Felt himself going mad with me. Then I said I understood.

I was still broken and sobbing because he had destroyed his letters to me, his poems, the real tender Huck, the understanding Huck. I almost struck him when he told me, and then broke into sobbing. When he talked about self-preservation I said, coming toward him, "I'm glad *you* are saved."

Then, sobbing: "What I want to know, what I want to know is . . ."

"What?" said Huck, more tenderly. But then I ran away. To this moment I don't know what it is that I wanted to know. I don't know why I said this.

Though I didn't love him, the parting hurt me terribly. I thought constantly of his sensitiveness, how absolutely he had given himself; remembered everything, regretted him, tried to realize my cruelty. Why, why do I always feel innocent?

My poor Huck. Forgive me.

There were times when it was so difficult to love him. Why do I always want to *answer* the love? His ugliness. I loved him through his ugliness, as you pierce through a carapace; loved a soul and a mind, this little man—this one little man whom I could not deceive.

At moments I think only of his loneliness.

Spiritually, I accept mine. Henry gives me the human closeness—the human warmth.

I gave Henry my version (for Henry) of the break.

But I will never again pretend to love—only, the truth is that I *deceive myself* as well as the others.

I fought off the pain. I know I buried it away, refusing to suffer. There was no storm, only the blackness. It was still dark when I returned to Henry from that strange six o'clock visit, through a snowstorm. I got into bed with Henry. Tried to sleep. Refusing to suffer. No. No. I have wept enough, now, over the others. At nine I got up. At ten I was out in the bitter cold, looking for a room for my patients who cannot pay. They cannot come to the place where I live under the name of Mrs. Miller because they know Mrs. Guiler. As I walked, in spite of Henry, in spite of his love, I felt lost. I felt again that same reproach I made to Allendy: I came for help, and I got no help, no peace anywhere. The only one who *knew,* or could know, me was Huck, and he too got all mixed up because he loved me.

There is no truth, no reality. We can only know with our feelings. Our head is false. All I know is that I love Henry.

That morning I could only think of the shock, of my dependence on Huck's wisdom, and of his failing me. Selfishly. He said I failed him. He had staked his all on me.

Henry looked at me during breakfast. "The face that launched a thousand ships."

"No," I said, "the face that baffled a thousand analysts."

I told Henry that Rank sent me away because he didn't want to suffer an unrequited love anymore. Again a *near*-truth.

At twelve I decided upon a solution. I would take a room at the Barbizon Plaza only two days a week—see all my patients on those two days—spend only six dollars, as I had to keep on taking care of Henry and the problem was serious.

All the time I meditated a letter to Huck: "Forgive me."

F E B R U A R Y   2 8 ,   1 9 3 5

*T*ODAY, THURSDAY, I WENT TO THE BARBIZON AT nine-thirty. Saw Richard, who said marvelously acute things: "You could not love Hugh. He is not alive. He can neither live nor dream. He tries to follow you into your dream world by astrology."

"I don't think Hugh failed to follow me. In astrology, he came quite near . . ."

Henry, whose picture he looked at, he liked: "He has a sense of humor."

I asked him point-blank, saying, "I'm asking your sixth sense: Is Rank the man for me?"

"No."

Adding, "Rank is the man you described in your novel—not Henry. I mean about the bomb throwing and the bitterness."

He spent an hour analyzing the analyst. Me. And then my patients began to come, hysterical, weeping, or joyous because of my care. Ironic. I gave strength to three people who were far from imagining what I was going through.

All day thoughts of Huck, Henry, tender, loving, thoughtful, and working well.

But the moment there, alone in the Barbizon Plaza, Room 2107, I remember Huck had said: *The creator seeks to be alone—he creates alone, because that is like God.* I created my life and insisted upon my loneliness.

So, I permit only intermittent companionship. With all sorts of excuses: One is inadequate, another does not understand, another cannot follow, etc. I do them an injustice at times. Because I liked Henry's badness, as Henry liked June's badness, as Huck liked mine (all exaggerating the others' badness in order to suffer, or to become human!). I exaggerated it in my novel too, and overlooked the change in Henry. For three years I have been expecting Henry to hurt me mortally, and he hasn't. Beautiful behavior, human, kind, tender, sacrificing, faultless.

Aloneness. Strength. Pride. I lost another Father. Oh, that craving for a father, for the Father, for God again, the God I saw after my operation, and then lost sight of.*

I think all man's ideology is contained in the fable of Huck's explanation of my wanting to return to the night whence I came, at night, when I could not sleep with him merely because he snored so hard.

---

* In the wake of her traumatic abortion of Henry Miller's child, late in August 1934, Anaïs Nin underwent a mystic experience in which she "melted into God." See *Incest: From "A Journal of Love": The Unexpurgated Diary of Anaïs Nin, 1932–1934* (San Diego: Harcourt Brace Jovanovich, 1992), p. 384.

MARCH 4, 1935

*A*S FAR AS I KNOW, THE SHOCK OF HUCK'S BRUTAL departure—the thought of him *trembling,* so hurt (it turned out afterward that he did tremble, could not stop himself trembling, like a racehorse), moved me to write a protective letter to Huck (I felt a desire to protect Huck from the *will* of Dr. Rank). I don't know. All I know is that during those days, between our scene and our reconciliation, I felt myself drowning. Neuroses, fears, tears, obsessions, hallucinations. Why, why wasn't Henry sufficient? What made me write to Huck the child, thinking that he wanted me, and that Rank was destroying his happiness? Why couldn't I just give up? Why did I think of this break with relief: no more caresses—and with anxiety: no more understanding? Why didn't I want him to think I had betrayed our love? Why did I try to restore this faith in a love which I know is over?

He answered: YOU: I feel the same way. I am heartbroken, too, that you forced me to act as I did. It was not my brain, my ideas; no, it was the human being, it was Huck. That's what you don't understand yet.

I can explain it all to you now because my pride is gone, too, and now I feel you would understand again as you did in the beginning, before you fell back into old bad habits!

YOU are not bad and never can be, your habits are; and I hoped my love—which of course I cannot kill—would help you to overcome them. The fact that it didn't was painful enough. But that you had to be cruel, too, was too much. I want to talk to you, to explain to you humanly what happened, also for your sake. That's the only forgiveness—mutual forgiveness—I can conceive of: to have a frank and human talk and blot out the ugly scene. . . .

Letter to Rank: Huck, my darling Huck, you have begged me for the truth, you have begged me never to lie again. I have had these days a terrible struggle with myself. Something has changed in our love. That is why I wept when we left the Adams. It isn't the same love. Something was killed the day I lied to you, and the day you left me because of the lie. I killed your faith in me, but you killed my faith in our love, or the woman-love. I don't know. I don't feel the same way anymore. I don't feel any trustingness anymore. The brutality of your going away was a shock you cannot yet fully measure, except in terms of that other shock which has cursed my whole life. I don't believe anymore in your ultimate love—or in your forgiveness. I believe you are too strong (and I am too strong in an indirect, cowardly way) to endure what I am—I mean my not being whole. I feel that ever since the shock I have desperately tried to withdraw and I have succeeded. We have both withdrawn away from *pain*—only, there were many precious things we could not give up. As man—lover, husband—you gave me up when you went away because you had a right to expect an answer to your whole love. I went away as woman—mistress, wife—when you hurt me by not forgiving; because now you have become to me, hopelessly, the severe, unforgiving father. What we couldn't give up, my Huck, was the understanding we have of each other—the only relief in our cursedly lonely life—and my desire to keep Huck alive—so many things outside of the man-woman love. I don't feel like a woman toward you anymore, Huck. Ever since the shock, I told you, the woman died, desire died, passion. The man in you died, too, on account of my hurting your truth, your reality, your most sensitive feelings. I beg you on my knees, Huck, to forgive me. But this is one time when I must be truthful. It was the need of protecting Huck, and of salvaging the precious things, which drove me to call you back. I want to see things as you do. Your happiness is terribly important to me—our happiness is tied up. We are twins, but you love me for the twinship, too. Today you write me that you love me for my understanding of you. Oh, Huck, understanding, sympathy, work together—all that is possible, but no longer the man-woman love. You said that morning, at six, that you couldn't live in that insecurity. Everything in me is treacherous, because it isn't whole. I want you saved from me, I do. I do, because of the nature of my love for you. I think of you continually. If you hate me for this—for failing you as a woman—then hurt me again, punish me, do everything that will help you. If it hurts you less to transmute our love into understanding, I want to do that with you. We couldn't be happy together, my Huck, because you are absolute and have a strong self-will. You have a great, a brilliant, a generous self to live for. You have, more than anyone in the world, the right to an *absolute* love. I am, in love, incapable of this. I am crippled. I came to you as a cripple. You tried to live an ideal life with a cripple—to overlook the defect, the illness. Forgive me for failing you, for failing to be your dream. I have never known anyone who deserved happiness more. You are generous, you have such deep feelings, such a rich mind, such a beautiful humanness—everything. I want to do whatever you ask me, to help you to forget me altogether, and that can be if we do it without bitterness. Forgetting by the will, as you tried last time, would only hurt you—or [I could] remain close to you, close to your work, your life, giving you all the strength you gave me. After you read this, telephone me tomorrow morning, or write me. I'll come and talk with you. I am not running away. If I don't hear from you, I will know you don't want to see me anymore. I will understand. Remember, oh remember, Huck, that you said once the happiness of those first weeks made up for the rest of your life—for me too. That was absolute. It is the best I could give—the utmost. Forgive me, forgive me, forgive me. Remember only that. I curse analysis, which puts everything on a false basis and conceals the true human connection or issue with false hopes. Please, please understand and forgive me, because this is the truth and the lie would have hurt you more.

Your heartbroken Puck.

MARCH 5, 1935

*A*ND NOW, NOW I'M PREGNANT AGAIN! NIGHT OF torture. Nightmares. Huck turns away from me. I sent him away. Nobody will operate me. The terror of anaesthetic. My Mother says I must bear the child. I must have a cesarean operation.

Huck telephones me that he understands and forgives—to come and see him tomorrow. Neurosis. Pain again. Always tragedy. Giving my strength to others. I need a father! I need a father!

Am I still the child, or is woman always a child?

I tell Henry, "I lean on you." He is marvelously tender—divinely tender—but I don't feel any strength there.

There is no strength in me either. My world crumbles too easily.

The reconciliation with Huck, based on sympathy? Talk in the dark. Hysteria on my part, weeping. He said, "The lie made me doubt the love."

"The lie was done for the love. All my lies were done for love. I suffer from the insanity of protection—wanting to protect."

"You are not bad—your habits are bad."

He said it was the rebellion of Huck against the all-understanding, all-forgiving analyst.

We said later, laughing, that we were not sorry.

I said, "Analysis is an artificial process. It hastens the attainment of wisdom. We cannot live by your wisdom. But biologically, life continues to evolve in its own rhythm. Analysis is only another form of idealization. You analyzed me—or created me—then you wanted me exactly according to your ideal image—the potential me, *your* creation—and to your own image" (his insistence on our twinship).

Last night I said, "Analysis gives vision into the potential self. Also false hopes."

I write to Eduardo: Have been a victim of another analytical situation. Such a relationship bursts suddenly, like a soap bubble, at the test of real life. No more passion.

Strange. As I lost the passion I began to see Huck from the *outside.* His ugliness, vulgarity. Inside, beautiful soul and mind. But exterior repulsive.

The sun is shining on what I write. But I feel a little crazy—a little strange and weak. My breasts are swollen and they hurt.

When Huck returned to me, he did not return the ring of love, but a tiny silver ring he got me in New Mexico, with two small turquoise stones, which he calls the twin ring. It fits on my little finger—on the child finger. He always knows. He knew I was, for him, no longer a woman.

MARCH 14, 1935

VISIT TO PHILADELPHIA—AFTER HUCK TELE-phoned me that he understood everything. A sorrowful, purified, chastened Huck. I, with the fixed stare of my neurotic days, determined to say "I no longer love you." He asking me what I want. To all my anxieties answering, "I'll take care of your Mother and Joaquin." But I showing that I don't want to live with him all the time, that I still love Henry protectively and must stay by him and keep my promise to marry him. We exhausted ourselves in talk. Huck was all acceptance. I told him the woman was dead. And the woman *was* dead.

(Describe wetness between the legs like desire coming after or during the weeping—a sexual excitement, nearest approach to pure masochism ever experienced. After our scene Huck touched me there and said, "Oh, you see, you see, the woman is not dead at all!" He mistook it for desire, and I was so surprised myself that I did not realize the meaning of it until today, while I was copying this scene out of the diary.)

Then, just as I have done other times, I subtilized the situation, I annulled the boundaries, I diffused the black-and-white-ness. All the definite outlines, problems, decisions, choices, melted into a vaster dream—into wonder. I enchanted him with a sea of talk, we enlarged and expanded our whole life, he loosened his clutch on me, he became cosmic again, his understanding was enlarged, extended. We talked ourselves into illusion and wonder, talked ourselves out of reality. We talked in the dark. What I did not say then because I only understood it later was: I do not want reality (life with you) because I do not want tragedy. I want only the wonder.

The word *sublimation* applied here is not enough. It is a lifting from the ordinary, it is a heightening, an enlargement, an escape from the insoluble and the ugly. Anyway, we plunged into a new realm, rising even beyond his Jewish humor into creation. He admitted that as a creator he had wished me to be what he wanted. When I didn't go south with him, it may have been because of my love for Henry, but it may also have been because I felt I had to escape from his possessiveness. I could not have endured much longer his intensity, the force of his clutch on me. All this he realized. If the break made me aware that I needed him, it also made me aware that, again, to be true to myself, I had lied; I had lied because—I didn't know why, but I wouldn't go on that trip with Huck. (I see now that being true to myself, and being true to my love for Henry, was one and the same thing, but that being true to myself could be told to Huck and would hurt him less because it is a deeper cosmic need!)

Anyway, he respects me for my integrity. My means are twisted, crooked, dishonest, but often because I act upon an emotional instinct which I cannot explain correctly at the time.

Since then, I have been again to Philadelphia. If, to evade my woman role, I transposed our love again into an imaginative realm, by arousing the creator in Huck and offering the artist in me, I only enriched this love. Huck already had begun to write a preface for my child diary.* I gave him the diary to read—after he wrote the preface! I talked a great deal about my work. I had been working on the various "Alraune" pages. I aroused his interest in my writing.

The first night in Philadelphia I felt no passion, but Huck was happy. I felt a great peace on the train, afterward. I felt I had escaped reality again, placed the relationship in the climate I desired, and that the temperature will be preserved by the absences in between, which permit the dream to develop in proportion to the reality. It is while we are away from each other that we embroider upon the love by creating around it. With continuous presence, the proportions are lost, Huck becomes an ordinary husband who is concerned only with the facts of my life, and the jealousy. Anyway, no tragedy, no victims, no violence. That is what I want, I know it now. Huck lost me when he tried to make me break away from Hugh and Henry.

The *dream.* I brooded a great deal on this subject, how I made Henry's life a dream, and how that alone inspires creation, that alone nourishes the artist—how, if I had made Henry the husband, I would have killed the dream.

The shock made everything unreal again, although the strange fact is that the last time I saw Huck I felt a sexual excitement and was able to respond—but I know now it was a response to his passionate intensity. Of my own accord I have no need of his presence, no yearning for his body as I have of Henry's. The shock started a process of sublimination and the dream was reinstated by deviating into creation.

---

* Anaïs Nin began her diary, initially written in French, in 1914, when, at the age of eleven, she started her "exile" in New York, after her father had deserted the family. An abridged English-language version—*The Early Diary of Anaïs Nin (Linotte) (1914–1920),* with a Preface by Joaquin Nin-Culmell—was published, for the first time, in 1978 (San Diego: Harcourt Brace Jovanovich), although since the 1930s Henry Miller had tried to arrange for its publication at various times. The complete French text was published by Editions Stock, in Paris, in 1979, in two volumes. Otto Rank's preface was never used, though it appeared, eventually, in *Anaïs: An International Journal,* Volume 2, 1984 (Becket, Massachusetts), pp. 20–23.

One of our talks in the dark, the very Saturday afternoon of his return from the South, was on the creator's pride—his willful isolation. His need to create alone, as God creates alone. His need, therefore, of lies, which are a creation, and which cause separation of his world from the other people's world (I said this). My lies are a creation. I have written, in "Alraune": "The worst of lies is that they create solitude." Difficult to surrender this pride and self-sufficiency. Huck has now surrendered it. He says that what I do is always good for us. When our life was about to become husband-and-wife, I went away (while he was down South) and toward my self again, because I began to create, I began to write again.

At the same time, too, when Henry and I have to choose between our husband-and-wife life or our writing, our free glamorous life, we choose the dreamlike life and not the human.

A few days ago Henry felt in conflict with American pragmatism and values. He was rebelling against compromises, felt defeated and panicky before the failure of our attempt to escape. I had to free him from anxiety, and for the first time not as a sacrifice of what I wanted but because I want also to live as an artist and not to create tragedies in which I will get choked. I was equally tormented when, for the sake of living a real life with Henry, a day-to-day one, I was going to sacrifice three or four people and sink with Henry into drabness! Life in New York in one room, two of us taking ordinary jobs, cooking, no traveling. No freedom. Writing in these surroundings, among empty people, in a big, mechanically run city. Mother and Joaquin hurt, Hugh hurt, Huck hurt. The other way: illusion, the dream, the fecundity of life as artists—that is, not life as others see it, but a deeper life. Henry and I could not have lived more deeply together than we did all these years. I want the dream. And Henry wants the dream.

In the bus I change rings instead of stations! Change now into the fifty-cent Indian love ring given to me by Henry. Change now into the turquoise twin ring because I am going to meet Huck at the Barbizon. Or I wear the ring Freud gave to Rank. Or I wear my Father's coat of arms!

But I have returned all the gifts. That part of the fairy tale was killed. They are not real gifts any longer. They are like costumes I wear for a part, which I put on when I go to Philadelphia. The fact that Huck could take them back when he got angry—that killed my belief in them. They have become unreal. I detached myself from them. I no longer care for them. I once loved them: the red embroidered Russian dress, the turquoise ring and bracelet and earrings, the silver box with turquoise, the jade cigarette holder, the red Spanish shawl, the lace nightgown, the black velvet negligee, the Persian cigarette box, the leather writing case, the seashell, the sea flower, the bottled aquarium, the tulle underwear, the gold-and-silver sandals.

Note importance of fact that I don't care for good quality of materials, permanent values, real gems, real silver, gold, mahogany, solid woods, quality of dresses, stuffs—unimportant. Everything only for effect, as on the stage. Contented with false jewelry, lacquered woods, painted walls, imitation woods. Exactly like stage settings. Or stage costumes. Everything in Louveciennes, on close inspection, shoddy, but beautiful. Interest in effect, in illusion.

When Huck took everything away and kept it in Philadelphia, it became unreal, like a costume and jewelry I put on for a role.

To a patient: Wearing the handkerchief you gave me and thinking of you. When we meet in real life it is difficult for us to get into communication. Some part of you seems aloof and withdrawn, although I am sure you do not wish it to be so. What is baffling is that when I read your book I felt that I understood your emotions and your sensibilities. And then I tried to reach you, to talk to you, by means of the language of your work, which is so familiar to me. If I understood your emotions, complications, and subtleties as artist, it seems to me we should also understand each other as human beings. I wanted to give you my novel to read for the same reason. It seemed to me that through the novel I could address you and communicate with you. You will find in my novel two women who are afraid of talking to each other for fear of creating a wrong impression, fear of disappointing or failing to show their true selves. Both of us are actresses, not in the bad sense of pretending what we don't feel, but in the sense that we can take on such diverse roles and transformations that we don't know which one to present to the world at times, or to each other. The least uneasiness or insecurity (fear of being misunderstood or criticized) will throw us into an unnatural attitude. You appear withdrawn and yet I feel you are not. And I, the other day, may also have appeared to be something I am not.

Answer to a proposal on board ship: "I couldn't be faithful to any man for six days."

MacDonald asked me, "Are you always as full of life on land as you have been on this boat?"

"Much better on land," I answered, "because there I never miss a day because of seasickness!"

MARCH 19, 1935

*M*Y NEXT BOOK WILL BE CALLED *WHITE LIES.* I am very happy. I stand at the center of my self-created world, where everything for the moment is *as I want it.* I have plotted, lied, tyrannized, struggled, until I have come to my real desire: life with Henry. Henry to touch, to kiss, to caress, to lie with—Henry and his slow, sensual, nonintellectual climate. Henry and his laughter and joyousness and lethargy. Meals with Henry. Sunday with Henry. Movies with Henry. Henry writing while I read what he writes. Henry fixing up my writing.

Huck—far away where I don't have to kiss him or touch him or sleep with him. Huck, his understanding, his mental activity, his mental climate. Huck to write to, to talk with from a distance!

Hugh—far away, working with pleasure, enjoying his new artist self (he is painting) and thinking of me, loyal to me, giving me the most precious of all the gifts—my liberty—on his way always back to me, but not here yet.

I am happy today. I am a tyrant. Huck wants me for good, definitely, and is sad not to be given that, but I can also make him happier than anyone else can. Henry alone is the satisfied one.

I am happy, selfishly, tyrannically happy.

I lie for a while on the bed at the Barbizon, Room 2107, on a rust-colored bedspread; rust-colored rug and chair and desk. The radio is over my head. The Japanese garden is on my dressing table. The room is small, velvety, like a womb. In the locked tin box is my "Incest" diary. On the table also manuscript of "Alraune" and two rejection letters from Simon and Schuster, for *Chaotica** and the child diary with preface by Rank. Letter from my Father: "Could not write you without moralizing and I didn't want to moralize." Hugh's hand mirror, which he gave me with a poem.

Every time something is taken away from me, every time I lose someone or something, every time I must separate from something or someone, my reaction is creative. Huck observed that when I had lost my Father, I became my Father; when Henry fails me, I become the writer; when Rank fails me, I become an analyst. Everything must be replaced and re-created. Everything must come out of me and be me, and in me. I create everything that is perishable, evanescent, treacherous. I create my self-sufficiency, self-reliance, self-fecundation. But because I am a woman I don't want to be without needs. And I continue to have great needs. Nothing replaces life or love. I needed a father; I needed Henry; I needed Hugh's protection, his loyalty, his faith; I needed Rank's understanding; I needed Henry's writing; I needed my Father's equilibrium; I needed love. Terrific, immense, devouring, shattering needs. Life forces me to prevent and remedy needs—to be a cosmos all by myself: man, woman, father, mother, mistress, child. All the roles!

Very strenuous!

---

* Apparently an early version of the novella "The Voice," which became part of *The Winter of Artifice*. Anaïs Nin had christened her workspace, where she saw her analytical patients, the "Hotel Chaotica."

Today I am happy. The only sad one is Huck—and even Huck is very happy because, as he says, so much is happening to him, so much! So many changes, so many emotions, so many ecstasies, so many experiences! He is living! Life includes pain. It's impossible to live life without pain.

I help Hugh the banker—analyze his bosses for him, to deliver him of fears and timidities and boguses, humanizing the vice-presidents for him!

Henry, when alone one evening, fears to lose me. Suppose, suppose he were to be swallowed back into drabness, limited surroundings, slavery. His selfish love for me, like mine for Hugh.

I push Huck's desire and sex life into the background by magic of talk.

Symbolism of colors, early girlhood colors. Taken from Mother, blue for spirituality and mind. Chose coral and turquoise in studio of Boulevard Suchet, and black. Then orange and green and black in Louveciennes (from coral to orange—expansion of primitive feeling).

With June and for June I adopted purple, for only a while. Color of neurosis and death.

Came to New York in white and black. Wore blue for Rank's first kiss. Blue for faithfulness!

After Rank, shock—craved violet again: death. And masculine clothes: to supplant Rank and have no need of him.

Huck tremendously impressed by what I wrote in my diary about lies: "fairy tale–illusions" (in a speech made to Henry in the garden one afternoon at Louveciennes, that summer after Father episode).*

---

* "When I told a lie it was a *mensonge vital,* a lie which gave life," Anaïs Nin recalled under the date of August 5, 1933. "Nobody has been grateful for my lies. Now they will know the truth. And do you think Hugo [Hugh] will like what I have written about him better than what I said to him or implied by my evasions?" See *Incest*, p. 235.

Saturday I gave myself to gay shopping. Bought a turquoise-colored dress, turquoise imitation jewelry. Rented a radio for Henry (substitute for Huck's gift, to achieve detachment from his gifts).

In terms of metabolism: Henry too slow and I too quick. People seek human alchemy for balance. I need to be slowed down and Henry needs to be quickened.

Now I seek (through medicine) to be slowed up naturally, without need of Henry!

Medicine given to me for delayed menstruation (all the symptoms of pregnancy) expected to take effect in a week, but after two treatments it worked a few minutes before Huck arrived from Philadelphia (like the abortion made possible when he returned from London).

In talking with Huck I get very tired of his constant explaining. He can let nothing stand still or be. His life consists mainly of analyzing. I feel the need to swing away inevitably from his intensity of explanation. Everything we do or say gets explained, although fortunately that does not keep us from doing or saying it. It is inspiring and stimulating, but I have to get away.

When Huck came Friday he was trembling with intensity and joy.

Passed by a bargain shop and bought a handsomely bound diary at a bargain price. Diary reborn, thanks to Rank's great enthusiasm for it as a human document.

Entr'acte: Analysis of violinist, my favorite patient. (I love her.)

To Richard (who writes me, "I am in a dense fog as to any possible way for me to find you"):   The mix-up is due not to you but to the fact that no matter how intelligent I grow I have no control over my moods. Every day is seen through the prism of a mood that is a changing and undependable element. Fortunately the predominant mood in this Coney Island of moods that I am is a sense of wonder, beauty, and the magical and the miraculous. As I said: When you tried to find me through my novel I had already changed. The trouble is, things happen to me, thousands of them, every day. And they change me. Do you mind very much having a volcano, Coney Island, and Niagara Falls for a companion? We agree on the essence, or core. Details, which are of interest to the artist—I mean color, dramatic facts, experiences, ways of expression—are different. But that's fun, I think. After all, a little resistance makes interplay. Stimulants—not hypodermics (I mean sedatives).

I'm happy today. Today it is the Sun. Do you mind moods that leap like grasshoppers, and looking at things through different windows each time? It's all mentally a puzzle game, isn't it? Do you mind so much not being too sure, or my not being too exact? You know in poetry and in life ecstasy is what counts and ecstasy is sometimes a bit diffuse, like drunkenness. Letting things happen, letting things flow a little, is fun. The arrangements, order, creative synthesis will always come. In life itself, in nature, there is always a slight disorder, and a bit of capriciousness. Do you mind? It's due to over-richness of material.

What I have not been able to write about will have to be lost. I can never go back now. I'm only interested in the present. The mood of the present is everything to me. The ecstasy of the moment. Day to day. The fullness of each day is astonishing. Yesterday the woman from the shop who lends me a sash because my only evening dress is stained from Henry's desire one night. [William] Hoffman's eager approaches in the evening. My stories to him. I tantalize him. Dancing in Harlem. My letter to Hugh on his first watercolor, stuck on the wall in front of me. Huck's inchoate special deliveries. Melting and dissolving with love, stuttering with love. Richard bringing me a package of cigarettes each time. Henry typewriting when I come home, having torn myself away from Hoffman's party, hating even Harlem because I am with Hoffman and other vice-presidents—white gloves, butlers, private home on Fifth Avenue. Special flowers sent to me from Savannah. Stockings repaired for twenty-five cents apiece. Letter to Father: "Please admire me—you're the only one who isn't satisfied with me. Please be an indulgent father." Radio going. Old Gold cigarettes. Making notes on analysis of violinist. She gives me the first money she ever earned. Someday I'll write her up fully. She will be one of my friends. I liked her from the first. Eduardo's bath salts are finished. My Paris sandals are wearing out. My Paris gloves have been thrown away. I read Hemingway and liked his truthfulness. He was hit on the face for it. *House of Incest* is growing beautifully. Each day a new plan weaves, reweaves, molds, and recasts it. But it contains the keys to all the mysteries. Huck says the child diary was a letter to Father because I signed off each time. I write with a pen given to Joaquin, inscribed with his name, which he gave me. Good photographs of me taken for and with Huck—sent to Hugh and given to Henry. Frances Schiff has gone to sleep; [Richard] Osborn has gone crazy and is in an asylum; Henry's friends are all dead men; Huck's letters, when not inchoate with love, are abstract algebraics of human emotions. Eduardo stutters in breathless notes, but our affection is solid and well fixed. Mother has not married [Señor] Soler in Mallorca. Joaquin did not abandon Mother when he came here alone but realized he couldn't live without her courage.

I don't want to spend a year of my life rewriting Rank's book on incest. I want to do my own writing. I am the writer and the artist for Rank—just as Henry was the writer for me and instead of me. But now I want to be all things myself. I want to be a world all to myself, because—well, because I feel like it. I feel like playing all the roles.

When I send my dancer patient out to dance, I feel I could do it, would like to do it. When I send my actress patient out to act, I feel I would like to be acting. When the violinist plays the violin I am breathing music into her, and I pour myself out into all these things, giving to analysis more than others give, my own strength, my own creativity.

But concentrate. I am concentrating on the poetic "Alraune."

But the diary—my diary, I'm so happy to have you again. At odd moments, between two patients, a furtive note is enough. It is my world, my ego. Avowed, admitted, honest. I will no longer be ashamed of it, or disguise it, or embellish it.

I think of it while Henry and I are washing dishes. I am happy because Henry has written more poetry, as good as the first *Black Spring* pages in Louveciennes, and I told him what I had been feeling about the dream reinstated, which made such writing possible. I am happy and amused to think of what Katrine Perkins would say if she would see me washing dishes with Henry, and Bill Hoffman with his white-gloved butlers and doormen, and Patrick, the Wolfes' chauffeur, and all those who think I am marvelous, fragile, and reigning! And this romantic love for Henry, this defense of Henry. I smile as I scrape the pans, and wonder. No one knows where I am when I leave the Barbizon Plaza. I say I am in Forest Hills with Hugh's family. Hoffman asks me to play golf and to go horseback riding. Huck awaits me with his golden cage. I am buying seventy-nine-cent gloves and the violinist is saying, "This is the most wonderful thing that ever happened to me. I am well but I don't want you to send me away." She has a religious attitude toward analysis. I have decided that if analysis is a hothouse, a hastening of wisdom and growth, nevertheless the life experience must be actually lived out and through, completely, in spite of it; everything that is lived out in the imagination is poison. I tell the violinist to go to Italy and live out the end of her love for the Italian violinist, even though she knows now that the love is not real, that it is dying off. I am really denying the value of wisdom as a life force. Wisdom is to be used only to conquer death, destruction, or tragedy, but not as a substitute for life. I advise the full living-out of mistakes, errors. I am against artificial acceleration of the growth process. To help only on the taking of a hurdle, jump when stuck.

I make eloquent speeches to animate, inspire. I give myself a lot of trouble.

I am not a writer, or an artist, but a diarist, or *documentaire*. Accepted. Diary my chief work. Post mortem. A few little minor works of art: "Alraune" and *Chaotica*.

My faith in Henry as a writer absolute. All the others are wrong. But I know, too, that Henry would not have been a writer without me. The inner and poetic illumination of his life came from me.

MARCH 21, 1935

*R*AIN. SLOW TO DRESS, SLOW TO GET ANYWHERE, because at one o'clock I take the train to Philadelphia and I don't want to leave Henry. It is like leaving the sun, the sea, food, sex, languor, wine, for geometry. Even though Huck is full of passion and emotion, I don't want them from him. I yearn for Hugh's arrival, to be saved from Huck, from *nights* with Huck.

I know that I go through life like a drunkard. I'm drunk on illusion. But no matter how drunk I am, there are things I can't help seeing, ferociously real things. I close my eyes, and I reel, I reel. I reel, I believe, I live in a fever and turmoil, I rise into ecstasy, but all the time there is the face of reality staring at me with ugly eyes. I know that if I open my eyes I will be intolerably hurt by the ugliness.

When Joaquin saw Rank he was overwhelmed and in despair: "Oh, the ugliness, the vulgarity." Henry says, "A most unprepossessing guy." Woman author writes, "I saw an ugly little man with bad teeth." How I have suffered and recoiled from his bad breath and his constant perspiring. He is always hot and apoplectic. He eats voraciously and yet without tasting. I dread going there, being shut up in a room with him for a day and night. He doesn't let me sleep. He rushes through the meals.

The intellectual banquet will keep me afloat. An orgy of ideas. The champagne of understanding. It is his creation, "Dr. Rank," who seduced me—not the man. At moments he feared this: "I'm like a rich man who fears to be loved for his money" (for being "Dr. Rank"), and that is precisely the truth.

Creation. The force of a man's creation—but, oh, the human tragedy. I felt compassion for Huck the child; compassion for the man so lonely in his created world of books. For each thing I lived out (Double theme, Don Juan, Incest, Truth & Reality) he wrote a book! In books he lived out his double, his Don Juan, and his incest. He belongs to books and among books. There he is great. It is in life that he is ordinary, vulgar, ugly, impossible.

I'm still in the age of tumult: Coney Island and Niagara Falls. I want to be. I don't want to sit. Play chess with explanations and erect a timetable (Where are you going? asks Richard) and an itinerary. *Voyage sans billet de retour.*

Sitting under the hair dryer, nails newly lacquered. The present. A briefcase containing "Alraune"—I hope to work on the train. Containing *Truth and Reality* by Otto Rank. Containing shoes and a hat, lipstick and rouge, and the diary.

MARCH 25, 1935

*T*HE MAN WHO TOOK THE DIARY AWAY FROM ME as neurosis gave it back to me as a unique work by his enthusiasm for it. He incites and inspires me to work. He admires "Alraune" and wants to publish it.

We are now starting another twin diary where I write on one page and he on the other.

MARCH 26, 1935

*H*ENRY'S PROTECTIVENESS: TO WASH THE DISHES SO I won't spoil my hands, which he loves; to cut my meat when it is too tough. But he won't cut out the obscenity in *Tropic of Cancer* to get it published [in the United States] and I don't ask that, though his integrity means separate lives—humanly separate. Very erratic and perverse when he sets out to make a way for his books. Gives them to the wrong people, chooses all the ineffective ways, rejects the intelligent ways. Frustration and failure. The other night I talked to him with an almost divine gentleness, tact, indulgence. He was affected. I revealed to him his contrariness, his cussedness, all with such gentleness that the next day he set to work again feverishly and lucidly. No one else could do this. Everybody else makes him combative, contrary, illogical.

Henry has a feminine nature in every way. When his hatred is fed by defeat he writes emotionally and badly. The same emotions can rise into poetry and ecstasy, prophecy, when I smooth the wasted, downward emotions. With Henry, somehow, I am at my best. I am soft, indulgent; I have a divine tact which I don't have for others. He is touched, he sees, he melts, he gets into harmony again.

We are all like partially insane people with areas of lucidity. When I am with someone who doesn't believe in me I act insanely, unbalanced and deprived of all my faculties. It is the same with other people. My Mother is at her best with Joaquin. My Father is at his best with Maruca. Henry is at his best with me. Huck is at his best with me. Doubt creates a form of insanity. Fear unsettles.

Hugh is supposed to be here, traveling around, and now in Washington. So I have to invent weekends in Washington with details. I talk about war, politics, because if Hugh were here I would be informed on all this. I talk about Ethel and Mother Guiler and golf, whereas an hour ago I have left Huck at the Barbizon and we talked about woman, psychology, truth, and reality. Have to condense what I learned and discussed with Rank as coming from an hour's lunch together because Henry, when I tested him out, didn't even want me to accept going to the movies with Huck.

Lies also to prevent Henry from discovering Hugh is not here (for example, Henry meets Mrs. Nixon here and she knows Hugh was in London). I cannot let any of my friends meet because the Maynards know Hugh isn't here; Frances Schiff knows I see Rank when I am supposed to be with Hugh; Henry thinks I am in Forest Hills when I'm not here; and Hoffman wanted to call for me at Forest Hills with his car and I cannot let anyone call up Forest Hills because I have told the Guilers I'm in Philadelphia in order not to see them. Huck thinks I have not been living sexually with Henry, yet my pregnancy dates from the time he was away in the south, and as I have no money for abortion I will have to borrow from Huck and the doctor may mention casually the date of my impregnation. Lorraine [Maynard], who knows Hugh is not here, invites me to Seabury's lecture and as I can't go Henry wants to go and would have sat with Lorraine— only an accident prevented him from going. We might meet one of the Guilers anytime on the street and they might blurt out in front of Henry, "When is Hugh arriving after all?"

The Spanish maid who cleans our room thinks I work on the stage. The lingerie-shop woman thinks Huck is my "daddy" and plots to make him buy me underwear, to be good to herself and to me! She winks at me behind his back. Ethel [Guiler] thinks I am dressing more youthfully in American dresses, that I become my girl-self again and no longer the pale femme fatale. I send *Chaotica* to [Jack] Kahane. Lorraine writes me starchily. Huck writes I have changed him fundamentally, and Father says I do not need him anymore. I send my actress patient to the Art Worker's Club, where I worked as a model, and wish I could live all that over again because I was not awake then. I drink whiskey with Henry and it makes me talk about the violinist, my favorite patient. I write to Huck that I like her just because she is full of emotion, full of poetry, full of ecstasy. One hates to cure people of the moment of drunkenness, because those moments of drunkenness are the most wonderful in life. When you are drunk on a feeling, no matter what it is (she is drunk now on an imaginary feeling) you don't see reality or ugliness anymore. Too bad to have to wake her up. She made me laugh, too, because she said I should warn people in advance of what I look like because otherwise they get such a surprise that they are put at a disadvantage and cannot think anymore. Always returns to the fact that she expected a masculine, maybe a prehistoric, horse. The idea that feminine women cannot do man's work.

MARCH 29, 1935

KATRINE PERKINS AND I HAVE LUNCH IN MY ROOM. She is flowerlike and hungry for reality. She is, says Huck, my poor, wan banker-wife self, starving for liberty; and I pity her and my old self, and I talk to her as one empties one's house in wartime for the benefit of the wounded.

Idea of enclosing facsimile of three passports in *Chaotica* to answer all concrete questions. Irony of giving color of eyes, weight, hair, height, address, nationality, etc., which is what people say is missing.

Henry wrote, at the same time as Rank, a better preface to *Child Diary*. More human, more artistic and poetic, intuitively deep. Rank, more cosmic, philosophical, ideological. While reading Rank's preface Henry said, "Most of this is too much for my slow mind. The casuistry. Christian versus Jewish mind."

Huck thinks my diary invaluable: woman's point of view—biological separated from ideological in me. Woman's psychology revealed (protectiveness of woman, aggressive like tigress only to defend her children. No masculinity, but whatever is positive mistaken for masculine).

On Henry's work: I have to *épurer* (refine) bad taste, ranting, excrescence. As I could have done for D. H. Lawrence. In *Black Spring* (childhood, tailor shop, epilogue) Henry has now created a work of art. But he tries to mar it by including imperfect early parts, like the tuning up of a symphony orchestra. Injects again the wild shots of his preartistic age!

"If I am an artist, as you say I am," said Henry, "then all I do is right."

"Oh, no," I laughed, "you're not an artist all the time. Only intermittently."

Hard for me to be rigorous, because I like some of the disorganized, dissonant, loose, flabby parts.

Henry, just as in life, has no judgment. Includes all. Cannot evaluate; cannot graduate, compare, or select. No taste. But intuitively when he reaches perfection or perfect parts, I have to struggle so that he won't ruin them. No judgment at all of people, or of his work, until later; he does see all I see later.

Child who wanted to go to Africa. Scrapbook of details and plans, timetables, picture of airplane, etc. His school was far away and it became Africa for him, but when he was moved next door to it he failed to attend, because he wanted the traveling, the adventure of getting there.

My reality world obtained from Henry and June—vulgar and bad taste—because other realities, refinement, did not seem real to me.

Huck and I are writing a twin diary of ideas.

Shaking the green Czechoslovakian tablecloth out of the window, Mrs. Miller always experiences the fear that she may be throwing out precious and irreplaceable things, jewels, manuscripts, gifts. Washing the dishes because Henry is absorbed with a watercolor fever. On her way home from the Barbizon Mrs. Miller stopped to buy him paints.

She was introduced to George Buzby, an attractive blond giant of the ideal type, a type manufactured exclusively by Northern races, the physical power and poise, the absence of ghosts, the face without memories, the ideal pattern, the Jupiterean kindliness and god-sense. A kind of royalty of some sort or other, as perfect as a mountain, a sea, or a sky. I was powerfully attracted—I mean, Mrs. Miller. Mrs. Miller is persistently drinking whiskey by the spoonful to overcome the ancestral infirmities, denying any organic weakness and impatient with her psychic hypersensitiveness. Mr. Miller is writing *Black Spring* and George Buzby consumes a glass of rye every ten minutes by the clock without losing his mountain firmness.

"Alraune" doesn't get done, but *Chaotica* and *Child Diary* are in the hands of E. P. Dutton today. I bought the black tailored suit with mannish pockets—such a hankering for that fourteen-dollar suit—a new role, the trim American positive woman, the sleekness and the youthfulness.

Violinist says I can't take away from her that feeling about me because it is warm and sweet and life giving and because it belongs to her. I inscribe my book on D. H. Lawrence to her: "To my favorite patient," and she reads it in the elevator and trips and falls on the street on her way out of the hotel—like the time she absolutely wanted to kneel to God on the street and did so by pretending to lace up her shoe.

Eduardo writes me so humanly; also tells me Saturn has been passing over my Sun and Jupiter so it is natural I should have had dark days. Dr. Finley says I'm not pregnant, and gives me thyroid treatment to fatten me, to attain well-being I felt during pregnancy.

Huck will give a lecture on the psychology of women. I have added to his knowledge of woman and life and he has added to my knowledge of my work. His insight into the meaning of "Alraune," in which I walk about blindly, stumbling and stuttering, has been a great gift.* He says he always wanted to write poetically, dramatically,

---

* "Alraune, the modern re-creation by a woman of this symbol of feminine badness, arouses our interest and curiosity in many respects," Otto Rank wrote in a preface to Anaïs Nin's story. "Is it going to reveal to us more of the inner secret of woman or will it merely confirm that woman is—whether in life or in writing—nothing but a reflection of what man wants her to be and has succeeded in making her into?" See *Anaïs: An International Journal*, Volume 3, 1985 (Becket, Massachusetts), pp. 49–54.

and that I am writing the fairy tale of neurosis, poetizing its language. Remember the night I could not go to sleep without first showing him page on fairy tale and lies in my diary. And now as I write "Alraune" I am aware that he knows absolutely what I mean and is becoming sensitive to the beauty I add in the telling.

Violinist relates what I have told her in analysis about her idealism to what I wrote on Lawrence and "dead ideals." Gives me three more books by Hemingway and says she will introduce me to him. Buzby says he thought my book on Lawrence one of the two best books on Lawrence (the other being Aldous Huxley's preface to the *Letters*) but cannot believe I wrote it after seeing "such a youthful, charming, beautiful woman."

When Dr. Finley tells me I'm not pregnant, I cannot believe her— I cannot believe in happiness. O God, why cannot I believe in happiness. Please, O God, I want to believe in happiness, I want to believe that good things come to me, that I have come to the end of my troubles. Because I feel so well, and look so well, I think I must be pregnant and will have to be operated, and where will the money come from, and perhaps I will hold on to my embryo again and bring on complications. The church bells are ringing while I sit at Elizabeth Arden's [Beauty Salon on Fifth Avenue] with my face covered by a mask, and I almost come near God again, like that other time at the hospital, and all I am saying to Him is to please let me believe in happiness. Henry cannot believe either, none of us who have been either very poor, or very sick, or very lonely. It is hard for me to believe in continuous, sustained happiness, just as it is hard for me to believe in love. I take whiskey and I think, Oh, to hell, to hell with caring so much, to hell with everything. Huck's emotions of longing for me do not arouse any feeling in me; they make me hard and indifferent. Henry's egotistical feeling that all he writes is of interest, that his letters should be published, his insistence that his fumblings, stutterings, and dissonances are invaluable, makes me cynical.

Rank prefers to give me gifts for which I have to be grateful instead of patients who would make me independent. The sun is shining on what I write; my hair is being curled—a day of frivolity because I felt black and sad and cynical. More reasons for becoming more and more independent and self-sufficient.

Henry started to fumble around and write a marginal work of scraps and odds and ends and came to the rock-crystal core of *Black Spring;* then he still wanted to include the didactic, the opinions, the boring dissertations; and he lovingly collects them all. Can't tell the difference, almost like a color-blind man! Collapsed at the first touch of my judgment, which was so gentle, saying merely this does not belong in *Black Spring,* that's all. Mediocrity. [Emil] Conason accused him of being surrounded by mediocre friends. It is true. They are as mediocre as the bankers, and I have been so disillusioned by their emptiness, weakness. Worse than the bankers because they are loafers. I have my days of lucidity and realism.

Huck is surprised because I give the number of his room in the Philadelphia hotel. I see all life dually, the real and the dream. I do see the pessaries, the douche bag, the wax earplugs melting on the pillow because otherwise Huck's and Henry's snoring keeps me awake. I know my heart beats too fast when I take whiskey, and that the blue vein on my right temple, which [my friend] Enric used to notice in Richmond Hill [in the early 1920s], now swells up when I laugh. I see all that Hemingway sees, all that Dreiser sees, all that Henry sees, but I hate it, and I get drunk on other things, and I like the things which make me drunk so that I can forget. I see that I outdo Huck in generosity, in acceptance, and in understanding. I see that Henry is difficult to live with; that if I learn to sleep late to please him, and learn to stay up at night, as soon as I learn it, then he awakes at eight in the morning and gets up briskly and teases me about my laziness. Contrariness. Exactly like my Mother, that negative way of asserting one's will. The fact that my plan was to write an imaginary diary of my innocence, leave it to Hugh, and disappear after pretending to have committed suicide proves it isn't the fear of being abandoned or of losing anyone which makes me lie, but a deep protective instinct. *Lying is the only way I have found to be true to myself, to do what I want, to be what I want with the least possible pain to others.* To sustain illusion I have to lie. Henry thinks my hair is naturally curly.

Huck thinks I am not sleeping with Henry. Henry frowns on the little tailored suit I wanted so much and so I have to play tricks to explain how and why I finally got it.

I, as a woman writing always "I," am more honest than Henry generalizing on his "Late City Man," modern man, when he only means himself and makes it appear cosmic when it is subjective. I accept being entirely subjective and cosmic only because I am woman, and woman is cosmic, as Huck says. Huck is weepy and sentimental and so grasping and demanding in love. He has realized his crises are due to change of life, that I got the brunt of his chaotic, emotional craziness. *Maladif.* His love is not love, it is a disease, it's absolutely neurotic and I feel devoured.

APRIL 1, 1935

I MET HUCK AT PENNSYLVANIA STATION AGAINST my will. I was sad to leave Henry. I was withdrawn and preoccupied. Slowly Huck won me back again with his mind, his generosity, his passion.

I just wanted to talk. I dreaded the moment when he would kiss me. I eluded it. I suggested we go out (he always wants to lock me up, just as Hugh did). We saw the marvelous Planetarium. We were awed and we laughed too, our own special kind of wit which is so quick. And then we had tea together and Huck talked to me about his restlessness in Philadelphia, his boredom. Slowly, it was as if I got used to the Beast and was able to forget everything except that luminousness of his mind and the potency of his passion. Slowly I am able to let him caress me, still thinking desperately of Henry.

As if Huck penetrates me with new tentacles, and penetrates new areas of me, and slowly, slowly Henry is eclipsed by an intense fire, the fieriness of Huck's aliveness and positivism, and Henry seems to be terribly weak and inert, the Henry who first came from Paris doesn't exist anymore, the natural Henry has come back, the lazy, inert, will-less Henry. And I am sad, I am sad, terribly sad, that there should be so many fissures and cracks in my life with Henry that Huck's strength could seep through and then invade. I feel imprisoned. I don't mind but only because I know I am leaving Monday. I can enjoy the new records Huck got, I put on the Russian dress, we eat delicate meals, it is raining outside, and we are talking with deep seriousness as well as humor, quick, darting humor. Huck said once, with astonishment, "My, but you are quick! I have to be on the alert every second." Such humor cannot be reproduced, because it is so elusive and improvised. And then the caverns, the explorations: woman psychology.

True, with him I am most myself, but I also told him I was wistful the other day because I realized that he was getting the natural, imperfect, selfish *me,* not the ideal me. Not the good mother I was for Henry, not the false gaiety, the put-on heroism, the forced sweetness, the abnegations. He has created the real me, and he knows it is always so. In analysis, too, when he is forced to reject the generously given love, the woman progresses from giving into *being*—being herself. I was ashamed, too, that for Huck I am almost what Henry and June were to me, the weak, the unscrupulous, the liars, the ones who used me and my gifts for others. When I came here (for myself, for my happiness, for my own egotistical ends) I expanded this self due to Huck, to his understanding, to his encouragement. Knowing that acting was useless before him, knowing he knows the truth, I abandoned all pretenses, all efforts, all ideal strivings. And I enjoy it. I have wistful regrets. We laughed about it, turned that into comedy, too, this time. I said to him, "Oh, Huck, you don't know how heroic I could be, how understanding, how forgiving, how selfless." We talked about the suffering I endured to be the confessor for Henry and June so that they could talk to me, be themselves, no matter what it did to me. How I had fought not to impose this suffering on Huck. Because of his understanding I am so tempted to tell him all, to forget the human being. We reached the conclusion that I *could not destroy*— that to create, it is necessary to destroy, that to create without destroying I nearly destroyed myself (lies, split, forced acting). Woman in general cannot destroy. We said perhaps that was why she was not a great artist. We read his horoscope and found marvelous things in it.

We talked about dissolution and will—how Huck saves himself when he feels he is dissolving, by an act of violence and destruction (the way he tried to save himself from me). He is trying now to be noble and less human. He wants to protect me. He asked me if I felt I wanted to marry Henry. Yet he believes I am not living sexually with Henry, because when we talked about my fear that I may still be pregnant he figured it would be two months now from before his departure to the south. He admits he cannot live without me. And yet he likes or loves me as I am, with what I call my weakness (not able to destroy) and my selfishness (living true to myself), which he calls by other names. Perhaps acceptance of human fallacies is necessary to enter life. Just as I had tolerance for Henry and June, so Huck is bowing to that because he is compensated by the wonders of life itself, the human life which I bring him. He is all softness and understanding. Someday he may explode (as I exploded a few times a year against the tortures imposed on me by Henry's egotistical expansion), but I can bear this because I have no fear of losing him and that is why I am strong and happy. We talked about his mother role in analysis. He was the mother to his patients as I was the father to Henry (the active, courageous, leading one). "So we have got beyond the need of father or mother," said Huck. I wonder. Perhaps I am on my way to this. Huck certainly finds it hard at times to be without a mother. I refuse to be that to him, I abandon him, I do not care about his human fate nor about his loneliness. I am for him just woman and whore; I take his passion without returning it, out of gratitude for his great love.

As I arrive here at the hotel I find two letters from Hugh, thanking me for fanning the flame in him and promising to return to me with all the qualities I admired in Erskine, Henry Miller, and Rank. He is intoxicated with his newfound material power, and meanwhile I deny myself to give to Henry, who refuses to take a job, and I create financial difficulties for myself.

Huck asks me to finish *House of Incest*. On the train I think about the flowers I want to include and what Huck wrote about me March 20: "You are great. You are great in life as I am in creation (writing).

You lived my creation (before—I didn't create you except as a woman). And in that sense you are greater, and your philosophy of *living* (not life—that's abstract) is *true*—it is the one which I arrived at in *Truth and Reality*—on paper! As an analyst I still tried the other. As a human being I want to live it out now as you did, with you.

"And because you are great in living, your writing is not only a rare—a unique—human document, but it is great. If it is presented in a certain way which will enable people to see its greatness. We will do that."

On the bus I wrote, "The very man who killed off the diary as neurosis has now given me back the urge to continue it." A day in Philadelphia, Room 1205, I had given him the "Incest" volume of the diary to read and then asked him not to read it, thinking that the details of my past might hurt him as a human being. But I did want him to read it for its content. On the train, on my way to him, it had come very clearly to me that all along I had been the one who had acted out and lived Rank's philosophy. His body of work contained the psychological insight into and interpretation of my life. I had been the actress. I had tried all the roles (also, added Rank, the poetic expression of them in writing). This was the opening page of a green-bound volume which afterward I got a twin for, red leather, and we are using both as twin diaries, exchanging them each week.

Returning always with the fear of having lost Henry, that he may have gone somewhere and got drunk and stayed with a woman. Heart tight with pain and perhaps with the feeling that I have deserved such a punishment. Calling him up with a husky voice.

He came to lunch with me; we couldn't wait for the evening. We got into bed together. Henry said, "You think I was off on a bat, don't you? Well, I have a surprise for you. I wasn't, I stayed home and worked, and I painted watercolors with Emil."

Immediately I am so happy, so happy, that he is still mine, still close. When we get home we take a rest, and I watch him sleep, with such a strange, full joy just that he is there, no matter what he is, or if he failed; I love him so much, in a blind, unquestioning way. I watch him sleep and it seems to me that this is all I want, Henry, just Henry lying at my side. Nothing else, nothing else. Immediately I forget the soaring with Huck—for the sake of one caress, one touch of Henry's body, Henry's hand on my leg, for the sake of lying beside him, his breath on my face, his full mouth near mine, I would throw away everything else—for the sound of his voice, for his laughter, for the hair on his neck, for his morning-blue eyes, for his brooding Chinese face, for his slanting hat.

If it is Huck who gives me the strength to be happy with Henry, and it may be, I couldn't be happy with Huck alone. It is true I don't know which one makes me happy.

APRIL 2, 1935

PHYSICAL TEST PROVES I'M *NOT* PREGNANT. HUCK knew it.

APRIL 15, 1935

HOW I HELP HUCK OUT OF HIS DIFFICULTIES AND how he likes to be helped for a change. After a complete sexual bout in Atlantic City in the afternoon after our arrival, he again desired me at night when I didn't want it. He felt this but could not deny himself and so he took me as I lay passive. As I lay there letting him take his pleasure, I felt far away, as when I had to yield to Hugh; only, Hugh did not feel everything as Huck does—not as knowingly. So he was sad at the end, and I let him be sad—there was nothing I could say. My passivity was as natural as his desire. No way to reconcile them. And if I talked I felt that I might blame myself for indifference and thus betray the fact that I am fundamentally indifferent sexually to Huck. So I let him fall asleep, feeling a bit hard and reckless. Not until the afternoon of the next day, after a very warm, blind sexual fusion which had reassured him, did I feel in myself sufficient assurance to mention his sadness of the night before, saying, "Was it because I was passive last night that you were sad? Why should you mind that—I gave so much in the afternoon, it was so full. I just felt quiet and peaceful last night."

"Yes," said Huck. "When it is just sex, when it isn't an expression of our togetherness, then it makes me sad, for just-sex is a separating thing, not a uniting one. I do know I should have left you alone last night. You were tired. I knew I was doing wrong because I can't enjoy it when you're passive. I just can't."

I talked about his clinging love, his clutching, saying, "You taught me to believe and not to clutch and now I want to give you that fearlessness you gave me." He said it was not fear but his age, his being closer to the end of his life, fear of coming to the end of his life. Whenever he talks about his age I say marvelous things, and now: "Organically you're so young, because you haven't lived, you haven't burned yourself."

"But they say, on the contrary, that the organism gets atrophied by not living."

"I don't believe that at all. And I'm certainly the one to judge your organic youthfulness!"

The truth is that he is insatiable. He demands more than Henry.

APRIL 16, 1935

Letter to Huck: You delivered me from both pain and un-reality and I want to do the same for you. You woke up the Princess (at six!) and you took all the pain of living away from me. I want to do the same for you. I hope I do. I hope what I said to you on our last morning was true. Do you know, that night when I went to sleep, after you spoke to me and I misunderstood you, I don't think I misunderstood you so much as I knew there was nothing I could do because you were suffering from the pain of living, from a sense of possible loss, of the danger of too-muchness, and the pain of taking back, but I do not mean that there is a need of taking back and of putting the lid on yourself again. There is no too-muchness of you for me. I like your explosiveness, I love siphons, I love your richness and your fullness. Don't hesitate. Don't hesitate, don't hold back. I know what you felt. I used to feel that way after I had confessed, after I had yielded up my secrets, or some of them! I have been concerned. I felt, strangely enough, that the only thing I could do for you was to go to sleep, to keep my gaiety and my insouciance, because that was what living had given me; and that I could help you to go on living, which takes courage, just be remaining *insouciante;* but I love you so much that in the morning your mood finally affected me, without changing mine, which is one of confidence, of painlessness, of fearlessness, of serenity. Thanks to your wisdom and all that I have already lived through. It's only the newness that makes one so shivery and sensitive and sad. Afterward, it's the sadness that wears off, and only the good, the solid, remains. The sadness is still a part of *creative* living. It's all that hunger for perfection. I'm going to make you more and more happy. I know how. I realized I learned how by living on and on, by going through many sadnesses and shedding them on the way.

Recollected the mood of loneliness I had one day while Henry slept on. It was, figuratively, as if he had continued always to sleep and eat joyfully, unaffected by my moods, not understanding them.

*Letter to Father:** You don't write to me. There is nothing more I can do for the two of us. I keep on writing you so that we won't be apart. I analyze, I talk to you, searching for an

* In French in the original.

understanding. Is this useless? Is there no way to reconcile our thoughts?

In your last letter you tell me one of the reasons you haven't written is that I don't need you. But don't forget that when I realized I had no role to play in your life, or at least no role commensurate with my energy and the riches that I have built up, because I am too overflowing and too alive to live "between parentheses," as you once said, waiting for the annual visits to Valescure—when I realized that, I didn't leave you. I stamped with rage and I wept; then I turned to a task, a role, a place for me that needed all I have to give. It wasn't I who left you first, but rather you who, having discovered a Vesuvius, thought you could put it in your window like a little flowerpot while you worked!

You see, I can laugh at all that now. But now you should be glad to be rid of Vesuvius, glad that I am asking others for what you couldn't give me.

Each of us was made to play a leading role. Last winter, when you thought that I should be satisfied to sit at my typewriter and talk to you one afternoon a week, I felt smothered. Now I am happy. I have a full life—a life that is wide, free, rich, and exciting. Between Henry and my analyst, you can imagine that I am running on all cylinders: wife, lover, critic, mother, muse, sister, companion, adviser, mistress, etc., etc. Yes, I have plenty to do.

Don't have any regrets, dearest Papa. Be happy. Write to me the way we used to talk in the dark, all our secrets. I am so natural with you now. Both of us have such a passion for perfection that it's hard, almost impossible, for us to accept a defeat. To resign ourselves. That's why I so often speak of our failure. No one is to blame, just life.

I try always to soften what happened by understanding. In the end, don't you think that once we understand, we can remember only the good times and forget the failure? It's so painful for us to admit defeat. There are days when I can't believe that *you and I* didn't understand each other. We understand other people so well. And it's strange, but when two people don't understand each other, it becomes a painful, destructive friendship. To understand, and understand each other, is positive and constructive. To build, to create, gives strength. Not to understand hurts and destroys. Letters are an effort to understand. Without wanting to, we hurt each other. But don't you think we could manage to do each other good?

I wouldn't want you to think that it was vanity that made me need your admiration, as I said jokingly in another letter; rather it's that I lack self-confidence and live on other people's love and faith in me. I need that, as they need my faith in them, my confidence and admiration. It's a weakness, but it isn't vanity. You thought Maman had destroyed my faith in you, but as soon as I saw you this time, that faith was reborn just as I felt it when I was a child, when I loved you so much that your departure almost killed it. I do admire you.

So where is my funny Papa, who loves harmony? How does he expect me to keep on writing letters like this all by myself, eh? Send me a little hug. I'm carrying you around America like a religious medal, an idol, my mute Sun King. Hey there, shine a little!

APRIL 17, 1935

*H*OW I SOLVED MY NOT WANTING HUCK HAS BEEN very strange. I take an attitude I have never taken about sex. I prepare myself for his embrace by thinking about sex—just sex for its own sake. The very opposite of what I feel for Henry, whose closeness I want. I excite myself by thinking and feeling myself a sexual, whorish woman. I close my eyes and seek to become aware of my desire for man—any man, any hand, any mouth, any penis—saying to myself: Any man, I want any man at all. I close my eyes and try to forget it is Huck, forget my picture of Huck; only a very passionate man. Even then I cannot bear his mouth (as I couldn't bear Hugh's mouth). Only lately I discovered from a talk with Henry that whores will always try not to be kissed, on various pretexts (because it isn't love, love gives the mouth desire). Henry's mouth draws me like a magnet. So I am whore to Huck. I even excite myself with gratitude, thinking of all that he has given me; or I excite myself with hardness: Well, here you are, he's given you so much, now pay for it, pay it back! Pay it back! I have no desire. I have to act sex. And Huck is so full of desire and love.

Life is full of deep injustices. Some of the injustices I try to remedy. For example, I have made Henry selfish by making him live for himself, by spoiling and adoring him, by fulfilling all his wishes; and now Huck has made me selfish by helping me to become more myself through analysis and my trip [following him to New York], through spoiling me and loving me, whatever I do or say. I can only help him to live also for himself and his pleasure. I do ask him: What do you want? But I can't re-establish the balance. He is the Giver! Our weekends at Atlantic City beautiful, even if we love each other for different reasons and in different ways. He has made me finish the "Alraune" manuscript. He helped me to discover the meaning and then I was able to make a synthesis. It is he who says, "Why, it ends here, with the dancer, of course. And this page on drugs (where I say to Alraune, 'I'll write for you—that will be our drug') can't be thrown out. It's important. It says just what I felt when I read the ms on the train. It is like a drug. I woke up when I got to the end, as if I had been dreaming. If people accept your language, then they will be drugged."

Acquiring a much-needed eloquence from speeches made during analysis. Acquired more sustained periods of lucidity. Art of language. Effect of artistic language in place of the scientific. Henry sits painting watercolors. Scene over work versus laziness. Said I was active because of misregulated glands. I accuse him of falseness, glorifying laziness when he is writing and therefore working. I didn't like his mocking and derision of men who work. Argument. I said, "I don't make you ashamed of your laziness, but you must not make me ashamed of my activity." He refused a job. I ask not for concrete change (that he should take a job) but for a change of attitude. I don't like the false lines in *Black Spring:* "I am snoozing while the factory whistles are blowing." Insulting all the workers of the world.

Because I said I was disillusioned, Henry was crushed. I said he had not lived up to his promise when he first came over. "Literature means nothing to me if I can't have you. I want to make a world for us." He has not made a world for me as a woman. I know that he is too lazy and too self-indulgent to do so. He will only write. I wept.

Futility. Weakness. I accept him as he is. He is painting. He is like a child. Obedient. Yielding. Almost dies when I seem to lose my faith in him. Crushed by my smallest doubts. In writing—a murderer, an assassin, a caricaturist. Vitriolic. I make no more struggles to demand of people what they cannot give. Each to his own nature. Henry has responded to my dreams of him as a writer. Wrote a marvelous preface to "night" part of "Alraune," showing tremendous new reaches in understanding.* I love him. I hate to thrust him out into the world, hardships, hateful jobs. I can't do it. I'm willing to work for him.

My belief sometimes wavering and uncertain, I need reality and realism.

Cafeteria. Preferring one's room not out of indifference to the world but out of hyper-responsiveness to it. Tired of pitying the doorman who sits brooding over his lunch at the cafeteria where I eat. Evading the place because the handsome Italian gives me extra sauce and is concerned whether I eat well or not, so that I have to be grateful, and I am tired of feeling. Rather go where I am unknown and where I can rest from the effort all human dealings require of me. Cashier's admiration. She thinks I am a dancer or actress. We talk about nail polish.

---

* Miller's comments about the first part of "Alraune," the "night" section, were incorporated, apparently, into a foreword to what became *The House of Incest.* "This is a language beyond the language of nerves. The effect is that of starlight carried over into daytime and this image is appropriate since the various personifications of neurosis are here caught and fixed in the night. . . ." Never used in connection with the book, this text first appeared in *Anaïs: An International Journal,* Volume 5, 1987 (Becket, Massachusetts), pp. 111–114.

While waiting for a patient I have to make changes in the photographs before me. Have to insert photo of Hugh on top of Henry's and Huck's and Eduardo's. To each one I can write truthfully, according to the hour: "I have your photograph before me."

APRIL 18, 1935

*P*ATIENTS. THEY WEEP WHEN THEY DISCOVER THEY are their own victimizers and not the victims of others. Psychically responsible for attitudes toward the world. Imaginative interpretation according to personal, subjective facets. World changes according to our concepts. Blame for all our concepts and creative part in its making a hurtful truth. Rank says analysis is a reevaluation. Here I paste label for the cleaning of my red velvet dress for the stain made by X. Seance in my cabin when he tried to force me and finally came all over my dress while I resisted him. I showed this label to Huck without telling him the truth.

Analysis: 1. Dancer: ordinary, uninteresting. 2. Her sister: actress, inert, passive, interesting. 3. Violinist: rich in feeling and poetry and original in her actions. 4. Russian Jew: poetical, sensitive, dreamy.

Huck said, "It must be wonderful to be analyzed by you." And we play at it. He needs help, but he never took it from anyone before. In life he lacks experience altogether. His quickness, intelligence help him, but he lacks the mellowness, the grace, the insouciance, the ease and flow.

Not homosexual love, but a love of different parts of ourselves incorporated or lived out by others. Henry loves his sensitive self in Fred [Perlès]. I loved my dramatic self in June, *realized* in June. Henry loves his own weakness in Joe O'Regan and in Emil Schnellock, reflections of his sickness and femininity.

Huck's distress because I spilled my handbag as I got into the train. The only imperfection in our weekend. The love and the need of perfection. Henry cured me of this but I still can't leave Henry on a dissonant phrase. My anguish at thought of losing Hugh altogether, inexplicable, except as an attachment to an ideal, unreal, romantic first love.

I finished the manuscript of "Alraune." Henry was impressed with its new form.

My extreme love for *all* people and things is not neurosis but *love,* attachment, passion.

Talking about Henry–June novel [*Djuna*] to Huck, I said, "You will be shocked by its unreality!" because he had been saying (to console himself) that my human life with Henry had not been real (only it is so now—was made real when I gave him pain). Huck said I had to write about it to make it real, I had to play role of living and then really live (with Huck). But I happen to know I make life real with Henry now, and that my life with Huck, so far as I am concerned, is unreal, because I am in love with a mind, a man's creation. It is real for him, more real than anything he lived through. That is the illusion I must continue to give him.

A P R I L   2 2 ,   1 9 3 5

*I*T'S LIKE BEING IN A BOAT AND STRUGGLING TO save oneself, and someone is always seeking help so desperately that I cannot be allowed to live for myself. Huck helped me and then, when I was strong, he collapsed; and now he wants care and help and analysis and he does not know how to live, or how to be happy, and teaching him pulls me back again into darkness, and back into all my doubts and jealousies about Henry's love.

Never free. He is so dark, so heavy, just like Hugh. No joy, no joy. He is tired. And I always come for strength and get weakness. I have barely come out of the darkness myself and I have to spend all my strength saving Huck. The worst of it is that I have no human love for Huck at all, I don't feel any tenderness or pity. I was angry and hard when he collapsed yesterday. Fatigue. But mostly sadness, because he can't have everything the way he wants it—me. The absolute.

The creator's will, I said once, which can only be satisfied in creation. Certainly never in life, where one has to accept so many limitations, so many imperfections and compromises, to be happy. Henry is the wise one now, wise from living. Huck is young because the wisdom gained from ideas is useless, in fact contrary to life. From a stimulating, creative relationship it has now become a destructive one because I don't love Huck and I have to pretend. And I can't pretend anymore. I have to live by my true feelings. And it is Huck who has helped me to learn what my true feelings are. The illusion I have to give Huck is intolerable to me now. I want to smash it right at the beginning rather than build it up. Because Huck himself said, "Happiness based on an illusion is not possible. Worse, even." He senses something of the truth, but I delude him. I counterinterpret. My illness on weekends is due to repulsion, dislike of being in lonely places with Huck because it means closeness to his body. I interpret otherwise. He wants to believe me. It is easy to give the love illusion. The other helps you.

Analysis: Young sculptor said what I have always said, that analysis is like a love affair. Produces the same ecstasy, liberation, renewal. *Discovering the plot of one's life.* Idea of creative limitation in life. Doors closing as one walks forward, curtains of silence and inertia. Obstacles like icebergs. Wild animals. Forests of hair, cactus. Idea that limitation is inside of one, a malformation, wanting the impossible. The imagination pulling one into *trop* (too much). Evasion possible by renunciation in life and creation in art.

Walking home and thinking, In my book I can ordain, rule, walk, laugh, shout, do acts of violence, kill. I am creator and king. This same will, applied to life, kills one. All creators are unhappy in life.

All creators are absolutists. Tired of struggling against the limitations of life. In art none. I think this is not my idea but Rank's.

Huck understands that it makes me angry to see myself in him, struggling with my old ideal sorrows, my old complications, from which I am already so far away. His sadness during living—like mine while Henry slept insouciantly, or ate joyfully, or watched a movie with unconcern. I, all alone, struggling with my doubts, my fears, my sorrows, my shocks, my surprises. After much experience comes the non-caring, the toughening, *Werther's* sorrows, big and deep, due to seeing one's life as a whole. No joy in this. Joy only in the little things along the way, the ones that get spoiled by big philosophies or too much knowingness. Just as most talk I hear I cannot enjoy, because I have too much wisdom. I went to sleep on Huck while he learned how to live, because that cannot be taught except by living. I learned how to live from the way Henry went to sleep. I learned thus that one should not care so much, that one ought better to sleep.

Analysis: After neurosis is cured there remains a more acute loneliness in a new world because there are more neurotics than non-neurotics.

If I had not rebelled against Hugh sexually, I would never have hated him. I love him as a brother, deeply. I only hate him sexually, as I hate Huck sexually.

I said to Henry: "I have accepted everything, accepted you as you are, your purpose, your need of faith, your need of liberty. I never tried to shut you up in a house and in a job. I want you free. I'm willing to make sacrifices. I want to continue to live our dream, not to make it real. My woman's desire, or world, has to be sacrificed. Life together impossible. Interruptions are concessions to reality. I will have to return to Hugh every weekend. But are you happy? Your voice sounds as if I had killed something in you, as if you were disillusioned. I am not disillusioned, but I have no more illusions. I believe in you and in what you are doing, but I don't expect happiness as a panacea. The day you have money you would only have it for a day. You would give it to Joe in a fit of drunken sentimentality. But I don't mind that. It's you. It's life. I can't ask you to play all the roles. I like the fantasy we live in. I am happier living out our crazy dream."

It was Henry who said, "I believe that in our own crazy, fantastic way, we will get further than other people do by realistic means."

But further into fantasy, not into human life. It's our human life and our togetherness that I fought for with all my trickeries. The pain in my voice is only what it cost me to come to this. I did rebel. I admit that. I rebelled as every woman does. Man's purpose: sacrificing always the warm and the human. That is one reason I came to New York. I wanted to get free of you, independent. I rebelled against not being your purpose in life.

We saw a movie, *Living on Velvet*, which upset us both. Man possessed by his airplane. Woman seeking to hold him on earth. One moment, defeated, she leaves him, saying, "You don't love me." The eternal complaint. The difference is that Henry only understood the man, his craziness, his soarings, whereas I understood both. I often say to Henry, "Give me only understanding and I will find it easier to live, to give up my woman's world." All this because Hugh's return threatens our life together, because I rage inwardly to have sought in Rank again (as I did in Father, Henry, Dr. Allendy) a more ideal, a closer marriage.

Ideal. That is what I first said: an ideal attraction to Rank. It was an attraction to an ideal. Instinct rebels against the ideal. I have to stick to Henry no matter how much I suffer. I can't live with ideals. So is Hugh an ideal? Nature is against the ideal. *Rien à faire.* I tried. I tried very hard. I tried to go against nature, Rank, the ideal, understanding, peace, happiness. Living only for me. And I, living an instinct and a dream—for an aviator! I tease Henry about his airplane. It's funny. That sacrifice I made to Henry does not seem like a pretense. I act, I pretend gaiety, courage—but it is more natural than to pretend to love Rank.

ARIL 24, 1935

CARICATURAL ASPECTS OF LIFE REAPPEAR WHEN the drunkenness of illusion fades: Huck, out of his apartment, the first time I saw him with a hat on, in full daylight, in the Bois. In New York, in his bowler hat and fur-collared coat, and with his cigar, like a Jewish merchant. The night he wanted tenderness here, the night I was so sick after two days of bilious attacks I could not bear to have him sleep with me in my small bed. I saw the varicose veins on his legs, and I smelled his breath. But when you love, nothing repels you. I see caricatures in everything. I see caricatures of myself in Huck, in my Father. I see all that Henry so savagely depicted with his hatred of disillusion.

Life with Henry coming to a temporary end, for a month or two, and great sadness oppresses me. I forget his selfishness, I forget the window open even if I am cold, the table in the middle of the room, like peasants, the light overhead instead of lamps and softness, the irregular hours, his caprices, phobias, craziness, contrariness. I forget all the serious selfishness. I love him.

He has been finishing the rewriting of *Black Spring*. He wrote the marvelous "City Man" section. The "Burlesk," in which there are parts that make me weep. He read aloud last night. I know it is great. I know it is worth many sacrifices.

I am tired.

I was happy to know Hugh was coming, as if Joaquin were coming. Yet it takes me away from Henry. But I fight off the sadness. I think of it as a new adventure. I pack. I prepare surprises for Hugh. Montreal. Moving again. Last weekend with Huck I sent Hugh a humorous cable referring to his multiple professions: "Will meet steamer. Hope to recognize banker, artist, painter, astrologer, sage, rascal. Will flirt with all of them." And before that, something about the everlasting adventure. What faithfulness to the past. I think of Hugh in terms of peace—rest. Everything else requires an effort, courage, strain, labor.

Henry misses the decay of Paris, the slumberous old age of Paris. I like the animal activity here, the whirlwind of a young race. I don't mind that it has no meaning, that it is a factory. I have my own meaning. It has buoyancy, above all—buoyancy. Springs. Nerves. Dynamism.

I am tired.

I have worked hard. I have acquired eloquence. But I always come to the same conclusion: I want to do my own living and not help others to live. I fret. I get restless and impatient in my analyst chair. Damn you, I can do it all better than you, I have done it all better than you, I have lived more bravely, I have done things, I have wept more, laughed more, moved more, I contain more; what you tell me is rarely new, rarely better than what I think, do, say every day. I was more sick than you. I still am. I suffer insanely from jealousy. Always will, from doubts of love. More than all of you. I have written in between our talks.

But no regrets. Love makes me yield again, love, compassion, interest. Love inspires wonderful vehement speeches to combat Henry's obsessions that he is writing in a void, that he is like a rat in a trap, while *Tropic of Cancer* is circulating [among American publishers], and *Black Spring* has not yet been shown to any editor. "What would you really say then if your books had been burned, like Lawrence's, or if you had really been persecuted and put in prison?" He can't bear rejections, the silence of conventional editors, the formal slips from magazines, the stupid comments of literary agents. He whines, he frets. What do you want, my Henry? You'll publish your own books. We'll get subscriptions. It will be done, and you know it. I haven't failed you yet, have I?

It is all anticipatory fears and frustrations that I have to combat. But when I talk he understands. So much he understands that the day I said, "Woman takes her ideology from man, as I took yours," he was doubtful! I have absorbed his philosophy of life. I like his whiny voice, but when I get a roomful of his friends, the "warm, whiny, indolent, flabby, insouciant men," then it is too much and I chafe and rebel under a pretense of joy and tolerance, chafe against this white trash. Yet I see there always the same warm flowering of blood and instinct and mindlessness, and it is good, like the tropics.

Father writes me like a Protestant minister, Joaquin like a Catholic preacher, Mother like a loving but permanently baffled one, Hugh trying to catch up, to become, he says, more than Rank and Henry and Erskine.

"I Believe in Miracles," croons the radio from every street corner. "Blue Moon," sings every radio from every open window. "Night and Day" comes plaintive like a primitive chant. Night and Day. Night and Day. Night and Day!

A patient says, "I am having a love affair with a voice. A voice that gets to things so deep in me that I can't realize what is happening to me. Magic." It is he who used the word. He says he has found it again, through me: his sense of wonder. Wonder.

The joy in little things is all we have to combat the tragic in life. The pleasure from a white handbag from Huck. The pleasure of walking through crowded streets. Elizabeth Arden bath salts: rose geranium. Ascot shirt in emerald green for Hugh, and the electric shaver, and the pocket adding machine. The set of miniature hand-blown bottles, found at Grand Central, as reminder of Huck's work in a glass factory near Vienna. My collection of rare, exotic fishes preserved by Japanese in painted bottles.

From dual diary kept with Huck: Lies necessary to her to maintain the split. The denial—always two—but rationalized as necessary for the other—to make the other happy. By keeping up illusion, or rather building up illusion. This has to be counteracted if too unreal by stark reality, life service which is not real, not life either, but through the pain is made real: creating reality (just as much as unreality) by having it pain, but again as a balance having unreality, which is happiness.

He tells me: Giving man the deception of love, of being loved the way they want to be (Maya), she uses her mother-instinct for that, turning it into deception as protection. From what? From life or from self? Self-deception necessary for deceiving the other, but if self-deception becomes truth (that is, a conscious lie) then the lie indicates the self-deception; that is, if the lie is necessary in order to assure love (to self and other) then this must be untrue also. Lying for fear of loss (anger), loss of love! Loss of being loved interpreted *for* the other, but maybe it is for the other too—creating a uterine world for the man in which he can live; uterine world means ego world, where everything is as he wants it to be, or as he needs it. She knows that in her feelings when and what he needs, that's her adaptability; she is man's environment, changeable, possible environment. Where is your true self—not in your writing, nor in your living, nor in your playing—where?

MAY 2, 1935

7 PARK AVENUE. RENT 125 DOLLARS. APARTMENT 61. I buy a white nightgown, as Hugh asked me, for our remarriage. *Tout ce que je fais, c'est pour me distraire de mon grand amour pour Henry.*

When I leave Henry on weekends he comes back home in the evenings, because he finds nothing else he wants to do.

I fight off intrusion of world, of politics, war, Communism, revolutions, because they kill the individual life when it is all we have, all I have. After talks with Emil or other men, Henry returns to me battered, pessimistic, and I remain indifferent to world problems, seeking to maintain a day-to-day happiness. Others want this outer disintegration because it is a good pretext under which to accept their inner destruction. No more art, no more books, because war is near. There is nothing left to live for but the woman's world—man-and-woman love. Woman is fundamentally right. I stand more and more for life. Hate politics. History. Which cheat one of individual happiness. War, which destroys individual life.

To Henry one evening: Why not take it humorously? We don't want to be free, economically, by living dully as ordinary people. You don't want an ordinary job. I don't want analysis, or anything, as a routine, but as an adventure. Well, then we will have to conform to my job as Hugh's wife. Think what it would be if you had married the captain of a ship (oh, significance!): "I have to leave for a few months." Imagine you're married to an actress (oh, significance!): "I am going on the road"—or a dancer. Accept the separateness. I will continue to play tricks for us to live together as much as possible. (What a trick it turned out to be! Huck getting me to come away from Paris and making it possible for me to live with Henry. What irony!)

Henry, solemn: "We need a printing press. We dream. In our own fantastic way we may get free. I don't know."

Speech to Henry, eloquent, to cure him of wanting my job as analyst. After our talk, Henry desists. He gets frisky and playful again. I feel I have gained a battle against tragedy. Gay, though separation breaks my heart.

I chose an apartment near Henry. Showed it to Huck for approval. If only Huck would stop wailing, perspiring, collapsing.

Pain of identification: When I am with Huck, I confuse and identify some of my feelings toward him as Henry's toward me because some of them are similar, and that makes me fear all of them (doubt of Henry's love), just as because some of the feelings of my Father were like mine I got all entangled and confused with him.

Twice now a black pall came over Huck. His depressions are terrible and like an animal's. He lies there sighing, collapsed, with an earth-colored face, with a breath like death. Death all over his face. And then I have no pity, only anger. I don't want to be his mother. He demands too much. He is too heavy, too tragic, too young in life, in living. I find no words of compassion for him, no patience. I loved his strength. I loved his giftedness, not a weak, sick, human Huck. He looks terribly ridiculous to me—because I don't love him. I'm not moved by his suffering—because I don't love him. He looks ridiculous, comical, in his nightgown, like a woman, like an old woman. I hate him then. I show it. I say hard things. I can't kiss him. He repels me. I scold him for not knowing how to be happy. If he is trying to act like Henry (because I said that everything I have done for Henry this winter was done because he was very sick), he will discover that I don't love him. Perhaps he has already. I explained my anger as rebelling against playing the good mother.

I am sitting in the Park Avenue apartment, in a stereotypical American salon with Adams-period furniture, expecting Huck, who has not been able to work since Monday. He says he is tired, tired and with no desire to live, but it is all full of implications about his need of me. And I hate his dependency. I could not write him. I sent him telegrams, on which it is easier to write empty words. I am ready to pretend again, whatever he needs, to make him well again, to see him through his American experience, which I alone made possible because in Paris he did not have the courage to carry it out if I did not promise to come over. I know I failed him—I would not go all the way with him. But he demanded too much. All I want is not to poison life anymore with tragedy. My tears are exhausted, my capacity for suffering is exhausted. I have caught up with Henry's insouciance and nonchalance and selfishness!

I can sit before a coffee while Huck is suffering, before coffee and toast, drinking and eating slowly, leisurely, and feeling infinitely contented, just sitting there alone, free of caring, free of pity.

I came to the end of my pity by discovering that it was I who created my own suffering, just as others create their suffering. I am to blame for my attitude, for my desire to suffer. So I know now Huck has to be left alone until he exhausts that suffering, his tragic attitude. Poor Huck. He made me strong and now he is jealous of what he has given me. I learn so quickly. He is old, more inflexible.

MAY 2, 1935

*H*UCK CAME. HARD AND ANGRY AGAIN. HE SAID HIS life had always been a mess, and would always be a mess, that he knew all the time there was no room for him in my life, that he did not like the role I made him play, that I had used him.

All this was true. I could only say, "And didn't I give you something in return?" Yes, that he was not questioning, but he, he had given his all, himself. He sat there contemplating with self-pity what he had given. I never count what I gave Henry; nor do I ever take it back. I saw that Huck even then had been less generous to me than I have been to Henry. But about the love—there was nothing to say or to deny. He knew all the time. He left, both of us having said little. I felt no regret and I could not even move from the couch where I sat. I let him go. I watched him out of the window. No feeling. He had his valise with him.

I sat down and wrote [George] Buzby: "Never mind about the publication of my ms." There was, anyway, a question as to whether it would not be too dangerous to publish it. Then I lay down.

The ring I gave Huck—my Father's—was given to a father and not to a husband. It never occurred to me to give it to Henry. But now I will, merely because Henry is everything I need. What he is not, I can do without. I gave Huck what I could give—pleasure— that's all. *Life.*

Huck asks me to forgive him. "You can because you know I was not myself yesterday. What I said was crazy and you should have stopped me. Having been that unjust to you made me sicker, of course. It was not right."

On the train to Montreal: My Huck, you were not unjust and you did not say crazy things the other day. You said terrible and death-dealing truths. It is true our relationship has been one-sided and all the giving came from you; it is true, unfortunately, that you were not able to be your real self with me—your human self. It is true that the role I gave you to play in my life is not big enough for your bigness and your absolutism. About the using of you, which hurt me most of all—I knew it and fought it off. I struggled not to use you, not to need you, and you know that. I struggled against your generosity. I don't justify myself. I did need you. I will never again. It is impossible to help you, or to give to you, but I could have done it if . . .

Huck, you always said you didn't want happiness built on an illusion. You were my ideal love. You deserve the greatest love, but I still love Henry and I can't give you what you deserve. That is my fatality and my destiny, the love of Henry, no matter how imperfect. When I realized this, as soon as Henry came, I tried to save our ideal love because I thought— more than that—I identified myself so much with you that I saw in your love for me the same kind of love I have for Henry, and I used to think: My love for Henry will die slowly, just as Henry's love for June. I could not help feeling it was the same. That you would suffer perhaps as I had suffered waiting for Henry's love for June to die. And at the same time I hated to see you suffer.

You say I did not let you have human reactions. No, but I knew all the time all the human reactions you felt. I felt them with you. Each step of the way was torture for me. I failed. I made you miserable. I had that faith in the outcome. I haven't got that anymore, because you are too truthful to live. I have accepted the inequalities in love. You haven't. You can't. And you're right. Why should you? You are not a woman. You are the one who has the courage to break away from what causes you pain. I have nothing to forgive you. You have been great and wonderful, you have done superhuman things, divine things. All you have given of yourself will not make you poor. Forgive me for my illusions, delusions, for deluding you and myself, for my false hopes that the ideal love can prevail over the neurotic, or whatever you called mine for Henry. Oh, forgive me. I feel terribly, terribly humble, terribly sad and broken, because though my love for you is not the kind you desire, not what you wanted in answer to yours, not human, I still feel bound to you somehow, and feel all you feel, and would give years and years of my life to make everything different. But it can't be made different. You are the victim of an illusion of human creation; you thought I could be cured, saved from an imperfect love by an absolute. I think nature fights off absolutes. You are the most wonderful being I know, Huck. I will never forget all you are. But I am bad for you, very bad. I hurt you. I made you play roles. I made you accept sharing and all kinds of sacrifices. It is I who ask for your forgiveness.

When you were sick I knew it was rebellion and unhappiness. I was angry that you could not keep up the illusion. I want to do something for you, yet I have to keep away. I'm the last person who can do you good. How ironic and terrible that is. I don't want to do to you what was done to me. I had to act a superhuman role with Henry. Believe me, I prefer that to acting the cruel and destructive role I had to for you. I care too much to do that to you.

I beg you, Huck, don't have any regrets. Every moment of joy I gave you was poisoned by a moment of pain. I know it. Nothing can be done, nothing. The strength you gave me disappears when you disappear, so I don't feel as if I had taken anything away from you. Nothing remains but the memory of what you are as a human being. At least I want you to know that you were fully, fully loved and all your love was answered equally from the time of our first kiss to the time of Henry's arrival in New York. Completely and absolutely. Think only of that.

Hotel Mount Royal, Montreal. Room 6022. Great emotion at meeting Hugh again, a tender love. Passion from him, constant outpour of desire. A new Hugh, who thanks me for having let him be himself by my persisting in being myself. Has lived fully in London, is freer, gayer. Sad to discover he is treated as a sage, adviser, father, and not as a human being. Women treat him as they treat Rank. But, Hugh consoles himself, spiritual power and sensual power are the same, just as strong. He has a lot to talk about, is alive. I met him all perfumed, in a white transparent nightgown. I can be more loving. His body does not repulse me. He is attractive. It is pleasant to submit to him, after Huck.

I think of Huck all the time, of what I have done to him, of how he will survive. I am haunted by him. There was nothing else to do, it's no use trying to protect men from the cruelties of life. They are not grateful. They hate you for the deception. They don't love the pretender. Yet it is terrible to tell the truth as I have done. He forced me to. He knew the truth. I am deeply sad.

My life with Hugh is absolutely unreal and meaningless. He touches me, moves me by his quality, his nobility. He says, "When I return to you I return to the only real—the only human life I have. I have learned to appreciate you more than ever, your responsiveness and expressiveness."

I think his life in London was a beginning, like mine in Montparnasse. Not quite real yet, but it will become more and more real, as mine did. Now he was acting, as Huck said about me; he was imitating me. He thought of me while he was doing it, he thought of my life in Paris with the artists, the life I did not share with him. He is young, and strong, and faithful, and loyal. Lives from day to day. At least I am just to Hugh now. I was deeply unjust before, in my fight for integrity. I hated him. Now I love him as I love Joaquin.

Living only from day to day. Canoeing on the Ottawa River for our honeymoon. Jokes. Acting little scenes of jealousy to please him. Laughter.

Resisting the impulse to go and take care of a sick Huck. Cannot be a mistress and a nurse, too. Some other woman will have to be the nurse. If you give life you also give pain. Poor lonely Huck.

Acceptance. Fatalism. Resignation. While Hugh talks about his business, I study the stuccoed walls. He is saying he loves power, he wants power. He has power now, a will, a dynamism. Power. Power. Power. He wants power and to play around with artists. He came back with a high-collared emerald sweater, delicately gray-checked trousers and coat as the artists wear. He lived on Charlotte Street. He did the painters' horoscopes. He met Epstein's mistress.* He stayed at the Royal Automobile Club. He drank beer and whiskey. He is living his own life. He is drawing. He gives me freedom. He wants my body. We exchange with tenderness. He gives me the freedom Huck could not give me, the freedom to be true to myself, to my love for Henry. He is happy because he is free and human with me. He is proud of me. Together we are a great force. He has a wonderful mixture: love of power on earth and love of art. "Rest on me," he says. Poor Huck. Too great a knowledge of truth, too great a probing destroys *life, which is illusion.* He has destroyed his own life by absolutism. He wanted to be Hugh and Henry and all people to me, the whole world. One always loses something. I am losing my great compassion, which made me weak; my tenderness, my softness. Audacity. One has to go on. I used to wince and be a coward. I had to hurt Huck; that was inevitable. The hurt I cause as a *woman, mistress,* I want always to efface because of my maternal love. I want to take care of the men I hurt.

Oh, God, I am not as free of caring as I seem to be.

MAY 11, 1935

7 PARK AVENUE. APT. 61. DESK IN THE SUNSHINE. Noise of 34th Street traffic. Sun on me while I am quietly pasting in the diary Huck's last note: "Thanks for your letters. I really could not write. It all hurts so much. I don't know

---

* New York–born Jacob Epstein (1880–1959), after studying with Auguste Rodin in Paris, settled eventually in England and became one of Britain's most prominent sculptors. He was involved, apparently, in a number of extramarital affairs with his models and sired five children with three different women while married to his staunch supporter, Margaret (Peggy) Dunlop, who died in 1947. The "mistress" Hugh Guiler met may have been Kathleen Garman, who became the second Mrs. Epstein.

when it will end, or how." Pasting this quietly, as if it were all very old. I only miss Huck acutely, deeply, as someone to talk to. Not physically, not humanly. Just that divine understanding and unique responsiveness and clairvoyance, the match to my mind. But my love affairs of the mind and my marriages of thought are over. It is better to be alone. Better to be alone than pretending to love. I wear my hair high, *à la Récamier*. I wear a flowered evening dress I bought to show Hugh when he comes home. It is for the weekend at the Perkinses'. I pack the turquoise jewelry to return to Huck. I send him a telegram because Hugh wants to see him. I feel cool, and fatalistic, and deeply weary of struggle, and indifferent. Analysis, happiness, makes people selfish. Even Hugh has become selfish, because he is more natural, and all the rest was pretending to be ideal. A less ideal, less false, more honest world, each for himself. Yet I still give to Henry.

Henry has finished *Black Spring* and is meeting William Carlos Williams. I told Henry something was broken in me, not my spirit, not my courage, but the absolute. The absolute. Another ideal quest. I have become resigned to reality—that is, to the fact that if I make Henry responsible as husband I destroy Henry the vagabond, and our dreams, for the sake of human life. But it was hard, terribly hard, to separate. Henry was as usual, resigned, sad, gentle, caressing, defeated. He never fights except in writing.

So here is Mrs. Guiler in a new evening dress, with something forever shattered inside of her, the absolute. What I wanted was Henry and life with Henry. To go directly for what one wants, as Huck reached unwisely for me, means to destroy it, to sink it into reality and tragedy. The rebellious me, the believing me, was broken exactly at the same moment that I broke Huck's overabsoluteness, intransigence, idealism.

In creation alone there is the possibility of perfection.

The train of my dress lies in circles around my feet. The aquarium lies exposed by the window. The sea flower blooms white, with specks of coal dust. The seashell has parted from its twin, which Huck kept. Huck has the diaries we wrote together.

A patient gives me thirty dollars, which I will give to Henry for his rent, and a book, Daniel Defoe's *Moll Flanders,* with a dedication: "Practically the first novel in English, to the first and finest lady in the world, from one she raised from the dead."

Strange: it says on the title page, "Moll Flanders . . . was twelve years a whore, five times a wife (whore once to her own brother), twelve years a thief, eight years a transported felon in Virginia, at last grew rich, lived honest and died a penitent."

I like all but the end.

Montreal. Playacting love for Hugh. I think sometimes he is too, but that he does not know it, that he is more a slave to habit and ideals. I can hardly tell now whether his emotions are real. I am so accustomed to thinking that Hugh is sincere. But I also wonder whether there is a Hugh, whether he isn't just my robot man, doing and being everything to please me.

But we laugh together. We are gay, I like his emerald green sweater.

I awake shouting, "Listen, you English fresh-air fiend, close the window!"

"Cough up," says Hugh, "*who* have you flirted with?"

"Give me a cough drop." Playing at love. Playing at the five months having been too long.

When I'm good Hugh says, "Oh, so you're afraid of me." Yes, afraid of getting another five months. Unconsciously, I prepare another escape by pretending the separation was painful.

Hugh says that he loves me more by comparison now with other women and men he has met. That he loves my weakness and the courage with which I fight this weakness. He regrets nothing; no regrets for the pain I gave him. It was all good, he felt in London. He lived. Says he loves above all my responsiveness. Met artists and models and remembered the time when I had been a model.

I'm tired of strain and efforts. Hugh wants to protect me. I will let him. He says I take away all his incentive for work when I work.

I felt a bit broken since my desire for an absolute has been shattered by life. I feel defeated, just as Huck was defeated. You can't have the absolute. The sooner you resign yourself the better. I'm resigned to life as it is, because making it over means a lifelong struggle and a loss of all its good hours. I have learned to accept limitations to my desires and dreams. It is terrible for strong-willed natures.

Hugh says he can't dissolve all the way with the artists. Neither can I dissolve all the way. He has become more dynamic and more human. He is loved for what he gives (horoscopes, help, protection), not for himself, and it makes him sad, just like Huck. Consoles himself thinking that spiritual power over people is as strong as or stronger than sensual power. It's like Huck saying that he was afraid always of being loved for his analysis, as men are loved for their money. Alas, that is exactly what happened!

Insanity, caused by seeing that Huck loves me as I love Henry (wanted to live on a desert island with me, wanted me alone, far from other people) and this made me doubt Henry's love again because I had, in relation to Rank, Henry's feelings of gregariousness, and this meant perhaps that Henry did not love me. Identification of Rank's love for me with mine for Henry very painful, and had to be dispelled each time by Henry's passionateness when I returned to him, his constantly renewed proofs of love. Could not have endured this analogy any longer. Cause of great pain, this comparison in ways of loving, asking if one way means real love and the other not loving.

Such speculations lead only to death and despair. I am curing myself by life, living on, daring, facing. Comparison and identification disintegrated and killed me before (entanglement with my Father). I feel saner now than I ever was, but I have terrible nightmares. I dynamited a city. I was in a room full of dead animals. I saw a baby who had been abandoned. I decided to adopt him. As I began kissing him, he began to look more and more like a baboon. His mouth was repulsive. I thought to myself, It is good I don't have to kiss a baby on the mouth. I was so appalled by his ugliness, I wondered whether he ought not to be killed because he would be unhappy. Huck told me once, when he was born his mother was deeply shocked. Says he looked monstrously ugly, covered with black hair. I spoke to Huck very often of adopting the little Huck, his own child-self, for whom he had a peculiar and tremendous self-pity. He gave me a picture of himself as a little boy. Eyes always very beautiful and soulful. Born old.

Dream: Sticking safety pins in my stomach, and then closing them as if it were natural. In China. Everybody leaves houses because there will be an earthquake. Thunderbolts come but fall into the sea. City is saved. Someone tells me Henry is dead. Tremendous grief. I look for him everywhere. (Henry's writing on artist in China. Depressed by American aridity.)

MAY 14, 1935

*L*UNCH. REBECCA WEST, WHO IS APPALLED BY what is missing in America: "You know, those rats they brought up without magnesium or something, and they lost their maternal love. Well, Americans—there is some element lacking. What is it? One doesn't say *soul*. One finds other names for it. It's everything deep; everything deep is lacking."

She wants my nail lacquer. She hasn't finished her new book because of an operation. She thought she was not going to live: "I won't see the spring again!" The human only a second thought. "Maybe I'm not human," she said. "I love the feelings between the two women in your book. I don't mind being mentally alone, as you seem to. But then I'm years older than you. Your husband is so sweet, but I was so surprised he should be your husband—aren't you?"

Crabmeat and strawberries. Indigestion. Soda. Nervousness from the whirlpool of invitations.

Henry again seems dead to me, so inert, so passive, so plantlike, mentally. I suppose I miss Huck terrifically, to talk to. This deadness of Henry pushed me out toward Huck. Henry is burned out. He can only write books and ruminate. Remember. He only came alive when I tortured him by leaving him.

Will I really be able to accept my mental loneliness? Will I be able to live just on human passion, and human protection?

Weekend at the Perkinses'. Katrine a victim of her bank life. Too late to save her. Buried alive in the tombs of ceremony, duties, obligations, rituals, family conventions. Victim of starvation. Anemic. People everywhere, hundreds of them—of no value. I'm surrounded by people made of cellophane. A desert. Yes, Huck filled it, but I had to *pay* with love.

To console myself for deep lacks, I swim upward, toward the surface, the cellophane surface of coral bath salts, new dresses, objects, sandals, sheer nightgowns, luxury. I'm starved again. It must be the tapeworm. And poor Huck, he is very sick, and what can I do? What he wants I can't give.

Letter to Huck: I just want you to know this: that no one can ever take your place, that I miss you deeply, that I will never feel as close to anyone, never as closely married to anyone's feelings and thoughts, that I consider it a tragedy that you, because of your too-truthful vision, could not live on what we had, on the illusion, the twinship and the disparity, because now we have nothing.

I miss you everywhere I go, all the time. If only you had not loved me. If only what I gave you had been enough. I can't help regretting you, every moment. I can't help telling you. Maybe it will make you a little less sick to know that in the deepest way, what I have for you is beyond human love. Someday, oh, Huck, when you have got beyond loving or hating me humanly, come back to me so we won't be so alone, so utterly alone. You may think I was cruel to admit all the truths which you knew all the time. I think you were perhaps cruel to yourself not to be able to accept the half-happiness. There is no absolute on earth. But I want you to know I regret you.

I want you to know that the only thing I can't forgive you

is for feeling I used you. I only took what you gave me because when I loved you completely I felt it was right. Later, when the division came (reread the letter I wrote you when you went away—there I already say what I say now: I did not want to separate from you, I did not want to lose you altogether, yet I didn't feel any longer as a woman toward you), I began to refuse the gifts.

I know I can't save you, because of your absolutism. Perhaps I can't save anything at all of the unique communication we had together, but at least you know now that I'm as sad as you are, that nothing that you do or say to destroy what there is, can destroy inside of me what we created together— the rhythm and the understanding. You have lost me, but I'm alone, and true to all we lived out together, what was so beautiful that you feared its power to last. No one will ever come so near to me, to my soul and being. I just wanted you to know.

M A Y   2 2 ,   1 9 3 5

I SEND MOTHER COPIES OF THE *NEW YORKER*. I write Father, Eduardo, Joaquin. I analyze the sculptor and prepare the violinist to go to Europe. I return to Rank one of his mss, which I had submitted to a publisher. I charm and lure Henry out of his depression, take him to dinner on Broadway.

We decided to go to the movies last night. We're standing awaiting the bus. He looks at me and at the same moment we feel desire. He says, "Let's go back to our room." And we get into bed. Afterward we talk about the future, giving up Louveciennes, traveling. I want to go south. Hugh will be doing more traveling. I paint very glowing pictures. I glow with normal health, absence of fatigue, acceptance, philosophical moods. I enjoy everything, even being taken to the theater by bank people.

Frances Schiff, a friend from my school days, buys a pink negligee and eyelash stuff and thinks she is on her way to imitating my life. Rebecca West introduces me as "the woman who wrote the best book on Lawrence," and as "beautiful." Mrs. X. says I look so fragile that she can't imagine me analyzing anybody. Mr. Y. is attracted and says he is afraid of me because I am the kind of woman who leaves scars.

J U N E   2 2 ,   1 9 3 5

*L*OUVECIENNES. HOME. RUSH OF MEMORIES. SLEEP-lessness. Resistance. Wistfulness. No. No. No. The Persian bed. The clock ticking. The dog barking. Maria serving us. Mother and Joaquin visiting us. Eduardo astrologizing. Tommy laughing. There are bulbs missing. The tenants took things away. The books are dusty. The colored bottles shine less. The colored rooms no longer twinkle. The rugs are worn. The glass top of my dressing table is broken. Curtain rods are missing. Where are the garden chairs? France is old. *Elle est faisandée,* overripe. I hated it, coming down on the train, because of the wrinkles, the agedness, the odor of stale cheese with green worms, the odor of pennies. On the ship I had dark fantasies. Doctor Endler would be waiting for me on the pier.* I would be taken back to the hospital and go through everything again. Everything. Then I would recall every detail of the *fausse couche.* Or I would picture my Father's brown house. Brown all through. I don't want to see my Father. I don't want the past. The house is rotting away. I used to love its oldness. I hate the musty odors of decadence. The past, oh, the past. Mildewed, with the smell of mothballs, of cheese, of dead cats, dead mice, so wrinkled and soiled. Sitting by the same fireplace four years ago, in this bedroom, with Hugh, and he was saying, "I know you will have an affair with Henry." The studio

---

* A German refugee doctor in Paris, friend of Dr. Otto Rank, who apparently assisted at Anaïs Nin's abortion in August 1934. See, also, *Incest (opus cit.),* pp. 375–382.

where I wrote about June/Alraune because I was suffering from jealousy. The garden where I had dinner with Rank. Where I lay with Henry behind the bushes. The wall is crumbling. My Mother thinks it is beautiful. Eduardo is glad to be in his nest again. I am sad. I don't fit here anymore. It has worn itself away. It is small. It is decrepit. I was on a mountaintop. I was free. I have to catch trains. I have too much time to brood. My past. Mostly pain. Hugh sitting at the foot of the bed, crushed, after reading the June–Henry novel, and I trying to convince him it is all fiction. The difficulty of getting bread, butter, milk. The sullenness of Louveciennes, the stony faces behind the curtains, the dogs barking. Peace. Home is peace. A prison. It's a prison for me. I feel shut in. I'm wistful. I heard "You and the Night and the Music" on the radio. A rush of yearning for New York. It is ten o'clock. We are tired. So much to do in the house. The village church bells are ringing. Mosquitoes. Ants. Flies. Mice. The dogs barking. The smell of honeysuckle.

The new things I brought, the gifts for all, the Persian cotton print dress with the large wide skirt, the white pajamas and white Bedouin cape lined with red, a white coat and white Greek hat, the new valise given to me by Rank, the blue wooden dishes with stars on them, the new things.

A new me, a new me who does not belong here anymore, living in a dead house. A new me, without home and without resting place, the adventurer and the nomad, because now *I have accepted my solitude* and so I have no home and no husband. Henry still on the ocean, the voice of my feelings always. I bought *two* Hindu dresses, one for Henry's studio. People around me don't change as I do. I seem to live too quickly and always forward. I have dropped so many people— the Bradleys, the Viñes, Louise de Vilmorin, Roger Klein, the Guicciardis, Hugh's family—spiritually and actually. To come back here was like being caught in a circle. I make efforts against the sameness. I say, "We're going to have an astrologer's dinner with the blue wooden dishes with the stars on them, and we'll invite [Dr.] Allendy and [Antonin] Artaud." But I don't want to do it. It does not interest me.

On the ship I had so many nightmares. I thought the lady at the table next to us looked like Mrs. Rank. Yet I walked in the Bedouin cape, attracting so much attention that they took my photograph. And I danced and I slept and I ate caviar and lobster and crepe suzettes but I didn't want to come back. Ten-twenty. The radio. The sameness. It is the sameness which seems a nightmare. Coming back. That is why men take ships, go through Africa, walk through Tibet, climb the Himalayas, live in shacks, and walk starving, beg, sell things, fly, crawl through Arabian deserts. To fly from the sameness, the staleness and the sameness. That is why men read and get on airplanes, change women, stamp their passports multilaterally, swim, ski, and commit suicide. Face-to-face with one's own soul.

Where will I meet Rank again? At the Café du Rond Point, where we met on our way to the room. At Villa Seurat, while walking with Henry, or carrying Henry's market bag. Paris is like a second-rate fair. Shoddy. Everything is askew and small. There is no wind. They say it has charm. But I smell the decomposure. I'm in love with new worlds. Possible in America only. The satin-lined drawers of the house in Jericho, Long Island. Symbols. The snow on the windowsill making the window heavy when I lifted it after lying down with [George] Turner. Taxis in snowstorms to catch Rank, with his hair tousled, writing about me at six in the morning in order to look at me from a distance and move away from his pain. Radios in the taxis. Fudge cake at the drugstore and "Are you a showgirl?" Vivid colors and large scales, vastness and abundance, pasteboard and a bigger and livelier fair. The dimes click in the Fifth Avenue busman's clicker. The nickel clicks in the revolving turnstiles. Shoot to the heights of the Empire State Building, where the city looks like a map. Canary-birds are singing up there. It is possible to sing without earth under your feet, without a branch resting on damp earth, where the rain brings decay and the wind papers and leaves which must be raked away. Pineapple juice for breakfast from tropical America, and news of the carnival in New Orleans. Big Negroes serving soft southern lunches on the air-conditioned trains. And people so grateful and humble for all you give them, a country where there is a great demand for one's originalities, where one can give.

———

Father is taking his cure for rheumatism; Joaquin does not get his First Prize at the Conservatoire; the plumber has waited three days to repair the water closets; there is a smell of mildew on the sheets; this house is now like our house in White Plains, from which all my life slowly ebbed away, leaving greasy walls and stained carpets and a silence which this diary has loudly tried to break.

JUNE 27, 1935

*I*HAD EXPECTED TOO MUCH, I HAD EXPECTED Rank to give me my liberty by letting me inherit his work, but he did not give me that. He made me a prisoner and dependent. I had expected to make a fortune and become a publisher for Henry. I had expected great expansions, tremendous outward changes to match the changes in me. Luminous, pearl-colored rooms, ships, voyages, India, China, and Spain, floating, swimming, and lying, a feast of speed and height and oceans and new sensations. But Henry is sitting at the typewriter. We're in the studio in Louveciennes. Hugh is in London. Fred [Perlès] and Roger [Klein] and Maggy are coming for dinner. Emilia is ironing. I'm happy again in a mellow, humid way. I'm trying hard for a soft *atterrissage,* a soft landing. I have landed, landed from fantastic voyages through all the levels of American life, through the world of Rank's mind and creations, through the experience of analysis, of freedom from Hugh, of excessive courtships, of triumphs, of acquiring that wisdom which Henry had. I told Henry last night that he was ahead of me in three things that I'd finally learned: wisdom from living and not from the head, liberation from the romantic absolute, and possession of one's own soul. Michael Fraenkel understands ideas and not wisdom, not Henry's wisdom.

Fraenkel telephoned me as soon as he arrived. I dream of the printing press, an impossible dream. I'm incurable. Father writes me whimsical letters. I write him equally humorous ones. False laughter. I have to move in a different way, not over mileage but from a center. I have to sublimate my love of adventure.

So—the printing press. The idea fires me, and fires everybody. Everybody loves the idea of bringing forth his own book, of working with his own hands. China again, as Henry calls it, the China of the artist. The house begins to work its magic on Fraenkel and Fred. They came last night for dinner. Fred said it was like the house in *Le grand Meaulnes*. A fairy tale. I have worked at it. Henry is blissfully working. Slow meals in the garden. I am at peace. Louveciennes becomes a center. When I don't move about, people come. And the coming to Louveciennes is an adventure for them.

And so I begin a *tourbillon intérieur,* a mysterious, inner whirlpool. I feel less intense, yet creative. I feel that I am a bad artisan. I won't slave, perspire, perfect, or rewrite, so I will never produce a solid work; but my constant shooting off ideas and plans, my starting and launching and inciting and animating will make others produce. I like only the freshness, the seed throwing, the first élan, the creative leap and opening of new roads.

Lively talk last night. Henry mellow and deep. Negligently run house, just enough carelessness to make everyone at ease. Beds made at the last minute for Fred and Fraenkel. I took the wood carving of a Negro head and lay it on the bed and it looks startlingly real—a big Negro asleep in rose sheets. We laughed. Eduardo came down, all flowing and strong with the bigness of his research work. I bring Fraenkel back with me tonight. Sunshine. Peace. It was hard only to stand still physically, to change level and tempo. I like it now. I like what Henry wrote about it.

Fred and Henry talk about my sincerity. We all write about the same people so differently. I am true to life, as a woman is. Fred's book *[Sentiments limitrophes]* is very much liked by everybody, including my Father.

JUNE 29, 1935

*B*E STRONG AND QUIET. BE STRONG AND QUIET. IN one hour Fraenkel destroyed my peace and strength by appropriating Henry, the printing press, dominating Louveciennes, talking uninterruptedly all night and all today. I'm shattered with antagonism, jealousy, loneliness. And Henry, as usual, in quest of nourishment and novelty and stimulus, is listening as he listened to [Walter] Lowenfels; and Fraenkel, just like Lowenfels, is so jealous of me that he excludes me from everything, saying, "*Black Spring* is a result of all that happened between Lowenfels, Henry, and me."

Henry spoke up during the evening: "This talk was wonderful, wasn't it? Well, I've had better ones alone with Anaïs, right here in this room." Henry was human and gentle, but Fraenkel was drunk with himself, with his own talk, a supreme egoist, in need above all of power.

Then I realized Louveciennes was a refuge, realized that if I opened it to the world I would have no refuge from the world. Fraenkel would not take the train home last night. Staying on and on. I left them in the garden, talking. I came here for strength. My diary, I'm terribly human and fallible. If only Fraenkel had been human and gentle and inclusive.

I was sitting on my bed. Fraenkel came, different and gentle. Why? Because he had found his book, *Werther's Younger Brother,* marked by me and he liked the notes I made on it. He stood very near me and said, "You alone know what that book means. Better than Henry." He touched his book fondly, tenderly, with the same self-love Rank had for little "Huck," the child in himself; only, that memory made me miss Rank. I miss him more and more, but I know it is only when I am in distress, sinking, nervous, when I lose my strength, and not with the love he wants. I dream of his goodness, of his understanding.

After the feeling of invasion I had this week I began to prefer that the printing press should be at the Villa Seurat, what I now call "Russia," and the collective life—in contrast to the "Haven" of Louveciennes. Could not bear them all here, so close. There I can come and go, and leave. And this will remain my refuge.

Intellectuals like Fraenkel have no tact, no sacredness, no sense of walls, no sensitiveness in relationship. It is anarchism and inhumanness.

At night, Henry and I worked out the printing press alone. I told him I thought an association with Fraenkel impossible, and why. Henry knew I was right. The rightness came, as usual, out of a chaotic, tumultuous, nervous state in which I knew my instinct was at work, but I didn't see clearly what was happening. Something warned me of the danger in Fraenkel's domineeringness, how in the end both Henry and I would revolt. We planned to tell him I had the money already so he would not participate. We planned to allow him to talk, which he loves, while we would act. Henry and I always in unison and happy to work by ourselves. Fraenkel as a stimulus, but not as an associate.

When something is wrong—what a misery. I do not come clear. I feel an upheaval. I suspect myself of femininity, jealousy, a coming period, neurosis, every conceivable weakness; but these factors only exaggerate and deform and enlarge, they don't cause the upheaval fundamentally. They are danger signs. I have to obey them. I don't want our independence blocked by Fraenkel. I can't submit to Fraenkel, I told Henry. He is not my feminine axis. I can't change my orbit. I can only work for Henry, not for Fraenkel.

Fraenkel talks a perpetual creation. An extremist. Highly sensitive. Completely mental. Has a repulsive side—it's only the glamor and brilliancy of his mind which are attractive.

I must get inside of myself again and sublimate the energy I feel. I miss Rank desperately tonight. I yearn for his understanding. With Henry there is an understanding of blood, cells, unconscious, moon feelings, plant communication, seed intermarriage, deeper and more unformulated harmonies. It is every day more marvelous. A moon love. Very little talk about the relationship, very little analysis, just a flowering and stimulation.

Last night Fraenkel was talking about how we got tired of logic, how surrealism, humor, and chaos came to break down that logic which was unlike life and which was uninspiring. New elements stimulating. The "living thing," as Henry puts it. I recognized this quality in Henry and yielded to it as against my own state of crystallization, yielded to his chaos, which I, as a woman, should have had but squelched in order to act the intellectual father and the husband of my Mother—to take the place of my missing Father (Rank) I went to Lawrence, to praise it in Lawrence, and then found it in Henry.

Planning never to come out of the diary again to write novels, but to perfect and expand the diary form. I am gifted for the diary and nothing else.

JUNE 30, 1935

STRETCHED MY SOUL AGAIN, EXPANDED, ENLARGED. Through astrology. Asked Eduardo about Fraenkel. Eduardo said he was the one who had given us the seed, he was the leader. So I abdicated. I talked to Henry. I would submit to Fraenkel if that were right for our Idea, our Plan. I prefer, as a woman, to live and work with Henry alone. Last night I felt such peace—Henry and I, working through, for, and with, each other. But I had to get bigger than myself. Henry said, "You are trying too hard."

As soon as Eduardo took me into the stellar regions, I could control the feminine revolt I felt yesterday! Today I feel at peace after a tempestuous struggle with my pride and egoism. I must not act too much like a female. Eduardo and I made a joke of it. I said to him with a bow, "Now, under your influence, I have written a note of abdication to Fraenkel." Eduardo applauded.

Yesterday the idea of sharing the press with Fraenkel was intolerable. For besides the fact that he must dominate everything he touches, he does not know how to answer my need of feminine mystical participation—the indirect one which Henry knows how to do. Henry knows how to give me the place I need, because Henry knows woman's place in the cells of a man's life. Fraenkel does not. There's a coldness in him where everything is just an idea. No sentimentality, no delicacy. A kind of ruthless mind. He considers me a good mind, but he offends the woman.

Won a battle over my ego. I'm all worn out and shaky. Oh, the monsters I create and have to struggle against! My jealousy, my hypersensitiveness, my need of assurance. But it is done and I feel a religious calm. Henry, all through this, is so infinitely patient, calm, tender.

JULY 1, 1935

*F*IGHTING THE MOST CHOKING DEPRESSION. NOTHing helps. Not the talk with Fraenkel, where he praised me and showed understanding. Not Henry's softness. Not the sun. Not Hugh's tenderness, nor Eduardo's. It is a curse. I am assailed by all kinds of small monsters, jealousy of healthy and dumb Joyce, Fraenkel's mistress. I invent interminable scenes where I see Henry abandoning me for Joyce. I torture myself with images, fears, self-doubts.

I didn't seem the same in New York, or was there more poise and glare to drown it? I feel weaker here. I yearn for New York, and for Huck. Oh, loneliness, among so much love and care from all. When I left Henry, Fraenkel, Joyce, and Fred at the café, I felt relieved. So grateful to be able to escape them, because everything is pain, the slightest look or word away from me or against me. One moment of relief driving in the small car, sitting close between Eduardo and Hugh, one moment. And then pain again, pain all over and all through, at nothing. The old pains, the new ones, recurring. The moonstorms!

Once a month, the moonstorm. Dust in the eyes and ghosts in the veins. The blood of woman is spilling and all the strength ebbs away. Neptune and the Moon. What nightmares, of treachery and persecution. Everybody put on earth to work malice and tricks. Fraenkel becomes the Roman Caligula who invents tortures for me. He brings the Follies girl, Joyce, my antithesis, just to take Henry away from me. Her healthiness and stupidity offend me. Everything hurts me. Everything is imagined. I know that much now. It is simply like looking at one's insanity, but it goes on, just goes on, like a moonstorm made of secret and obscure sorrows.

JULY 5, 1935

*E*DUARDO SAYS, JUSTLY, THAT CONSCIOUSNESS IS not painful if one is going somewhere, doing or creating something, with it. If one stands still and conscious, one rots away. I'm suffering deeply because I miss the electric rhythm of New York (or Rank?). It was like having a fiery racehorse under you, giving you animal vigor. Here it is like a garbage can. Henry says that the soul expands in this garbage can. Not mine. I was drunk on liberty and sensation and bigness and space and dynamism.

Paris is a vegetable patch. Where are my wings, my airplanes, my ships, trains, and the luminousness of New York? I want to go away. Louveciennes is too small for me. Henry's life is too slow and sleepy.

I'm chafing. *Je piétine sur place.*

I'm awaiting a lover. I have to be rent and pulled apart and live according to the demons and the imagination in me. I'm restless. Things are calling me away. My hair is being pulled by the stars again. I feel I must obey—what? Fickleness. I'm awaiting this *man I used to dream about while Huck talked to me—this man who would deliver me from all of them.* Not one has been strong enough to deliver me from ambivalences and divisions. In Louveciennes there is an order, a divine Order which I need to continue work. Continuous life with Henry is impossible because I am not myself there. Everything is as Henry wants it. We eat, sleep at his hours. We go to his café, his movie; we read his books, cook for his friends, everything is for him only.

In Louveciennes everything is for me.

Today I wrap Henry in love, in tenderness. Another day I wrap Hugh in tenderness, because he is sick with a carbuncle. I take the most complete care of him. I have to visit my Father for two hours because he is leaving for the south.

This self is growing beyond control. I'm less happy than when I was selfless.

When I turn to Eduardo with questions I call his answers Astroanalysis. He says Mars is in my Libra so I am living out my own Mars instead of letting Henry do it. I ask him: Shall I sail tomorrow? Go somewhere? Obey myself or laugh at myself?

Why can't anything hold me? Henry is writing, not living. Fraenkel I can't come too near to, as I should not have come too near to Rank. I gave Rank too full, too complete, a life together in New York. Afterward he could not be just a lover. If I had not done that he might not have demanded all of me. And we would still be meeting in the ugly French room for a few hours a week.

I feel so strangely released; no boundaries, no walls, no fears, nothing holds me back from adventure. I feel blind, mobile, without home or axis. It is now that I become really dangerous to the happiness of Hugh, Henry, Mother, and Joaquin. An untrammeled, unleashed tigress.

Sacrifices. I came back from New York, away from my work and my liberty, because Hugh came to fetch me, believing so candidly that I would return. I came back because Henry did not want to stay in New York. I would have come back for Huck, for my Father, for Mother and Joaquin. Not for *me*. For me, I wanted New York, my work, and independence. Henry there, the vastness of a new role to make, to re-create. I would have given so much there, infused soul and mind into all who approached me.

And here?

J U L Y   6 ,   1 9 3 5

*F*ATHER AND I IN THE GARDEN. FATHER SAYING, "After what happened to us, which was so intense, so fantastic and magnificent, I could not have any more ordinary affairs. Everything seemed too stupid and commonplace. I knew that was the climax of my career."

It might have been the climax of mine too, only I was not ready for that; I was weak, dependent, and clinging. I needed someone close to me. I did not possess my own soul, as I do now. Now I have learned to live alone. In a way, I do live alone. I am more isolate and self-sufficient. Now I can understand what you wanted a year ago, but a year ago that was too austere and lonely for me. After that, there was a peace and a great wave of love and tenderness. *Les fiancés éternels.* Maruca still says, "We must leave the fiancés alone."

Notes made on the boat: Flirtations in New York with George Buzby, Donald Friede, Norman Bel Geddes, Cuban vice-consul at the last moment, one hour before leaving. Attracted to so many people all at once. But all superficial. Bill Hoffmann not angry at all my tricks. Parting kiss.

Seeing Henry off the night before Hugh and I sailed. So much love always. Immense tenderness. Yearning to leave with him. When I came to awaken him that Friday he was already awake and he was thinking, If only we could have sailed together. And he said, "But this time everything is all right, we're both sailing in the same direction."

He sailed on the SS *Veendam* Friday, and Saturday Hugh and I sailed on the SS *Champlain.* So I felt him near. We sent each other radiograms. On the same ocean, at the same time.

I came away loaded with triumphs as woman, as analyst. At the last minute two patients came to me for help, women of fifty, clutching at me. I developed a great, gentle firmness.

Lowenfels capitulated when he read my Henry–June novel and "Alraune." He said I was a human being, a creative artist, and that he had underestimated me (his insistence on regarding me as a rich society woman patronizing Henry, putting the cheapest interpretation on our relationship!).

Amazing, astonishing, incredible, to be able to enjoy a meal no matter where or with whom. Before, I could not eat well before strangers. I was always nervous and tight. To be able to write letters casually, to telephone without shyness, not to be intimidated by anyone. No longer afraid of Fraenkel's intelligence. Out of the prison of my shyness. No more need of Father, nor of being understood. I don't care now about the thoughts which belong to me alone. I don't need to share anything. I learned the destructive power of this with Rank.

What a rest and peace I really feel, away from his constant probing and never letting anything alone. As soon as I separated from Rank I entered into my true feminine world of uncerebral perceptions. The mental exaltation I used to feel with Rank, the banquet of ideas, have vanished into smoke. I sank into a great serenity, a psychological moon life.

I miss him, but I don't want any more analysis. I need motion and sensation; it is as if we had never lived together, which proves that it was Rank's creations and ideas which held me, and his love, but that there was no love in me.

When I met Henry at the Gare du Nord: happiness. We lay on the couch in his studio, which reminded him of all he had suffered when he thought he had lost me. Tossing and unable to sleep, finally going to sleep when he saw the moon and felt I was watching him.

JULY 10, 1935

I HAVE BEEN VERY SICK, NEUROTIC, REPRESSED, and finally ill. I feel too big and too full for all this, as if I had been riding a racehorse and were suddenly pushed into a snail house. Repressing a tremendous force which I can't use here. Have lost the big rhythm I had in New York, an intoxication. Rank had my rhythm. Here I feel stifled without my work. Nobody keeps my rhythm. What will help me? Taking another boat. I can't write, I can't read, I am *frémissante,* restless, feverish; I leap, I pace, I run, aimlessly. Tremendous struggle to quiet down. Everyone else is content. Henry is in his element. Hugh and Eduardo are discoursing. I have lost Rank, and now? Henry timorous and passive, but his creative rhythm is large. Rank was daring in every way. I'm awaiting someone. A new lover with seven-league boots like mine. My Father, too, is timorous. He is thinking of nothing but preserving himself from sickness, old age, and death.

JULY 11, 1935

H ENRY'S PASSIONATE RECEPTION, HIS JEALOUSY OF Fraenkel. A movie which took us to Egypt. We experienced the infinite. All this helped me to get out of my torture and choking moods. Moving away from the petty fears of life, the pain of all relationships; creating with a hope, bringing people to Louveciennes.

Oh, the effort I have made to fit myself into Louveciennes and Villa Seurat—the human me so satisfied and the demon in me always pushing me, my body so warmed by Henry's passion, my life so secure on Hugh's loyalty.

Divided life: Villa Seurat, disorder and gregariousness. Louveciennes, order and isolation. But I can't sit very long with Fred, Brassai, Roger, Maggy. Aside from Fraenkel they are all flabby, weak, whiny, and without grandeur. Something has awakened my grandeur now and I get restless.

Fred describes my novel as a hymn of love. Today he is a reputed, admired novelist.

When my woman's jealousy calmed down before the fact of Fraenkel's leadership, I then realized Fraenkel was the one Henry needed, and that I had admitted this need long ago when I tried to give Rank to Henry. I told Rank then, in the course of analysis, that in his book on Lawrence, Henry had got beyond me, and that, although I could follow him, I certainly could no longer guide or help or criticize his work. A bigger and stronger mind than mine was required to put order in Henry's instinctive and lyrical visions. I thought Rank would fulfill this need. Fraenkel is the one. He nourishes Henry's intellectual explorations and relieves me of a too-heavy burden, because for years I have been everything to Henry, there has been nobody else. I remember my struggles with [his] Lawrence book at the rue des Marronniers* and, finally, my discouragement. During the Clichy period, surrounded by Fred, etc., Henry had no equal, and I had to be the receiver, stimulator of ideas, far too difficult for me. Spengler, for example.

Now that a separate and personal understanding exists between Fraenkel and me, I am glad Henry has found his man, his world, and his intellectual equal. A strange thing happens. In discussions Fraenkel is always the subtle one, the wise one, the understanding one. Henry does not talk as wisely when faced with several persons as he does all alone with me. I am forced to take Fraenkel's side.

---

* During the winter of 1933 to 1934, on the advice of Dr. Rank, Anais Nin had moved by herself from Louveciennes to a hotel near the Bois, where she also rented a room for Henry Miller, who had given up the apartment in Clichy that he had shared with Alfred Perlès.

Then the gibberish in Henry seems to become accentuated and I feel resentful toward Henry for his primitivism, his lack of understanding (he caricatures Fraenkel), and I feel I have been trapped biologically into loving passionately a man who is not close to my mind at all, but close to my blood and body—the real mental marriage is with Rank, and now with Fraenkel. Fraenkel knows I understand him, and as with Rank, he has very few people with whom he can make contact, and so he values understanding highly.

At these discussions I finally grow silent. To talk more would reveal to Henry a whole body of thought in me which I never show him because he laughs at it, and betrays to Fraenkel the feelings and instincts which emotionally, obscurely, bind me to Henry. Henry does not think of me in terms of mind either; he does not know I can leap faster and further than he can, and away from Fraenkel too, but then he feels that I am different because I have a body and a blood different from Fraenkel's, which belong to him, a Moon being.

That moment of body warmth can seem to marry one so closely and mysteriously, those caresses of Henry, this voice, that tenderness, those silences. I am reality to Henry now. He has love for me and no love for Fraenkel, no body warmth. He turns and jeers at him. They would let one another starve. On another plane they meet at banquets of another kind, like mine with Rank. But for Henry, ultimately, that is not of supreme importance; and it is no longer, for me either, the Idea.

Peace. I have killed at last my despair. From the movies Henry and I walked clear across Paris, from the Opéra to Montsouris, more than an hour. I exhausted myself, voluntarily. I drank wine. I thought of our voyage to Egypt and of infinity. New York, we said, was not built with a sense of eternity.

Alone with Henry for the first time since our return, peace and silence and depth, and sleep together, and I courting fatigue, experiencing an orgasm in the train while reading a book of pornography.

Saying good-bye to a sad Father. What we have in common is this profound melancholy, masked in gaiety for all the world.

Peace.

Fraenkel is coming tomorrow night. No more tightening of small jealousies and fears. I loosen my deep, savage clutch on Henry. Again. Conquer my own primitivism. Rise. Seek a suprapersonal destiny. Oh, the pain nobody can measure, the courage it takes to live, to love, to laugh, to forget, to liquidate each day as Henry does, Henry who can start afresh each day.

Annis: Celtic Moon Goddess. Goddess of Earth.

Anahita: Celtic mother goddess and her son Myhtra; Persian moon goddess.

Anatis: Egyptian moon goddess. Nana of Babylon.

Anu: In southern France, known as the shining one, patron of fertility, fire, poetry, and medicine. Also known as the Black Anu, who in common folklore devoured men or turned them into lunatics.

Anaïtis: goddess of sexual love, not chastity. Mazdian moon goddess.

J U L Y   1 4 ,   1 9 3 5

W E PLAN TO DO OUR OWN PUBLISHING, EVEN though we don't own a press yet. Fred baptized the press "Siana," reversing the spelling of my name, a thing I did as a girl once in my diary.

All I have suffered from is falling from a motion life—action—into a slow rhythm. I can't sit with Henry and his friends for hours in a café. I just can't talk for ten hours, as Henry and Fraenkel do. I crave motion and life. I'm trying to subdue my energy, but I can't write, read, or go to the movies, or listen to music. It is as if my heart were beating too fast, as if I had broken into a running pace, and I am alone. Fraenkel is full of understanding but he is uncoordinated and vacillating.

He came here. Loved Louveciennes, harmonized with Eduardo.

Henry was jealous. Fraenkel wanted to stay for good. Henry impossible just now. Working on *Tropic of Capricorn*. As soon as his life settles into a mold he likes gibberish, cafés, idleness, foolishness, childishness. He clowns with Fred. I feel resentful, bored, and unhappy. Secret rebellion again, as when I left for New York with Rank. His fears, cowardices, rantings. I resent the fact that sensually we are in such deep accord. He does not think as I do. Anger that the men who think as I do (Rank, Eduardo, Fraenkel, Hugh) are not the blood answer. Anger against nature.

Henry's gregariousness. People for breakfast, for lunch, all day, and they almost sleep with us. No. I hate his way of life. His clownish, wasted life.

I come back with relief to my kingdom in Louveciennes. I hide from Henry a certain austerity and laboriousness in my life which flowers in Louveciennes. I have always concealed, out of fear of ridicule, my great seriousness and love of work. I have played enough with Henry's childishness. I'm bored. Again my feelings seem altered, my love seems to fade. When I arrive in his room and find him asleep and snoring, with the taste of wine on his lips, and Fred has just left and Fraenkel will come in a little while, and there are only a few pages on the desk for a whole ten days, I hate to lie down beside him. Yet I do, and we sink into sensuality, touch bottom, and something in me is left intact and lonely and unmatched always, unmarried, and I can't accept this; deep down, I can't.

At last I think I have twisted the neck of my martial spirit. After another evening and morning of the blackest misery I sat down with strong determination and to warm myself up I began to copy the New York diary. But I felt like writing in between the lines of the diary, felt like expanding and dramatizing the notes in the diary. Wondering if I am doing this because I have lost Rank and I miss him, his deep soul and dazzling mind. Why don't I begin on the book on my Father? The truth is my Father means very little to me now; I have finally torn him out of my life. I love him as I love Joaquin, a blood love, but I am not close to him. We live in separate worlds. Without love or hatred I can't write about my Father. There is an indifference. Whereas Rank, in one sense, I still love and think about.

I think I have found my style, however. Take the diary and write it more fully, more artistically, but keep the sincerity and directness. Diary as an indication of fever charts and developments.

To re-create New York because I have lost it, because I'm lovesick for the splendor and expansion of its rhythm. Longing for it. Must I write always under the leash of longing, calling out to what is far away and lost?

When Henry telephones I am relieved of the pain of jealousy. It seems to me that with Henry I have suffered continuously from all the jealousies. June, the supreme one; the whores; and the women who were least like me. Relieved only by my other love affairs. Distracted by incidents with Eduardo, Allendy, Artaud, my Father, Rank. And now I find myself lost because I have nothing to keep my mind off Henry. It is unbearable and comical, because Henry feels the same way. I had only to say George Buzby was handsome to arouse his anxiety.

In my Louveciennes kingdom, Eduardo alone now, close to us. We play badminton, we eat together, we talk.

Eduardo and I on Henry's absolute lack of understanding, of a consistent point of view on people, movies, books. Everything distorted, which permits caricature, burlesque, and invention. Contradictions and chaos and irrationality. He is writing about June and it is not June. What he knows of me is only what I have told him, what I write, and the diary; but I would not trust him to paint me. Caricatures of Fraenkel, Fred, of everyone. It would be comical if I pictured the same personages, the sensitiveness of Fred, the shrewdness of Fraenkel, the wonder of June.

I see the malevolent Henry so often now because I see him with his friends, but the Henry I made for myself exists for me as long as I believe in him. Henry is acting this role for me because it also gives him a higher opinion of himself. How I hate my eyes opening on Henry.

When we are alone all is well; he talks wisdom, he is tender. But I have seen him so much with others and it revolts me. Treachery, contrariness, inconsistency, shiftiness, cowardice, exploitation, malice, destructiveness.

—————

Maggy: "Before I read your novel I was full of resentment against the world, bitter, cross, and all tight inside. I was hurting others, but when I read it, it moved me so much that it did something to me. It was so moving, so full of feeling . . ." Maggy is Greek, with coal eyes and dazzling teeth, and a fear of life. Roger, her lover, is one of the few Frenchmen I like. He wrote a romantic letter about Louveciennes and his childhood. He is swerving away from France toward the chaos, the genius and depths of English.

J U L Y 1 7 , 1 9 3 5

J'AI FINALEMENT TORDU LE COU À MARS.
This great living force which was tormenting me has been finally tamed, *for the moment.* I am taking refuge in writing, but I will only write until the time comes for my next explosion and expansion. Fraenkel is writing. Henry is writing. He is more mine than ever. Joyce sailed today.

I copy the New York diary every day. It nourishes me.

I lie playing possum. Vesuvius is internal. I will not be cheated of adventure, blood, love, sex, motion, trickeries, full noisy action. I have no use for literature.

For visionary writing: get very quiet, mediumistic, to see more, further, and to feel the cosmos.

"The pounding of my heart woke me," wrote Gabriele D'Annunzio.

JULY 21, 1935

*T*HE FIXED, SOMNAMBULISTIC WAY I WALKED OUT of Sylvia Maynard's studio in New York. Not there, what I want. I feel big, inflated. No room anywhere for me, and no match. Henry so timorous and passive. Rank was daring.

Eduardo on my "Alraune" story: "An apocalyptic vision. Writing which may have a great tomorrow. Clairvoyant visionary writing."

It was via the dream record that Henry leapt into his own reality, his world, where four or five songs are sung together and flesh and spirit are truly made one.

Fraenkel needs to be always right. Also appreciates me. "You and I have the same kind of mind. A system ruled by the mind." Says Henry's influence is delatinizing me (chaos, instinct), has sidetracked me. But how it stimulated me! Fraenkel says I know just where to stop, sense of form. Henry can ruin his best pages. Fred calls my novel a hymn of love.

Anaïs to Henry: "Would you like to meet Brancusi?"
Henry: "I don't like prophets. It's a pose."
Henry to Roger Klein: "You don't understand Maggy because she is on a higher level. A level of health and reasonableness. You're all crazy."
Henry in love with the colored face of the Trinité clock.

A week or so ago Henry began to write about June. Reading what he wrote hurt me a little, and yet I felt Henry so close—he was so passionate in his caresses, so aware of me, so all there, not a nuance changed in his love—that I was not sad. The other night when I

arrived he was writing. I told him about Hugh's new way of express-
ing his jealousy. Every time Hugh knows I am going to the Villa
Seurat (he is home all day now, on vacation), he makes love to me,
never fails to; even at the last moment, while I am dressing, he throws
me on the bed, saying, "I want to tire you out before you go, to be
sure of you, to be sure you won't have any desire left." Or else, "You
have to pay me or I won't let you go out." He says this laughing, but
also seriously. I lie passive or I struggle to make believe I am excited.
It all nauseates me, hurts me.

As I told this to Henry he said, "Now I understand why I used
to do that to June before she went out to meet Jean."

I was silent. Then I said, "It's strange, your thoughts revert to
June; instead of connecting this incident to our life, you use it to
illumine your life with June." Henry understood what I felt, but he
said very sincerely, "It isn't what you think, though. My interest now
in my life is almost scientific, like a detective's, not human. It just
happens that I am struggling with several mysteries. And I want to
be truthful. I want to show you the pages. Do you mind? I can't tell
what I am doing."

I said I did not mind. I read the pages in which he describes
the way June talked, and their first kiss, and her first lie. I
commented on them. I sat near Henry. He said, "I am writing so
coolly, so slowly. I am not in love with what I am writing. The only
thing which could hurt you is if I had returned to the past to hug it,
but I haven't."

"I thought you would fall in love with June again."

"No, I haven't," said Henry. "It is my mind that is working. I
feel that I was asleep during my whole experience with June, that it
was a dream, that I was a somnambulist."

"She wanted and needed you to be asleep."

"I realize she was my creation. Do you know, Joyce irritated me.
I could see in her some of June's faults. She made the same crass,
ignorant remarks. She had all the defects of American women, the
self-will, the lack of feeling and understanding. I realize, Anis, how
much I learned from your novel, how much I learned from your
directness and sincerity, from your wholeness."

I realized again I had made Henry whole, that I had given him back the soul killed by June. He was moved as he talked.

We would not go down and see Fraenkel.

We talked about Fraenkel's world, his image of the world, which matches that of [Oswald] Spengler. I said I understood his world but did not feel connected with it, that I felt connected with tomorrow.

Fraenkel said, later, I was merely taking a hurdle, over and beyond war, destruction, death, into life, because I stand for life.

"All the world," I said, "suffered from the pain of consciousness. It had to be cured by exploring the unconscious, to find its source again."

Henry: "But all the world has not been analyzed."

Me: "Oh, yes, it has, not individually, but by infiltration, contagion, contamination, through that which travels by air; through literature, music, painting, philosophy. Everything that happens to a group ultimately happens to the mass, to the world."

Yesterday I said to Fraenkel, "If you want to see Fraenkel alive, look into my eyes . . ." Again the miracle. He shed his scales, his hardened skin. His soul, buried alive in order to live in the world, bloomed. The believing, the sensitive Fraenkel awakened.

He is here for a few days. He calls June an alley cat, a hybrid.

Villa Seurat: Chana Orloff, Richard Thoma. Rue des Artistes: Fujita, and a visit to Brancusi, his *Forêt Blanche, Colonnes sans fins dans les nuages,* Old Prophet, Café Roumain, Bali disks, black eyes and white beard. Snow-capped regions. Mountains of plaster.

Plant life with Henry. Love sensations. Moisture on the leaves, the rustle of all things coming to life. Nothing in the world like melting and yielding. Each time I surrender some part of my being, give up an idea, accept, sacrifice to Henry, accept the Other, it is as if the inflexible chain of Self breaks. When I discover the story of the whore he met was true, I kiss him. I surrender continually: my self, my jealousies, my claims, my egoism. Each time I melt, something happens to my femininity, to my woman-self. Each rush of feeling, of selflessness, brings a strange efflorescence. I'm happy in a divine way, not in a human way, as if this were a religion, not an ordinary love, bigger always than myself.

J U L Y   2 4 ,   1 9 3 5

I'M IN LOVE AGAIN. NOT ALONE WITH HENRY. JUST in love. I felt it this morning. I was listening to a record of "Blue Moon." I had just served Henry his breakfast. The sun was on the balcony. The studio was full of light and of living cells. Henry cannot follow me. He sings only in words. Not with his blood, not in my way, not with wings. A human love. I feel that someone is coming, someone is coming. I'm on tiptoes, and so alive to his coming.

Coming out of 18, Villa Seurat, Chana Orloff called me out of her window. Seeing her meant Rank. If I could have Rank without his body or his sexual love. No. Not Rank, though it stirred me to think I might see him again on account of Chana Orloff. What can I tell her? Not the truth. Shall I invent something like, I was in love with Rank, could not bear to see him anymore? Then she will tell him and he will be furious to think I am still lying, or he may believe it.

I am in love while I buy coffee, "San Paulo," melon, bread, and butter for Henry. I just came from his arms, but the world seems more alive and wild than he. He has done with wandering. I am only beginning. Chana Orloff at her window, asking me to come and see her, gave me a little stab because she sees Rank.

I am in love walking down Villa Seurat in the red Russian dress and white coat, in love with the world and the one who is coming, who is on his way, the one who will travel with me, whose body I may love, no matter if our minds are not twins; a body I may love, for now I am in love with bodies, with youth, with blood and flesh. I do not look for the dream—or the thought. I am in love while I get on the train to have lunch with Hugh and Eduardo in the garden, and while I take a sun bath, I offer my body to the sun. It is a little too slender, but the skin is beautiful and soft and it looks so young. I have no age, just as others have no physical age for me. Eduardo asks me, "How old is he?" I don't know. I never know. I know only the ages of their souls, of their experience, of their desire, of their audacity. No time. No age. I am still Bilitis; I love man sensually, at last, and my soul will not stand in the way. I await the *man* and no longer the *child,* or the *father.*

I was brushing Henry's coat because he was going to see his publisher. Oh, God, I forgot, [Jack] Kahane has accepted my novel of June–Henry, is making me sign a contract. Yes, I have a contract in my pocket.* I was brushing Henry's coat and he wanted to have his shoes shined because he was timid, because he is timid. He is becoming a celebrity, getting letters from Ezra Pound, T. S. Eliot, a review by Blaise Cendrars, 130 copies of *Tropic of Cancer* sold to date. When he awakes he takes me in his arms. Will anyone ever be as tender— always a hand on my body, always a caress slipping into some nook of the body, always a warm and caressing hand, an open mouth. So that we forget our discussion, in which I fight again his tendency to catalog everything because he thinks everything is interesting.

When the record was playing I felt moved right down to my toes, right at the pit of my stomach, everything in my body stirred and opening.

I look for Him in the crowd.

This love will either kill or save me forever.

Fever in the train, and then I sat down at home and tamed it by copying out for Fred my story "Waste of Timelessness," which still

---

* Though Anaïs Nin had been offered a multibook deal by Jack Kahane, his Obelisk Press only published the "Henry and June" novella—eventually titled "Djuna"—as part of the volume *The Winter of Artifice,* in June 1939, just about two months before Kahane's death. The volume then also contained the "Father" story, titled "Lilith," and "The Voice," based on Nin's New York experience with analysis.

seems ironic.* Where is my irony now? Rank made it flower and now it has gone again. I want to find my irony. No irony in my love for Henry, though he deserves it so often; and I am hurt by his "Scenario," made out of "Alraune," because it contains nothing of "Alraune"— nothing but the shell—and he has added mountains, masks, sand, temples, buildings, noise, space, skeletons, groans, dancing, but no meaning, no meaning. Death and disease and objects. I could carica- ture the empty Henry who walks the streets with idle eyes observing everything in order to understand less, and who amply makes up for this when he invents with his genius—invents, creates another world, yes. But only in his book, as Fraenkel said, not in life.

Give me back my blindness! Where is my blindness!

Fraenkel came for a few days. Revised "Alraune" thoroughly and with acuteness. Advised me to continue writing as I had in the intro- duction to the "Father" story, beginning with, "I am waiting for him. I have waited twenty years." Made me critical and so I made impor- tant cuts and slashes in "Alraune."

The Siana Press will publish Henry's "Scenario." He put that first. Then my "Alraune." Then a hundred-page letter to Fred on the New York trip, *"Aller Retour New York"* which I consider unimportant,** but there Henry shows his lack of values and critical faculty. He is in love with his letters to Emil, et al.—all that represents his philosophy of imperfection, the cult of the natural.

I curse Fraenkel, I curse him because he reawakens Anaïs Nin,

---

* Unpublished during Anaïs Nin's lifetime, "Waste of Timelessness" became the title story in a collection of sixteen of her early fictions, first published in 1977 as "a book for friends only" (*"Waste of Timelessness" and Other Early Stories;* Weston, Connecticut: Magic Circle Press. Reprinted, Athens, Ohio: Swallow Press/Ohio University Press, 1993).

** As it turned out, *Aller Retour New York* appeared under the Obelisk Press imprint in October 1935, in an edition of 150 copies, signed by Henry Miller. Anaïs Nin's "Alraune," eventually titled *The House of Incest,* came out in 1936 under the Siana Press imprint [18, villa Seurat, Paris), in an edition of 249 copies, printed through Michael Fraenkel's con- nection at the Saint Catherine press in Bruges, Belgium. Miller's *Scenario,* under the Obelisk Press imprint, was published in July 1937, in an edition of two hundred signed and numbered copies. This "film with sound" was, as the dedication read, "directly inspired by a phantasy called *The House of Incest,* written by Anaïs Nin."

the critic of writers and of men. I hate it, so I fall in love. I want to love. I don't want to see a hideous reality or laugh at it. Fraenkel saying, "You used a story with two faces, and the night and day symbolism, but you did not use the day face or the night face. I coined that: the *day face*. I think it is wonderful."*

The day before Rebecca West came to Paris I had a dream: I was working as a whore in a pink chemise. Was expelled because I used too much *thread*. Someone picked up the fragments of thread to hold them up to me. (I wonder if this relates to my pattern, my need to relate things, to *sew everything together*.)

Rebecca and I go out together. Henry insults her. She gives me a room with bath salts, perfumes, vanity case, etc. Showers me with gifts. I realize she is a lesbian and that she is waiting up for me. I use her gifts to fix myself and go to her room but it has taken me a half hour and she got tired of waiting.

The day after I got her telegram, she came to Louveciennes with her husband. All our afternoons and evenings were on the key of humor. I lost my timidity and became very comical and sharp. I was able to keep on her level of talk, which is one of beautiful brightness. Her ardent eyes. She would not sit with me in the rumble seat at first because we looked neglected, but in the dark she liked it, Hugh and Harry Andrews driving our car, responsible, while we looked at the stars. She said [Joseph] Delteil's book on Jeanne d'Arc was written by a brassiere advertising company: "All about Jeanne's bosom." I sensed her lack of faith in herself. She said she could not even bring herself to feel like the very ugly genius regarding himself contentedly in the

---

* Michael Fraenkel eventually published "The Day Face and the Night Face," in the Christmas 1938 issue of *Delta,* the short-lived magazine edited by Alfred Perlès, Henry Miller, et al. from 18, villa Seurat. Presenting this as a fragment from *The Personal Experience,* Fraenkel writes to a departing lover about the duality of her personality: "It was only in those moments at night, as I say, when your day face fell from you, that I could come to it—this other portion of you, your other self, hidden from you, unknown to you. . . . You leave, and what is left is just myself again with a world of ideas, but without an idea of a world."

mirror and saying "To think that I have talent." She is hypersensitive to criticism.

The next day she and I went shopping together (the bath salts). "What nonsense we talk about, Anaïs!" Laughing and discussing lipstick. I painted her eyelashes. She will wear a copy of my white hat. She is wearing my nail polish. I like her body, which is earthy, fulsome. Fine breasts. Tan skin like a Creole's. At the bottom of her eyes, the melancholy of Rank, but for the world a sparkle and humor.

Two hours, alone in her room, of intense talk, trying to cover our whole lives. She finds me stronger than she is. She is still the victim of her pain pattern. I am free. "You are dancing your life," she said. All the *grandes lignes* of our life the same. Hard childhood: her father left her at nine. She ran away with H. G. Wells at twenty. Had a child at twenty-one. Her husband could be Hugh's brother, and her lovers have much of Henry. She tells me all about "Tommy." I want to give her strength. "You are the most remarkable woman I have known," she said. Emotion and chaos. She has not been as true to herself as I have been, neither in her writing nor in her life.

J U L Y   2 9 ,   1 9 3 5

WHEN I HEAR FRAENKEL AND HENRY TALK I REmember Rank, who knew so much more than they know and who was more human. Why do I know already all that passes between Henry and Fraenkel, as if I had heard it all before? Rank was so far ahead, in spite of his failure as a writer. Between Fraenkel and Henry the language is better: They are artists. Rank was deeper and bigger, but he could neither write nor talk well. His magic was beyond art. He knew too much.

AUGUST 2, 1935

I SAW CHANA ORLOFF. SHE TOLD ME RANK HAD left for New York a month after he arrived. I felt a great pain. Then I realized I had hoped to see him by accident—to meet him as he came out of the Cité Universitaire, or in the Café Zeyer, or at Chana Orloff's. I knew then I had hoped for that, because I am still in love with his mind and soul. I fear this sudden poetization of Rank. The ideal father must always be far away and inaccessible. But how I yearn for the distant thing. I miss his greatness. Rank the lover deprived me of Rank the father. A father must always be wise. When I said to Henry that Rank had been the ideal father, he said, "I am the father now, father and son." But that is not so, because Henry is the father only intermittently. He does not live by his wisdom and he has no strength except with words. I am always in love with wisdom, with divinity, with creation in man; always in love with the closest manifestation of the god in man.

I wrote Rank a note to be forwarded to him: "I have not been able to separate myself from you altogether. So much in us was deeply married. Will I ever see you again?"

AUGUST 4, 1935

B RANCUSI'S NAME FOR ME: LA CASTAÑUELA.

I realize I dread discord because I think it destroys love and connection. I always think when Henry and I disagree, he will never come close to me again. It is all based on a feeling that love (closeness) is fragile but that there is a love (love as desire or antagonism) which is tough and thrives on hatred. That love I don't know. Just like Rank. I can't believe enough in my connection with Henry, because it has no continuity. I often think it has died in between the times I see him. I don't trust distance or time. When I return to Henry I feel the estrangement until we lie in bed and his caresses reestablish the current. That is why Rank said he could not believe in our life or love unless I lived with him all the time. I need that phrase that Hugh utters every day, that gesture always made by Henry, the possessiveness of Rank. Henry's faith does not need that. He believes because he does not think in between. He believes as a child believes.

To Rebecca: There is a great deal to make clear about what you tell me. We have to talk about it. I can only say this for the moment: Keep your faith in the love, for that is apt to waver in you. It is a part of your faith in yourself and its occasional waverings. Don't give too much importance to the gestures, the letter which was not written, etc. Keep very quiet and believe and wait. All that happens in London depends more on you than you can ever believe. Everything is created by the image you carry within you. If I can help you to leap out of this once, you will really stand on the other side of pain. There is an escape. Just as one can awaken from a nightmare. I want to give you strength to awaken. I am keeping very close to you.

Neptune causes worry over things that never come to pass.

I love Henry less in proportion to my antipathy for his friends, his life, his cafés, his falseness to others, cruelty to others, his cheatings, imitations, borrowings, plunderings. The analyst in me he had to rival and imitate. He had to write about Lawrence. He now takes all he learned from me and analyzes Fraenkel, and gives it to him as his own. Identifies himself with the role of Rank, while hating Rank. We all do that but we do it sincerely. I became an analyst. Henry plays with the wisdom of the analyst one day and destroys all his work the next day.

Once a month I become instinctual and neurotic. I went to Henry one day when I had my period. He began to talk about "Alraune," that I had muffed it, that Fraenkel had succeeded where I had failed, in describing sensation before the crystallization of thought. This coupled with the fact that whenever we talked about the press (a myth) Henry eluded mention of it and thought we should do my child diary. So my anger got fierce, though it did not awaken instantly. I nurtured it for a day. Then I burst in on him one morning: "If I had muffed 'Alraune,' as you said, it wouldn't have meant anything to you, to Fraenkel, or to Rank, as it did. What happens is that you are a *girouette*. Now you turn to the wind of Fraenkel's egotism, your need of him. It smells of alley cats here. Why don't you three fuck each other, it would be more honest. All you do is sit in cafés and gossip. But all you say won't kill my faith in myself. I won't let you. It takes a lifetime to build this faith and I won't let you kill it."

But Henry was in a very gentle, very wise mood. He answered me gently. He ended with, "Don't you see what all this means? It has to do with your faith in yourself. When that wavers then you see the whole world and me differently. You see me malicious and destructive now, but I have not changed toward you. About your writing, you're always too sensitive. I have not changed, and I know those storms come whenever you feel our relationship threatened by a third person. It happened with Lowenfels, Fred, and now Fraenkel. Then you begin to doubt me. You imagine the three of us gossiping against you. As a matter of fact I defended your 'Alraune.' I was against some of Fraenkel's corrections. I said it was like a coral reef in a bowl of water. Some of your thoughts are like crystal, like coral. But around them there is water, sensation. Fraenkel took some of that water away. He wants nothing but the mineral thought. I believe in your vagueness."

"Henry, I need your faith in me, or I can't fight the world. With Fraenkel I have to fight because he never gives anyone their place. He has so little faith in himself he has to shove everybody off."

Henry said he had to fight Fraenkel for his due, too.

After a while we realized we were agreeing. Henry was very caressing, full of understanding. But he can suddenly stop being wise and become foolish. "If you keep a clear head all the time," he says, "you miss a lot. When things get foolish and you leave, very often things happen right there."

Henry tells me this while we are lying in bed.

"Yes, I know, I miss those things, but they are small and unimportant, whereas because of my thirst for bigger things, the nonfoolish bigger things happen to me, big adventures like Allendy, Artaud, Rank." And I talk, I talk about the big important things which happen to me while he sits in a café with Fred, the clown, and Fraenkel, the mental trapeze worker.

Hard for me at times to believe that Henry is what he is to me. Rank used to say that this was not the real Henry. The real Henry was the man of hatred, of cruelties, of cold-blooded deformities and indifferences.

Henry describing his mockery of Fraenkel, how he helps Fred to steal from Fraenkel, gives me the same feeling as when I describe to Henry my treacheries toward Hugh, my tricks, and he, seeing the devil in me, loses for a moment his faith in my loyalty.

He is jealous of the red Russian dress, Rank's, which he says I wear too often. The difference is always the *love*. If you don't love, you are capable of this and that. But it's hard to believe in this love when to everyone else Henry is primarily the taking one.

When Henry adds wisdom to his warmth and mellowness he becomes the man I love madly. Instinct and the ideal then meet—but that is rare.

Fraenkel wrote me such an airtight, watertight, ideological Chinese Wall of theories on guilt that the only way for me not to sit for the next twenty years splitting hairs with him was to dive below and strike at his neurosis. This he answered even more magnificently with a perfect analysis of himself—to which I answered, "But the *other*, the other is altogether missing from your vision." Meanwhile Henry was attacking him too—and Fraenkel, all alone in his studio, felt personally persecuted and had pains in his chest. The same night, while he answered me, "You have cut off my head," I wrote him a human letter to counterbalance the ideological cruelty. He, of course, was overwhelmed by both the violence and the sweetness. He came to

Louveciennes. We made peace. Peace. At night in the studio, when Eduardo and Hugh had gone to bed, he said, "I resisted your protectiveness and warmth. You know why. You tantalize me when you approach me as a woman who can't be mine. I'm an extremist; either you are mine or you must be a man. If I were Henry I would never share you."

"Good night." He was so moved he pulled me toward him for a half-kiss, an unreal kiss. And that was all. We understood each other. His admiration and attraction to me grow every day. In his knowledge of woman he is like a child. He loves my strength.

The next days in Louveciennes were taken with the dropping of scales, shells, crusts, masks. He became more and more sensitive, more himself; he began to grow luminous. This small body, like a skeleton, without flesh. All thought and sensibility, warmer to touch than I had imagined.

The day I had to go to Paris to see Henry, he tried to make me miss my train. Played with the idea of taking me to Mexico instead of being taken there by Henry and me. Eduardo, he said, could come along, because he did not take me away from him; but Henry and Hugh took me away from him. So fascinated by his plans I did miss my train while Fraenkel said, "You should be so carefully preserved, taken care of. I never felt that about Henry or Fred. They are strong and they are not attempting such difficult, such rare things as you. Your life is remarkable, how you kept it balanced while yet so full, everything so full."

Reality. When you are in the heart of a summer day as inside a fruit, looking down at your lacquered toenails, at the white dust on your sandals from quiet somnolescent streets, looking at the sun expanding under your dress and between your legs, looking at the light polishing the silver bracelets, and smelling the bakery odors, the *petit pain au chocolat,* watching the cars rolling by, filled with blond women like the pictures in *Vogue,* and then you see the old *femme de ménage* with her burned, scarred, iron-colored face, and you read about the man who was cut into pieces, and there, before you, is the half-body of a man on wheels, and still the perfume of the coiffeur sings of reality.

AUGUST 5, 1935

WHEN I ARRIVED HENRY HAD RUN THROUGH ALL his money and he had not eaten lunch, so we began by eating at the table, in the center of the room; and then we lay in bed, and it is strange how Henry and I place our bodies so far from the ordinary positions of human bodies so that in the paroxysm of our joy our two bodies do not look human but like animals, satyrs, roots of trees, Negroes, savages, Indians. Unrecognizable. Not Henry, not Anaïs, so twisted and altered by sensuality. Then it seems as if we are making dinner again, and I am slicing eggplant and striving, thoughtfully, for succulence. And we fall into a deep peace, lying on the couch, talking about opium—the opium of sleep and the opium of action. Henry had said, "When I am sad I go to sleep." And suddenly I understood that when I was sad I had to act.

When I come out of the little kitchen our bodies collide, brush, stick; and meanwhile I am writing the Rank story of how our blood would not stick, in spite of passion.

With breakfast there is sun on the balcony. I throw the bed things over the balcony rail exposed to the sun. We wash dishes. We write. Henry, after my criticism of certain too-factual parts of his hundred-page letter to Fred, is piqued, and he adds to it and makes a fine small book of it.

I suggest we open fire with that letter to gather a group of subscribers around Henry, instead of with the *Scenario,* which is esoteric and limited. We baptize it *Aller Retour New York.* We talk about the differences, the ultimate differences between Fraenkel, Henry, and me. Henry talks about soul differences, and about how even when Fraenkel seems right Henry is more deeply right, somewhere closer to soul and something more divine. While he talks of Fraenkel, I think of Rank and write about Rank.

Fraenkel admires my letter to him, which had a more deadly, accurate aim. He gets lost in the sea of Henry's fifteen pages of instinctual bull attacks. Henry's nose is good but not his mind. But his nose is so good. Wherever Henry sniffs, smells, pisses, there is surely something wrong! And after I come upon the *lieu,* we know. Together we are deadly! When I see his nose palpitating, when he perspires and curses, I know we are on the track, but often he gets lost halfway. And that is when I come in, sniffing the air with a nose more like an airplane or a lighthouse!

Sometimes I fear the diary gives a petty image, because I leave out art and ideology, the actual content of the talks with Rank, criticisms, books, discoveries, ideologies. But I am not writing the book that contains all books. I encompass only the life that goes on around and behind the books. Finding motives of acts, in my case to excuse and justify others. I am like the keeper of the python Rebecca [West] was talking about. When questioned on how he fed the python without endangering his life, he said, "Oh, I feed him on a stick, because he has not enough sense to see the difference between a hand and a stick."

Henry was, I said, afraid to move out of his groove (our unity in studio) for fear of losing it. "You think you'll come back as one does in dreams and find 17, Villa Seurat and 19 but not 18."

Henry, becoming more and more Man, begins to resent Hugh's father role. To be told by Hugh (money situation) where to go, what to do. Good sign! When we talk of travel he says he would like it if the money came from him. Negative will. He objects to moving in October because he is happy. But I have to move away from Hugh.

Hugh has found a language in astrology. Now he can say all we say, and understand all we are and say. All I complained of before was his inarticulateness. He is creative in astrology and active and expressive.

Henry believes in life, love, money, as a child believes. It will always come from God, from somewhere.

Work on this diary, copying notes I make quickly in a small notebook at Villa Seurat. Notes made on the Rank story and copying New York diary. Reliving the beautiful New York intensity. Typing for Eduardo. Sun baths. Badminton. A day in Louveciennes. Letters from John and [Norman] Bel Geddes. But I write no one book. I write circuitously, peripherically, around everything. The lover, the *lover* I expected so keenly was the state of pregnancy again, which is bliss. How I regret each time its end, the medicine which makes the uncreative blood flow again. No use. No child possible without cesarrean operation and cesarean dangerous to my heart and general condition.

Whose child?

Instantaneity of thought produces crystallized thought—the purest, according to Fraenkel. I say fear of the world produces crystals in writing. Faultless, crystallized phrases, perfection and hard polish of inhuman things, as my first style in "Alraune." But such crystals are repulsive to people. No human imperfections, moisture, water, perspiration, halo, breath, body warmth and odor. *Inattaquable,* the invulnerable surface of words. The big things left out of the diary can be found in Rank's books, in Henry's books, in Fraenkel's books, in surrealism, Artaud, psychoanalysis, Breton, in the magazine *Minotaure.*

AUGUST 10, 1935

*T*WO DAYS OF WHITE HEAT BURNING.
Too full of Denis Seurat's *Modernes,* of ideas, phrases, plans, pictures, ecstasy. I hurry to fecundate Henry. Threaten to write a lively book about his writing, himself, so he gets on fire. We talk about Spain. I feel clairvoyant, burning. Talk about

classical period. We write joyously, having lost the misery. The cult of pain applied to writing. I'm so surprised to be writing without pain that I think I'm not writing again.

In October I move. I sacrifice New York to Henry. What I want is to go to New York, with Henry, to analyze, to enjoy, to be free. Henry wants Europe. I'm young. I can wait. He lacks the courage for conquering new worlds. I can wait.

When I was writing that I was in love, John Erskine was writing to us that he was coming, Allendy was asking for a rendezvous, Fraenkel was falling under my spell; but none of this is big enough or good enough. *Alors? J'attends.*

Now that Rank is gone I can love him at my ease and better; I am free to love in him what can be loved. There must be distance.

I spill out everything I create. Showered Henry with fire, ideas, visions. Told him to give up impossible synthesis of Lawrence book and accept its perfect fragments.

Packing to meet Rebecca in Rouen.

Dwell on, write fully on Henry's nose, ears, mouth, hair, hands, skin, mole. The body of the loved one should be explored completely. To describe is an act of love. Maybe I want to write about him instead of my Father or Rank, as another act of love. The most real love.

The day before yesterday I worked until the little veins of my eyes began to crack.

Am I writing about Rank to be near him? I was stopped by feelings of compassion while reading his letters.

I got drunk in the evening, with Eduardo and Hugh. Was comical. Hugh said all the way to Paris in the morning he was thinking about how much he loved me and how marvelous it was to live with me. Yet Eduardo says he feels the greatest pity for anyone trying to be my husband!

I don't need suffering any longer. I have created myself a soul, big as the world, that leaks all over, and I have to keep calling for the plumber.

To write all I see in Henry and around him. Just to write what I see. I see always a hundred dimensions. I see like a drunkard.

In New York I eluded John when I realized he could still stir me. Now he is angry. Last night, in the car, singing in the dark, I knew I had wanted him sensually and that I would still like his body over mine, that's all—a very animal reaction. Just a desire to chew into that big sensual body and to hear that sensual voice grunting sexually. I like to think of the day we were both in heat. I like thinking of that, John all "stiff in his pants," as he said then, which shocked me at that time—I mean the phrase, not the feeling.

I never wrote about the evening with Rebecca in New York, about the nights in Harlem, about the juggling and the *foire* selling objects on Broadway, about the burlesque, to which I took a great liking. I liked the vulgarity. Broadway shows. Broadway at night. Dinner at the Rainbow Room with my old admirer Mr. Freund, who still remembers Monte Carlo, Nice, the Eden Hotel dance. George Turner coming on a snowy afternoon, a slightly faded Don Juan, body too much like Hugh's, and reminding me of Hugh, pleading. Easier to say yes than no. Easier to lie down than to struggle, as I did on other occasions. Every invitation in New York a trap, every visit a struggle. Feeling very light and untouched after George, enjoying the treachery to Rank. When he came in a few minutes later, intense, so shaken with love, I enjoyed having betrayed him. No one has a right to clutch at a human being as Rank did.

Importance in modern books of moments *de bonheur simple.* Glorified because as rare to us, the neurotics, as ecstasy and tragedy are to others. Harriet Hume eating from a bag of cherries, Colette's cup of chocolate, my cup of coffee at the Roger Williams'.

AUGUST 12, 1935

*R*EBECCA LAUNCHED ON HER HAPPIEST LOVE AF-
fair. Says she feels it was due to me. I gave
her faith, during our talks at the Crillon, to take the hurdle. I divined
the situation accurately. Met in Rouen, all of us, Hugh, Eduardo, and
Rebecca, in a chablis and Bourgogne mood. The foamiest talk, with
sudden drops into depths. Ferment of admiration. I for her rich
breasts, her gypsy skin, her ardent eyes, her humor and irony. She for
my "beauty"! and for my accent. Walking across the bridge she
stopped to kiss me because I said *cow*-webs, emphasis on cow, the
milk giver. Great warmth, and she humble and timid: "Were you
bored?" Expanding to the tolerance of France. Eating heartily and
fantastically at all hours. Wandering through Rouen in the morning.
"What beautiful feet you have. How lovely you are." The night before,
while Hugh put the car in the garage, I go to her room and we talk
about "Tommy," and I kiss her good-night, very ardently, on several
places on her cheek, laughing. Vigor and warmth between us. I drunk
and drugged, elated. Drive back. We make a comedy of the loosely,
slackly run house, Louveciennes. We laugh at the deficiencies of Emilia. I have got beyond blushing. We laugh. She lies in bed in the
morning. Hugh and Eduardo are gone. We spend most of the day
pouring out our life stories, which are uncannily similar. I give her
the introduction to the Father story to read. She has to stop because
it makes her weep.

We take a walk and get lost in the maze of our talk, and find
ourselves in Marly at the hour we are expected home for dinner. We
have to telephone Hugh to come and rescue us.

Her tongue is sharp, and she does not suffer from naïveté. At her
age, will I be as sharp? Her descriptions of people are merciless. Her
humor. Her gestures are informal, earthy, very delightful. She looks
at her best lying on the couch, untidy and slack, with her very strong

legs and accentuated curves causing me somewhat the same uneasiness as Dorothy [Dudley]. I wore my pajamas and felt tempted to make love to her, to her breasts.

Reading about my childhood, she said, "It was all like that. Do you remember the colored stones in the windows, too?"

In her analysis she uncovered a memory—her father raped her. The analyst said that was a frequent delusion in women, a dream, a wish, a fear; questioned the reality of the memory. Rebecca said it was real but now she did not know.

Two things I have not dared tell her: about my love affair with my Father, and that I killed my child. I don't know how far she will follow me into strangeness. She comes out of her rigid English life liberated by France and free and passionate, and a "pig," as she says, but how free?

"How full of life you are," she said.

She admires the serenity of my bearing. I do not show the chaos, ever, outwardly. And in life I have been stronger and freer. At forty-two she says, "I will also take a studio for 'Tommy.' How cleverly you manage your life, Anaïs."

While waiting for her to wake up I copy my New York diary. So Rank mixes vividly with the present.

Rebecca definitely does not like Henry's writing. Thinks my preface to *Tropic of Cancer* a beautifully alive thing which bears no relation to the book. "He has no vision," she says.

In the studio she observed she had never seen such serious books in an atmosphere of gaiety and lightness and play. Yes. All seriousness enveloped in castanets, lace shawls, glass aquariums, colored stones, orange walls, costumes. Analysis enveloped in poetry and perfume.

I wore my black dress yesterday, the one I wore so much for analysis and for Rank. The two slits show the birth of the breasts. Rebecca said, "Of course, it was right for analysis, which is a giving of the breast to nourish others . . ."

Rebecca liked Hugh and Eduardo taking us to eat langoustines at eleven in the morning without rhyme or reason, just because they looked appetizing as we passed. And Hugh's hysterical fit of laughter in the garden over Emilia's slow service, a humorous hysteria born of years of patience for bad service because I have an affection for Emilia, and Emilia a worship of me.

Rebecca likes imaginative chaos and that we had to break the langoustines with our fingers because we had no pincers.

Seeing the end-car of the train: "Do I have to get in? It is so indecently exposed."

In the train, kissing me, she said, "I can't tell you how marvelous it has been. It is as if I had another love affair!"

A magnificent period. Breaking her conventional rhythm, the broken rhythm by which Henry always lives. A continuous broken rhythm *assouplie la fantaisie,* it stretches the imagination. The other, conventional life kills it. She said to be in Louveciennes was so lovely she would address it as *the womb:* "Let's have a toast to regression!"

My feeling of protectiveness toward her though I am thirty-two and she forty-two.

She said she was broken down by our extravagant goodness to her. Everything the three of us contrived, a truly royal reception without much gold.

I am the mother of the group in the sense that I am always ahead of Hugh, Eduardo, Henry, or Fraenkel, in my creation of life and giving of life. I am the All-Mother giving Henry strength and wisdom to stand alone; giving Hugh analysis, inciting him to live; pushing Eduardo, for years now, out of his solitude. And finally, when I succeed—Henry self-sufficient and amazingly evolved, guiding Fraenkel now; Eduardo having made friends with Fraenkel and staying with him; Hugh at one time enjoying his bohemian life in London—when they are out of the nest, Joaquin, too, or the violinist, all of them—then I look at the empty nest and I weep. Eduardo, in a great mood of expansion, fraternizing with Henry at last, all of them in motion. Henry talking like Rank and discovering what I knew before, long ago.

In motion, when I look at the whirlpools I create, the changes I bring, the transformations of life, then I feel afraid, afraid of being abandoned. To Henry and Fraenkel, to Rebecca, to each I say the thing which brings faith. The milk that comes out of my breasts is psychoanalytical, something beyond analysis, made of sympathy, understanding, vision into others' destiny. Rebecca's life, too, I feel I will influence, toward freedom. They obey and follow me, they hurl back my own words at me. Henry says now what I used to say about Allendy in the darkness of the garden in Louveciennes. But Henry, with the deepest humility, says, "You know all this. You have said all this."

But my children come back. Henry never loved me as much as right now, as last night. Hugh comes back. Eduardo comes back. Fraenkel is the most perverse of them. I have less patience with him because he is so *envious,* ungenerous. He fights as a woman does, with petty instruments. *Il est le plus malade.*

Hugh, for some strange reason, was excitedly in love with me while Rebecca was here. It is as if seeing me live, seeing me afire, they want to make love to this dancing figure.

Eduardo discovering now the pleasure of full talks I experienced in Clichy, shedding his reticences. So often I had tried to share it with him. It was I who invented his staying occasionally with Fraenkel. I said, "Oscillate between Paris and Louveciennes. Stay there a few days. Enjoy talks and people." And now he obeys and goes there, and likes it, and I get dark and brooding over my empty nest!

When I arrived at the Villa Seurat yesterday morning for breakfast it was Eduardo who leaned out of the window of Fraenkel's place to whistle good morning. Breakfast with Eduardo and Henry, who try to give me a summary of three days of Fraenkel. Telling me how the description of schizophrenia also applied to him. How *Tropic of Cancer* was a book of cannibalism and sadism. The Henry of that period, to whose room I went and into whose sensitiveness I entered directly, passing right through and beyond this edifice, this attitude, this book which he placed between himself and the world to parry the blows.

With Fraenkel we talked about Rebecca. He liked her as a woman, her healthiness. We talked about my being ahead on account of my power to act, to play tricks, to deceive, to lie, in leading a more adventurous life. I said to Henry, "Instead of calling it tricks, why don't you use a nicer word and call it my creation?" This creation Fraenkel admires. We agreed Rebecca was more realistic than I. Also a classical writer, while we are romantics.

At night, Henry in love. Showering kisses. Henry placing my hand on his penis. Half-asleep, half-dreaming, we fuck, until he arouses me to a paroxysm. Waves and waves of desire. We fall asleep holding each other. I tell him I said to Rebecca I would marry him. *There was a harvest moon.*

AUGUST 17, 1935

M *Y INCONSCIENCE DU MONDE, WHICH MADE IT* possible for me to wear a cherry red velvet dress in the morning in Richmond Hill to go to New York and pose for Richard Maynard.

Yesterday was an important day for my writing. The night before, we went out with Eduardo, Rodina and her lesbian friend, Carol, and Hugh. To the Bal Tabarin. I was tired from the orgiastic day with Rebecca, from the day and night with Henry. Several phrases rumbled through my head: *rêve éveillé,* dreaming awake. (Proust's analysis.) *L'extase joint à l'analyse.* Dislike of my female realism so separate from my dream self.

Yesterday morning I went to Elizabeth Arden to refresh my skin. Lying down there induced a kind of half-dream which reminded me of being under ether, only pleasantly. Then I saw both reality and the unconscious together; they fused, or alternated, harmoniously. Hugh had also said that there were times when I was crazy. The state between, the passing from normalcy into fantasy and neurosis, that was what I wanted to do. I began again to monologue about my Father, not Rank. I rushed to Henry. He had an errand to do. I sat at his typewriter and with desperate quickness wrote five pages in a new way which begin in the present, the salon of Elizabeth Arden, about my Father's feet. I know now how I will write that book.

Notes: Ether always. In and out of tunnel of consciousness and unconsciousness with full realistic details and the utmost of the *rêve éveillé*.

At the same time I get encouragement from Dorothy Dudley, warm praise of both my novel and "Alraune." In the novel I am a pioneer in description of woman-to-woman relationships, she says. "Alraune" is the blue flame, the pure communion. The novel to me is the fire. I am most myself in "Alraune" because it is communion with my vision. The character of Henry in the novel could be smelled. So dramatic and powerful. On top of that an enthusiastic letter from Katrine, who gave my work to read to her son-in-law, a publisher.

On top of that I now can drink wine without feeling sick. So to work!

AUGUST 18, 1935

*A*FTER RECOPYING "ALRAUNE" I WROTE ABOUT THE diaries burning in the Father book. It seems to me that this way I can never get stuck again. I am imitating the diary, approximating the tone of sincerity and the fullness.

A U G U S T   2 2 ,   1 9 3 5

CAME HOME FROM VILLA SEURAT VERY INTENSELY
alive, copied ten pages of the New York diary
(I need to keep reliving the feverish adventures and triumphs of New
York); then in a state of great exaltation I wrote two pages on music
for my Father book. Music. That is one of the key words. Music. He,
the musician, did not make the world sing for me, did not let me
sing or dance. "I never could dance around you, O my Father. No
one ever danced around you. As soon as I left you, my Father, the
whole world began to sing."

Neurosis: attributing to pregnancy every physical gain. Because I
gained weight I rushed to the doctor to be examined. I cannot yet
believe in happiness. Yearning for New York, the romance and the
pleasure and the intensity there. No longer for Rank.

Joaquin sends us his first royalties on his sonata, seventy francs.
Henry's first royalties are going to the printing of his *Scenario*. Henry
is so human.

Rebecca writes me a merciless letter about Fraenkel's book, which,
she thinks, is a pathetic book because it has nothing in it that could
not be said in two pages. She thinks it is empty and repetitious. She
feels that neither Fraenkel nor Henry seems to have any sense of
reality, which is the basis for literature—or life, for that matter. They
sit around and talk about an imaginary England, imaginary readers
of D. H. Lawrence; they spout platitudes. She does not think they
gain anything from contact with me; it is merely a tremendous waste
of energy and time, and they are takers who satisfy my maternal
instincts, but I should not be distracted, should forge ahead with my
own work . . .

Sitting in the studio tonight, drunk on music, writing letters, dancing letters. Music a stimulant to me of the highest order and more potent than wine. I'm drunk. Communicating with the world. I write only to communicate with people. I love people.

Henry's jealousy as intense as mine. He does not let me meet his young and handsome friends. It has taken me a long time to trust Henry's love. I never wanted to leave my clothes at the studio, because I remembered the story of his wife finding June wearing her kimono. I imagined him letting a whore wear my things. Remembering his other desecrations and my own love of desecration.

In monologues there is no punctuation.

I love all things in their abnormal, unreal sizes. Either too big or too small.

Louveciennes. Hugh is my sanity. Otherwise the world would seem always topsy-turvy. In Hugh there is health, peace, no change, eternal love, habit. But Henry is showing the greater protectiveness. When Fred said some parts of my novel sounded ridiculous in French (just as Lawrence does) and I broke down, Henry defended me and came over to me and took my head in his arms, standing close to me as he talked.

S E P T E M B E R 5 , 1 9 3 5

ONE AFTERNOON IN FRAENKEL'S PLACE, EDUARDO, Henry, Fraenkel, and I composed a play together on the theme of Fraenkel's death. He asks us to believe in his death, just as people believed in Christ's death, because until we believe in his death he can't be resurrected.

Henry never died that way, although he reached the same abyss of suffering. It must be because he lived out his suffering; it was not a suffering caused by frustration. Frustration causes death. Suffering, absolute and real, does not kill.

I told Henry that it is because he knows so well that wisdom stops living that he always insists on a balance, one day of wisdom and one of foolishness! That he is more right when he writes nonsense— fantasy or burlesque, as in his letters from New York—than when he offers his descriptions and impressions of New York as wisdom. He can't write with wisdom like Keyserling, or with the seriousness of a Duhamel. He doesn't know; he only has his crazy, mad, fantastic vision. He is all twisted. One evening he said very seriously, after Fraenkel had proved to him that Henry always caricatured people, "I don't wish to be twisted anymore." He is attracted to wisdom; it fascinates him. He does not have it, except in great divine flashes with many relapses.

I found the way in which I can pour all that I think or feel each day into a book that is not the diary. My Father book is written like the diary. Of course, everything does not go into it, but almost every day I think or act something which is related to that story. My Father book is well done because it is immediate writing. In this book I am doing Henry more humorously, more carelessly. Henry had a fit of laughter over his first appearance and my takeoff on "Everything is good." I have less respect, or naïveté, though no less love. I work slowly by hand while Henry writes the Max story.*

Fraenkel against Henry. Hugh against me. The colorless ones, who make no grand gestures, are accused of lacking generosity. Henry and I give attractively, illusory giving, not in reality. But the world needs the illusory giving, or giving of illusion.

The regrets for Rank are over.

I'm stuck again, in too narrow a life, though God knows it is full enough. I have written about one hundred pages of my Father book. Monday morning I leave Louveciennes with Hugh; I stop at the bank

---

* The story of Henry Miller's chance acquaintance with a panhandling refugee in Paris first appeared in the collection *Max and the White Phagocites,* published by the Obelisk Press in October 1938, and in the first volume of the American magazine *The Phoenix* (Fall 1938).

to put the New York diary in the vault, having finished copying it. I take a taxi to Villa Seurat. As I arrive I see Eduardo carrying milk for his breakfast with Fraenkel. We kiss each other on the corner of the mouth. I run upstairs. Henry opens the door just as I am about to knock. He feels me coming. He is in a good mood because he got a letter from a new admirer, and we set to work on the mailing of the subscription blanks for Number One of the Siana Series, *Aller Retour New York*. I write a lot of letters. Then I market for lunch. Eduardo carries my market bag so that we can talk. The boy he loves is a prostitute; he "does" the Café Sélect; and in spite of the horoscopes which indicate love between them, the boy feels he must stick to his career and Eduardo is sad.

Henry and I have lunch together. He is very caressing. We take a nap. He takes me so violently that I tell him he must have reached a supercunt. I am so elastic and pliable, I lie with legs so high, back curved, offering the whole like a bouquet, and Henry likes to watch it, to see it, all red and glistening, sliding in and out tantalizingly. At a certain point I lose my head completely, becoming frenzied and like crazy, all sex, blind sex, without identity or consciousness. And Henry, beside himself, says, "You son of a bitch," which makes me laugh. We fall asleep laughing. The black velvet curtains are drawn. Henry falls deeply asleep.

The *femme de ménage* is washing dishes. I take a bath. I put on the coral dress with the Medici collar, hide it all under a black cape, and call on Richard Thoma for a while to get back the "Alraune" manuscript I loaned him, and my copy of the magazine *Minotaure*. He tells me he designed a dress for me. He does not belong to our age of surrealism. He is a romantic and a decadent. He does not tell me fantastic stories, such as he told when he visited us, because he knows I don't believe them, even though I like them and know they are the prolongation of his writing.

I return to Henry. I bring him a bottle of talcum powder. I make coffee for him. We work until dinnertime. He corrects what I have written on my Father. He says it is good. He wants to go to the movies. At the exciting glimpses of China he holds my hand; we communicate our emotional moods by touch. We come out of the movies perspiring. Henry is hungry and eats the leftover soup. I hate soup in Louveciennes, but I like to make soup for Henry because he likes it and because it steams on the table and it looks like a haven, this steam, while it rains outside; and Henry is happy to have a permanent place, and does not want to move.

Tuesday afternoon I go to the Harveys'. Kahane is calling on Henry, so I stop and ask Fraenkel to come with me. He is alone. He is glad to see me. Henry keeps me out of his way. Dorothy told Fraenkel that he is in love with me. I knew that. I knew it would be *Werther's Younger Brother* again: Henry, just as in Fraenkel's book, and "Matilda," the wife of his brother, the taboo woman.*

After the visit to the Harveys, Fraenkel and I sit at the Sélect. He is a bit drunk. When I say it is time for me to go because Henry is waiting for me, he says, "Oh, that's exactly like Matilda." We are all victims of obsessional patterns and themes. When we return, Kahane is still there, so we all go out to dinner.

Wednesday. Eduardo comes up with a volume of the *Encyclopedia Britannica* on "Color" to talk with Henry. We are having lunch. Henry has been kissing me every half hour; between each letter, he either massages or kneads me. At five we get restless and walk out. Drop in at the bookshop to get paid for the twenty-five francs' worth of books I sold, our motto being "From surrealism on." We buy a tenth of a lottery ticket. At the post office.

I talk again about the need of anonymity to protect Hugh, my Father, Mother, brothers, friends, lovers. I have written to Kahane to try and convince him. At six-thirty I have to meet Hugh and thank him for the flowers he sent me at the Villa Seurat with this card: "Hugh. May I see you tomorrow?" Beautiful red roses, to the place where I am supposed to have a room alone. Drive back to Louveciennes.

------

*Inspired by Goethe's *Sorrows of Young Werther,* Michael Fraenkel used his own experience of having fallen hopelessly in love with his elder brother's sweetheart (the "transforming pain of my life") as the subject of his novel, which he self-published under his Carrefour imprint in 1930.

Thursday. I never do any good work. I feel uprooted. I miss Henry. I am alone all day with the radio, orange juice, work, a letter from Katrine saying my novel was not understood by Jim McCoward: publication in New York is out of the question.

I had to tell Emilia we are leaving for America, because Hugh can't bear her anymore and has engaged someone else, and I must let him because I don't intend to be home very much and I want him well served and taken care of efficiently when we move to Paris. She cried, and I too. But for him I would have kept Emilia until my death, out of pity and protectiveness and affection, until the cobwebs choked me, until the grease dissolved me, until my clothes rotted away, until I fell apart from lack of care and efficiency around me.

I started to rewrite the novel in the first person, trying to add a little fullness and subtract the naïveté at the beginning.

SEPTEMBER 12, 1935

*T*HE FULLNESS IS NOT ENOUGH.
My Father and I don't write to each other. I refuse to act as an obedient child who must keep writing to him, as I did from New York. *What I hate above all is a whole day in Louveciennes in the company of my past.* I have to move forward very fast, to place a great many incidents between my past and me, because it is still a burden.

Last night a frivolous night with Bill Hoffman, the Barclay Hudsons, Henri Hunt, and Hugh. Bright lights, savory dinner at Maxim's, Cabaret aux Fleurs with Kiki.

Hoffman was again intoxicated with me. He is in love with my gaiety. He asked me again, "Would you not . . . ?" He was very red after a month of hunting in Scotland. With champagne everything might have been possible right there, with the help of the lights, the music, the friction of dancing, the warmth of bodies pressed together, the bare breasts of the dancers making him curious about mine. But the next day I know it's impossible.

Toward Henry I never have any remorse. He always took from life everything life gave him. He taught me to take. Nothing can ever prevent me from daring anything I want, but Bill, who hunts in Scotland and wears silk shirts, is not tempting. But now I know real gaiety, away from Henry, real forgetting of myself, and I know drunkenness, and when I'm drunk I'm witty and my gaiety is contagious.

Pleasure. Henry denies me pleasure always, instinctively. He limits me. He asserts himself exactly as Eduardo did, by saying "No." If I want to light a fire, it is No. If I want to go to the Sélect, it is No. If I want to see a good movie, he does not want to go so far, and he takes me to the local cinema, Alesia, where I suffer from boredom and fleas.

Today I have seriously considered becoming a high-class *cocotte*. I want money, perfume, luxury, traveling, liberty. I don't want to be shut in at the Villa Seurat cooking for imbeciles like Fred, and Henry's timorous, bourgeois, weak, whiny friends. And the *waste*. I can't lead such a wasted life. I need to create constantly or enjoy myself intensely. I can't sit around with Fred, Benno, Max, Roger, Brassaï, Fraenkel for hours, either.

Eduardo is where I was with June. Suffering from the same difficulties in entering life, the nervousness, the upset stomach, sleeplessness, overexcitement, anxiety, fears, drawbacks, the need to retire alone to find strength again, the fear of abandoning himself to the flow, the need to play chess. *Il vit encore en jouant à la vie.*

He identifies himself and the boy he loves with June and me. At the same time, as is usual with lovers, he finds his capacity for love increasing and spreading, so he gives each one his due, and I am getting showered with it! We sit in the Sélect watching his boy looking for clients. He has a new green hat and tie. Marcel Duchamp passes by, looking like a man long buried who plays chess instead of painting because that is the nearest to complete immobility, the best pose for a dead man. Eyes of glass and skin of wax.

And Dorothy Dudley, who never knows anymore where she is, looks like a Pomeranian. She recognizes certain people, food, drink. But the rest of the time her eyes look on the world as from a rolling ship, and without any sense of distinction.

Inside of me there is the American jazz microbe. A jazz globule predominates, neither white nor red. I am expecting someone. He is not in France. I feel that. Where is he? If he does not come soon I am going to wander by myself into some dangerous ordinary adventure. I have such a fear of ordinary adventures. *J'ai la fièvre de nouveau* (I'm feverish again), *Il est en retard* (He is late). *He* does not pass before French cafés, where I have a rendezvous with the Present.

Anne Harvey passes by, saying Brancusi is *en arrêt*. He has found his philosophy and will not be dislodged, which is applicable to my Father. They do not wish to be moved.

I dread going to Spain with Henry because it will mean cafés, streets, whores, streets, cafés, and movies. No real enormous, or fantastic, adventures. Cafés. Just as I am sitting here with Eduardo, drinking *vin d'Alsace* and watching his minor June—oh, so much smaller—collecting clients.

I want to become a whore but I don't know how it is done. Shall I sit at the Café Marignan and let a man with a yellow roadster and a Scotch terrier drive me away? Banal. He, the one I am expecting, must have ears. He may be in Spain.

I add pages to the book on my Father, on the eclipsed period of my life, of our lives. Eclipses. My posing for artists. No savour. My life in Havana. The first year of my marriage. The flavor of events. Why was it that it often comes only *en retard,* while living another life, while telling the incident to someone? During my talks with my Father the whole flavor of my childhood came back to me. The taste of everything came back to me as we talked. But not everything comes back with the same vividness. Many things which I described to my Father I told without pleasure, without any taste in my mouth. Some portions of my life were lived as if I were under the effect of ether, and many others under a complete condition of eclipse. Some of them cleared up later; that is, the fog lifted, the events became clear, nearer, more intense, and remained as if unearthed for good. Why did some of them come to life and others not? Why did some remain flavorless and others recover a new flavor or meaning? Certain periods, like the posing, which seemed intense at the time, violent almost, have never had any taste. I know I wept, suffered, rebelled; was humiliated, and proud too.

The story I presented to my Father about the posing, and to Henry, was not devoid of color or incident, yet it has remained without flavor. It was not unimportant in the chain of my life, since it was my first confrontation with the world.

It was the period when I discovered I was not ugly, a very important moment for a woman. It was a dramatic period, beginning with the show for the painters in the Watteau costume and ending in being the star model of the Club, the Gibson girl, and the model for so many magazine covers, paintings, miniatures, statues, drawings, watercolors. I even wrote a novel about it.*

It cannot be that what is lived feebly or in a condition of unreality, in a dream or fog, disappears altogether, because I remember a ride I took through Louveciennes many years ago, when I was unhappy, ill, indifferent, in a dream. A mood of blind remoteness and sadness and divorce from life. This ride, which I took with my senses asleep, I repeated almost ten years later with my senses awakened, in good health, with clear eyes, and I was surprised to see that I not only remembered the road, but every detail of this ride which I thought I had not seen or felt at all. It was as if I had been sleepwalking while another part of my body recorded and observed the presence of the sun, the whiteness of the road, the billows of the heather, in spite of my inability to taste. Today I can see every leaf on every tree, every face in the street—and all as clear as leaves after the rain. Everything very near.

---

* Anaïs Nin eventually abandoned her novel *Aline's Choice,* begun in 1923; it suffered, she felt, from an "unbalanced view." "I evaded squalidness, grimness, naturalness, cynicism, physical and mental ugliness," she noted in her diary in February 1926. "I falsified in order to beautify." Though the name of her heroine echoes that of *Aline et Valour,* Nin was then apparently unaware of de Sade's novel.

It is as if, before, I had periods of myopia, like a psychological blindness to the present moment, and I wonder what caused this myopia. Could a sorrow alone, a shock, cause blindness, deafness, sleepwalking, unreality? Everything today absolutely clear, the eyes focusing with ease on the present, focusing on the outline and color of things as luminous and clear as they are in New York, in Switzerland under the snow. Intensity and clearness, besides the sensual awareness.

Neurosis is like a loss of all the senses, all perception through the senses. It causes deafness, blindness, sleep, or insomnia. But why do certain things come to life and others not? Analysis, for example, reawakened my old love for my Father, which I thought buried. What were the blocks of life which fell completely into oblivion? What was alive intensely sometimes disappeared because the very intensity was unbearable. But why did things that were not important return clear and washed and suddenly embodied?

SEPTEMBER 18, 1935

EDUARDO IS ACCOMPANIED BY SURREALISM. THE afterglow, the shadows cast by long-past things. Where is Rank?

Tendue vers l'impossible toujours, moi. I'm always reaching for the impossible. When I write I eat my neurosis. Out of my neurosis I write. Thus the process of creation for me is a sad one. I would rather be a nightclub hostess and dance jazz until I die.

Yesterday, moonstorm. So I made a drama of two things: his [Henry's] ordinary, worthless friends, and his using of people. I rebelled against his using my friends to help Fred, and against helping Fred, who is merely a minor edition of Henry.

Anyway, I revealed to Henry my restlessness and disillusion. To leave Louveciennes, which is out of the world; to enter Villa Seurat, if Villa Seurat were only Henry—but Henry is surrounded by Fraenkel and Fred. What poverty and drabness. I can market for Henry because I love him; I can't market for Fred. In New York it was the same. Now I see it more clearly. Henry has ordinary friends and he makes them appear extraordinary by caricaturing them. He invents them.

I, like June, attract unusual, extraordinary people like Louise, Artaud, Rank, Eduardo, Allendy, Rebecca, Bel Geddes.

Using people: Henry lost the friendship of [Aleister] Crowley by borrowing from him and then being too timid to approach him, thus convincing Crowley he did not really care for him but had used him. And now he writes an apologetic letter. This time he was sincere. But all the rest of the time, he only approaches people to use them. One after another I have seen him use people. He does not understand that it hurts people to be used. He does not know that only love makes using right. In love there is no using. But the rest of what he does is whorishness.

I remember when I first met June and Henry I had never heard the word *use*. I did not know what it was to beg or to use someone deliberately. I learned. I have done a lot of it for Henry. I have imitated them. I don't do it very well even today. It is imitation. In Henry it is a serious vice. He is a whore by nature. And how nastily he begs, arrogantly, cynically. Sometimes humorously. Then it is easier to forgive. His begging letter for Fred,* which he is going to send around, is humorous. But his list made me angry. Everybody. Everybody I have just met and want as a friend. That is easier to understand—he feels they have cheated him of something and he wants compensation—but what an idea of compensation. Just like June: when she lost Henry she wanted money.

---

* A twenty-page pamphlet, "What Are You Going to Do About Alf?," soliciting contributions to send Alfred Perlès to Ibiza, so he could finish his novel, was printed in October 1935 with funds supplied by Henry Miller, and distributed free.

The storm has passed. Henry just bows his head and lets the storms pass. He looks gentle and contrite. I wept. Nothing gained, nothing changed. The realization that I am alone. We lie in bed and he covers his defects with an outpour of caresses. I go to sleep. Nothing gained. Nothing changed. Adventures, glamorous things away from Henry, not with Henry. His life is crazy and like a circus. I can't laugh all the time. It isn't always funny. It's like having a child who wears you out playing. Nothing tremendous can come of that. Always a circus. Fred like a monkey. Fraenkel like a mouse, nibbling words. I said to Henry he was always trying to make a joke out of everything in order to evade the responsibility for all he does.

I'm sick physically now. Return to France was a step backward.

Perhaps I'm endangering my happiness. There is happiness and there is adventure. Since Rank, I have been without adventure. Rank was an adventure which he took too seriously. One should never make it real. Perhaps I have made my life with Henry too real because I love him so humanly, and his reality hurts my love.

But his love, our love, keeps us alive. We try to repair the fissures, the cracks, with passionate kisses. We hold on to each other. We are jealous. Love. Love. Love. He won't take me to cafés. He is afraid to lose me. If I speak of London, he asks, "What do you want to do in London?" New York is condemned because New York has glamor for me.

Coming back to Louveciennes with Hugh, finding two letters from my New York patients, both swimming in life because of me, thanking me, I again forgot my own sadness.

When I'm sad I sometimes tire my sadness away by walking. I walk until I am exhausted. I give myself a *fête des yeux*. I look at every shop window. Rue Saint-Honoré, rue de la Boétie, rue de Rivoli, avenue des Champs-Elysées, Place Vendôme, avenue Victor Hugo. I buy fashion magazines and live the life of *Vogue* aristocrats, wondering where I could wear these things—neither in Louveciennes nor in Villa Seurat. The theatrical ephemeralness of my settings. No solid values, because I know it is soon to be changed to match the inner changes.

I never buy for duration but for effect, illusion. A quick deterioration sets in, as upon stage settings. Unreality. Nowhere to stay.

The creator's mobility, change, transformations, do not inspire human confidence. We all have a need of a *fixed* thing or being. And the fixed being is stagnant. Henry is Knut Hamsun, even when he says he does not wish to be twisted anymore. The next moment he says, "Maybe I don't mean that."

The next morning he was off again in his Max story. He falsifies Fraenkel, for the sake of his story, but also because he does not know Fraenkel. When you know, it is hard to falsify. It's like now, when I know Dorothy Dudley's sensitiveness and understanding, in spite of the caricature I made of her.

My fixation on Henry is his solid axis. While I believe in him he will not need to be locked up!

Hugh is my axis and keeps me from going mad. If I lived with Henry I would go mad. I owe Hugh everything, all my strength and courage to live out other things. I am so grateful to him for giving me liberty, for letting me be, and for being always there when I return, always rather scarred and battered. My sweet, young father.

I know what I want now. Someone who will help me be bad, help me into adventure. Henry, Hugh, my Father, Rank—they all hold me back, hold me back in seriousness, for themselves.

The glamor, the glamor of New York even on a drugstore counter. So many men there in love with me that I did not taste: Buzby, Donald Friede, Bel Geddes; and now Frank Parker, Katrine's son-in-law, because he read my novel. I want to go to New York with Hugh in the spring, yet I don't want to leave Henry. I get possessed with my desire to wander, and I risk losing what I most love for adventure.

NEVER KNEW AS MUCH PLEASURE AND AS LITTLE contentment. Pleasure: the entrance into the family of Feri, the Hungarian boy loved by Eduardo. A pretty boy much like Joaquin. I like him. He is only twenty-one. He loved me before he came to Louveciennes. Had seen me sitting at the café with Fraenkel. Sent me perfume via Eduardo. I love him as I loved my brothers. With him gaiety entered the house. I used to be the only one dancing, restless, mimicking, playing. Now Feri and I together enliven Eduardo and Hugh. We dance. I taught him to dance. We play charades. We go to the races on Sunday afternoon. To Prunier to eat oysters with white wine. I dressed up in his clothes, which fit me. Could not look like a man, but a fairy, yes. He does not want to return to the Sélect or to his profession. He puts flowers in the vases, shoots, carves wood, repairs the phonograph, and writes his diary in Hungarian. Climate of laughter, playing; what I needed so much in my life with Henry, who restricts me to drabness, who refuses to travel, who wants to stay put. An outlet. I want to dress up as a man and go adventuring. Pleasure. Those things which I could not enjoy before, now I do. Food. Drink. Automobiling. Walking. Drink. Brioche at Cernay-les-Vauz. Nightclubs. Gambling. The Champs-Elysées fountains playing in the sunlight. Elegance. Aristocrats. Pedicure. A new Borgia hat in purple. A black oilcloth bag and gloves. *Vogue.* Dancing with American Roberts and in love with him for one evening, and he the same, because of the rhythm of the dance. Feeling of freedom from guilt, from restrictions.

Despair because Henry's life and mine cannot fuse, in spite of passion. Bitter explosions and revolts from me. One about his foolish acts of sending June a begging letter for Fred (macabre humor, I say);

a subscription blank to Dreiser, who snubbed him in New York; begging letters to Buzby, who always snubs him.

"I want to irritate him by keeping on asking," says Henry. "Why do you continue to beg?" I say. "I have made you a free man. Meet people as an equal, not always to get something from them. It ruins all your relationships. You lost Crowley that way. You have a whore complex, and you forget people have a complex about being used. Remember what I told you about the Dreiser tragedy. The day you're a celebrity you will know the pain of having people come to you not because of love but because of the glamor of your name and because of what you can do for them. Women will even want to sleep with you because of your name and power. You never understand what others feel who want you to like them for themselves and who feel you're merely using them. I'm trying to make you aware of your own value. Why must you always come in at the door like a beggar?"

Henry said it gives others pleasure to give.

"Yes," I said, "but not to be forced to give, to be held up and insulted as you do. I refuse to go on begging for you. I imitated you and June playfully, against my real nature. I hate to beg or use people. What you used to do in Clichy as a prank is now, in real relation to the world, just childish, ridiculous."

He did not protest. He was convinced. But I too was convinced of his innocence. He does not know anyone but himself, or what he does to others. Absolutely incapable of understanding other people. I fell asleep saying, "You're innocent. You're an innocent."

Henry was hurt. I feel again, on account of his passivity, his not fighting, that I have wounded him. Then I feel guilty and weak inside at having to operate on him. I feel crushed and tired. Ready to accept his crazy and foolish acts for the sake of our poor love.

Fraenkel is sore at his caricature, and Henry does not see why.

And so—I have to live for myself, separately from Henry. Give up the absolute.

For a day and night I hated him. Then I went back to him. His passionate kisses and apologies. Our caresses terribly enjoyable, perhaps because of the suffering and antagonism, the despair. That is all I have. That is all he gives me. I take it, desiring it should solder everything together at the same moment. But I'm frustrated by the impossible dream. Separation necessary, and ultimately the passion will die.

With this despair, I throw myself into sensation, pleasure, analysis, drink, the games with Feri. I will go to London alone. I will find another Rank. I feel close to Hugh, who is so good to me; I love him with a profound gratitude. About him, too, I refused to accept the limitation. Turn around, abandon the absolute, flow to the left, to the right, disperse?

Henry! Henry! Oh, my Henry! All your women have to be unfaithful, have to abandon you, because you are not man, you are the child who sucks one's breasts until they bleed.

O C T O B E R   6 ,   1 9 3 5

*J*AZZ ON THE RADIO. FERI HAS DANCED ME INTO serenity. But I have been physically sick because my strong desire for adventure and intensity is frustrated. Limitations all around. Money, Henry's inertia, Henry's hatred of New York. After days of pleasure with Hugh, Eduardo, and Feri, we were sobered down by the end of our money. I felt deeply defeated at not being able to go to New York, to work and to live freely. I have to make the best of Paris, which I hate. Henry sacrifices me to his every need. To live with him and to be dependent on him altogether would mean my death as individual, as artist, as woman, everything. Hugh alone has kept me alive and Henry has given me nothing but what a great passion gives—the chance to give one's self. But beyond a certain giving to Henry lies death.

And so: adventure.

I don't know how to find it, where to begin. I'm going to London alone, the first week of November. I would like to go to Venice and to India.

What I cannot do: finish my book on my Father—analyze people to earn money for luxuries.

OCTOBER 14, 1935

STILL FIGHTING THE DEMON. FOUND TITLE FOR MY novel just before giving it to Kahane—*104° Fahrenheit.* Took great care of Henry while he had the grippe, but left him because it was the weekend—feeling deeply his love.

The other day, when he boasted of his happy condition of insouciance, unconsciousness, guiltlessness, a world like a child's without concerns of any kind, saying, "I feel so happy," I couldn't help saying, "Yes, but you don't make others happy. That is how you lost June." He said, "You really mean that is how I will lose you." After that he got sick, as if to call me back. But I feel hard and lonely and disillusioned. Henry said, "I don't feel anything can go wrong between us. All people who give anything to the world also cause great suffering. I am one of those." Henry lives by the laws of his ego, so I must do the same. Later at night, when he got drunk, he said he wanted to go to London, after a miserable evening at Kahane's, where he talked crazily. I went to sleep at Henry's side, calling for Hugh like a lost child. Suffering from *differences.* In the morning, half-awake, we kissed and I forgot my pain. Beautiful harmonious day. Savage fucking.

Feri is vain, charming, proud, timid, home loving; loves like a child, not like a man; is martial, boastful, and a lover of sensation. Thoughtful, gallant, aristocratic, not soft. When I dance with him I feel his sensitiveness and nervousness, like a racehorse's. He has a cult for me, and a sort of attraction. We come very near to love. If he were double his age! He looks wonderful in his clothes, not effeminate but neat and dashing. We are the same height and build.

The truth is that I am slowly returning to my real nature, to all that I gave up by loving Henry, to my deep love of beauty, of harmony, of order, of an imagination which does not run to waste and folly. With this, gratitude and love for Hugh, who lets me live my true self. An unconscious desire not to go to Villa Seurat, where every hour is wasted, frittered away, dispersed, lost in chaos, talk, emptiness. I can't work there. I long for Louveciennes, which I hated before. I dread Monday. I feel I am falling apart, that Villa Seurat is eating into my creativity. For love I return, but I know now this love is a compromise, a cowardly yielding to love, against my soul's need and yearnings, against everything I need and love and am. With a religious attitude, I love Hugh, all that he lets me be, do, feel, think. My true ideal father is Hugh. Henry, my child; and so I shall die without a mate, without a love equal to me, a love that will be as old as I am today.

OCTOBER 16, 1935

*T*ERRIBLY PROFOUND HAPPINESS WHEN I SAW Henry yesterday and everything was as before. I exhausted my storm of criticism. I refuse to sacrifice life and love to an idea of how Henry should be or live. Deep tenderness, passion, peace.

Henry at work on *Black Spring,* pages on the obsessional walks. My love of this book. Henry trying to be thoughtful, after his fear of losing me. We go from separateness to the most passionate closeness.

But we were alone. He discourages his friends because he is in a serious working mood. Again I recapture my joy and send all ideas and ideals to hell. I want my love, Henry, pure, dark, wordless, instinctive, a denial of my plans, desires from the head. Oh, the one who can destroy one's criticalness toward life and human beings brings us closer to divinity. I cook—quietly singing. I wear my hair like a gypsy, curls on the nose! Henry is jealous of Feri. "Don't make a man out of him!" And when I left today, saying I would return Friday, Henry said that was too far off!

To be uncritical always, to mock the absolute, to mock the ideal. Close your eyes.

OCTOBER 19, 1935

YESTERDAY, WHEN I ARRIVED AT VILLA SEURAT, Henry met me with kisses and wanted me immediately in bed. He was in a mood which affects me still so much that I lose myself with love and yearning. Soft, vulnerable, serious, dreamy, tender, and so near to me—beyond all words. We looked and looked at each other. Someday, if the words come, if Henry says or writes what may seem to prove we did not understand, I must remember this *silence* and *nearness* which the mind has nothing to do with, a *nearness* which is deeper than understanding. If we talk or a scene reveals that when he uses words we are not close, it only proves the falsity of *words,* of *thought,* of *expressions.* Everything that has not been said between Henry and me, everything that will never be said, is what there is between us, that which can only be said with the fingers, the lips, the penis, the legs, the touch of skin, the smell of bodies, the voices when they utter only moans, sounds like the animals', the touch of hair, the divine language of the body.

This symphony and this dream. We lie on the couch listening to *Le Sacre du printemps, Black Spring* pages on the desk, dinner cooking. I wear my Persian dress. Almost every caress I have written here, because that alone is life and the rest I don't care about. Let him be.

I come back to Louveciennes to live my own life—to find my self, but that is a dismal necessity compared to that of loving. Loving comes first. Loving, losing, yielding.

I found my true love for Hugh, admitted my need of him. My love for my sick patients.

Pleasure. A night in Louveciennes with Eduardo, Feri, the Guicciardis; playing charades, splitting with laughter. I am finding my wit and my sharp tongue when I am not timid. I act comically. Joy. I don't want talk. Talk does not satisfy me, except talk between two people, which is relationship. Talk last night between Kahane, the Robertses, Henry, and Fred so foolish.

Colette Roberts makes a subtle distinction: "Your novel touched me. It is human and real, but it is *experience* re-created, and because it happens more deeply than where people usually experience, there's like a glass around it, like the glass over the paintings at the Louvre. One sees the real painting all right, one almost feels it, but there is a glass."

Note: Fear of death comes when not living; being alive is living out all the cells and parts of oneself. Parts that are denied get atrophied when dammed, like a dead arm, and infect the rest of the body with a death germ.

I learned from Henry to make love laughingly, with gaiety. This was what Rank most loved about me, that I laughed with pleasure during lovemaking instead of being intense or dramatic. He said all the women he had known were too serious in love.

Fraenkel: "June was a pathological child who made beautiful color patterns accidentally, as the insane do, not as *creator*."

I took away the artist from Hugh or in Hugh by my being one so completely. He took away my livingness and joyousness. That was our effect on each other. When we separated he became an artist and I won back my buoyancy.

I am perpetually lively, enthusiastic, smiling, although I am, deep down, sad about everything, and I have a tragic sense of life. Insanely jealous of *all* my loves and friendships.

Reading *Vogue* in New York to learn about stylish weekends and how to treat the butler!

At Henry's. Henry, Fraenkel, and I were talking together. Henry went out to get things for dinner. Fraenkel rushed up to me, calling, "Anis, Anis!" and kissed me, and asked me to kiss him. We kissed several times, standing up. I felt nothing. I feel that my face was smiling, perhaps mockingly. I felt as I did toward Artaud—a desire to arouse, but not to respond. I was dazed. I didn't say anything. Fraenkel said, "I have been expecting this. You're wonderful." I felt cold.

I cleaned the rouge off and powdered my face. Then I saw on the table Henry's wallet, which he had forgotten. Mechanically I looked at all he had in it. I found a photo of his little girl* and one of me. This made me so intensely happy, finding that he carried my picture about, that I almost cried. He loves me, he loves me. And the whole evening was transformed.

Moving to an apartment in Paris [sublet from Louise de Vilmorin], packing, seeing the New York tags on the trunk. Yearning for New York. But I again talked this over with Henry and he won't go. For him it is depressing and hateful. Packing. Thinking of Rank.

OCTOBER 28, 1935

*T*HIRTEEN AVENUE DE LA BOURDONNAISE, 6ᵉᵐᵉ. Well, my airplane sailed from Louveciennes and stopped at Paris. It seems to me that this is merely a stopping-place. I try to make myself settle down. I came with the fishbowl on my knees, my crystals, my aquarium, my seashell. I changed Louise's furnishings about, hid the porcelain figures, the French mosaic

---

* Barbara, born September 30, 1919, when Henry Miller was married to Beatrice Sylvas Wickens, was his first child. After their divorce in 1924, Miller had no contact with his daughter for many years.

clock, the French *bon-bon* pictures, the bric-a-brac Louis XV, XVI, or XX! A feeling of sweet luxury because the telephone is at my elbow, like in the movie stories, and I lie in a white satin bed with sheets embroidered with Louise's initials. I found her seashells tucked away.

After her divorce from Henri [Hunt] she stays in Verrière and comes to visit her children. Henri and his children live at the other end of the big apartment until he sails for New York.

I rushed to see Henry, so happy to be nearer to him. A white satin bed, a telephone, a big apartment. When Henri sails, my two children, Eduardo and Feri *(Chicuelo y Chiquito)*, will move in. I like Louise's presence here. I will see her.

New York seems a little nearer. I am sending one of my patients there, freeing her from the rule of her father. Vicariously, mystically, this year I have danced, acted, played the violin, and gone to New York. My patients did it. I earned a thousand francs for twenty sessions, which I gave Hugh because we are short. I am sweetly, stupidly happy. We see the Tour Eiffel very near. People study piano and sing badly. It is all sweet and lifelike and real.

I cannot rest, ever. I try to create a new life. I couldn't live June's gutter life; perhaps I may live one like Louise's, on the upper crust, and carry into it all that differentiates me from them: my depth. Luxury is sweet and beautiful. I need externals because I awake sad, deep down; then, with the help of beauty, of warmth, of decor, of the sun, of lulling things, of voluptuousness, I climb into joy. Climate, ambiance—they do affect me, help me to dream.

How Rank helped me to dream. I remember gratefully my arrival in New York, the room ready, the flowers every day, being waited on, meals in the room, taxis, plays, beautiful restaurants; the ideas we fed on, several each day, flowering with the day. One can be in love with what a man says. In that little room, warmed by his worship, I went into a trance. I dreamed. I was lulled. His protectiveness was immense, his possessiveness. He enveloped me. I was joyous. I wrote merry letters. I did not work. I cut out newspapers to make him laugh. I planned and played life: letters shooting down the glass tube, elevators with copper doors, maids in starched, light green dresses, elegance, soft lights, radiators boiling, whistling. Snow outside. I cutting and pasting for our humorous scrapbook, which he destroyed. Going out to buy symbolical things, a little house of logs on whose door I wrote, Do Not Disturb. Puck—Huck. A miniature automobile before we chose the real one, pencils with heart tops, or two small candles stuck together, burning, which he found when he came home from a lecture. He played. He wore his coat like a cape and danced the Continental all over the room, as we had seen it in the movies, stepping on and off the couch, on and off chairs. I dressed up for him, danced for him. Every night a different costume.

He came in between analyses: "My darling!" To laugh at the note he found under the door, or to tell me how he handled his patients, what happened. So quick, so intense. His happiness like a fire, burning and using him.

One Sunday afternoon I wore the red Russian dress. My room was flooded by sun-and-snow reflections. There were white flowers in a vase. He sat on the couch, and he noticed the luminousness. I, too, was luminous; it dazzled him. We were in a trance, a dream. If the dream could have continued, if he had known that for me it was a dream—the closeness, the same rhythm of thought and feeling—if only he had not wanted it so real! How the real marred, destroyed, the most beautiful of all unrealities; for now I know that my joys with Rank were mystical, of a kind I may never know again. What a tragedy that his body should become so important, should blot out and destroy the twinship. I, seeking a mystic marriage, remembering only the marvelous talks in the dark, in bed, and not one of his caresses—none except the feel of his hair in the morning, when he got into my bed like a child; surprised his hair was so soft. The talks we had were of such magical effect and profound content that today, in spite of what happened, I still feel mystically married out there to a little man who was not able to transcend the littleness of man, who destroyed a dream, an illusion, a fantasy, and with it—life.

I know that we understood each other completely. I know that today if Henry talked he would reveal all that he *does not understand.* Our love must thrive on silence and caresses.

OCTOBER 30, 1935

YESTERDAY I BEGAN TO THINK OF MY WRITING—life seeming insufficient, doors closed to fantasy and creation. I had written a few pages now and then. This morning I awoke serious, sober, determined, austere. I worked all morning on my Father book. Walked along the Seine after lunch, so happy to be near the river. Errands. Blind to cafés, to glamor, to all this stir and hum and color of life, which arouses such great yearnings and answers nothing. It was like a fever, a drug spell. The avenue des Champs-Elysées, which stirs me. Men waiting. Men's eyes. Men following. But I was austere, sad, withdrawn, writing my book as I walked.

No money. So I close my eyes as I pass the shops.

Henry is working. He cut out the pages I didn't like in New York about "I snooze while you work, brothers." Two things he has to beware of: one, the ranting and moralizing of a second-rate philosopher; the other, the personal, trivial feminine passages—the petty ones.

It is clear now that I have more to say and will never say it as well, and he has less to say and will say it marvelously. It is also clear that surrealism is for him and not for me. My style is simple in my Father book, direct like in the diary. *Documentaire.* His is rich and meaningless to the mind.

NOVEMBER 2, 1935

THE DAY AFTER, I BEGAN TO WORK EARNESTLY. Fell into a grave, intense, thoughtful mood. Have lost interest in life, in everything that touched me last month; turning inward, writing my Father book all day, even while I walk or go to the movies. Feeling austere, lonely, bitter, defeated. Life failed to materialize, to be what I want, so the book grows. I look pale, withdrawn, isolate. I hate art, work, writing, but it is the only remedy. I feel dark joys when I have worked well. Certain pages on my Father are deep and moving. I am thoroughly honest. My style is bare—I never think of how I will say it—only say it.

I met Christ on the Champs-Elysées, begging. Christ as a Hungarian artist begging. I am going to see him.

Life has lost its flavor of the marvelous. Everything looks realistic, like Henry's life. I write, I write all the time, while I yearn for new lovers. What has died is my talks with Henry. There is no more companionship, because he talks nonsense. Proust is not profound because he wrote about society!

NOVEMBER 7, 1935

*I*WROTE THE LAST PAGE OF MY BOOK ON MY FA-ther, about the last time I came out of the ether to see a dead little girl with long eyelashes and slender head. The little girl died in me and with her the need of a father. The great emotion with which I wrote the last pages, and only understanding the last lines after I had written them, while Eduardo and Chiquito played cards noisily and Hugh worked on a horoscope.

The book is not finished, only half-done, because I write the emotional pages first, without order, as I wrote the June–Henry novel. And then I have to fill in and construct. Ever since October 28 I have been serious, moody, deep, solitary, withdrawn, knowing only the austere joys of creation. Last month I could find pleasure in falling in love with a hat, a rich purple velvet hat with a long feather, exactly 1860 epoch, cancan—and wearing it, causing a sensation everywhere.

And now.
God the Father.

Nine-thirty. The Hunts' departure for New York—the three little girls getting ready. Mother and Joaquin preparing to leave for New York brought on a storm of yearning. *There is no doubt that whatever I desire strongly I must do or it kills me*—but that I seem to desire always what I cannot have: my Father as a child, John, New York.

Second storm, when Roger throws Fred out of his place and so Fred comes to the studio. I have already given him translation work to keep him afloat—not because I need it done. So I beg Henry not to spoil our life. I'd rather pay Fred's hotel bill, anything. Henry was sweet and really felt bad that I should be forced to keep Fred when he knows I despise him. I was aware all the time of the *exaggeration* in my feelings but I couldn't stop it. When my period is coming, I am crazy. I was trembling, wanted to weep, was immersed in a sense of tragedy. I had to leave Henry though I was free, and in the taxi I cried out to Hugh. Without Hugh I would today be in an insane asylum. There is a weakness in me—a need of others which is terrible. At a certain moment everything crumbles inside of me and I get desperate. I understand so well Louise taking drugs. June taking drugs.

Fred in our studio! Henry talking about wanting to make sacrifices. "But you know I won't let you starve, Henry. Go and make a real sacrifice, then. Ask for your royalties and give them to Fred instead of publishing the *Scenario*—then you will know how I feel about helping Fred when all I can possibly do, I want to do for you."

Meanwhile Kahane tells me I still have to work on the June–Henry novel. Stuart Gilbert admires it. He says whoever reads it feels Henry is just a lucky swine, a genius who gets away with everything and whom women shouldn't love!

But Henry, very tender, very serious, would not let me leave him until we had walked ourselves into serenity and understanding. About New York: I talked reasonably when he said, "I feel so selfish." I said it would be no use his going to New York to make me happy if it made him suffer. That our needs are different is no one's fault. I was more just, fair, gentle than I felt—inside of me everything was storm and pain and madness. Hatred of Fred, who is flabby, weak, *sournois,* inert, a parasite, helpless, foolish, worthless. Sitting there with his mouth open, imitating Henry, dirty, a caricature of Henry's worst faults—a sort of smaller, weaker, shabbier Henry. Revolt! Symbolism: Fred as all that I hate in Henry's life. Just to see him there enrages me. But Henry and I are walking about arm-in-arm, talking in the night, to find another way, what to do. Henry understanding I don't want to give Fred more. I suddenly grow very quiet, accepting. To help, somehow, if only Henry won't spoil our life. I can't come to the studio with Fred there. Strange and terrible, this exaggeration. I'm not all wrong, but crazily intense. No faith in my rightness. I feel ashamed of my outburst, because Henry is tender. God damn my desire for justice, justice only to others, for others. Then shame toward Hugh, worried about money, and so generous. Hugh, my soul, my life giver, my brother, my father, my strength on earth.

There comes a moment when I feel joy in yielding—like a religious expiation of the self. This enormous self in me, so egotistical, so hungry, so devouring. I must annihilate it, and so I bow, I bow. Is that necessary?

November 8, 1935

*I*AM FAR FROM THE DAYS WHEN I LEFT CLICHY because I was worn out or sick from bad food at irregular hours. Now I leave to save my happiness, to save the beauty. I wonder when—just before it becomes drab, or when I feel myself choking, or impatient?

Tonight I didn't want to leave Henry, because he was in a soft, passionate mood. But I had to then, out of gratitude toward Hugh, who saved me from despair last night. I came away thinking perhaps one minute more might kill my happiness. Fred and his air of a sick street of failures. Fraenkel sick with his thoughts, smell of death. But I left in time. Sad to leave, with a taste of Henry's kiss. Henry regretting me, hearing him say, "You make me so horny . . . so horny . . ." Seeing his face changed by desire, grown old, cruel, convulsed with desire.

Saw Louise weeping at her children's departure. Incapable of a long sorrow. Like June—only a storm. Life not real.

Writing Father book. Page on Amazon. Write on symbolism of Champs-Elysées. *Angoisse*. To lose what I have, to be trapped in either one life or another. Both intolerable, alone. *Angoisse,* fears, doubts.

What *helps* me to dream: luxury, beauty. Nobody understands. They think I love luxury for itself, intrinsically, not as the objects which muffle reality. Sordidness aroused my curiosity, but my hatred too.

I try not to take Henry out of his element, as other women do. Mrs. Rank took Rank out of his element. He likes what Henry likes, but she made the home, the surroundings, the friends, the life. Secretly, he wanted to live as Henry lives.

NOVEMBER 9, 1935

*A*LLENDY COMING TO DINNER. EDUARDO AND CHIquito moving in. I, weakened by the moonstorm, losing blood. Weeping with my Mother in unison, both emotional, she trying to understand my *motives*—ending by believing me innocent although I live with a "homo" and go to Montparnasse. "I believe you can touch filth and not be defiled."

Kissing and feeling very close to her. I explained to her that if society exiled homosexuals they would become dangerous—bad—like the young, guilty of light offenses, who are put in prison and then become criminals. Emotional talk. Why do I keep Eduardo? To give him a home, understanding, faith in himself. All Havana society talks.

I am talked about over teacups. Bah. I don't care. "Only, I want you to understand me, Mother. You have to try and see why I do things, even if you don't accept my ideas. Just to know, and stand by me."

NOVEMBER 13, 1935

*E*VERYTHING HENRY WRITES OR DOES IS "BUR-lesque." Now he and Fraenkel are writing a burlesque of *Hamlet*. Burlesque: the bicycle on the wall of the studio. *Burlesque* talks, breakfasts, letters, relationships. I don't know what I am doing there. Every day I must grin and go hungry. Everything I feel is too sincere, too humane, too human, too real, too deep. I write my book on my Father and I am hungry.

I am terribly, terribly lonely, terribly lonely. Full of rebellion and hatred of Henry. Hatred of the love that keeps me there. Why can't I break away?

Tremendous conflict between my feminine self, who wants to live in a man-ruled world, to live *with* man, and the creator in me capable of creating a world of my own and a rhythm of my own in which I can't find any man to live with (Rank was the only one who had my rhythm). In this man-made world, altogether made by Henry, I can't live as a self. I feel ahead of him in certain things, alone, lonely.

NOVEMBER 15, 1935

*H*AVING TOUCHED BOTTOM, I SPRANG UP AGAIN to reconstruct my life. Awoke and wrote fif-teen letters to call people around me and create a whirlpool. Then struggled with Henry to understand what was happening, and with his help realized my resentment and storminess were due to his sacrificing me—depriving me of New York and of all possibility of expansion and *modern* living (New York kills him). I love him and don't want to sacrifice him. On account of this I began to struggle against Henry himself. I think that is over. I am making the best of it, knowing it is my destiny to love *with sorrow,* and always what is bad for me, to be limited, stifled by love, sacrificed to love, to Henry's lack of modernism, and now definitely stuck inside of his bourgeois life. But I must find compensations, *chemins détournés:* London. New York in the spring. A feverish life here in Paris. I feel blocked and yet I must expand somehow.

In Henry's arms I can yield. As soon as I leave him my desire is so strong it kills me—my desire for adventure, expansion, fever, fantasy, beauty, grandeur.

Everything changed by Louise's visit—transported into the dream. I can dream with her. She read "Alraune" and was completely affected. She read me from her second book. Unreality. The fairy tale. Enchantment. Out of life. Her eyes madly open, like Artaud's. Her life has the grandeur I love; she has the wings, the power. Her talk is a creation. The mistake I made before, which put an end to our relationship, is that my timidity and my love for connection did not harmonize with her incapacity to connect with anyone, her schizophrenia. *"Je ne bâtis rien de durable"* (I'm not building anything lasting). I have learned to do without this human thing . . . to accept the same floating my Father has . . . to live in fantasy, without the human.

Her presence carried me away. A few hours before, I was writing in my diary and feeling everything crumbling inside. When I saw her I realized where I could find my ship again, my voyages: only in the dream, in drugs, creation, and perversity. I have decided to be reckless, to do and try everything, because nothing holds me on earth, and I am not afraid to die. If I don't die first, my love for Henry will die. I will live out my fever, disguise myself as a man, intoxicate myself with people, life, noise, motion, work, creation, and everything that, to know and feel, I will try. No fear and no respect for life, which is not worth dragging out.

Jazz. New York, on certain days, is nearer to me than other things. Now the New York I dream is perhaps Rank, the happiness he gave me in all that was outside of reality. Perhaps all this that lies outside of human reality is what I may reach alone.

Louise is coming back to change her dress here to go out in the evening. *Les métamorphoses.* These are very important. I will live through metamorphoses of myself rather than by any trip away. Louise can help me to stay put. My desires seem to be so strangely inhuman. Why New York—away from Henry, Hugh, Eduardo, and Chiquito? Why doesn't love, my love for all of them, hold me down? Hold me? What is it that haunts me away from what others call happiness?

What was so important, and so beautiful, with Rank was the games we played, games of talk in the dark, going to the theater and rewriting the plays, discovering, note by note, the symphony of the world, its meaning; our games of thoughts, marrying in space, this running and singing and shouting down the corridors of our inventions! He destroyed a dream for the sake of holding me in his arms, for the sake of penetrating my body, touching my skin! He destroyed a world, a great exaltation, such as I feel again tonight. Louise, Louise, Louise, Louise. What estranged us once was her jealousy of me. She has so little faith in herself. I will not do that to her. We shall not try to meet in the world, but always alone, for our opium dream.

Nine-thirty. I have finished writing the emotional pages of my Father book.

Struggling with Henry's duality and ambivalence in writing about ideas. At the same moment he expresses an idea and simultaneously the burlesque or denial of it. His book on Lawrence suffers from this. A vigorous argument in which I tried to show him that a man could be contradictory but not ambivalent, because then creation was impossible.

Slowly he discovers my wisdom.

I predicted how people would feel about helping Fred, for whom Henry wrote that humorous begging letter. No response.

His *Aller Retour New York;* no subscriptions to cover the expense, and the response feeble. As a woman I hate being right. Right about Fred, about how the world hates to be used and held up. I'm afraid now of the void Henry has created around me. As soon as I beg for him I lose a friend, he insults and alienates. I have to start creating a world apart from Henry, just as I had to start writing differently and far away from Henry and Fraenkel. But, oh God, how I hate solitude.

It is also true that jealousy makes me draw away. There is something between Henry and his men friends that I cannot share, an acrobatic, insincere, burlesque element, and I feel jealous and lonely. It is true that makes me abandon them and go off alone. Henry now smells of Fraenkel, as he did before of Lowenfels.

NOVEMBER 21, 1935

FACED ALWAYS BY THE IMPOSSIBILITY OF REACHing the absolute, I began to dance again. From the day I saw Louise I began to create a *tourbillon,* a ballet, a symphony. I wrote letters calling everybody around me, [René] Lalou, [John] Charpentier, [Salvador] Dalí, Anne Greene. And simultaneously invitations came from Colette Roberts, the Ferrants, from everywhere. Out of despair, deep, fundamental despair, I began to dance. I wrote to Monsieur le Verrier, who had deeply admired my book on Lawrence. A man of fifty, tall, a Jew, an intellectual-religious type. He fell in love with me at first sight. And I feel exalted and repelled together, always ensorcelled by minds, by age, by spirit. He telephoned this morning, exalted by my June–Henry novel. Kahane refuses to do it, *as it is,* in favor of my Father book, of which he read a few lines and said, "First rate. I have no doubts about it."

Feverish evening with Henry, Fraenkel, and Colette. Fraenkel tells Henry exactly what I told him, only expresses it better as the little voice in Henry that says, "Shit, shit, shit, crap, crap on the side" and will end by destroying his vision of relation between things.

Radio going. Writing. Nerves on edge. Dancing so as not to die. So nervous I could jump out of the window. Fever. Despair at life. The absolute. Henry in love with me. I learning to live from him; that is, to compromise, to yield, to accept; and so I go to the other extreme of the absolute—dispersion, fever, split, tension, illness, fever.

Started pages on orchestra in Father book in which I include violin and woman's body seen in a picture on the quai Saint-Michel. Already idea of orchestra had been fermenting in my head. But the great suffering I felt last night, due to my jealousy of Mrs. Ferrant—who has a wonderful head and luxuriant breasts, a vulgar type of beauty which is much to Henry's taste—drove me to hysterical pages.

This is my disease, I know it now, the greatest cause of suffering. In the taxi last night on my way to the Ferrant studio, already alarmed by Henry's description of a "woman with a very interesting face," I was singing, struggling to be strong, deciding I would seduce Ferrant, feeling strengthened by le Verrier's admiration. During the evening I felt Henry would not love Mrs. F. It might be only sex. Feeling resigned, remembering how often I had been wrong in imagining, how much useless suffering, how I tried to laugh at Henry's jealousy, his fear of losing me, which is even greater than mine. If I lose him I lose my pain. If he loses me he loses his life and happiness. I would be saved without him. He would sink.

Cancer of jealousy. Life too difficult. I come back like a drowning woman to the shelter of Hugh's love, to the white room, to sensation of warmth, softness, luxury as palliatives. I wrote ten pages without a stop, for an hour and a half. I suffer from little miseries, neuralgia, stomach trouble. I am thin, nervous.

Rank was right. I thought I would be happy without him. I can't. There are times when I feel ready to give up Henry and Hugh for Rank, as he wanted it; as one gives up the earth life for the monastery, for the peace and strength he gave me. I would force my body to obey. I think wildly how I could force my body to obey, to yield to Rank, by looking at erotic pictures, which have such an effect on me.

Later: After these lines written in bed, I masturbated, because last night when Henry took me after the Ferrant party I didn't feel anything. Then for a moment I was quiet, saying to myself: Be very quiet and still. Then I wrote two more pages. And I am exhausted.

NOVEMBER 25, 1935

THE SUFFERING LASTED A NIGHT AND A DAY. ONE night of real agony, imagining everything to have already happened. A day made more terrible by Fred telling me Henry had said Mrs. Ferrant resembled June. The rational me saying, "It is good if something happens to separate us. I was not able to break away of my own accord. I am not happy with Henry. The day we are separated my life will be saved, my life will begin."

Then I saw Henry with other people there. I got quieter, resigned, indifferent. That night we met at Kahane's to meet Jonathan Cape, who held my hand in the taxi in front of Henry. This little victory amused me for a few minutes. But I feel dead and cold. All this on top of my sacrifice of New York. Too much.

Again pain drives me to write. And finally today my book took possession of me. Life, New York, Henry—everything became less important. I am obsessed with my book.

I am waiting for a change in Henry, but it is so dangerous to measure the love by his desire, to measure it by sex. Yesterday, when we had an hour together, he was cold and tired, so I warmed him with my body and he fell asleep like a child. Another time this tenderness would have been good. Yesterday it seemed like an omen. And I must lose Henry, because I cannot abandon him. It is always the same thing. I have abandoned him so often, but I can't break altogether. Such misery.

I got up this morning and worked well, but so grimly and joylessly. Again I have to work with discipline and order. I have to get up early. I do gymnastics, take medicines, struggle to be strong for this labor of creation which kills me. I hate it. But it is the only thing which makes life bearable.

Today I stayed away from an evening at Colette's. Cannot face people—too great an effort. Henry was gloomy and intent on his work. I feel desolate and ready to do something mad. If I were not writing the book I would go to London.

I know this now: that my passion for Henry has been dying ever since I left him for Rank, that my rebellion these last months proves this, that I am no longer enslaved by him but that jealousy can make me suffer because I am a slave to pain.

But today the slavery to pain has ceased, and I see with clear eyes how far I have been from Henry; that, as the love lessened, I separated my life more and more from his. No more love of his childish acts, wasted gestures, foolishness.

A great calm came over me. It was after I said yesterday to Henry, "I feel divorced from you." He attributed this to our hectic life, in which I have given him less time. But when I could go to Villa Seurat, I chose to stay home.

Feel calm and detached, possessed by my book, and free of this slavery to pain which has nothing to do with love, because my love has been breaking down at moments when passion is not strong enough to fuse all the discordant elements. The Passion is over.

NOVEMBER 26, 1935

*H*ENRY MADE ME A *SCÈNE DE JALOUSIE* OVER JON-
athan Cape. He thought I had not wanted to
go to Colette's Monday evening to go out with Cape. He feels uneasy
and has doubts of me. He spoke of our difficulties. We tried to get
married again and only found a momentary reassurance in the very
depth of our sexual pleasure. I did say, in talking about my book, that
I would never have written it if I could have had what I wanted out
of life. "What did you want?" "Independence." "That's bad," said
Henry. "But I don't mean independence from you." This he doubted.

To come out of my crisis of jealousy I sprang up with the desire
to hurt rather than to be hurt, to make Henry jealous, which I succeeded in, due to Jonathan Cape.
Or I love him less. I don't know.

I see one thing clearly, that his exchange and talk with me gave
birth to *Black Spring,* which is divinely beautiful; that his talks with
Fraenkel are giving birth to "Hamlet," which panders to Henry's
disease of trying to be a man of ideas while at the same time creating
nothing in the world of ideas—nothing but imitation of other men,
a travesty, a burlesque—and which is so confusing that Fraenkel is
lost now, just as I got lost inside of Henry's book on Lawrence at the
time when I was taking Henry's thinking seriously.
Now I see the insanity of all he writes, which is only valuable as
poetry. When he expresses the ideas of Rank, Spengler, Lawrence, he
expresses them better than they did: He is a writer.
But here, with Fraenkel, the imitativeness, the parody of ideas, is
flagrant, and I believe "Hamlet" is going to turn out a comedy,
whereas I know that Henry thinks he is contributing original attitudes, original ideas. He will be laughed at as a philosopher and a

psychologist and a critic, as the world laughed at Mark Twain's *Personal Recollections of Joan of Arc,* because they knew Twain was a humorist.

Henry is only writing "Hamlet" because it is easier, discursive, everything poured in, but he does not intend it as a farce. I see him serious, hear him serious; the world will see only a farce.

And I can't say anything: first, because I hate the role of critic (prefer to encourage—not to kill); second, because it looks like the jealousy of Fraenkel; third, because Henry persists in certain perverse courses and if I fight him he gets more obstinate. I tried so hard to orient him away from his book on Lawrence, tried so hard. But he is obstinate, no matter how gentle or tactful I am.

What he likes is something he can drop in Fraenkel's letterbox, to get letters from Fraenkel.* I now believe Fraenkel is a brilliant mind without a spark of originality. Both of them plastic, but both *writers, poets, yes.* Fraenkel's expression of neuroses marvelous. Fraenkel's contribution to thought on psychology absolutely null.

Thought, psychology, philosophy are products of seriousness, not of playing with words. They are juggling with bright words and other men's ideas, while I am quietly writing seriously and humanly. When Henry read my orchestra pages he said I had outdone him.

I also feel too tired to try and save Henry. No man was ever given as much with which to become great, no man on earth. Because in addition to the love, I had the wisdom.

I cannot save him from clownishness, and what touches me is that when he imitates the philosopher or psychologist he is so inadequate. Why isn't he content to be a great poet? I was hypnotized, ensorcelled, for a long time by Henry's language, just as his presence and my love

---

* The so-called "Hamlet" correspondence (another title, first suggested, was "The Merry Widow Waltz"), which continued into 1938, was conceived somewhat prankishly as a way to preserve their endless talks. It would be published at the moment it reached one thousand pages. "These talks," Henry Miller recalled many years later, "were anything but discussions. Though I seemed to get nothing from them I was fascinated. Two people could hardly be more unlike than Fraenkel and myself. It seems to me that it was a sort of bowling game we played . . . he would set up the pins and I would knock them down as best I could." Fraenkel published volume one of these *Hamlet Letters* in Puerto Rico in 1939 and volume two in Mexico in 1941, in editions of five hundred copies each.

hypnotized me into happiness and enjoyment of things which were utterly empty. As a woman it distresses me to be so lucid.

Evening. Fighting to keep my head above water. Taking gymnastics lessons after leaving Henry. Writing ten pages a day. Receiving visitors. Writing letters.

Joaquin is in New York with Mother.

I sent Henry a message: "Everything is good." I felt the need of reassuring him. I think he is not to blame for anything, for being old and wanting peace and a groove and no change. For hating telephones, airplanes, traveling, glamor.

DECEMBER 5, 1935

SEXUAL CLOSENESS—ALWAYS—BUT NONE OTHERwise. If I had the courage I should break off, simply because Henry is now a stone around my neck. He gives me only unhappiness, because he is really impossible and cheap as a human being. He will never break away from his Broadway, his gold-digging. Now he is asking for Rank's address through the newspapers, to send him Fraenkel's book *[Bastard Death]*, prefaced by himself. He extracts names from everybody. He is inflated in his egoism, glorifying himself and Fraenkel. Wild schemes, cheap tricks, whoring—everything goes. So I told him, "Fine—carry out your publishing schemes—but leave me out of them."

I divorced myself literarily from them. Spiritually. Ideologically. Also in living. I live my real life here. If only I could divorce myself completely. Henry can take care of himself, and I am tired of sacrifice. I am trying to save myself. I want happiness, understanding. I don't want to hurt or destroy Henry by my needs. Just as I discovered I should not expect certain things from Hugh, I must also learn not to expect fulfillment in Henry. Rank was right. Henry's life is cheap, vulgar. As soon as I talk about someone he wants their address, to circularize them, beg from them.

I'm drowning. I feel I am being destroyed by Henry. No joy there anymore. No expansion. Just jealousy on both sides. He feels me going away. Why must I await an external accident to separate us?

I am weak. Weak.

I feel weak and small. Hugh's love is my most divine force. I lean on him. I hide in his arms. I give him love because I trust him. He is my strength.

If by a "neurotic" relationship Rank meant that which gives pain, I am only trying to save myself from pain today instead of years ago. I can't bear this slow disintegration of our love. I would like it to end quickly. I try a hundred ways to divert myself from this sorrow: interest in other people, Colette, Maggy, de Maigret, le Verrier, Charpentier, Allendy, Zadkine. I swim with my "court." I go out with them. I fight for my own publishing, alone. I have tea at Smith's, at the Hungarian café. Eduardo and I are so close. Such a knowledge we have because we suffer the same way. He and his shallow Chiquito, who is incapable of passion. I have fits of asceticism. A hunger for peace. I've lost my way again because the way of my ego—to live for my ego—doesn't make me happy. But there is a giving which is not this death-giving that Henry produces.

Evening! After a week of moonstorm—sudden peace, without reason. Nothing changes around me. When I come out of my *folie de doute* I hear Henry's voice over the telephone: "I'd like to see you." We meet at a café. He is tender, human. For him nothing has happened. Nothing has happened, I say to myself. But what happens inside of me? I am pretending gaiety because I carry something in my handbag. I am like a woman who has a revolver and feels gay because she can put an end to it. A few minutes before seeing Henry I called Allendy and cajoled him into giving me some *chanvre indien* [Indian hemp]—a drug which he said is harmless.

I have realized that one week a month, the week before my period, I am crazy. I see everything enormous, ominous, tragic; my doubts, jealousies, and fears are intensified, magnified: pessimism, destructive criticism, destructive acts which follow upon the intensification of pain.

For this no remedy. Out of these intensifications I create. My book on my Father, for instance. But humanly it is unbearable. The facts are so small: Henry's preoccupation with Fraenkel; Fraenkel trying to make Hugh go with a whore; shortage of money; Kahane's hesitations concerning Henry–June novel.

Then suddenly, just as they were the cause of my suffering, they just as easily turn into causes for laughter, or at least understanding. When Henry showed preoccupation, and a love for me he does not have for his friend "Boris." When I saw the beautiful women at the Bal Tabarin and understood how a man could want them. Kahane saying to Henry, "I have three important contracts to fulfill next year—yours, Anaïs's, and Cyril Connolly's."

Walking toward Allendy's place, I thought: I feel paralyzed by restrictions. I feel doors closed, New York, money, publication, analysis, adventure, everything I want. Instead I am carrying fruit to poor Monsieur Lantelme. Writing paper to Fred. Money to Henry.

But I have the little box of *chanvre indien*. I will not use it until I have to. I can keep my head above water. But I am terribly tired of struggling. I struggle, *je me débats*. Against all my problems I have fought. I fought for New York. For analysis I tried to get Allendy's help. I saw Dr. Jacobson. I talked to everybody. I wrote letters. For publication I have been equally active, both in New York and here. For money I tried to work at analysis. Adventure? No one attracts me, no one stirs me, there is no one my size.

Henry and I walked along the Seine. Henry was saying, "I feel a bit depressed by the inertia of the world." I remembered Lawrence returning to Frieda, battered from his fight with the world. A Henry not brutal and a bit discouraged. So my feelings flow again, like the Seine at our feet. *Encore un moment de bonheur.*

Henry and I, arm-in-arm one more hour, walking. He in need of me. The fog makes one cough and tightens that nerve on the left side of my face which hurts me also when I drink wine. *Chanvre indien* in my pocketbook. Day by day, to be able to live only by facts. Henry is here, at my side. That is a fact. While he is here, believe, be quiet, then work.

I feel like writing about Rank.

Henry's faith in facts, ruminating, nothing ahead or afterward. No analysis—no deterioration. Jealousy, yes. He tried to reconstruct what I have been doing with little questions, behind each little question a tremor of anxiety.

DECEMBER 6, 1935

*T*ALK WITH HUGH LAST NIGHT IN BED:
Anaïs: "I'm going to write another book."
Hugh: "What about?"
Anaïs: "About Rank."
Hugh: "I might have known that. When you write you're always one man behind. What I'd like to know is *who* comes after Rank."
Anaïs: "That is what I would like to know myself! I wish you could tell me!"

Tenderness can often rise to a peak of love, as it does between Hugh and me. Its very continuity and solidity can give birth to love. At this moment my tenderness for Hugh resembles love. I take an interest in what he does. I do all to please him. When he comes home he finds his bath ready, with salts in it. I typewrite letters for him with patience. I am patient about his bad memory.

Eduardo and I, twins in our neurosis, hypersensitivity, our way of loving, often lean on each other with immense tenderness too, great understanding.

During my active week I wrote to [Jules] Supervielle. Today we met. Face like Erskine, but wet, dreamful eyes. A haunted man, with human roots. In love with mystery. He read me his new poems. We talked about surrealism. He doesn't like it, is trying for simplicity, human symbols like those of the myth. "It's chaos and ridicule," I said. "I think dreams have a clarity, a luminousness." Supervielle dreams all day.

More and more I'm against surrealism, the belief that the dream is reached through absurdity and negation of all values. To put a bicycle in a room, to dwell on the absurdities, the umbrella on an operating table, to put anything that has a value like psychoanalysis next to a music-hall turn, is pure destruction. To describe what in life deserves destruction is different from making all life appear without value by chaoticizing it for the sake of laughter. Henry just wants to laugh. The surrealists just want to laugh at the unconscious. *Ce sont des farceurs.*

Supervielle creates a world. It has houses, seas, people, climates, humor.

I see now my mistake has been to take Henry seriously. I have been looking for all kinds of wise men, philosophers, where there was just a humorist.

I am looking for men like Rank who are not humorists. Poor Rank, he wanted to laugh in his biography of Mark Twain. But he was not so good at laughing. I am glad Henry has made me laugh, but I don't want to *live* in a circus.

People criticize *Aller Retour* as of little value.

I can't save Henry from being treated as a schoolboy. Kay Boyle thought he was a very young man, writing her a letter of admiration couched in her own language! Henry is joking, but believing himself serious. Like the time he thought he could step into Rank's role and imagined himself an analyst. Everything is a joke: the brochures, the self-advertisements, the schemes, Fraenkel's sudden desire to publish all my diaries as a set, out of which he would make thirty thousand dollars. Remember this, poor Anaïs, with your dreams, your seriousness, everything Henry does is a joke: kindergarten, circus, music hall, burlesque. What ideas, knowledge I brought him were to be caricatured. And I listened to his talk about Lawrence so believingly.

DECEMBER 9, 1935

*P*OUNCED ON MYSELF WITH CLINICAL SEVERITY. Accused myself of destroying my life by criticisms, morbid doubts, obsessions. As soon as I am alone a diseased flow of morbid images begins: self-torture, jealousy, obsession with Henry, doubts. All of it neurotic because I have no facts to go by. Anyway, the motifs are those I describe in the diary. But I have not described the time I spent on this torture. So I am treating myself as a sick person. Suggestion: I read, write, try to act and feel actively. Jealousy and doubts are negative. But the struggle to live positively, that is, to read, write, love, talk, is so tremendous.

I must go to New York, which saves me from myself. Life at a slow rhythm kills me. Melancholy devours me.

I plan to go for a month. With five patients awaiting me I can pay all my expenses and return with three or four hundred dollars. For a month Henry will come. We can pass through a few copies of *Tropic of Cancer*.

Action saves me from great misery. I am a sick person. I devour my life with analysis. I must have more life and less time.

Here nothing interests me. Nobody holds me. The slowness kills me. I have decided also to throw my body to the winds! I am tired of deep love, which causes me only pain. Oh, God, I want happiness, happiness, happiness.

As soon as I decided on the plan for New York I was well, energetic, alive, buoyant. Electricity passed through my body again. I wrote letters announcing . . .

Big work. Full days. Pressure. A big city to battle with, to conquer, men to lie with. I can't lie here with museum keepers. Henry wants to mold away because he is old now. But I am young. I need fire and electricity.

*I*T IS CLEARER NOW. I HAVE BEEN REBELLING against my mother role. And Henry has not become man. So I find myself forced to continue to play the mother, because he is always the child. I can't make him wiser. I can't save him from errors. I can only be indulgent, blind. It is I who have changed, not Henry. My self-effacing, self-sacrificing love is over. When I have the moonstorm, my instincts reveal themselves. Jealousy and doubt and possessiveness in contrast to my conscious ideal-mother role of understanding, faith, tolerance, self-effacement. The *décalage* has been too great, so I got sick again, as in New York. Terribly sick, vomiting and dizziness—the whole physical being revolting, splitting, poisoned.

My conflict is that instinctively I still need Henry, but instinctively I don't trust him. I know he lives only for himself. He is passing through a veritable phase of megalomania. Planning a brochure of letters received about *Tropic of Cancer,* with photo of himself, his horoscope, etc. To be done humorously. But his humorous effects are often most earnest in intent. To compensate for Kahane not doing enough. It will cost five thousand francs. Now Fraenkel is willing to back Henry—but not willing to let him do all he wants. Henry is circularizing thousands of people. He got sick because Fraenkel didn't put the money in his hands, because people resist him, snub him. Because the "letter" from New York was a failure. Everyone says it is sour, not humorous, and too personal, unimportant, too much Henry.

Again, when he got sick I said, "I'll give you the money for the brochure. But come to New York with me to get it. If I go to New York I can make $750 in one month. I can return with $400. Consider that a month sacrificed to your ambition."

Henry had already said he would go with me—this only helped

to make New York more bearable to him. A gentle bribe! I said, "You know I'm the only one who will give you money without questioning how you're going to use it." But I know well he will use it foolishly—that he may get the attention of the public but that serious people will think him a freak. *Tropic of Cancer* is not a book to excuse megalomania.

Out of guilt he includes me in his fantastic schemes. He will ask Fraenkel for money to do "Alraune." But I see the impracticability of it all and I say gently, "Ask Fraenkel only for yourself. From his point of view it seems strange to ask him to help me when I have Hugh. Don't bother about me. Work for yourself."

The truth is that I am here revolting against begging, publicity, exaggeration, and pretensions. It gives me nausea to do things that way, to use people, to play pranks, to be cheap and noisy.

So the mother is no longer blind. She has no hope of giving birth to *man.*

To Allendy: I have now to be clever and live out my life as mother and my life as woman. In New York I am going to take every lover who comes my way, to live my life as woman, as sex, to make up for my stupid role of mother, my slavery, and in mockery of the instinct which binds me to Henry. I feel bitter and without illusions. I want to mock my body; my blood; my sex, which binds me to a child; the instinct which destroys me.

Fraenkel on Father novel: "Structure always magnificent. Powerful. But bad bricklaying." It is as if I saw the steelwork, the structure, with my power for vision, like a clairvoyant person. But I could not see the bricks. I won't take any more help. I stand or fall as I am.

Evening: Henry came to see me. How humorous it is to me, or how ironic, when he expresses his jealousy: "You're not going to New York just to see Rank?" Jealousy—when he keeps me from life; jealousy, when I criticize his collaboration with Fraenkel. Perhaps Henry is jealous too of the subjects I love, like astrology. So he tries to destroy them. I believe he is more jealous than I am!

DECEMBER 15, 1935

*H*UGH LEFT FOR BIARRITZ. I RUSHED TO HENRY. HE was still obsessed with letters received, letters written, business, plans, his brochure, money, self-advertising. I have heard nothing else for months. And "Hamlet." Toward midnight I felt a terrible discouragement. I exploded. I said I would go home and return when he was human again. I was blind with despair. I said, "I could understand your being obsessed with creation, because I could respect that. But I can't understand your being obsessed with the business of pushing yourself . . ."

And I left him. He thought I would come back. He had been gentle, as usual, with nothing to say for himself. I didn't come back. I went home and went to bed and took the drug.

I saw a dreamlike picture. The black sea, still, stopped by a wall, damned. But as I looked it became a wall of books, enormous books. Paper. How clear the meaning. I was sucking the penis of a man without legs, who was in midair. Nothing else. Bodily sensation of heaviness, fever. At four I awoke and thought, I made too much of last night.

I worked this afternoon. I yearn for Rank's strength, under-standing—the mystic marriage. And last night, sleeping with Henry, I dreamed of Rank, even of desiring Rank. In the dream I said, "Once, just once."

I gave away most of Rank's gifts to me. The turquoise to Maruca, the white handbag to my Mother, the book on ships to little Paul. I only kept the lace nightgown and the valise.

Le Monocle with Eduardo and Chiquito. As soon as I entered I saw a woman dressed like a man who attracted me. I danced with her. I asked her her name. "Fred." That was a shock. But I thought a lot about her today and I want to see her again.

"Fred." Fred is half-French, half-Russian. Blue eyes, like Allendy's, round face, small nose, soft, negroid features, but luminous eyes.

Comte de Maigret [Henry's neighbor] comes for his birthday dinner. I leave after dinner to meet [Joseph] Delteil.

Now that I know it is all Saturn's fault I seek ways to subdue the gloom without fighting limitations, without blaming Henry, or money, or Paris for my discontent.

DECEMBER 18, 1935

*M*EN—HERBERT READ, LOWENFELS, OR FRAENKEL— can say to Henry that *Aller Retour* is no good, or that one thousand pages on "Hamlet" are too much, or any other comment or criticism, and he takes it well. If I say it he takes it personally. So I am silent, although I think at present Henry is simply a bore. Coming out of a humorous movie, he starts hacking it as a manifestation of America's worthlessness, like a reformer.

But I have to be silent. The world will strike at Henry with sufficient cruelty. I am not here to judge and criticize, only to love. So, to bed, and to hell with values.

I did forget "Fred" of the Monocle because Henry possessed me so thoroughly Tuesday morning. Tuesday was a day of body warmth and bed joys, of much kissing and little talking, of dreaming, eating, touching, grunting, humming, hemming, and other expressions of primitive communication.

Write about Henry as *nature*.

I came back Tuesday evening tired, happy, a real female.

Differences between sexual moods. Some like fury; nature aroused to anger and hatred, need to destroy almost. The peace afterward. Because Henry has no will, his whole body, hands, fingers, have a malleable, soft, insinuating, relaxed quality which is better for sex than the tense, nervous love gestures of Hugh or Rank. At least to my liking. Henry softens me. The others make me tense.

DECEMBER 22, 1935

*P*REPARATIONS FOR CHRISTMAS. AGAINST MY WILL, because Hugh and I are tired of Chiquito's shallowness, vanity, and selfishness, and the tree, etc., are all for him. Discovering the childishness in homosexuals. Because I give de Maigret a birthday cake, they sulk and spoil the party.

Peace with Henry because I have resolved to play only the woman role, the mother role, to consent, encourage.

No pleasure in seeing my Father for a few hours. When we kiss good-bye we almost break down, but there is a wall between us.

Dark, nervous moods better controlled. Concealing my joy at going to New York. Will arrive in time for Joaquin's concert. Control of morbidity by saying *"merde,"* or "and what of it?" Treating myself roughly. *Eh bien, et quoi?* Understanding jealousy as imaginative suffering, I mean, when there is no cause for it. Keep tears for real catastrophes.

Hardening. Fighting for health desperately. When I cannot write, making a rug to keep my hands active. Wondering if I will see Rank in New York. Sacrificing Henry only for one month, as against seven months I spent here in hell. Was it all because I like to move forward and out of levels of life, and to return to unchanged spot unbearable?

Manias: I can't see bottles on a shelf without working to put the medicines in bottles without labels, where they won't look like medicines. Throwing out bottles or boxes in which there is hardly any content, putting the remains in another bottle, reducing, embellishing, eliminating waste, making good use of everything, giving away what I don't use.

Manias for order when I am unhappy. For leaving no loose ends, finishing. Papers always minimum, filed. Automatically I always arrange my desk, my working table with utmost precision. Every time I go out I have to return to see if iron boxes are locked so Hugh won't see diaries and letters. Once during an evening with Henry I thought I had left the key at home. I turned pale. Heart dead with fear, cold, to imagine Hugh's pain. When I found the key in my bag, what relief!

JANUARY 3, 1936

GREAT HAPPINESS WITH HENRY EVER SINCE I GAVE up struggle for ideas. Sweetness. Passion. Laughter. He is correcting my Father novel. Says it reads like a translation.

Plans for New York trip make me strong and unified. Action pulls me together. I'm whole, tense, like a horse ready for a race. I set myself goals. Fraenkel won't give Henry the money he needs for the Siana Series, only in exchange for something Henry can't do: becoming a salesman for Fraenkel's book, going from shop to shop. I delivered Henry of guilt about accepting this work. He always gets into a conflict. Feels he should make sacrifices to earn money. Waits for me to tell him not to do it. Says at times he feels he should not accept the ideal life I give him.

If he is at my side I can work joyously in New York. I want to give Henry what he wants. I want to get myself published. I don't want to beg or await anybody's laws and orders. I love analysis. It is what the world wants of me. They don't seem to want my writing.

In analysis I know the nearness to human beings is illusory: they are disciples, not friends. But I have friends, lovers, everything I want. I want to come back with a thousand dollars. And I want intensity of life to drown the morbid introspection and obsessions.

JANUARY 4, 1936

*H*UGH BUYS ME A WHITE MANNISH HAT AND white scarf and white Russian wool blouse for the tailored suit. We have tea together. The last hours always so sweet. I have such a deep love of him. I get letters from New York. About ten patients are awaiting me. When I hear jazz I feel a tremor of adventure, as if the analysis I am going to do is a romance. I dream of the miracles I will perform. It is with joy I buy myself new garters, a new perfume, a new pair of gloves. I ask Kahane for the money coming to me on my investment in *Tropic of Cancer* to pay for Henry's trip. Inside of myself I feel ready for a new rhythm, the rhythm of New York. I will take care of those whose lives are broken, who were crushed in the machine. But I am not the victim of that machine. I stand outside and I can enjoy the enormous, fantastic heartbeats of it, and the noise.

The pains of parting from Hugh, from Eduardo, are only felt by the *woman,* the human being, but I am otherwise possessed by my need for a fruitful activity, for an expenditure of myself, for fever, fullness, excess.

The Christmas tree is withering. Lantelme is saved. Joaquin is playing in Havana. My Mother is writing gay letters. Thorvald is planning to go to New York. Rank is not in New York. Eduardo and I are drawn close by our suffering in love. Louise sent me a bottle of champagne. Roger sent me roses. James Boyd, his novel. Katrine is "dancing on her head" because I am coming.

I take with me six bottles of Dr. Jacobson's fattening powders. I must fill out all the sexual parts in the diary. When I idealized my posing experience I submerged the truth, which came out violently one night while I talked with Henry. The shocks I received during posing and modeling were so strong they sank in like heavy stones. And I went on embellishing, not seeing, not hearing, as in the novel, and even today when I mention that period. Henry forced that open, because he has such a nose for truth, for naked reality.

The life here so tame. The pretty apartment, the pretty dinners, the pastel-colored friends, everything feeble. Money restrictions. Publishing restrictions. Open the windows! Let's have magnificence, splendor, hard work, miracles, coffee and toast, smiles, miracles, coffee and toast, smiles, health, jazz, schizophrenia, swift elevators, men with lovable bodies, unobtrusive minds that don't mar happiness, primitives.

JANUARY 5, 1936

DREAM OF A GARGANTUAN MEAL FOR WHICH A woman comes to ask money. I say I will pay it although I know I have not the money. Given a gigantic umbrella which I can hardly carry. I try to get rid of it and give it to three attractive priests. Fantasies on reading newspapers. Where the rivers overflowed the cemeteries were inundated. Dead could not be buried. But those who were buried, did they change places? Could the coffin of a betrayed husband float to his house? The cash rotted away in the water. The body lay on the bed. The couple were drowned and lay on the same bed.

The coming separation exalts the love between Hugh and me. He tells me he depends on me for life. I make him happy sexually and with great tenderness.

January 12, 1936

*E*XULTATION GROWING. FRAENKEL LENDS ME ONE
hundred dollars spontaneously and writes me
a beautiful letter. All my loves exalted, heightened. Love of Eduardo,
of Hugh. Immense hatred of France. Its water-covered, inundated
areas. Wish it would get sick altogether.

Fever growing. And weakness too, wondering why I must seek
struggles and difficulties. A desire for sensuality, to escape absolutism
of woman. Woman sensual only when in love. It makes me angry. In
this I wish to be like a man. A voice like Erskine's at the movies can
still stir me. I felt it in my stomach, guts, womb, down to my feet.
Hell, I'm going to have him before I die. I'm going to hear that voice
of his groan with pleasure.

America, which is not sensual, represents sensuality to me because
there are men there to lie with. Harlem, jazz, and the burlesque.
Potency of physical vitality, of beauty. I suppose I'm talking about
aesthetic sensuality. Henry can be satisfied more easily.

Eduardo and Chiquito are playing cards. Hugh is reading Rank.
Ever since I decided to go to New York he reads Rank and reads it
aloud to me with admiration, enthusiasm. He analyzes Eduardo. He
participates in and enacts my role as analyst. I think both Henry and
Hugh are women whom I fecundated mentally, and Henry fecundated me sensually, and Hugh takes care of me. Symbolically, today,
he gave a few ounces of his blood for me to help combat an attack
of eczema, like my Father's!

I find it hard to separate from Hugh even for a moment. I have
a fear of losing him. Symbolically, I seek pretexts for going to the
avenue des Champs-Elysées, which means Hugh. For instance, while
I am at the Villa Seurat I say I have to go to the hairdresser. Once
there I feel relieved. I pass by the bank. Hugh is there. Then I go

back to Henry. On Mondays, after the long weekend, I have the same feeling about Henry. A feeling of insecurity. I get impatient to get there, half fearing a change, a shock of some kind. Peace not here on earth. I get anxious even when Eduardo or Chiquito strays from me.

The time I left Henry at eleven o'clock, angrily, and came home when Hugh didn't expect me. I said, "I returned just to be with you," so that Hugh could interpret it as love for him. I imitate the spontaneities of love. It is easy, because I do love. Love inspires me to demonstrate to Hugh, so as to nourish this love, so that it may appear like an absolute love, a chain of thoughtfulness.

Henry wants to do analysis, too. I am going to let him!

JANUARY 13, 1936

WENT TO HENRY AND HE TELLS ME WHILE WE ARE sitting in the bus that our housing problem is solved forever because Fraenkel will rent him a room in Villa Seurat and at the end of three years Henry will own it and pay no more rent.

At this I went suddenly insane. In a low voice I uttered violent words: "If I thought I would have to spend the rest of my life in France I'd commit suicide today. Henry, you're always taking the easiest way out. To be able to sleep mornings you'll have us living in a hovel soon. I know you love France, but you always said you didn't want to spend your whole life anywhere. I am only happy because we live from day to day and I hope always for something else. Owning a place in France kills all my dreams of a marvelous life. It is ironic that you of all people should become so fearful as to live like a neurotic, or a bourgeois, and prepare for your old age. You never make plans, and now you make plans for death, and to bury me alive. You want to kill me." It was like a tropical storm. Henry said nothing. He gave up the idea—that's all. I begged him to understand my outburst. It was as if I had said to him, "You know, I've been given a room free in New York, so we have to live there . . ."

My breakdown in studio. Real anguish. Real despair. Henry finally touched. We again go to bed, caress, love. But this time something is broken. Henry has killed my hopes for the future. My struggles are futile. My destiny is to be buried alive by Hugh, then by my Father, then by Henry. Hugh now gives me life by letting me seek for it outside. My Father only gave me death. Henry gives me life as a sensual woman and kills my real self.

JANUARY 18, 1936

O N BOARD SS *BREMEN*. CABIN 503C. AT FIRST I WAS not going to bring you, my diary. To have to hide you, to fear discovery. I am getting a little tired of that. I thought I would travel more lightly, but then, at the same moment, I felt again what a *personage* you are, how abandoning you was abandoning a real part of me. Tonight, alone in my cabin, with Henry sleeping in Number 565, missing Hugh, I realized my loneliness, my weakness, my need of you. With a pang of pleasure I took you out of the tin box in which I carry copies of my diary—a presence, a consolation. I didn't want to break down before Henry and say, "Sleep here. I am lonely." It is my sentimentality I have to hide from him, because he does not have that. I don't have to hide it from you. I feel stronger with you on my knees. I am not made for the world, for what I want to give to or wrestle from the world. My desires are immense, and so is my weakness.

I present you to the detective. Listen to his report: I followed Anaïs to her apartment at avenue de la Bourdonnais and saw her carrying two valises full of books from Villa Seurat. On examining these valises I saw on them tags of a trip taken by Henry Miller on the SS *Veendam* in June. These valises were left in the hall. Mr. Guiler came in for lunch, commented on their presence, but did not examine them. Anaïs

Nin also went to the Chase Bank yesterday afternoon and cashed a check for two thousand francs signed by Jack Kahane. With this she went to the German Line and with Mr. Miller she bought a passage, Cabin 565. I heard him ask for "the cabin nearest to 503." To Mr. Kahane she pretended this was money for her own trip, which was of practical necessity. She did not say it was for Mr. Miller. This money is due her on her investment in Mr. Miller's book. Any day Mr. Kahane might meet Mr. Guiler, and the fact of the two thousand—franc check will be revealed.

Don't worry, Mr. Detective, I have already found an explanation if this happens. I will say to Mr. Guiler this money was due Miller, his royalties, and was only paid to me because I have more facilities for cashing checks.

Dancing always on the brink of discovery, I gave a party and put all my friends together: Supervielle, Charpentier, Maggy, Colette, Roger, Genevieve Klein, Kahane, Zadkine, Anne Greene, Roger's brother Jacques, Colette's husband, Barclay Hudson and his wife, Madame Charpentier, Madame Lantelme, etc. The party was unusually beautiful.

The Detective thought I was very rash.

I wrote Henry a note of capitulation: "I have no joy in going to New York. I cannot want something you don't want."

Too great a struggle against my femininity; tired, deep down, of struggle.

I will continue to record the Detective's adventures: Anaïs Nin was met at Cherbourg by Henry Miller shouting "Anis!" through the train window. His capacity for enjoyment predominates. He didn't want New York, but he loves the good food and the luxury on board, which he has never had.

Thursday. The trip was a sad one. Henry becomes a schizophrenic when traveling. I had the same feeling of frustration, emptiness, that he gave me in Chamonix. Only, this time I have understood why. He himself told me, "Every trip I ever took was dramatic, tragic, a shock, a failure. I don't feel anything."

He was so dispersed, vague, so unreal, that I felt I was traveling alone. A ghostly Henry, unemotional, indifferent, not human. I sought to get near him, and I couldn't, no warmth, no awareness. It all became unreal, and each night I felt alone and I thought it was because he was unhappy. One morning at dawn I went to his cabin and slipped into his bed. He kissed me, but it was not real to him. He took me last night, but that, too, was unreal. No Henry anywhere. This morning we talked about it. He spoke of the shocks each trip had been. When he came to my cabin I kissed him tenderly and said, "I'll be your shock absorber from now on. You will never get shocks again. I'm a good shock absorber, I'm so fat."

But I'm glad to be landing. This is symbolic of what makes my life with Henry so hurtful to me, because at the least move he loses his integrity, he falls apart; his wholeness is only transitory. He becomes weak, dispersed, without identity, emotion, or self. And this is the man I try to keep close to, this sand, water, wax, cotton, cloud, called Henry. He looks pale, effaced, lost. No more vitality; pale eyes, unreality, unconvincing, floating, no self or will to collect himself. It is worse for me than being alone. My other trip, alone, was easier. And this one, which I thought would be so happy because I felt so whole with Henry, this one I want to forget.

New York. Barbizon Plaza. Before I landed I knew it was not New York I had been craving but my lost companionship with Rank, and Henry's most passionate climax, which comes when he is tormented. I landed with realistic eyes, eyes opened on a naked New York, on spiritual and mental solitude.

Henry continues in a kind of catatonic state, bad headaches, etc. I feel sorry for him and offer to sail back. I try to understand his neurosis, to help him, but my own neurosis makes it so hard for me. My own disease, which is doubt of love, interprets an attack of schizophrenia as indifference. What I could understand as an analyst makes me suffer as a woman. "I feel distance like a wound." I woke up crying. New York seems cold—it is literally painfully cold, violent. I feel weak, exposed, lonely. When I need strength I realize Henry is my burden, my child.

Joaquin's concert was like a shock, a strain, a plunge into the world. All kinds of ghosts from the past sprang up, people from Richmond Hill. Joaquin was not at his best.

I feel *unequal* to facing the world.

JANUARY 27, 1936

*P*EOPLE. PEOPLE COMING FOR STRENGTH AND WISdom. And I look at them sadly and feel weak and trembling, secretly. One patient is well and says, "I need a friend." Another is well and says, "I need a friend." At one moment, sitting in Henry's room, listening to his friend Emil Conason talking, I thought, When they go away, I will telephone Rank. I will not go to dinner with them. And I didn't. I lay on my bed.

Pleasure from the admiration of the literary agent Barthold Fles. From feeling my power over people's destinies. But the human voice in me wails, as it did in Rank, to be permitted weakness. Such timidity that I get a shock when the telephone rings.

Neurosis.

The emptiness of a world full of power. Not enough love—I need more love. I sit having dinner alone, thinking of how I played with one patient and with Conason. I laugh to myself. I laugh at my own magic tricks, which don't seem like tricks while I do them. Afterward I chuckle. Just a little more coldness in me, a little less feeling, and I could become diabolical, the way I play upon souls. I don't believe an adoring patient's love to be real. So I play hide-and-seek. When I think I am convinced she no longer needs analysis I accept to go down and have a cocktail. But while I am powdering I think, If I take a cocktail it will make me sick. So I must find a way out. So I make it appear I am not sure yet. *Et le manège recommence.*

With Fles I disguise myself in my foreignness. Joaquin's visit, lunches with Mother, all begin to seem unreal to me, remote.

JANUARY 31, 1936

ONE NIGHT, LYING WITH HENRY, WE WENT deeply into his mood. I understood his numbness, his remoteness. The past was too painful. He was trying to shut it out. I offered to sail back. I understood he was suffering. I told him nothing mattered to me but his happiness. Then he talked out of his own life wisdom. "But maybe this will be good for me." He always accepts. I always struggle. The next morning he began to work on *Tropic of Capricorn*. To alchemize the past. The pain became creation, and at the same time his passion returned. He had been without desire for me.

The next night we went out with Fles. We took whiskey. We sat at the bar, Henry became imbecilic. "Like soup," I said. The whiskey didn't make me drunk. It made me feel despair, weakness. The whole despair of my trip came to the surface; anxiety, solitude, Henry's mood of misery, my fear of the old Henry, a thousand dark, twisted, fears, images, pushed me to leave them. Back in the hotel I took the drug, hoping to become unconscious. Instead of that the anxiety increased, my heart seemed to fail, I lay on the bed and sobbed hysterically. God, God, bring Henry back, bring Henry back. I got up. I listened for the sound of his door opening. I imagined he would stay out all night, I imagined he would treat me as he treated June. I saw a cruel Henry. I lost my strength. In place of my heart there seemed to be a hole in my body, the vital core missing, life crumbling, faith crumbling, strength crumbling. I sobbed, I prayed. I cried out to Hugh. I tried to telephone Rank, a father! I couldn't find his telephone number.

Two hours of nightmare. Henry came. He was not drunk. I lay on the bed and sobbed hysterically. Henry leaned over with the deepest, deepest concern: "Anis, Anis, it breaks my heart to see you crying.

What have I done? I wouldn't do you any harm. Anis, don't, don't."
I poured out my fears. "I wouldn't do that to you. You must have
faith. That was a Henry of thirteen years ago . . ." He was wise, he
was tender. He understood. I was torturing myself over nothing—my
fear of drunkenness, of a different Henry. He realized I felt guilty at
having brought him back into his past. But he is writing. He accepts
what life does. He says I must not try to protect him.

Sobbing, I said, "I couldn't stand the way Fles talked to you. I
saw you hurt again, by America. I saw you crazy with hurt again, I
saw you drinking because you were hurt."

Henry said once that one had to accept—accept. He is writing
now while I see patients in the room next to his.

After our storm there was peace. I had felt his love, his gentleness.
He had felt my love. What I cried out, lying on the bed, was, "Henry,
don't do that to me, don't do that to me, I love you so!"

Do what? Drink—and from drink to cruelty and sensuality. I
expressed my fear of his *instincts*.

We decided to stay, to accomplish the practical tasks we came for.
Henry has people to see. He felt it might be good for *Tropic of
Capricorn*—all this. My strength came back. What a fear of pain. And
Henry was surprised that one could suffer when *nothing had happened.*

To descend into darkness. I wanted it when I wanted to die, with
Henry and June, but now it gives me anguish, terror. I want to live,
without pain—please, oh God, God.

FEBRUARY 1, 1936

*T*HE DRINKING HERE IS MY GREATEST ENEMY. BEL
Geddes had to drink, and to make me drink.
Miriam had to get drunk, and tried to make me drunk. I don't enjoy
getting drunk. But I also hate to kill others' enjoyment. And it is
something which must be shared. At last Henry expressed an under-

standing of the fact that I live in an Elysian world where it is not needed. Where real relationship takes the place of it. Here, there is no relationship, a fear of it—and so to drink! And I'm lost. It kills me physically. I couldn't stop last night after the champagne with Bel Geddes. My real joys are sunk in aftermaths, hangovers, frustration. No sense of richness, fullness, joy. Just sottish sprawling. To not be alone, to come close to them, I drink. But I'm not happy. I don't belong in this world. I love people, but to get near them must I become like them, drink with them?

Bel Geddes was disappointed to hear I was not alone here and wanted to take me to Harlem. I told him about Henry. I don't want to play comedies any longer. I feel myself growing so deep, so grave, that it is frightening.

Salvation through love: the sufferings of the violinist more important now than I am. I feel my power growing again, blooming.

How terrified Americans are of intimacy. Why? Of their emptiness! Wine barrels. Whiskey bottles. Miriam, who was rich during analysis, can only face me outside when drunk

Sunday supper at Mrs. Thoma's. Aesthetic surroundings. Exquisite food. Intelligent conversation. Mrs. Thoma with a porcelain face. But her mouth trembles strangely, as if her teeth are chattering. I feel an immense pity. She has had a breakdown. We all go to a hockey game. Madison Square Garden. Violence. Speed. Physical power. Strong lights. Strong smells. Strong music. Hoarse voices shouting. Noses broken. Intensity. Round table at the bar for members. A dozen whiskey-and-sodas. John Huston talks to me with his face one inch away from mine and his knees touching mine. Bel Geddes, who thinks I am a most exciting person, gets jealous. He has not yet digested the fact that there is a Mr. Miller in my life. Here the talk gets hard, glazed, scathing. More so at Reubens while Eddie Cantor gives a stag party, and director Max Reinhart shares his supper with two actresses and a stage designer. Mrs. Bel Geddes has a weasel nose and a viperous tongue. Mocking eyes. Bel Geddes is good natured and weak. John is decidedly vital, rough, cynical, but I like him. Raymond Massey interested me at first, with his thyroid eyes and gaunt, drugged face, but John was more tangible. I could not enjoy the evening from midnight on. I made efforts to keep myself in it. The sophistication discouraged me. After a while I wanted to run away. Bel Geddes's squeezing me now and then didn't comfort me. I grew afraid of being mocked, ridiculed. It seemed to me they ridiculed everything, everybody. I felt strange.

Went to bed at two-thirty and dreamed: My left hand had been replaced by a new one. I looked at it and said, "How strange it is to have a hand that is not your own. I wonder where it has been before." A swimming pool. Mocking people. My Father in a bungalow. Big dinner being prepared. I don't want to upset Cook but there is something I must get from my Father by crooked means. I hide under his window. He catches me.

John Huston said, "John Erskine was trying to be facetious."

I had quail and wild rice for lunch at Greenwich.

I called on Mrs. B. Stepped into her house with a grave feeling of the sacredness of healing. Wondering if I'm going to become a saint. Fear of my spirituality. I see the damn concrete world so vividly but I feel detached from it. I smell flowers, eat wild rice, seek heat, hate cold, take trains, enjoy hot coffee, but I am far away. All New York is nothing to me now, without Rank. I carry his book about.

In the middle of the supper at the Thomas' I suddenly remember Henry, and I say to myself, Is it possible I have enjoyed myself for two hours without him? A life separate from Henry is rarely achieved by me.

I sit in his room now. He is painting a watercolor. He has been in a morbid mood and then he draws close. I don't know whether this is schizophrenia or saintliness. I feel closer to people who are suffering than to Eddie Cantor's laughter. My disease is winning out. Melancholy is setting in. Everywhere I can dream, my reverie in the train, in the bus, while resting, while bathing, is a fight against melancholy.

The evening starts very well. I'm introduced as the woman who wrote a book on Lawrence and as the friend of Rebecca West. Everybody is always surprised that a writer should look like this or that. People are drawn to me.

But slowly, though I enter with vivacity and ready to give myself, slowly my pleasures and exhilaration diminish. Why? One careless phrase, inattentiveness, irony—even when not directed at me—begins to freeze my blood. My voice trails off. I talk less convincingly, I fall back into "form," into conventional phrases. What is worse? I lose my confidence. I am afraid to leave because I imagine their mockery after I leave. This malaise grows. Everything I wanted to say freezes in me. My throat begins to contract and I can neither eat nor drink. I want to leave. I feel the need to leave so imperative. I give bad excuses. Every minute I stay becomes torture. I smile almost pleadingly, as if to ask to be left alone. I come home angry. I know I have cut off the evening. I have often done that. With Henry too.

Meanwhile Bel Geddes would like to sleep with me. And John Huston is aflame with interest. It is only jealousy which makes Mrs. Bel Geddes's nose longer and her tongue more venomous.

Slowly the fullness I came here for begins to come to me. Patients come. The violinist with his sweetness, trustingness, childishness. Mr. M., whose leadership obsession makes analysis a duel—but at the first sitting I broke down his false construction and made him say, "This is wonderful. I never felt anything like this before." Mrs. B. gets up from her sickbed and prepares herself to come to me. Katrine lies down almost as soon as I arrive at her house, as if analysis were a pleasure.

In a snowstorm I go to see Waldo Frank, whose eyes are so intently bright and clairvoyant, who is gentle and human, mellow, and who talks like a real artist. He receives me with such a look of marveling that I talk freely. I can dance for him. There is a core to touch, seeing eyes, and richness. So I can talk with my own voice, and he reads to me out of *Virgin Spain* his description of the Catalan woman because he says it fits me. We drink port. His room is simple, orderly. There is a sense of wonder in his eyes. And so, he can detect that I know neither death nor finished things, that nothing is finished, that my discontent is a creative restlessness and not a grouch, a curiosity, an expectation of still new miracles. He gives me a feeling of youth, of wholeness, sweetness. He seems taken quite out of himself, as if I were the sudden materialization of a fantasy, and admits me into the seclusion he seeks, in which he lives with the book he is writing. I do not break into creation. I have silent footsteps which dance noiselessly and my voice doesn't make handwriting shake. We meet in quietness. Elation in royal blue. White too.

Out in the snow again, I do not feel my body. I am in the dream. So I am glad to find Bill Hoffman waiting for me with his air of coming back from hunting quail in Georgia, or of riding a horse whose picture appears in Sunday papers. With him I walk gaily in the slush to the Plaza Bar while he is saying, "Do you think we will ever sleep together?"

He has forgiven me for the time I had promised to, before he went down South, and then refused when he had spent three weeks imagining the scene. His ordinariness, the Plaza Bar make the world appear to have four legs, and the askewness in my blood seems to have ceased. William has an erection while we dance, and when I return to the table I play at crystal gazing through the water bottle and say, "I see a *cinq à sept* romance in the future." But not for the reason I said yes last year.

Last year I got weary of refusing, eluding, lying, saying no, and I had such a desire to become *une femme ordinaire*. This time I have a fear of becoming a saint. My body is slipping from me. Henry takes me feverishly and quickly when I am about to meet another man, his desire whipped by jealousy. He fucked me thoroughly before I saw Waldo Frank. It is as if he wants me to meet other men with his sperm in my womb. I carried his sperm to Hugh, to Rank, to Allendy, to Eduardo, to Turner, to many places. But the depth of my response, the fulfillment of our desire, a savage desire, leaves a tremor through the body, like a wire continuing to tremble. From Henry's penis I take my reality and I go to Waldo Frank and Bill Hoffman with a fear of becoming a saint, of being lured back into the whitest corners of the dream, nun's wings like small ship sails, snow, and the painted porcelain birds of Christmas trees. From Henry's penis flows the sperm I'm dancing with, and my body feels Bill's desire and has ceased to slip from me, and I would like many men to come and place their penises between my legs because I am so far from desire, so far from this flesh I covered with musk and patchouli, this flesh walking over wet snow with sandals because I have so strong, so strong a sense of wonder, of the marvelous, the miraculous.

I cannot believe my feet will get wet, my throat ache, because isn't it magic which made Mr. M. realize his soul today, and the violinist realize his dream? And my love for Henry spills over into a desire to be absolutely woman, in order to keep at his side, to stay in his world, because it is his world and he is in it. I see the dirty snow like the soiled bandages of a crippled city piled up. I see the line of the violinist's mouth, which is like my Father's. It is strange, I love the world so much, it moves me, no hatred pours from me, I see it so clearly, with eyes that see the body and the appearance   yet I have to be grateful to a Bill Hoffman because of his desire, his hand on me, everything that is lifelike, ordinary, simple, the whiskey, the bill, the waiter, the dog tied at the *vestiaire,* his words: "I love your gaiety, your humor, and you're a thoroughbred."

Oh, I'm a thoroughbred. He has not said I am a saint. Nobody has said it. The sacredness with which I heal, the emotion I feel at the miracle of man being born over and over again, this makes me fear to wake up in white, transparent, forever removed from sensuality and the earth!

FEBRUARY 15, 1936

ONE NIGHT HENRY WAS OUT, GIVING ME, AS HE often does, the feeling of his belonging to the crowd, to the street, to exterior life, never to silence, to himself, to me.

Waldo Frank came. I knew because of the look in his eyes that he wanted to come close to me. I dressed and perfumed for closeness. I don't see him even today, consciously. The night he came I knew he would say "Let me come close to you." Those were his first words. I felt that we had met in a strange silence, in an unformulated, mysterious manner. It seemed very natural, very simple, very much like music, to let him kiss me, to take my clothes off. A dream. No sensuality. No desire. No passion. A meeting of eyes, a blind meeting below the level of consciousness. *La Catalana.* Sweetness and delicacy and musicality. No dissonances. No strain. "I am the child who is not afraid." Clear, intensely bright eyes. No reality and no sensuality, though we lay together and I thought, Henry, why do you always leave me so alone? I did not respond sensually. But I did not strain to act, to pretend. I was yielding and quiet like a plant. Yielding and quiet, as I had dreamed of being with men. Unafraid and peaceful. Unafraid to yield, to show my nakedness. Henry, why do you leave me so alone in my soul, in my soul, that I must let others come nearer to my soul, for the loneliness? You are the man of the crowd, of the streets. Here I lie with a stranger, to feel wholeness as a woman. Waldo Frank was delicate and natural. A poet riveted to reality, as poets are in America, tainted with the drabness of the life here. No madman, and not a man big enough to abandon and transcend America, his soil, the commonness of America. But a poet, delicate and sensitive, full of God and simplicity. "God sent you, *la Catalana,* so that I might finish my book." What makes me lonely, Henry, are the cheap and gaudy and common people you go to. I am lying naked with Waldo Frank and these are the caresses I felt when I read his book, *Rahab,* eleven years ago, handed to me by Hélène Boussinesq.

We met in silence, sweetness, and naturalness. I was happy, afterward, untouched, like a virgin, yet aware of having been touched, warmed, of having touched and warmed. He knows I love Henry. Yesterday he reproached me, "You are not filled with me." As a woman would say to a man. He wants nothing else, not to go out. He wants to be shut in with his book and me. He wants the dream and the isolation, he wants that tender shelled-in feeling in which the soul finds strength. Henry is in the street. Henry is at the movies. Henry is with noisy, empty people. Henry's eyes are looking out, always out—no innerness. A meeting, like a prayer in a dark, chaotic world, with Waldo Frank. The quieting touch of hands like Lawrence's words. "Blindly, blindly we touched each other's bodies and saw peace."

Snowstorm. Streets like the *mer de glace*. Mrs. B. weeping. Antonia Brico filling my little room with the breath of an animal, sitting with legs apart. Mrs. E. tightening the thin lips of Anglo-Saxon women in the bitterness of passionless lives. Dorrey weeping while telling how her poems were discovered in school and read aloud jeeringly to the whole class. Helen saying, "You have given me more than one human being can give to another."

I am saving the artist who is maltreated in America. I am saving the child who is brutalized, I am saving the individualist who is submerged by the mass here. I am buying one ounce of musk and one ounce of patchouli to make my own perfume. I am tormented and tortured by my own sickness.

One night Henry went out to the burlesque.

I came home at midnight, too tired to sleep. I tried his door—no answer. I tried to sleep. Images came before me. Henry and his white-trash friends drinking. Henry and whores. All night. A fever burning me. A despair. I knelt to pray. My feeling of loneliness immense, deep. I, sneering at myself, working while Henry amuses himself. I, too tired to play—just as when I was a girl and I watched my brothers playing in the garden. I had housework to do. And after the housework I didn't have strength to play and laugh. And so today. All day people coming, people who use me, treat me as a symbol, as an oracle, people asking for strength and wisdom. And I weak because I am only strong in two-ness, in twinship, and Henry does not give me the feeling that he is a part of me.

I prayed. I cried. My heart beat fast. At dawn I went down to the lobby to get his key. I wanted to be in his room. I wanted to kill him and to die. The old man at the desk would not give it to me. It was against the rules. At six I went down again with a story. Mr. Miller was my brother. He was away. He had a medicine in his room for sleep. I hadn't slept all night. Wouldn't he just let me take the medicine? He sent the bellboy. The door was opened. Henry was asleep.

He had come home early. He had been asleep the first time I knocked. I was trembling, crying. I got into his bed. He was tender. I fell asleep.

This was the moonstorm too. All because I am giving all my strength away. Too many burdens on my shoulders. I give all my strength away, to everyone who comes near me. None of them bring me strength. I have no friend. I am alone, teaching, and Henry is playing. He tries to work, but he plays at it. He doesn't do analysis seriously. He is not capable of it. He plays at it, and it is for himself, and people feel it—that it is for *himself.*

Waldo Frank came again, also for himself, for his book. I didn't want him anymore. He is not a man. I pretended a little. He felt it. I don't call him when he telephones. He is hurt by my indifference. He is trying to stay away. He said he was afraid of falling in love. We had dinner in the room. I aroused him to exasperation, but I was not moved. He was beside himself. Indifference.

As an analyst I imitate God. And that brings me so near to God— to his solitude. So I feel him near. I have felt his presence twice—in music, and in the sun this morning. But being an analyst makes it harder to be human. The sick ones are cripples. They are not equal to a man or a woman. They only want a doctor, a father, a mother. I want to be human. I'm tired of imitating God. I would rather have friends.

I have given to the point of death. Superhumanly. And so I cracked, physically, and in my own strength as a woman toward Henry. They drained me, the cripples.

Henry does not give himself. He does not care about the others. This is for himself, a game.

Thus, as an analyst he is egotistical and out for himself. He is playing at it—to write about it. Misery does not touch him. If I did not believe that Henry is attached to me I would shiver at his lack of love. I see his ugly side when he plays the analyst.

He wants to prove my technique (or Rank's) wrong. He lacks understanding. We talk long hours. He fumbles about experience being better than analysis. But when he tried it, he found the neurotic incapable of entering experience. We agree only upon one thing: Experience teaches acceptance of the imperfect as life. Analysis carried to extremity, as Rank carried it, leads again into an idealistic conception of a life without neurosis. Rank thought my life with Henry neurotic because not happy, and did not understand I could not climb to a life without difficulties because it was a life without passion—life with Rank, for instance. Almost as bad as the idea that pearls and automobiles are better for a woman's happiness. Rank pushed his belief in analysis to an expectation of a human life without pain. But that is not always life. I have accepted my nature with its limitations. For instance, it is my nature to give, to love. I could not be happy being loved by Rank—being given to—though it was good for me. It took away all pain. My life with Henry is not happy. But my nature made it, chose it. Everything but happiness is neurosis. So speaks the man of wisdom, not the man of experience. I learned experience from Henry.

One night with bank people, dinner at the Plaza. Luxury. Music. Getting into the taxi, host says to wife, "What's the name of the theater? The Henry Miller Theater. Are you sure? Yes. Driver! Henry Miller Theater! I didn't know it was at the Henry Miller Theater!"

I thought I was far away from my life with Henry. Other levels. It is as if I were in an elevator shooting up and down—hundreds of floors. Up into God's cloud garden—no floors above. A planetarium. Sun. And bars of shadow on the walls of a room. A bower. Why? Lying in bed as I was lying in the hospital, the presence of God in light and then in darkness. A bower. Why? Something to lie on, to lie on. Faith.

Red lights. "Down! Down!" the telephone operator announces. A man who limps; a man whose hand is paralyzed, who cannot play his violin; a man in love with his mother; a man who cannot write his book; a woman abandoned; a woman blocked by guilt; a woman cringing with shame for her love of woman; a girl trembling with fear. Free the slaves of incubi, of ghosts and anguish. Listen to their crying: I feel soft and iridescent. Isn't it a weakness to listen to the complaints of the child in us? It will never cease lamenting until it is consoled, answered. The child demands to be understood; then it will lie still in us, like our fears. It will die in peace and leave us what the child leaves to the man who must survive: the sense of wonder. The telephone announces: "A cable for you. Shall I send it up?" Yes. "Happy Birthday, Hugh." "Happy Birthday, Maman, Joaquin."

Red lights. Down! Virginia is waiting to take me to lunch. Oh, you didn't wear your boots. I must keep on making pictures for the world. Virginia came to look at my boots, at my nail polish. Virginia wants boots like mine. We talk about perfumes. She looks like a Byzantine jewel. All gold, green, russet, shimmer, and breasts I would love to kiss.

White lights. Going up! Henry, in his room, is writing to Fraenkel, the same words about playing at being God, preferring to be human. He is writing a great deal about analysis. He is painting watercolors and studying music. This makes me blissfully, ecstatically happy, I don't know why. Music. He is spending hours studying music. It seems to me that it is through music that we rise in swift, noiseless elevators to the planetarium, together.

Red lights. Down! At the drugstore, I ask for coffee and for calomel. Physically I am cracking. It isn't the change of floors, the sudden rises and descents, which make me dizzy, but the giving. Parts of my body, my life, are passing into others. I feel what they feel. I identify myself. Their anguish tightens my throat. My tongue feels heavy. I wonder whether I can go on—no objectivity. I pass into them to illumine, reveal. But I cannot remain apart. I look out of the window. People are skating in the park. The band is playing. It is Sunday. I could be walking with Hugh through the Champs Militaires, along the Seine. I did not recognize my happiness then. I yearned for fever. The children are laughing and the laughter rises to the twenty-fifth floor, to the window where I stand.

Red lights. Down. All the way down I am thinking of the problem of spiritual symmetry. Retaliation. Revenge. Need to balance. In the mailbox there are letters from Hugh, Eduardo, Chiquito, Lantelme, Hanns Sachs, a note from Waldo Frank: "Why don't you telephone me?" A rejected manuscript. An invitation to a cocktail party. The week's bill. A book.

Thurema is taking me out to dinner—the woman Joaquin loved, the monk. Joaquin, the son, repudiated her for the sake of his mother. She attracts me. I am empty with weariness, but I still have to struggle. She came with prejudices against my work. I had to win her.

White lights. Going up! As Henry opens his door I sit on the doorstep laughing with tiredness, and when I lie on my bed he runs his hand between my legs and takes me with swift excitement from behind. While I am talking to Bel Geddes over the telephone, refusing for the eleventh time to go to Harlem with him because I don't enjoy the debate over the bedtime plans.

In the basement there are my empty trunk and empty valises, waiting for sailing time. Where the elevator strikes bottom there is hysteria and darkness. On the main floor there is the luminous Anaïs who rides on waves of musk and patchouli to be greeted by gentlemen from Norwalk, doctors from Brooklyn, artist models from the Bronx, literary agents with slick Russian tongues, celebrities, obscurities, poor people, timid people, bankers, bank presidents, social workers, Communists, revolutionaries, the flower of Southern aristocracy, snobs, social leaders, musicians, commuters. Men with big voices still stir me sensually, but most Americans have voices like women, and the women have masculine voices. Thirty-six floors, with maids cleaning, men carpet sweeping, letters falling down the chute. Thirty-six floors to my activities, thirty-six cells. But I can't do more than five analyses a day. I find a limit to my strength. Always the body setting a limit.

MARCH 2, 1936

*H*ANNS SACHS CALLING. THE MONSTER AGAIN, THE inhuman face, the lips which seem to be peeled of their skin, the bulbous eyes, the joyless flesh, a caricature of Rank, a shock. I had expected . . . expected? He was seduced, and invited me for a weekend in Boston where he lives. "I hope you are not disappointed," he said. But I was.

Thurema, the woman Joaquin loves and denied himself. A woman my size. I love her. She loves me. Two evenings with her excited me. Her strength, her active self destroyed, as I was, by the passivity of the men we love. But she and I, bubbling, exhilarated, all the cells alive, response, rhythm, timing, electric quality. Her husky voice, strong body, open manner. Joaquin asked her to save me. But I won her over to my life. She believes in me.

Meanwhile my mind works with keenness. I apply trickery, cleverness, nimbleness. Clever manipulations. Mrs. B. says, "What a mind you have!"

Henry so honest, always, about himself: "I hate work" (analysis).

"Even if it is to get something you want?" (publication of our books).

"To work for what you want, yes, that's the honest way, but I don't believe in that."

"How will you get what you want?"

"I'll steal it, borrow it. Yes, plunder." And so here ends his desire to be an analyst—again into a farce, a humorous experience. While I keep on. Laughing, too, but laughing at my victories, at my daily mastering of difficulties, laughing when I win, guide, save, discover.

I cried because I thought maybe Henry would become Rank by

some miracle. No, I was wrong. Then, like Rank, he wouldn't laugh, his flesh would be without joy, his hands without their softness. Yet, God, how I miss the dynamism, the will, the strength. I crave it. Crave it. It is that I have missed all the time—the force which gave me life.

Henry is jealous. "Don't go to Harlem." As jealous as I am. Bel Geddes got tired of telephoning. Then mad. Then jealous. At dinner, at their house, his wife says, "Call up Henry, make him come."

"No, Henry doesn't interest me."

All night he fought her. She wanted Henry to be there, but Bel Geddes wanted me. In Harlem, dancing, I was a little drunk, and I flared up, sensually. His desire. His desire—so little do I want of men sensually, outside of Henry. Why? Why must all my hunger be for Henry? Scatter, divide, relieve intensity, jealousy; the clutching. I electrify Bel Geddes. He can't dance anymore. He is angry that I resisted him. But I don't resist in Harlem. I want earth, this appetite which my desire for other things perpetually destroyed. No desire for Waldo Frank, because he's a little man. No desire of the body, but for what lies in there, what lies in the flesh, the world, the thought, the creation, the illumination.

Thurema is there—palpable. I said to her, "You've given me something marvelous. I don't know what it is. A feeling I have a friend. You have a lot to give me."

"Oh, Anaïs," she answers, at the other end of the telephone, "the night I left you I didn't sleep. You worried me so. You looked so tired. I thought I had tired you. You don't know how happy you make me. I don't know when I've ever been so fond of anyone."

Tremors in our voices. Fullness. To be able to say all one wants to say. We had dinner in my room because we were talking so excitedly—Joaquin, her life, my life. She lost Joaquin because she did what I have so often done: leapt, acted, expressed. And all of them, Joaquin, Eduardo, Hugh, John, recoil in fear of nature, woman, passion, fullness. And we love those men who are negative, afraid. Henry afraid of dogs, afraid of a thousand things. The body is an instrument which only gives music when it is used as a body: in sex, sensuality—as body. Saintliness, or religious ecstasy, is only reached by a triangle of body-life, mind-life, soul-life. Always an orchestra, and, just as music traverses walls, so sensuality traverses body and reaches up to ecstasy beyond moral forms, in love of all kinds and sorts, between men and between women! The orchestra is reached with a fullness which rises to God, whereas the soloist talks to his own soul.

Ecstasy. I feel it now because my lame ducks are dancing. My cripples are singing. So I am happy and Henry and I lie together in a frenzy and he bites my breasts.

The snow has melted. Hugh cables: "I miss you terribly. Try to sail back on March 14."

Henry is working. I play the god with love, with love. Love goes to all of them. I write notes to strengthen. I undercharge. My bills are small. Thank you, God, for letting me taste all things, no cords untouched, no cell closed, no nerve silent, at the tip of my nerves a million eyes, contact with the planets, and my moisture dripping in snow white drops everywhere.

I see my patients now as victims of the American life. Survival-of-the-fittest ideals. No forgiveness for the weak. Mass molds. Loss of individuality and respect for self.

Henry's head when he bows down to lace his shoes: so humble, so delicate, the skin and the hair. There is a peculiar glow to his hair, a light, such as I saw on Paderewski's head. Said by materialists to be due to reflected light on bald scalp.

Dreamed of this phrase: "How strange it is to have a hand that is not your own."

Alone, in bed. Deeply contented. Henry has taken me with passion. My patients are getting cured. I am almost a cult. I am desired, loved, worshiped.

It isn't that I want other men. It's that I have such a fear of reducing my life to an absolute (life with Henry) that I feel I must spread out, I must enrich, expand, to save myself from the madness of clutching. I don't want Bel Geddes as a man, but I want a night during which I can forget Henry. When I deceive him I am happy. I feel prepared for his constant wandering, spreading. Twice now, he has given me a shock. It is when he talks about his daughter. He has heard that she is beautiful. He thinks about her. If he had money he would seek her out. He only hesitates because he is ashamed of his life.

When he mentions her my heart grows cold—I feel the shock, the sudden stillness. It is like a stab. I am expected to go and see her and unite them. Everything beautiful is expected of me. But I am no longer the woman who was noble. I feel I could kill to defend my only happiness on earth. I feel that now that I have convinced the world of my goodness, under the cover of this goodness I could commit crimes. No one would suspect me. There was a time when I would have gone out to Henry's daughter, loved her, served her, given her to Henry. But now I think, Perhaps the same thing will happen between them as happened between my Father and me. And I want to die, to kill, to murder. Wild plans rush through my mind. I will pretend to go and plead for Henry. I will estrange them. Then I dream that Henry and I seek her out and she is only seven—a child. I say, Reality is always less terrible than what I imagine. What I imagine is this daughter sharing Henry's life and idolized by him, and I unable to bear this. I have to have a love for myself alone, and Henry is the man I have to share with the whole world, and now with his daughter. What I know about life, my Father, myself, only gives me fear.

Last night I was to go to Donald's apartment at eleven. I had dinner with Henry and we went to the movies. In the afternoon we had enjoyed each other in bed and rested together. He was very soft; he took my hand in the movies. And I didn't feel like leaving him to go and be made love to by Donald. I stayed, because he was holding my hand and because he was tender and clutching and clinging to me.

I felt cleaved by goodness and evil. To love or to kill. To destroy or to give life. Never before did I stand at such a crossroad, between my primitive emotions and my noble impulses. No one expects anything of me but nobility. But I know now I forced myself to be noble. Deep down I want to kill, to possess, to hold. Oh God, oh God. When I awoke this morning I awoke with sweetness: I will love his daughter too, and take her into our life. I will try to love, as I have loved June.

I don't mean this. I won't do this.

MARCH 5, 1936

THUREMA, A BLUE-EYED GYPSY. WILD HAIR. Strong body. Dimples. So warm and alive. We talk with passion and excitement. "I want to give you things, Anaïs," and she gives me a beautiful silver medallion she carries around her neck. Because she loves it. She didn't win Joaquin, but she shook him out of his death. Since June I have not felt for any woman what I feel for her. The whole evening passes like a dream. She has danced, she speaks Spanish, she was brought up in Mexico. She is a musician. She is fiery, direct. When she left me at midnight, and while she waited for the elevator, I paced up and down in my room with nervousness. Then I rushed out. She was still standing in the hall. I went up to her and kissed her. She held me close. She said, "Oh, you sweet thing. I could squeeze you to death."

MARCH 6, 1936

THE LITTLE TREMOR LEFT FROM THE DANCING AT Harlem, where I said yes, made me dress excitedly, and in the mood in which one should dress for such events, and meet Bel Geddes at the Ritz Bar. For pleasure. Drinking, eating. Kit Kat Club. Burlesque. At his touch I respond. Broadway.

Anaïs Nin in the mid 1930s

Hugh ("Hugo") Guiler, Eduard Sánchez, and Anaïs Nin in the garden of the house at Louveciennes in the early 1930s

Louveciennes, partial view of the front of the house

Henry Miller in the garden at Louveciennes in the early 1930s

Henry Miller and Alfred Perlès in their apartment in Clichy in 1933

*Joaquin Nin y Castellanos,
Anaïs Nin's father, in 1933*

Dr. Otto Rank

Louise de Vilmorin

Rebecca West

NOVEMBER 19

Donald Friede. Anaïs Nin clipped this photograph from a newspaper and pasted it in her diary.

Thurema Sokol

Helba Huara, Peruvian dancer, in one of her elaborate
costumes, likely designed with the assistance of Gonzalo
Moré

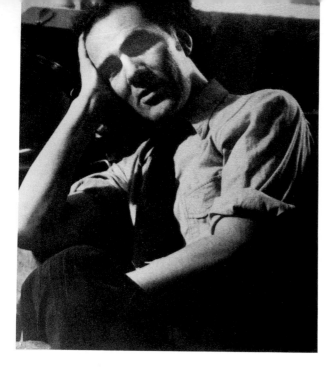

Gonzalo Moré

Gonzalo Moré's drawing of the houseboat "Nanankepichu"

Bel Geddes thinks I'm exciting. We talk completely off-key, and nothing clicks but the blood currents. He is generous, friendly, promiscuous, experienced. "You seem very free," he says. I leave my phrases unfinished. Ordinary life. Pleasure, this, because there is no love. No love, no pain. I don't care what he does, what he sees, who he squeezes, as he squeezes me. Down into adventure, with an open mouth, to light and the lascivious Negresses, to champagne and promiscuity. Names flashing. "When I saw Reinhart . . . Miriam Hopkins . . . When Eva le Gallienne and I had dinner in Paris . . . When I produced . . ."

At one o'clock he drives me to his office, where there is a large salon with a divan and a fireplace. He lights the fire. The first collision is fiery. I am all body, all flesh, all blood, aroused by his vigor, by his sensuality. "You've got talent," he says. "Those quiet persons with dynamos inside." I surprised him and roused him.

Stepping out in the night, at three, I wondered again whether love alone would make me respond with orgasm, the absolute, or whether I could be free and experience a body appetite. Play with sex. This seemed alone what could make me free of Henry. I think of Bel Geddes with warmth, although I have no love whatsoever of what he is.

How strange it is, this mingling with a stranger. "You're marvelous, you're marvelous, you're marvelous." At three in the morning the hotel looks strange. He was angry that I should have resisted him so long, that we wasted time. So many places he wanted to take me to. How sick he is of the baby faces and uninteresting Broadway beauties. His fraternizing with the world amuses me. For an evening I enjoyed myself.

As soon as I forget Henry I enjoy myself. That my deepest love should be mostly pain, that is a disease within me. My imagination leaps, always forward, to imagine torture, to imagine the worst. Even last night I imagined that the day Henry gets his wish, which is precisely to be on terms of fraternity with Broadway and Hollywood, I will have to leave him. He has such childish and cheap desires. A night with Bel Geddes is an incident for me, but Henry could spend his life with empty people and be happy.

At ten in the morning I am saying to the violinist that to withhold from living is to die and that the more you give of yourself to life the more life nourishes you. I advise him to dance, to go to Harlem, where the Negroes are natural.

At eleven o'clock I am explaining the sense of guilt of the artist.

At twelve o'clock I am talking to a motherless girl, so gently and tenderly.

At one, I am having lunch at the Saint Regis with Mrs. Hunt, and we talk about our husbands, the bank, clothes, Elizabeth Arden, and other people in the bank. After lunch I am dizzy from the drinking, and sleepy.

My patients are doing so well that I'm beginning to have free time in the afternoons. Katrine writes about me: "She has the most extraordinary understanding of human problems. She looks like a slip of a child but she has the wisdom of the Sphinx. She was a very sensitive child and her suffering gave her such a compassion for the sufferings of others that she longs to help them. She is very beautiful; she has long slender fingers with flame-colored nails. She looks like a little Oriental princess."

Schizophrenia looks like indifference. Easy to interpret as such. When I left Henry in Paris he was in a schizophrenic mood, and I thought it was inertia, indifference, and I wanted to hurt and rouse him. Danger of schizophrenia is to seek another shock to awaken, to seek pain.

Rank is back from the South and I have done nothing about him. I have a feeling I am living out my instinctual life at last, all my impulses. I thought I would feel the way a man does after he has been with a whore. But it's different. I have a bit of nausea toward sex. Last night, at the burlesque, when Bel Geddes chose the box seats, I thought as I looked at the chairs that they were all stained with sperm, and suddenly the gaudiness, the bawdiness of the whole thing revolted me, although I was laughing at the jokes. I thought, I'm in the wrong world. This is not my world.

MARCH 7, 1936

*T*HUREMA AND I KEEP A CLOSENESS SUCH AS IS unknown between man and woman—I mean by *signs:* thoughtfulness, expressiveness, by what we say to each other. When I described my whole life to Thurema she said, "You need a woman in your life." Eduardo had said the same. But since June I have not loved any woman. I love Rebecca, but she is too sick, too neurotic, too difficult as a friend. I like Louise imaginatively, not humanly, and she also is too far. Thurema is so warm and comes out to me, so that we collide with a great impetus, not in space, and our impulses toward each other are in rhythm. I love her face, which is gypsylike except for the blondness. Her mouth is large, generous, humorous; her eyes are intensely blue, almost darkly so; she wears dresses like mine (she got the same Persian flowered dress I have), jewels like mine, capes; but she is more *laisser-aller,* reckless, negligent, which I like. Her voice is beautiful, not as low as June's, but rich. There's a nobility to her, a primitiveness, an emotionalism. But her life has been so poor, so restricted. In living she has not had courage. That will be my gift to her.

MARCH 9, 1936

*I*T'S LIKE A GAME OF *QUILLES.* ONE DAY IN PARIS I had made a list in my notebook: Bel Geddes, Donald Friede, Waldo Frank, Cuban vice-consul, Buzby—except for the order. When I saw Donald with Kay just before leaving America last year, I was attracted by his sensual body—a face and body made for lovemaking. Fleshy, disintegrated, lax; and his eyes recognized in me a direct curiosity. He said on Saturday, "As soon as I saw you I knew your attitude was like mine, your emotional reaction. You see, I'm a realist. Everybody around here fools himself about what he wants. I don't. I want sex. In fact, it is the orgy I like best, and which I consider the most satisfying."

The night I chose to stay in the movies with Henry, Donald was awaiting me in his hotel room with another woman. His attitude just answered to what my mood is at present, the extremely handsome Russian Jew, tall, fat, like a Spaniard, a golden skin, glowing eyes, a feminine beauty of features. I knew, instinctively, that here was the answer to my painful flight from love, from orgy. I knew I had sensed Donald's pleasure, the cult, the perversity.

And so to bed. I displayed the maximum of my skill. I was at ease, relaxed. I didn't feel the orgasm. I was as faithful as a whore is to her man. But I played the game. And he was ravenous. It was strenuous. Coming back to the hotel I said to myself, My only exercise in New York consists of fucking. No sensual enjoyment—quite the contrary. I kept thinking, It will soon be over! The laughter with which I dressed for the occasion and the precautions I took beforehand clearly revealed what I expected to happen. No sensual enjoyment, but a kind of relief at escaping from *feeling*—as if by way of gymnastics I expected liberation from emotion and the pain of love. As if through gymnastics I was learning not only physical suppleness but a domination of my sensibilities, another *souplesse*.

Arithmetic: one man, two men, three men. Gymnastic: how to fall on a bed, how to fuck, how to get dressed. Pleasure instead of happiness. Donald kneeling over me, with a stomach like Bacchus. No more talk. Men are not worth talking to. If you talk, you discover you disagree. If you talk, the idea of lying naked in bed with such a man becomes ridiculous. Very little talk with Bel Geddes. Hardly any with Donald. As he gets dressed, I like him better. Better and better as he gets ready to leave with me. A very handsome man as he stands saying good-bye to me. I know nothing of him. I know his body. To hell with knowingness. Fuck. Fuck. Fuck. You may drown your soul that is always wailing. Drown tears. Drown jealousy. Curiosity and adventure. Reportage. Motion. Out of the Fifth Avenue Hotel.

To Henry. Henry is resting. The next day it is Henry. Fucking other men makes me easier with Henry—less sentimental. Fuck. Fuck. Fuck. I'm always glad to have deceived him. In this I take pleasure. Revenge for what he is not.

I have forgotten him for two hours, for an evening—good. So much relief. Now thoughts about war upset him, not because of others but because his haven in Paris may be destroyed. He is afraid for his security—he whines.

The war. The first time I hear the word I feel a shock. Hugh will be in danger. We may get separated.

When I made Henry a scene—because I said he could take analysis seriously for at least a month in order to get what he wanted—though he protested, the scene had a great effect on him. It made him *whole*. Suddenly he began to work, and to preach to Emil Conason about his dilettantism, and to realize that I always keep him from falling apart.

Now he is working, not because I believe in work as such but because I believe in wholeness. I said to him, "You and Fraenkel would sit eternally around a table discussing, like two Russians, all the things you want, and do nothing about them. I have desires and I must fulfill them. It isn't morality which pushes me to work but the fact that there is no other way to get what one wants."

Bel Geddes wanted to come at five. In my sober day-mood I didn't want him. I have to excite myself into it by dancing, eating, drinking. After that there is William waiting, then an orgy with Donald, and then I'm through. I've abandoned Waldo Frank. I'm giving myself a real chance to test gymnastics and loveless adventures. I know already that this can't hold me on earth. Keep my body on earth please, man, with your desires, for I am ready for departure and flight.

MARCH 11, 1936

*M*ONDAY EVENING. THUREMA CAME. HER HUSBAND wanted to get home early (to the country) and so she decided to stay all night. We both wanted this. Back in my room after dinner we talked endlessly. I gave her my white rug because her room is white. When we began to undress we began with laughter; she was laughing at my underclothes, the lace, the transparent nightgowns—she wouldn't wear one. I fixed her a perfumed bath. I wanted to see her body—not that I felt any sexual impulse, but I felt such a love, such a need for caresses and softness. But we were both shy. I saw only her back. I let her bathe. She was so natural. She admired my hands, my feet; she finds me beautiful. We joked and teased and laughed. How did I look with cold cream? I would show her. I'd wash my face. We would sleep crosswise, her head next to my feet. She opened the window. New York was covered with mists. One could see only the lights of the buildings. One could hear the muffled sounds, the noise of the Park *canards,* the ship sirens from the river. A damp, mist-laden air filled the room. I would get neuralgia, but I didn't care. Thurema was lying there, with her vibrant voice, her voice which contains laughter and sobbing together, her wide mouth with dimples. She talked about her life. The story of her marriage was so sad, I came right over and took her in my arms. She resisted my pity because she didn't want to be like the people who come to me for help. She is full of doubts about herself. She thinks she does everything wrong. She thinks I'm like Joaquin and that I will suddenly turn away from her. "It's in your blood."

We talked, and kissed, and sighed, and marveled over each other. Our love just welled over without a shadow of sexuality but with physical fervor, a passion. We talked and laughed and tried to sleep, and it was she who felt protective, then it was me, and there began a seesaw, a well-equalized seesaw of concern, sympathy. She is all emotion. In the dark such loveliness, such a new experience, to feel her softness and warmth. I did want to touch her breasts but I didn't want her to misunderstand. There was no misunderstanding—again a separateness from the experiences around us. We laughed at Antonia.* At lesbianism. She seems like a woman who has lived, as I seemed to June. There's no lack in her, though she has only known a husband and her frustrated love for Joaquin.

As soon as she left me in the morning I missed her. I felt tired but elated and happy. Felt so happy and strong. Thurema came when I was beginning to commit suicide again (killing my feelings, my soul, my real self so as to suffer less). But as soon as I saw her I knew this was a real love and that, having her, I could no longer live falsely. I immediately gave up Bel Geddes, Donald. I'm in love, I'm in love with love, purity, wholeness. Thurema's face, everything—her vividness. Thurema's voice in my ears. That evening, as I returned from the concert, as I opened the door of my room, I expected to find her there. My solitude was over. Passing by Henry's door, I didn't ask myself where he was. The next morning, when Henry began describing how he had spent the evening, I didn't feel the icy shock of pain when he came to the phrase "The Matisses introduced me to a girl—a case they wanted me to treat." (I have had three fears here: that Henry should get a woman patient, because I am sure he would not resist the sexual offer as I resist the desire of all the men I take care of; that he should drink; that he would fall in love with his daughter.)

Antonia's concert was one of the climaxes of my career as analyst. I went there filled with a sense of my power, knowing I was going there to give her force. I looked at her and said little. She wanted to go on the stage immediately. She conducted marvelously—a demon, a force, a compelling, magnificent performance. All Carnegie Hall was electrified. People said it was her best concert. She telephoned Thurema: "Do you know who did it, who made me conduct—it was Anaïs." Antonia said she felt me all night as she played, felt my strength behind her. And I felt the whole orchestra, and her strength.

---

* The organizer and leader of an all-female orchestra, Antonia Brico was well known, apparently, for her numerous relationships with other women.

Her power thrilled me, but it was Thurema's face I saw, Thurema I longed to see.

The concert left me ecstatic, drunk with music and magic and my power to create—to save, to build. Compassion and love, and a religious feeling, led me to analysis. Then I fear holiness. I fear to be the religious type rather than the artist.

The next evening Thurema came only for dinner. I broke my engagement with William (which meant dinner, dancing, fucking). I was entranced with her. We went to the dining room and ordered something to eat—then we walked out and asked to have it sent to the room. We wanted to be close and together. I was sick. But I walked with her in the rain to Carnegie Hall. I came back and went to sleep. At midnight she came up. She wanted to take me home with her and take care of me. We embraced passionately.

The next day I went to White Plains, to her house. When she played the harp I cried. She plays vigorously and delicately, just as she is, and I was happy. Waiting for the train, we kissed. We were exultant. It was misty again. She was counting the days I had left.

Today her voice over the telephone was hurt. I knew it immediately. I asked her why. She would only say she was sad. I called her back at the end of the day and finally discovered she had finished my June–Henry novel. "It has hurt you, then, Thurema. I have hurt you? What is it? Nothing wrong between us? That is all I care about!" She couldn't say. She is one who doesn't know what she suffers from, or why, or what she feels. She is all unconscious, music, motion. She is coming tomorrow.

I refused Donald's orgy. I told him I had fallen in love, laughing, and had no more time for "pleasure." What relief when I stop pretending, living with my head, and become true to myself again. Loving Thurema is real to me. I also got rid of Waldo Frank. Read him what I had written (skipping "a man not big enough"), acknowledging the delicacy of what had been but refusing to continue it. Thurema swept everything away.

Waldo Frank was surprised by what I read him, by the accuracy of it. How could I see and say all that so quickly? Also surprised by the brutal way I tried to push him off—a talk about reasons that were off-key, such as, "You don't like to play." Vulgarizing or betraying what did happen—a sudden gesture of destruction because the act of pushing someone away is so difficult. I was aggressive and martial. But he was quiet and began to talk about it just in the way I had written about it.

MARCH 16, 1936

*T*HUREMA WAS JEALOUS OF THE NOVEL AND AFRAID that everything I did was perhaps insincere and "just to write about"—afraid of literature. I took her in my arms and gently explained the difference between human life and literature, just as I learned it from my life with Henry. She was afraid of the "falsities." I told her how well I recognized my real emotions from my games, how very real love sweeps away the games for me. I reassured her, I forced her into confessions. She is such a hurt, nervous, trembling woman—I feel so protective. She is the hurt one—not I—she has real sorrows. I've forgotten all my moods and imaginary dramas now, to take care of her. My love gives her strength, but I also seem to have the power to hurt her. My life, the fullness of it, what I give to others, the numerous people in love with me—all of it makes her afraid, just as Henry's past and friends make me afraid.

A friend writes in her diary, "I had lunch with Anaïs today. She's exquisitely lovely and feminine and I enjoyed the calm of her subtly perfumed presence. She's the first woman I've not minded wearing perfume. I think she understands me uncommonly well. She's fascinating. There's a reserve about her, yet I don't feel at all constrained in her presence. Despite her allure and exoticism she's very human and close to me temperamentally. I'm always relaxed completely with her. I met her agent, Barthold Fles. He's head over heels in love with Anaïs."

Jealousy motif: The day I bought an alarm clock to wake myself up, my wristwatch stopped working!

*A*NOTHER NIGHT WITH THUREMA, WHO IS NERvous, highstrung, unhappy, explosive. I try to help her. She says it's not a father I need but a mother. Perhaps she's right. I was expecting from man something only a woman can give me. It is hard to give to her, because she is all emotion and has no power of analysis, hard to help her. She is hurt and shocked by life. As I talk to her, even about my lies, I see her wide mouth smiling in the semidarkness, forgiving. Telling everything about my life means Henry, June, Rank, and Waldo Frank. Something is left out: my Father, minor affairs, the abortion. At the moment I forget these things. They do not weigh on me. When she decides that I am sincere, that Joaquin's fears of my degradation are unjust—when I have won her and given myself with utter faith—then I wonder. If I told her the rest, would I lose her? She is not ready. Only Rank could be told everything, because he understood everything. And I can look at her with clear eyes. In the dark I'm saying, "Don't worry now about my lies and trickeries. I'm like a magician in a vaudeville show. It's the only thing that is humorous about my life!"

"But some day," said Thurema, "you'll be discovered and all of them will throw you out, and then you'll have to come to me."

"I live from day to day. I am reckless and courageous. Laugh, Thurema." And I begin to tell her how I have promised both Henry and Hugh the money I'm making here. How I owe Fraenkel a hundred dollars, plus money for the printing of my book. How I don't know yet how I'll manage all this.

"The point is, I always find a way. Rank used to say that's how I used my creative energy. He used to call that my creative lies!"

Then we kiss. I lie over her and kiss her repeatedly, amorously, kiss her wide mouth with the dimples, and I feel myself growing passionate, the wildness mounting. She feels it too. "Oh, Anaïs, I could almost . . ."

Then she sobs.

"I know. You're thinking of Joaquin. You're wishing he would be as I am now." I grow tender and quiet. I console her. Every emotional upheaval brings the picture of Joaquin. It makes her sad. "Your mouths are different." Joaquin's mouth is thin, like my Father's.

We fall asleep in each other's arms. I tell her I'd like to be a man, and to be her lover. She dreams that I undress before her and that I have a penis, and she says in the dream, "Why did you conceal that from me? Why didn't you give me that?"

I dreamed once that June had the penis, yet in each case I'm the one who plays the lover, though I look more feminine. Henry thought Thurema was decidedly masculine.

Meanwhile, all around me people are coming to life. Friends and patients. But the ones I have left—Hugh and my Father—are sick and sad, and I cannot resuscitate my brother, Joaquin.

Henry feels the power of earning money and doesn't want to sail back. He wants us to stay here and work, to make the break. He is afraid of France now because it no longer represents a haven. He shows a strange and terrible cowardice, always a self-preservation instinct; he is driven to this by fear, not by love. I am hoping he doesn't mean this, because Hugh writes me love letters which break me to pieces, and I wouldn't leave him. Henry says, "You're a mixture of wild emotions and analysis."

I left Henry at the public library and walked slowly back. The weather was soft and windy. I felt as if I were June walking when she was sad and full of compassion.

MARCH 18, 1936

I HAVEN'T SUFFICIENT CONFIDENCE TO LIVE OR love except when I am at the center, when I enslave or possess wholly. That is my failure. Henry is possessed only by his ego—himself. And that will always hurt me. I believe in Hugh, Rank, and Thurema, because they give themselves. I only saw Henry possessed and enslaved once, when I eluded him, betrayed and abandoned him. Is it lack of faith in me that makes it hard for me to accept Henry's inhuman love, or is it that I am not strong enough to live with anyone who belongs to himself? It seems wrong that I should need this slavery and believe in slavery alone. Hugh's last letter affected me deeply. For the first time I felt the powerful bond between us. I ask myself how it was I ever hated him, ran away from him, tormented him. When he wrote, "Am I crazy? I'm obsessed with you. Have you made me crazy?" I felt his mouth, his whole body, his sensitiveness, his emotion, and felt my love—or was it a love that does not want to hurt—no, it's love, because I don't hesitate for a moment to hurt other sensitive men, to hurt Turner, or Waldo Frank, or Rank. But Hugh I won't hurt. I love him. It isn't just pity, it's in my blood, in my soul. He is not just my slave. He has taken hold of me somehow.

Henry last night, after saying "I'll come back about ten," went off book hunting and to drink with a barman. He came back after midnight, gloating over some Goethe phrases. I waited for him, then when he came I told him our life isn't human, that he isn't human. He said it was only the "situation," our work, the hotel rooms—but it's me. Rank and I could make a world, a home, a complete world, in any hotel room, anywhere, at any time.

But when the moonstorm is on, I doubt all I feel and analyze. I just want to believe him, as Hugh wants to believe me. As soon as he comes back and is there I feel he is innocent. It is only because deep down I am so honest that I know it is wrong to want to possess another's soul and body, that I feel the ordeal of my life with Henry the egoist is a good punishment, a good, well-deserved punishment, for I have made the others (Hugh, Rank particularly) suffer from the pain of not being able to possess me.

MARCH 19, 1936

*T*ALK WITH HENRY AFTER THE MOVIES ABOUT THE barbarian and the Christian. Attila and Christ. Both in the end conquering the world, one by force, the other by love and gentleness, both doing harm and good. I told Henry *Tropic of Cancer* was "barbarian," and his writing in general was barbaric. It is so contradictory to his gentleness, but under his gentleness and softness Henry is inhuman—that is, for what he wants he will do anything, and what he wants is always for himself. He gives nothing; that is, he doesn't give himself. Christ gave himself.

Henry began to corner me about why I still wrote in my diary— because I couldn't live out my real self; that is, I couldn't get what I wanted because I always gave it up, or gave to the other. But I said, "I'm not doing badly, with tricks and all that." Suddenly Henry's eyes filled with tears, his mouth twisted, and he said, "It's my fault, of course. It's my fault. I've done just like the others. Drained you. I used your sustaining qualities to grow. But if I must grow at the expense of you and choke you, I won't let that be. Please do what you want, always, from now on . . ."

His emotion was tremendous. He lay over me and kissed me. I said repeatedly, "I'm happy, I'm happy. I don't know why." Then he took me, with great wildness, and I cried but felt nothing. I was too emotionally upset.

It seemed to me that those moments of humanness in Henry make up to me for everything. I'm the only one who can make him feel human. The rest of the time Henry is Attila, conquering force, eating, warring for himself, his ego.

Before this talk, in an agony of solitude (Thurema is a drain and someone I have to carry), I wrote to Rank, asking to see him. Now it seems less important, and I realized it is as the giver of life that I turn to him.

Thurema had a headache. "My father used to get headaches like this and he went mad. Do you think I will go mad, Anaïs?" She dreams of being under ether and awakes in terror.

Letter to Hugh: It hurts me still to think that you were sick. I have no business to be giving all my strength away here while you're alone in Paris. I don't know what inhuman demon drives me, my darling, to fulfill an inhuman destiny, and I ask you humbly, humbly, to forgive me for all the inhuman things I have done to you and asked of you. I humbly thank you for the sacrifices you made of your happiness to allow me always to do what I wanted, even when it hurt you. It hurts me to think of all you have done, and with what love; and I only hope that you yourself found some happiness in doing it. I only hope that what I have to give you is worth all that, that when you gave and gave, understood, forgave—that this may bring you riches, that this horribly monstrous ego which drives me to create, to live in strange and difficult ways, out of my home, away from the man I love, may be able to enrich your life somehow. Can all this expansion which I owe you, can it flow back always to you, its source flow back and fill you with life and joy and ecstasy? Oh, my darling, if you love me, it must be that these inhuman things I do are not so monstrous; yet tonight I would give everything up, writing, analysis, the cult which is growing around me, my action in the world, for a moment at your side, a moment of closeness to you, body to body, when I would caress you and love you and take you into myself, you who are already forever engrooved inside of me, part of me, settled in my soul and body. . . .

This love, I know, is born out of gratitude, out of a bond that is not free will. The love I feel is fraternal, but as I pour it out—let him interpret it as he will—it's love.

To Eduardo (who suffers from insane jealousy): I've come back to the desire to give directly to those I love: Hugh, you, my friends, instead of collectively. It doesn't seem human or satisfying to be helping people I don't know when I could help *mon petit cousin,* my husband, my women friends. I'm returning to the intimate, the personal. Maybe the truth is that relationships hurt—but analysis doesn't hurt, it just tires me— but the personal female in me ain't satisfied. I'm coming home soon, to devote myself to my loves and that means you.

And it means Thurema, who is hysterical and whom I have not had time to help.

MARCH 20, 1936

*A*NOTHER VITAL TALK WITH HENRY ON OUR friends. He thinks I am aloof and that I don't give myself, because I can't give myself superficially to everyone but form vital, intense attachments to a few. He doesn't see or know what Rank meant, Louise, Thurema, Rebecca West, Eduardo. I told him how we look for different things. He is contented with a flow of people who are not vital to him. He says himself any one of them could drop dead and he wouldn't mind. To this flow he gives his time, energy; he talks, but he doesn't give himself. I do. And I hold back from the flow. We talked about his being an extrovert. I said he had only had a year or two of innerness, in Clichy and Louveciennes when he and I were practically alone, and that a world with his work and a woman means only with himself. It's a complete circle which produced *Black Spring.* After that, when he got restless for the world again and I gave him a home and a life which became open to the world, then he turned outward again. He let Fraenkel invade him, Fraenkel who makes demands I never made, egotistical ones, who doesn't care about Henry's writing; and so Henry lived all last year for Fraenkel, for the letters, the "Hamlet," and the talks, and *lost himself.* Coming here did something to him—reintegrated him. When I take him away it isn't only for myself, God knows, because he becomes himself. I influence him to *become himself,* not to give me himself.

Anyway—the friends—we clarified everything. We joked. Henry said, "We'll line them all up and shoot them." I said I didn't care about anything as long as our differences didn't separate us. He mistakes my aloofness, which is partly timidity, for criticalness. It's true I criticize them to myself as not being important to me, but I don't dislike them or maltreat them.

Henry's work, which he now does seriously, does make him understand more. He understood that I was being true to my nature, even though I wept when we talked, because I said I had dreamed of finding his friends and his life to be my life, but that it had been hard for me to separate my life and friends from his and to create a third one of my own. It had not happened without pain, because my dream is marriage. I see now that New York means the place where I can best live this third life that is neither Hugh's nor Henry's but mine. In Paris I pass from Henry's bed to Hugh's, there is no time or energy left for anything in between. *Here,* yes, I can even materially escape from both. Henry doesn't know at what time I come home. The result last year was the relationship with Rank; this year, with Thurema. Difficult to believe in love. Passion is easier because it is intense and obvious. Write on Suicide of a Soul.

MARCH 23, 1936

SATURDAY MORNING ON THE TRAIN, ON THE WAY to see Thurema. Sunshine on the letter I am writing to Father. Thurema in a red raincoat, hair like a lioness's, losing her way in the car. Little seven-year-old Johnnie, her child, skating while we take a walk. Thurema and I lying on the couch after lunch and I saying, "You don't believe in love. You've lost your faith in yourself." The telephone rings: "Your boy has been run over by a car. He's at the hospital." Thurema sobs hysterically. We drive to the hospital. On the way we see the bicycle lying on the road, all smashed. "He is dead, oh God, he is dead." His little shoes are lying next to the bicycle. "He is dead, oh God . . ."

"No, no," I say—"no, no." Johnnie is not dead. He is all scratched up and hysterical.

Driving to the station, Thurema says, "What I feel for you, Anaïs, is so strange that I'm beginning to think it's abnormal—we're abnormal."

Then I went dead. Playing God every day, saving people from misery, tragedy, sickness, death—and then Johnnie is struck by a car and suddenly I don't care anymore. There is a stronger destiny. I relinquish my efforts against it. I don't care about tomorrow, about my work, about Hugh or Henry. I don't care. I haven't any more feelings.

Last night, with the hardness, there came a freedom and recklessness. Fear of death, nearness of death, plunges us into reckless living. Rank said when I decided to die, to go anywhere, to do anything (just before I met Henry and June), then I began to live. So, again, I feel reckless. I feel that I live in the moment.

Last night I carried to the [Hilaire] Hilers a riotous mood, a hard comical mood. I danced humorously, dialogued in an *accent du Midi* with Hiler, and he said, "You're the only one who has come in here who's not gray. You have color." Curls over the nose, a perfume which brings comments from the elevator boys, green eyelids, a sharp tongue, cruelty. I make Henry jealous. Jealousy arouses his desire. All cruel instincts arouse instincts. I feel that if I stopped feeling for a moment I'd become a demon. When I have no feeling I'm cruel and harmful. So I strike fear into Henry, which makes him forget to make me jealous, as he does by his past, his love of woman, his superficial susceptibility to all women, and the deep faithfulness to me, which I see but don't altogether believe.

I feel more like June today than ever before. It's the recklessness, through not believing in tomorrow, through feeling the violence of life, which whips the instinct to live, a whip, a smashed bicycle on the road. Little shoes lying next to it. Anger at God.

I smoked a marijuana cigarette at Hiler's.

You care when you create, you save your strength for creation. You don't drink because you become unconscious, you cease to live, and you loved your awareness, and violence makes you blind with anger and hatred, perhaps impotence, no supreme power then. Very well, God, if destruction must be, I'll smash first of all my soul, which hurts me, which keeps me from laughing, from breaking too, from living, from striking, hating. I know nothing between pain and hardness, noncaring. Either to feel all that happens to Thurema or not to feel anything but violence and anger, such as Henry feels. I cannot save all the wounded. I want to kill this soul which *sees* the wounds.

MARCH 29, 1936

*D*ONALD WAS NOT DISCOURAGED. HE TELEPHONED that he must see me before he left for Hollywood for good. I couldn't come that afternoon. But Friday evening, then, about eleven. I had dinner with Henry, who was groggy and sleepy. I left him at ten-thirty, saying I was going to hear Sasha play at a party. I had heard Sasha play that very afternoon. I was drunk with music and with fatigue. Thurema and I had slept together the night before. And because I did not show any passion she urged me to kiss her. I kissed her more and more wildly until she moaned and sighed and we both stopped again on the brink of a gesture neither one of us really wanted. I teased and laughed and was comical. When she asked me, "Do you think we are lesbians?" I answered, "Not yet." When we grew passionate she remembered Joaquin. She wished Joaquin were as free as I am.

In the taxi, on my way to the hotel, to Donald, I planned my visit. I would be very self-possessed, poised, mature, mysterious, but very firm about not wanting to go to bed. I would draw him into talk about himself. I would say, "I'm interested in you and curious about you." I would charm him with talk.

When I arrived I was shown into his apartment. He telephoned that he was detained at a party and had left a note saying to help myself to cigarettes, a drink, and a pornographic book called *The Prodigal Virgin*. I read the book. I was slightly stirred by the descriptions of the sexual bouts. What stirred me more were my own erotic longings and images, all my curiosities, my desire for woman, for the orgy.

Donald telephoned again: "If Arline comes, give her a drink and ask her to wait." So he had invited the woman he wanted me to know. The one who was there the night I stayed at the movies with Henry. The idea pleased me. I was alone in Donald's apartment. I could have walked out. Instead I looked all around me. The place was French. I hated it. It smelled of oldness and urine. The bed was in an alcove. I picked up the book again. Two things I always pictured and wanted: to slip my hand under a woman's skirt and to feel her backside; to feel and kiss beautiful breasts.

I felt no hesitancy, but a certain timidity. I asked myself would I know what to do, would I do it well? I knew what physical gestures were expected of me. I was intensely curious about the woman.

Donald came in and, a moment later, the woman, Arline. Luminous, clear eyed, simple. Open blond face, lazy gestures, a well-rounded body under a simple skirt and blouse.

The three of us sat on the couch drinking whiskey. Donald

caressed me. Arline began by admiring my hands, then she began to kiss me like a man, giving me her tongue. And all the things I had wanted to do to a woman I began to do, to caress her breast, to slip my hand under her skirt. Meanwhile Donald had knelt before the two of us, and he was looking under our dresses, and he had a finger inside of her and inside of me. My honey began to flow. Her mouth tasted like June.

We all shed our clothes. She stood up for a moment as if about to leap, full breasts pointing upward, beautiful soft, rounded body. Donald placed me on his bed and began sucking me. He was making more love to me, perhaps because I was the guest of honor. For a long while the three of us lay entangled, caressing, sucking, biting, kissing, with fingers and tongues. Donald did not penetrate either one. He allowed himself to be sucked off. I tasted a woman's vagina with my lips. I did not like it. It was a strong seashell dish. I did not like the smell. But I did like it when she offered her backside. I loved her breasts, her mouth, and it amused me that while we caressed Donald and fulfilled our female obligations, our real interest was in each other. Over his body we looked at each other with something like closeness, whereas Donald remained apart, neutral. Sometimes her head and mine were next to each other while we both kissed Donald. We enjoyed finding our mouths near the same place, and we would stop and kiss each other. When Donald, satisfied, fell asleep, she and I went on kissing and saying *How lovely you are, how soft, how beautiful.* She said, "You've got the softest skin, a body like a girl's. We must see each other again." I had felt no orgasm, though the moisture was flowing and I was excited. I was not free enough, deep down. I was pretending. But soon, soon, the complete abandon will come. I am still yearning for love, for love, for love.

I felt that she'd had no orgasm. She was not even wet. I wondered why she should be pretending. It seemed to me she was merely eager to please Donald and me. I said to her, "I never did this before." She laughed. "Why not?"

It is the abandon I like, Donald, Bel Geddes, Arline. Their freedom from care and jealousy. The smoothness. There is a world where people play joyously and naturally the tricks I play for alibis, without being blamed. I heard Arline telephone to whoever was waiting for her and say she was at a party. Then she and Donald invented who she might have seen. Gracefully they move, fuck, forget. She stood in front of the mirror fixing her face. Donald said to me, "I'm sorry I won't see you again. I like the way you do things, your directness."

I took her home. In the taxi, before an Arline all dressed, I felt shy. She said Donald was always telling her he would introduce her to a beautiful woman but that he never had until tonight. She called me darling. I would never have asked her if I could see her again. I did not know whether my body had any value in that fucking world. But from all kinds of tests I find now I am considered a valuable animal.

I wanted to ask her if I had caressed her well. The intimacy when we were naked and now the strangeness, dressed. But I have learned one thing about the pleasure world: that is silence. Things are enjoyed in a kind of silence and unawareness. That may be the law of enjoyment: not to think or feel. I have learned this silence, this noncaring. I ask no questions. I slide along.

I thought to myself, laughingly: If someone asked me, Do you know Donald, do you know Arline? Well, I would answer, I have slept with them, I know every part of their bodies intimately, their smells, their tastes, their textures of skin, but for the rest, please introduce me.

Arline took my telephone number. I did not believe in her interest in me. I thought, She is more knowing, more sophisticated, more experienced. She won't like me. I was afraid she would think me unexciting, would discover my naïveté.

But she telephoned today and I felt this warm body knowledge, body friendship, body warmth, when I heard her voice. The immense loneliness was attenuated by this body contact with Arline. While I analyzed people during the day I pictured her physically, not Donald. I saw her vulva, her tuft of hair, her backside. So marvelous. Woman. The woman in her. Her freedom, her naturalness appealed to me. She made me forget Thurema, all bound and knotted and choked. As the sun makes you forget cares. Sun. Sea. Nature. Silence of feelings. Relief from feeling. The difficulties, the emotions, the complexities with Thurema. My soul is tired. Or maybe it is giving out.

April 4, 1936

*A*BOARD SS *BREMEN*. DRUNK AND CRAZY WITH PAIN, loneliness, regrets, emotions. If only Rank had not tried to possess me exclusively, if only he had remained the lover. I don't know what I am saying.

When I arrived at his place, he was standing at the door, with such sadness, eagerness, gentleness in his eyes, I was profoundly moved, moved as I did not expect to be. Everything beautiful came back in one flash, I was overwhelmed with regrets.

When we talked the magic was set on again, just as before. His eyes and mine clung to each other. Oh, the loneliness, the loneliness. He, thinner, younger, sunburned, gentle. And the smile. The knowing smile. No longer physical resistance but love, just love. One hour to see him, smaller than I remembered, leaner, healthier, less ugly, so soft his eyes, so knowing his smile. Fatality. Totality. Yes, it is as I wrote him, I have remained faithful to what we had, and no one else has come so near, mystically. I have lived out the partialization. He is saying this. He could not be less total. The [Hudson] River lies under his window, he is resigned, he is working as before, there is no other woman in his life. But he is afraid, he is afraid of woman, of life, of me. He is controlled.

Our eyes say everything. Our words nothing, except when we agree laughingly to sign a blank contract. Not knowing what we want. Why didn't he take, take all I could give him? Why did he clutch at me, clutch, clutch, clutch? One hour worth my trip to New York. The instant flash of understanding. Nearness to him. "Will I lose you again? Will I lose you again? It would be better for life if I were less total," he said. Better for life. I could give my body to Donald, Arline, Bel Geddes, to Frank—why couldn't I give it as easily to Rank? Why not? They demanded no feeling. You give the shell, with wet lips and wet vulva. Possession. What does it mean to be possessed? Henry had totality from me, yet this totality, when it became unbearable, when I discovered he was not whole, out of fear, I split up and I went out to Allendy, to Rank, and the others. In New York I lived in a million pieces. A million pieces. Love fragmented. When I began to turn away from a fragmented, elusive Henry.

I turned so far.

I got lost again. I lost him. I was relieved of my obsession for days.

Other loves.

The passion for Thurema died. I don't know what killed it. Something in her paralyzes life. Her fear. Her fear. Her fear of life kills life.

The pain of leaving Rank, Thurema. It seemed to me that all my being was so aroused that I felt all my loves at once, and it was unbearable. So many loves. What am I? The Lover of the World. Crazed with love. Crazed with love. My whole body in pain, the pain of separation, loss, change.

Henry came in at eleven, when the ship had begun to move, asking wonderingly, "What's the matter?"

Henry was there. During all those last days when I saw so little of him, when I spent my evenings with Thurema, in the morning I used to look through the slit in his door, the breakfast slit, and I could see his shoes, his blue shirt on the armchair, his pants, and I would think, *Henry is there,* and feel a great peace, and go down and eat my breakfast with a kind of grateful joy. Henry is there. Henry is there.

APRIL 5, 1936

*H*ENRY AND I TALK QUIETLY BUT EMOTIONALLY about the changes in us. He realizes now what I wrote on the ship on our way to New York last year, that he and I, by interaction, have exchanged souls. He is classical, wiser, has gained tremendously in understanding. I have become emotional, primitive. He has less need of direct relationship, direct experience; he knows men now by wisdom, understanding. I am swimming full into direct living, passionate experience. We're traveling in opposite directions. I observe all this with a tragic tone. Henry doesn't. I say, "Because then we're going to be separated, like two planets traveling in opposite directions." Henry says, "You say this because you always have a fear of separation, but I have faith. Our relationship is tough. It can stand all this."

He has faith. I haven't. In everything I see a threat, an end, a break. In quarrels, in differences. I am afraid to expand *in my own way fully, only for fear of losing Henry.* I try to suit my rhythm to his and it does not work. Those days in New York when I lived out my adventures, I forgot Henry, but I thought too, Perhaps we'll never find each other again.

On the ship I suffer if I have to be alone. Distance between us— a long afternoon. It so happens Henry is not one who lives close to anyone, ever. He was always independent from his parents, his wives, never like Hugh or Rank, the kind that melts into the other.

When I have to listen to my desires, like the trip to New York, I suffer a horrible conflict with my feminine self, which is afraid to lose its personal happiness in the drive toward fulfillment. It turned out well for Henry; his experience with psychoanalysis increased his understanding. He really helps me now, when I get personal and emotional. That means that most of what I have done for myself has enriched both Hugh and Henry. I must remember this. But the woman in me wails and dreams of yielding, losing herself, giving up, surrendering.

Henry fights the diary. I say it has a simple human raison d'être. It is a friend. It makes me feel less alone. But Henry maintains it is harmful to me as artist. It is a search for truth. It kills my imagination. (Strange how I picked out the science of psychoanalysis, which could alone make me more truthful, more sincere.)

We straightened out so much between us on this trip. Henry says the figure I present to the world is still not the real me. It is an idealized me, the Christ in me. Henry talked to me about the mask.

He tries to expose the real me. Henry and psychoanalysis make me honest.

In New York I had an evening to myself once. I rushed through my dinner with excitement at all the ideas in my head. I was joyous to be alone with the diary. I was full of things to tell. It is *communion!*

I said to Henry, "All men's thinking is hypocritical because it is impersonal. Woman is closer to the truth because she is personal."

Rank consoles himself with *ideas*. I could not accept totality because it was perfection and I felt guilt at accepting the ultimate love. And I have learned the language of men; I use his interpretation, which seems bigger and which hurts less. Guilt. Anything you want. He doesn't know that it has all to do with body-love, touch, caress, mouth.

Strange, however, that since the sexual barrier has broken down in me (not entirely!), since I have learned to lie with strangers, learned to like bodies, strangers' bodies, since I am no longer the *"sauvage"* Virgin, everything bodily seems easier, Hugh and Rank too. There is less personal feeling and more of a general womb feeling. Men, not man. Henry wanted me to lose my totality (which means eyes, souls, sex turned toward Henry) and so he made the Whore. And now, for the sake of Rank's greatness of soul and mind, I could lie with him. And why speculate? That will never be recaptured. He has grown afraid to give himself. He will never give himself again.

Patients who say they were trying to think over the analysis. Henry said to one of them, "Don't think. This is an arithmetic that goes on in the dark."

Henry Mann said, "Henry has not got your skill or subtlety. I can see by his analysis of C. that he does not plumb the depths. He is more superficial."

None of his patients suffered at parting from Henry. There was no deep attachment. Henry is honest enough to observe this in contrast to the behavior of my patients, and to say, "Maybe I didn't give them analysis."

He does not want anyone to depend on him.

He was amazed at what I suffered when I left New York. There is a hardness in Henry, a lack of attachment and of love.

To a lot that Rank said I answered, "I don't know. I don't think anymore."

"I envy you," said Rank.

It seemed to me that in front of him I was the dissolved sensuous one, living only through feeling, not ideas. Perhaps it was this, my emotional life, that I saved from his analytic power. I minded his not letting things be. But I miss so much his strength when I am with Henry.

I would willingly have let explanations alone and tried physical contact. That was the way June fixed everything. It is a way of being happy, blind. The idea hurts. Awareness hurts. Knowing hurts. Lucidity hurts. Relationship hurts. Life hurts. But to flow, to drift, to live as nature, does not hurt. My eyes are closing. I am drifting, drifting into a world of sensation.

Henry is reading Emerson, Emerson, who moved me so much when I was sixteen. Henry is sobered by Emerson. I don't want Emerson now. I don't want the Arctic regions anymore.

Letter to Rank: You said you didn't want to write, but you didn't say you didn't want me to write. Only one letter, please, because there are things you must know, things that may wipe out all that hurt us. In the letter I wrote you from Montreal, the separation letter, I was utterly wrong. I didn't know it, didn't know it until I saw you a few days ago. I would never have separated myself from you, never, if you had not wanted me to give up my maternal loves. I never stopped loving you. When I saw you the other day I felt exactly and completely as before. Everything complete, whole. There was never a change in my love but a fear of your totality, which made me draw away physically, for a time. I don't know why I must tell you this. I know it is too late. I saw everything all at once, in your eyes. I felt that everything was as it was before, yet that it would never live again, because you no longer believed. Your eyes were soft, but you were ironic. Perhaps I'm wrong. My understanding is failing. That ultimate marriage, failing, I don't care anymore. I live blindly, like nature. Maybe we gave each other fatal wounds. You, when you said I used you, struck me fatally. I, when I thought we were not meant to be lovers. I was wrong. Maybe it is all too late. What I wrote you before was true—I didn't separate myself from you, I have not yet done so. I tried to. But perhaps you did from me. This letter is full of contradictions. You will understand them. It's between what I feel and what I think, just as I see every moment a contradictory you, between what your eyes said and what your words said.

Tuesday. When I first began this letter I felt that I was false, that it was based on a lie, but that I wanted so desperately to keep the man who thinks and feels as I do that I would do anything or say anything. I stopped in the middle of it to have coffee with Henry, a walk on deck, dinner, during which we had another intimate, personal talk, the kind that makes everything click again; Henry saying that there is so much latent in me, in Emerson's sense, so much that I don't express but that people feel; people feel all the mysteries, the secrets, the infinite layers. "Do you think I have character in the Emersonian sense?" I asked. "That's your greatest asset," said Henry. Then I read Emerson and was inundated in the purity and grandeur. I told Henry he must have a bigger over-soul than mine, because he was simple, not as I was, vain, and noisy, and glamorous. We read until midnight, then made love with the usual exact timing of the orgasm and spasm, such a harmony, then Henry very tenderly covered me, left me. I could not sleep. The rest of my letter to Rank was forming in my head. I turned on the light and finished it, feeling as I did a tremendous communion with Rank, right after my communion with Henry. Two currents flowing strongly.

Then today, after more sweetness with Henry, he acts very close, very tender, very near. I felt a surge of power. I want Rank on my own terms; I want Rank on the peaks, for drunkenness, not for daily living. I remembered walking down Fifth Avenue with Thurema on our last evening together and I saying, "We'll go to the top of the

Empire State Building, and I will leave you up there on the top of the world until I come back."

Drunkenness. Why did Rank want to capture this flame that I am and make it a wife? I'm not going to stay put anywhere, because of the many sides in myself, the layers and the latent mysteries, the things I am not yet.

Wholeness is not possible, because I can only be whole in relation to myself.

Henry and I talk about the personal in woman, man's superstructure, my fear of invention, my lies, my search for truth, for a superstructure in art. I think I am afraid of deformation in art because I feel I have this in life.

Those days when I am not only in love with the whole world, with man and woman, with my old loves, my past, with everybody I know, but also with myself, then the way I see myself is this: alive. I see and love the dancer, the light feet, the efforts at laughter, at lightness, the gravity, and my audacity. What I like best about myself is my audacity, my tricks, my courage, the way by which I am true to myself without causing much damage or pain. The fire in me, the way I excuse and embellish others, my faith in others.

What I hate is my vanity, my need to shine, my need of applause, and my sentimentality. I would like to be harder. I cannot make a joke, tease, make fun of someone, without regrets.

Landed in Paris with joy. Contented. Sun. Liberty. Peace. A Hugh who gives me peace, who never hurts me. Sweetness.

Hugh had planned a trip to Morocco. Morocco was a dream.*

---

* Anaïs Nin and her husband embarked at Marseilles on April 15, 1936, for Algiers and proceded from there by train to Fez. Two days later, from the hotel Palais Jamai, Nin wrote to Henry Miller, "Are you glad I came without the diary?" Her subsequent recollections, from which only a few paragraphs are included here, and which appeared in full in *The Diary of Anaïs Nin, Volume Two, 1934–1939*, were added to the original diary volume, apparently, after her return via Cádiz, Granada, and Seville. Some of her impressions were also conveyed to Miller in a number of postcards and short letters (See *A Literate Passion*, pp. 299–305).

Fez. I have just left the balcony where I stood listening to the evening prayer rising over the city. Overwhelmed by all I have seen.

Mystery and labyrinth. Complex streets. Anonymous walls. Secrecy of the houses without windows on the streets.

Fez is the image of my inner self. This explains its fascination for me. Wearing a veil. Full and inexhaustible. Labyrinthian. So rich and variable I myself get lost.

Fez is a drug. It enmeshes you.

The layers of the city of Fez are like the layers and secrecies inside of me. One needs a guide. Traveling, I add everything I see to myself. I am not merely a spectator. It is not merely observation. It is experience. It is expansion. It is forgetting the Self and discovering the self of affinities, the infinite, limitless worlds within the self.

Return to a passionate Henry, a Henry more loving than I ever remember him. Attentive. Awake. I so passionate, to my toes and fingertips. Last night incredible—that one can reach greater and greater physical paroxysms. I had my whole tongue in his mouth, as I never placed it, still a new abandon, just the whole tongue, which he kept between his teeth; and the sex, mouth, wide open, a tremendous climax. And a talk over dinner about the deepest difference between us: my *noblesse,* my pride, and his peasantness. He said it was something he could not understand, no more than I can understand his begging and self-humiliations. He brought this subject up. I was happy, because there were times when I felt Henry was trying to break down in me something that was integral, something he could not see, possess, understand, and at such moments I felt he was trying to destroy me. I begged him not to try to change me, familiarize, vulgarize me. During the trip, as during my stay with my Father, I had discovered a core which could not dissolve. I can yield to Henry to please him up to a point, I can be flexible, supple, understanding of him, but I have something I can't change which baffles him. Last night he said, with tears in his eyes, "But I see now it is a *noblesse,* something I will never have and cannot understand."

"As long as it is something you do not hate."

But it does arouse his antagonism, just as his crawling and clownishness humiliate me. At such moments I feel always compensated for all that Henry does not see (and therefore does not love); I come a little nearer to real happiness and closeness. Every now and then miracles happen. Henry *sees,* and then is moved to love.

I am in such a healthy mood. Have learned to turn away the tide of melancholic thoughts. The demons which devour me seem to be defeated. I came back from Morocco plump and peaceful, psychically speaking. I don't let myself brood. Less self-torture, anxiety, dwelling on cruel pictures; realizing it is all in the imagination. I don't know what has made me so healthy. I went to Morocco without the diary. Thoughts of defeat, dreams of suffering, emphasis on limitations, defeats, discord, all that has gone. I work with suggestion, too; *I guide my dreams.*

Seeing how Hugh suffers at night when he does not sleep helped me. I could see the exaggerations, dispelled by the day.

Joy. Hope. The present and future strength. No fears. No anguish. Laughter. Henry and I even laughed about my finding a condom in his pocket. I am aware of the strength of our bond. I can laugh at the small things. Laugh.

Désinvolte.

Henry so obviously in love. He teases me about New York. He dreamed of a ship sinking but he was holding me in his arms and had no fears. Hesitated to pick up the diary. It is linked to disease. A healthy diary possible? I don't know. Why was this return so different from the last? Because I finished with New York? Went to the limit? Exhausted my fevers? I am like a pregnant woman. Full and rich. Blossoming. My body too.

Health?

End?

J U N E   1 2 ,   1 9 3 6

O UTSIDE. OUTSIDE. FIRST THERE WAS FEZ OUTSIDE, the sun, the sea. Then there was Paris outside, and I on the streets, running between avenue de la Bourdonnais and Villa Seurat. There was the book, *The House of Incest,* arriving in huge bundles. There were letters to be written. The hairdresser. Turquoise-colored paste for the eyelashes. Betty to analyze. The new apartment chosen, on the quai de Passy by the Seine. Letters to Thurema, to whom Rank gave life. Henry to take care of, Henry passing through an air pocket, as he calls it.

Lost, dispersed, sandy, frivolous, disconnected.

There were injections for the whooping cough, and a lot of coughing at night, and fatigue, but fighting, fighting to keep healthy.

Then there were beautiful letters from Charpentier and Madame Charpentier on *The House of Incest.* No money from New York. Henry's taxes to pay. Shopping for the new apartment, which had to be modern at all cost, a psychic necessity. New surroundings, a clock made of seashells, white wool rugs from Morocco, and circulars mailed to friends all over the world, and new friends made, and dreams which predicted the things that happened. No clouds yet. No jealousy. Outside.

George Turner getting feverish again, disobeying my order (in New York): just once and then forget all about it. He and I, with his wife and Hugh, crowded in the elevator, pressed against each other, and great excitement through the red globules and the white. We feel each other through this excitement. In the taxi, his knee against mine makes me feel as in the swift elevator in the Barbizon Plaza shooting down, oh, so aware of this warm life between my legs while I walk. And so when he telephones and pleads I concede some meeting in the future.

Then the sun vanished somehow. It vanished. Our money ran out.

Stop mailing books and circulars. Outside. Walking outside. Red flags waving.

Newspaper headlines: *"C'est donc une réforme? Non. Sire. C'est une révolution." "Les grèves"* (Strikes). *"Grèves terminées." "Grèves nouvelles." "Grèves en cours."*

Outside it is all winter, and ugliness.

JUNE 13, 1936

FRAENKEL IS LEAVING FOR SPAIN BECAUSE HENRY is faithless to ideas, faithless to relationships. No continuity. Roger asking me for lunch. The Sakharoffs simpering, overaesthetic, too much art. Astrological dinner, looking for a Sun in Capricorn and meeting Marguerite Svalberg, writer, dreamer.

In Louveciennes, dressing up again in Chiquito's clothes, and Fraenkel so roused he stole a kiss.

Walking along the Seine, thinking of Rank's quickness. Rank's quickness. Shall I now write about him, to have the joy of reliving all this? Shall I? The Seine is flowing. I am in life. I want to stay in human life. Jonathan Cape rejected my Father novel.

When did the poison begin to work again, insidiously; when did the bright outer shell break? Choking, suddenly again in melancholy. Choking. Tired of helping Henry to live and to write. No. Not Henry. But the poison. Nameless.

Is this the agony of the diary? The last vestiges of the cancer? Healing? Scars? I find less to say about the malady. There. Diary. Doctor. Here I am.

It is seven-thirty and I am hungry and tired.

JUNE 5, 1936

*T*HERE IS GONZALO [MORÉ]. GONZALO IS A TIGER who dreams. A tiger without claws. Gonzalo and his wife, Helba Huara. Hearing about them, the Peruvians, the woman whose dance without arms inspired the dancer in *House of Incest*. Hearing that for two years she has been ill. Dreaming of her, pale, worn, instead of the brilliant dancer I saw, then seeing her enter Roger's studio, looking just as in my dream, and loving her immediately, and she me. Gonzalo is tall, dark, dark skinned, with animal eyes, coal black hair. He disturbs me, with his physical presence and his dreaming. Walking today I felt so warm between the legs, ready to fall into someone's arms, because of love of love and love of life and love of men, because I felt so warm between the legs.

Gonzalo. Or George. Always the unusual and the ordinary, and from the unusual, from Gonzalo, I fear suffering, as from Artaud and Eduardo. So I am outside again, dancing with Helba Huara, talking with Gonzalo, kissing Henry passionately, weeping because Henry is writing about June. Here is the pain, here is the malady. Loss. The fear of loss.

I feared losing Henry to Helba, to the Budapest woman he was going to see. When Budapest was being discussed one evening, when he was invited, I suffered so much I couldn't talk. I was sick with pain. The demon, there is the demon; diary, doctor, world, God, cure me, help me, save me. I suffer, humbly I suffer.

Because Henry is not whole, not an absolutist, he betrays everyone, even himself and God (he writes in his June book). Henry has only been sincere with me, which saved him also as an artist.

After one of our strong talks, Henry retired from a silly café life. He would come to everything alone, but so painfully, so awkwardly. Even today he begins his book on June with a laborious quotation from Abelard. I say quotations are literary. They are good only when dealing with ideas, not with experience. Experience should be pure, unique. You wouldn't say to me, "What I feel for you was put by Nietzsche in these words."

Henry fears to starve or to be sick just as much as I fear losing those I love.

When I am in a reverie among people, then my voice comes from another world. Henry has noticed the contrast between my warm, near, passionate talks (mostly with him) and my feeble, ineffectual, other-world attitude when there are several people and I lose interest.

I am grateful to the men who can make me a little drunk physically because they free me from my emotional and obsessive bondage to Henry. Pleasure.

J U N E   2 6 ,   1 9 3 6

*T*HIRTY, QUAI DE PASSY, PARIS 16ᵐᵉ. 7TH FLOOR.
    New background, created without hope or joy, without feeling of permanence or conviction of its rightness. But inevitably beautiful. Beautiful and modern, simple, summerlike, joyous. Orange walls, white wool rugs from Morocco, chairs of natural pale oak and cream leather, a huge table of pine wood with a surface sandblasted to look like pale sand on the beach. Luminousness, lack of formality, of sumptuosity.

Created during hot days and the torment of a period of separation from Henry, suffering from his inhumanness while he writes, and from jealousy.

Grateful to George Turner for his power *de me distraire de ma douleur.*

Yes. Turner. Since the night in his apartment when we danced together and felt a violent desire; then New York, where I did not want him because of Henry and Rank and yet yielded; then Paris, in the elevator and in the taxi, the drunkenness again; then, one afternoon, he came to see me and I felt shivery and desirous, and we lay on my bed but I was nervous and did not enjoy it.

But yesterday, yesterday he came here, and there was Madeleine in the apartment, the moving man, Chiquito in the next room; and George and I sat on the couch and felt surge after surge of the most violent desire and our mouths were opening with a craving to kiss and bite and his eyes were drunk and he said, "I felt excited at the very thought of coming here. God, you're the most exciting woman I've ever known, I'd like to take you right now, it's painful how much I want you. Let's imagine, then—open your legs, open your legs. Last night I imagined you, there, and I playing games, doing wild things together." We stood up by the window. "Can I slip my finger there, can I?" By the window he lifted my dress and felt the honey flowing. And the dizziness, the sense of falling, melting, yearning for mouth and sex.

"I'll show you the apartment for rent, you'll come and live here," I said. "Let's pretend." I ran down with him but the apartment for rent was occupied, so George and I stood in the very small elevator and I said, "Let's stay here and push the button to the eighth floor." And there we stopped. I had his penis in my hand, it was so hard, so big and a little wet already, and he took me right there in the little elevator, wildly, oh, wildly, as we went up and down several times, so now I never go up and down without feeling drunk with desire. And who is George Turner? It does not matter. Nothing matters but this drunkenness.

Today I saw Henry. I had taken my ring off. We had a scene. He threw himself on me with such love, such love, clutching and clinging, all my fears and doubts vanished. I told him I felt divorced, as during other cycles of his deadness. I asked him, begged him, to tell me the truth: Was everything all right between us? But how can I believe in Henry, when yesterday I could desire George voraciously and today could melt with love and passion for Henry?

Such a relief, the absence of love for George, the pure sensuality; such a refuge from pain. How I like George's words, erotic courting, lovemaking, his emotionalism, his feminine mobile face, passionate blue eyes.

Henry has been worrying about his age, agedness.

Strange how I danced with George about eight years ago and he charmed me (his charm was proverbial in the bank; his amorous career, the way women pursued him). But there was not that violent spark set off so that charm could become desire.

I seem to suffer more from the fear of losing Henry when I am betraying him. I suppose I expect punishment. I don't know. The night. I seek the night, to feel, to live, to know only by the route of the night, the senses, visions in the fire. Whenever Henry is removed by his creation, I plunge into night, sensuality, and it comes always *after* a dark moment of pain (as in New York) when I feel Henry to be all sand and sponge, without core, nothing to hold, an abyss, dissolution.

The nights of torture in New York, the night he began the June book, when I wept: "Hold on to me, Henry, hold me close, this will be hard for me to bear humanly. I love you in that absolute way you said did not exist anymore. I believe you gave yourself to me, as you wrote me that first time I was in New York." Exposed all my feelings, like: "Today I need to hear you say everything is all right between us. I need to hear you say it." Instead of saying it, Henry kissed me deeply, and after taking me he went on kissing me—this is where love begins.

JULY 3, 1936

OH, MY DIARY, WHAT AN OVERFLOW OF LIFE! ALL jealousy and pain dissolved in the richness of sensual living, desire for George. George and I dancing again at our housewarming party, dancing under dim paper lanterns to Tahitian music played by three Tahitians while their sister dances. The Seine flowing, shining, the Tahitians dancing and singing, orange walls, lantern light, and Gonzalo so magnificent, *le tigre qui rêve.*

Gonzalo, Inca Indian, coal eyes, hair, a beautiful face. I remember our first meeting, a shock at his beauty, darkness, intensity. Gonzalo, mystic, dreamer, pure; *noblesse,* grandeur, quality, depth, race. Gonzalo whispering while we dance, "Anaïs, Anaïs, you are so strong, so strong and so fragile, such strength. I fear you. What an influence you have on me. I fear you, Anaïs, the most beautiful music your Father ever produced was your voice, it is so strange, you're all sensitiveness, you're the flower of everything, you're stylization, the perfume of all things, how unique you are, Anaïs."

All this in Spanish. My blood hears Spanish. I hear Spanish through dark subterranean channels. Always I awaited Spanish love language. To hear him better my cheek touches his dark Indian cheek and I wish he would hold me as George holds me a moment later, holds me only to feel, to press me hotly, and we dance, sexes soldered, hot, burning, saying: Open your legs, God, I want you like hell, I could take you right here. Whore, whore, whore at last.

But dancing with Gonzalo is the dream. Anaïs, you have bruised your head a million times against the world's reality, you don't see the city, houses, men, as such; you see beyond.

"Anaïs, I have seen thousands of women but never one like you . . ."

Why, Gonzalo, don't you hold me as George does; why must always the body go one way and my dreams another? Gonzalo, I sit here tonight with your eyes like the night, a night without moon. I live in the night now like the moon I am, like the name of the moon I bear, I sit here with you because you have wrapped me in dreams. I fear you as much as you fear me. I fear the dream, the dream tearing me away from George, dancing hot, lascivious, erotic, mouth red, eyes languid. George jealous of Gonzalo, always emotional, erotic, George pinching me, clutching me, breathless, sick with desire. Gonzalo jealous too, intuitive, seeking me, finding me dancing in the darkest corner with George, the Seine glittering, flowing, the lights laughing, people dancing, kissing out on the balcony. Allendy watching, de Maigret, Henri Hunt, Marguerite Svalberg, men, women, handsome women, soft sensual faces, sensual ambiance, everybody sensual, thanking me today for a beautiful, beautiful party, like a nightclub night, just night on the balcony, poetry, Gonzalo the lion with the pride.

The next day Henry seems diminished, and with him the constant pain of his destructiveness, for now I know Henry destroys everything he loves, eats into it. If I am poetry and illusion, as June was poetry and illusion, he eats, he eats into it with his realism, he destroys, he has to destroy, to eat. It is subtle, I don't know how it happens. I live again, alone, with Helba, Gonzalo, illusion again, poetry. I begin to flower anew—new creations, a white cape I flaunt while the revolution growls around me—there must be more poetry, more and more.

Gonzalo. From the first, his voice calling me. What tenderness in his voice, what fervor. The first time we met he said to Henry, "Your wife is wonderful, marvelous." And I was afraid as one is of beauty. My house like the inside of a seashell, with the cream-white and the pale orange, with the luminousness. With Gonzalo everything unspoken, he feels all I am, no talk, but waves and waves of mystic knowingness. Dreamer. Dreamer. He had gone to sleep with my book next to him, read it over and over again; like a drug to him, he said, *The House of Incest*.

Circles. Twenty years seeking this moment, this moment when I lie down on a hotel bed in Cádiz without a diary because the flow of the poisoned waters of regrets and recapitulations is arrested. Diary as a mirror, diary as assurance, diary in place of talk, now at rest as I am resting on the bed of a hotel in Cádiz with nothing to ruminate, nothing to chew over. Life passed as I passed through Fez, leaving no shreds. The sun is on the water, my eyes and my mouth are open, my body is open, I breathe and I love without need to say *I am breathing, and I am loving*. When I was caught in the dark cellars of the cathedral as a child I was afraid of being shut in within the walls of my own terrors; I was bound and bandaged by my hurt, like a mummy, because of a twenty-year calvary of doubts. A long circle of struggle with a crippled self.

In living sensually there is only pleasure, in loving everybody rather than One. Gonzalo, you are One. What will you ask of me? The day George could give me drunkenness like passion's drunkenness I was grateful. Gonzalo, have you come again to remind me of love when I am a whore, when I have slit my skirts, made a new little jacket out of red Moroccan cloth, when I want to reach for nothing that is not within reach, no moon, no stars? Gonzalo, you haunt me. In Spanish you said, "Could you ever mix with anyone who was not of your blood?" He talks of blood because of the Spanish words we speak.

J U L Y 5 , 1 9 3 6

APARTY. A STUDIO. THE TAHITIAN MUSICIANS. Many people I cannot see or hear. Gonzalo taller than all, dark eyes like infinite caverns, brilliant, Gonzalo whose golden brown arms are bare, Gonzalo still talking in my ear, "Anaïs, what a force you are, spiritual and vital, you are all wrapped in myth and legend, you are like a whip on me, when I saw you I felt a shock, you arouse my pride, for the first time I feel awake, I want to *be,* Anaïs."

Dancing together, but without sensuality. The dream enveloping us, ensorcelling us. Peru. His hacienda. The Indian culture, legends, the distance between people. The crushing immensity of nature. The beauty of his body, the smell of his hair. Below the studio, down the stairs, there is a room. When I go down Gonzalo comes down; we are pushed, moved, blind. I go down and we stand facing each other, I saying Hugh will take Helba home (Helba had asked to be taken home). "I'll take her," says Gonzalo, but he does not move, he looks at me. "Don't go," I say, and the magnetism pulls, pulls body and heads together. I say, *"No se vaya, Gonzalo,"* standing very near, and he looks fixedly at me and kisses me, kisses me. Silence. I run upstairs. He comes and opens his arms to dance. Passion mounting, a passion light with dreams. We go to the balcony, out in the night, this is the night, a night pierced with a million stars as in the tropics; we stand overhanging the river, the night, the stars, the studio behind us, and kiss drunkenly, fiercely, wholly, he presses me against the wall, passion pierced with lights and stars, passion bleeding poetry, passion in ecstasy of recognition, kisses that rise, his head falls, his long black eyelashes in my mouth, his mouth, his body, *mi chiquita, mi chiquita, dime cuando nos vemos.*

I had thought once, in the studio, when he left me after he had talked like a song from the Incas, talked in a dream without moving: Are you going to remain on the edge of the night, a dream? I won't let you, there will be fewer words, Gonzalo, your body is eloquent, the dream intact. But kisses, kisses like rain and lightning, kisses and eyes proudly holding, opening, gazing deep through the body. I took his body, reached out for it, reached out as a woman reaches, by opening, opening, electric, Anaïs, Anaïs, *chiquita mia, chiquita mia,* deep the bowels of the night and high the dream above the world, thick the clouds and light the air, heavy the river flowing carrying fallen stars, myths and legends, minerals and cactus.

"With cruelty," he said, "with cruelty you can whip me into action, with cruelty. We are so old we cannot reach out for the food."

Alone in my apartment, we continued kissing the next day.

At night through the streets, kissing, smelling. "Anaïs, you drive a man mad. I feel drugged. I feel as I did coming out of the opium dens, blinded, drugged. How your mouth draws me, and what a beauty you have, Anaïs, your gestures are incredible, to see how you move and walk gives me ecstasy, it takes centuries of race to make a body like yours, you obsess me, haunt me, I am so full of you I can't do anything else, I can't think of anything else. Do you know the seven mystical circles—seven circles had to be broken through to reach the core. I am reaching you slowly, slowly. I want to possess your soul before I possess your body. I want you all to myself. When we meet finally it will be tremendous."

I am ensorcelled by his beautiful dark face, his vehemence, his poetry. He creates as we walk, between kisses, a white passion, which he subtly, perversely intensifies by denial. He won't take me.

Through the ugly city we walk blindly. It is the middle of the night and we are sitting by the river. For the first time I feel his desire, but it awes me too. Too beautiful, too exalting. I am awed, the honey flows between my legs, but the burning is high in the sky. We are so drunk on kissing, we reel through the streets. His bare chest golden brown, the softness of his outline, no bones showing, yet he is lean, the heavy curled black hair with some white in it, the eyes more brilliant than the Arabs', intense, hypnotic, animal; the mouth not sensual, delicate; the brow high and noble; grandeur and nobility, like a lion. Incredible to me, all that I could desire physically, and his vehemence, head thrown back, poetry pouring. I cannot believe he is mine, I cannot believe his words, they are too beautiful, like the marriage in India—the lover woos for days, approaches the bride so delicately.

Filled, filled with Gonzalo, in a dream, floating, drugged, I went to Henry, whom I did not want to see. As soon as I saw him it was as if nothing had happened. Henry, mellow, at work, in love, rushing out to meet me while I was shopping, because it had begun to rain. Henry standing me up against a ladder and taking me deliriously, and taking the climax of a whole night of kissing Gonzalo. I untrue to the exaltation, on earth again, for a few moments, incapable of wholeness, yet with Gonzalo in me. Henry could still enter my body so simply and destroy the dream for a moment.

A few hours later I meet Gonzalo. He says, "I telephoned you at twelve, the maid said you had just left. I felt I knew where you were going, you went to Villa Seurat, Miller has a hold on you sensually. Oh, Anaïs, but I want you all to myself."

So lies begin.

He was so much like Joaquin: the pride, the intransigence, the renunciation. When he is thirsty he places a glass of water in front of him and does not drink it. "We have a world to create together." I had been yearning for the night. Here is the night, in Gonzalo and drugs. I feel, as he talks disconnectedly and feverishly, that he is weaving strangeness around me, perversities, and I feel helpless. I feel caught in his magic game of waiting and reaching frenzy. He is too old, he says always, to live in an ordinary way; too old, too subtle, to reach directly for things. He leads me into dark ways, adds perfume, torture, denial, exaltation.

*Letter to Eduardo:** About myself I can tell you that this man, the noblest, most magnificent, serious, dedicated and unconditional man, has rescued me from an ordinary life, from being a prostitute. He holds my entire soul in his golden hands. He keeps me in a state of ecstasy, as if I were taking communion. He doesn't want my body until he can possess my soul. He is subtle, deep, intense, and he loves me madly, with a madness I have never seen before, a mystical madness with no danger of dying because it is a mystical and human passion, as I feel it. I can't write or think or eat or sleep. I am being transformed, lifted up.

He searches for the Anaïs who used to be, one who is not common, one who has pride and purity. He struggles against Henry, against reality, against everything that has done violence to my nature. He wants me to be a passive woman. He dominates me, Eduardo. This man of my own race dominates me.

Gonzalo, I write to be with you, as when I breathe you in, when I breathe in your breath, your flesh, your hair. At first I didn't see you, not with the eyes of my soul. The eyes of my soul were closed, Gonzalo, when you came. Men had bodies. Life was simple and physical and without music. You were more beautiful than the rest. But I did not see you. I felt you darkly, Gonzalo, to be with you tonight, and our insanity. Walking the streets, kissing in full daylight. The world destroyed, fallen.

"Anaïs, you were not aware of your spiritual force. If I could have you here, tonight, I wouldn't take you, that is not how one penetrates a woman like you. I want to penetrate the deepest part of your soul."

---

* In Spanish in the original.

Gonzalo, I want always to remember your words, because you spoke like my own soul; you spoke for both of us.

"Anaïs, I have loved you since the first day." Even in the garden at Louveciennes he was saying, "You love Miller," and it was true until that evening when we stood by the river and I looked at him, deep into his Arab eyes, asking, What do my eyes say, what do my eyes say now?

Not writing, breathing in his life-giving words. He would not take me simply, directly, that was desecration. He built a web of words, he breathed, poured out magic, kissed me, held me, let the honey flow, undressed me, knelt before me, adored me, worshiped me, ensorcelled me, but did not take me.

All alone in Louveciennes, in the Louveciennes bedroom, the end of Louveciennes, Louveciennes dying out in the splendor of a new passion. Louveciennes dying, the wood rotting, the rain falling, the ghosts creaking. The odor of age, the threadbare red velvet cover; and Gonzalo the Indian, blindingly beautiful like a dream of Spain and Arabia, with his head between my legs, worshiping.

"Your skin was made for me. Your body is the loveliest in the whole world. That place at the root of your nose, the space between your eyes—I would burn down all the museums for that line of antique beauty. There is such beauty in your every gesture, in every line of your body. Anaïs, you make me weep with happiness. The warmth of your skin, such tenderness, such ardor."*

When I walked naked he was in ecstasy. All night, all night we dreamed. He slept a moment. Awoke desirous, slipping into me and out, swiftly, pushed away his desire, our fever mounting, words like caresses, caresses like words, like drugs. His desire again, renunciation, fever, the dream, ecstasy.

He broke in me the false roles, that of active courting which Henry asked of me, his Spanish-lover instinct opposed activity in the woman. I wept with joy, I understood instantly. I found all I was before Henry, the passivity, the yieldingness. I wept with joy at his

---

* Largely in Spanish in the original; the text alternates freely between Spanish and English.

subtleties, all that was lost in my life with Henry, the voluptuousness of the dream rising, smoke and fire burning, two lovers now, not I the lover; two lovers answering each other.

I close my eyes and I see his, intense and visionary. Anaïs, this is you, we are in Notre-Dame cathedral, the organ is playing, I am weeping, purple clouds are falling from the windows. I am seeking *you*, angel and demon. In the darkness we kiss, his face a dream before me, so grave, mouth delicate, not sensual.

What is the blood he stirs? Old race blood, blood of my past, the pride of my Father, the *noblesse* of Joaquin, the beauty of royalty. What is this he stirs, my soul, my God, my purity, and the honey is flowing. I told him, in Louveciennes, for three days it has been flowing and it delighted him so he is still laughing, remembering, *mi vasito de miel,* the honey he won't drink. And now I have understood, and I am tasting the waiting, the deepening, we cannot stay a day without seeing each other, but we are traveling through a kind of purification by fire, through the seven magic circles, to the center of our beings, traveling slowly, strangely. Talking little through the drunkenness of our love, breathing hair, smelling skins.

"How you have filled my life, Anaïs! The other night was a night of love, the most beautiful of my entire life. I want to watch you live. What a wonder you are, *mi chiquita.* Your body a marvel of mystery. You know how to stir passion. I cannot think or write or eat. Such drunkenness, *chiquita.* I am falling. I can't think of anything but you." His voice, his voice is low, heavy, dark, rich. Indian smoothness, quick gestures, brow so high, a black heavy curl which comes behind his ear evokes a storm of desire in me. The smoothness of his neck, his golden-brown chest, his leonine head. Goodness and nobility, the quick intelligence, alive, burning.

Writing to breathe him in. A sense of fatality, of extreme; a fear I never had that now, now there was madness. Madness to kiss on that balcony where Hugh or Helba might have seen us, and others. Madness to always dance together, talk together. I can smell him on my fingers. His flesh, as he smelled me drunkenly in the cathedral, with the incense. I cried to be so naked, so stripped of my hardness, of my human life, the labyrinth of my life retraced to find roots, in incense.

What madness, where will it take us? I was not afraid of anything while I was the lover and the one with open, visionary eyes, but now that two pairs of eyes are burning, and that there are two of us chanting, smelling, adoring, in words, prayers, with sex and vision, body and dreams, where will it take us? Where? Where?

Letter to Mother: I sound a little mad, but I'm just very happy, that is all. I was in Notre-Dame yesterday afternoon and I heard vespers, and I cried and found my old soul again. I don't know where I was. I had found it once in the hospital, you remember. I found it again yesterday. I stood there in the church and cried and today I am happy. It is all so good, we are so quiet, Hugh and I, the house is sweet, the cat is so funny, and we have bicycles and will go to the country soon, but there is no sun at all, no heat, and we were not able to rent Louveciennes because of that, nothing has happened. I will pay your rent tomorrow, and let Joaquin read this too, it is for him, it is what they call the modern style in writing, with all the phrases running close together, I am doing it to make you laugh, because you like surrealism so much. I hope Alida liked my book, you will like it too, someday, I don't know when, when you realize it is all a dream and that dreams are necessary to life, and you know not all our dreams are holy, are they, you had some which were not so holy, our dreams are not holy but that does not hurt and does not change the fundamental soul, maybe someday you will believe so firmly in my fundamental soul you won't mind my crazy little fancies, you won't frown, you will just listen and smile as I imagine you smiling and listening when you are far away, I never imagine you cross or displeased with me, or disillusioned, when you are far everything is sweet and as it was before and always when I was wholly devoted to you, as you were to your children, and this devotion has remained even though my life split up and I live with Hugh, only you did not believe it so much and you sort of pushed me away a bit, scolding me for things I did which were different from the things I did as a girl, but fundamentally, *Mamacita,* nothing has changed, if one is good, nothing ever changes, I love you so much.

July 14, 1936

I LOVE ALL THE WORLD, ALL THIS EARTH, ALL men—this is my passion and my death, into darkness with Gonzalo, darkness, fighting against possession and invasion, seeing all my life at once, and little shreds of me out of his hands yearning back toward Henry.

Henry and I sitting together after I read seventy-eight pages of his book in which he states the most tragic of all truths: "Life does not interest me, what interests me is what I am doing now (this book), which is parallel to it, of it and yet beyond it. . . . With June's faith as it was, I should have become a god."

Now that he has lost her, he loves her with words; when she was there he hated all she was, he destroyed, attacked her, as he insidiously diminishes me by an absence of worship, by not holding; no present act of love but a perverse pushing away, losing.

I said, "Henry, I have been going away from you. I felt death setting in through your deromanticizing of our relationship. It was too big. I don't want it smaller. There is something in you that is perhaps not incapable of love but that destroys what it loves. I knew this, and I thought I could be stronger than it, but you have harmed me. I have only begun to live again lately, to get my strength back, from being loved. In life I have found what you denied me, something too subtle to define, a death you spread by loving always aside, elsewhere, by not being whole."

Even while he writes about June he cannot be true to that passion;

he spreads and loses himself into other women, other desires, like too wide a river. He never loved her actually in life, in the present, in reality, but only in his loss and through pain. The truth is so stark, and all the perversities of our love choking me, my own sufferings, my concessions, forgiveness, faith, giving, and Henry negative, passive, unreal, and real only in the prosaic, and I giving up poetry, seeking it elsewhere, crying out for the lack of it in him. No soul in Henry, though two women gave him their souls. I don't know.

We sat very silent and Henry said, "I know there is something very wrong with me, some perversity."

It is I, and June, talking out of the tomb he makes of the present moment, where passion is demanded, and both June and I went to receive love elsewhere and cried for a Henry unborn, the lover in words, the poet crying out to us only after we died.

We sat so silent and one tear fell out of my eyes, one blue tear because of the blue-painted eyelashes, one blue tear at the exhaustion of my pain, my aloneness in Henry. "One blue tear, how funny," I said. "Look at it. We won't be sad. I don't know if it is the end. I love you, Henry, but I am going away from you, to rebuild the dreams and myself, which I lost; ecstasy. Write to me, care of the Dream. That is where I am, laughing. And we won't be sad; perhaps my power will be stronger than yours, yours for death of life. I am going out to find the life you strangely eat into, by your hatreds, denials, and renunciations."

I stood at the top of the stairs. Henry was laughing hysterically. Henry crazy. Henry in fissures. Henry in fragments, all slits, losses, dispersions, laughing, then holding me, kissing me. No, I am dead to you, Henry, Gonzalo is waiting for me. He knows I have been with Henry all afternoon. I let him know, malice and cruelty, because I love him one moment less, one degree less, one breath less than he loves me. Henry is kissing me and I fall into water, obscurity, disso- lution, marriage in a void, marriage in dissolution, the dissolution of Henry, water, desire, I fall, he carries me to the couch, he is all desire, he cannot love, he desires, his sex is hot and erect, that is how he loves, his sex hot and erect and his fingers soft, but I am thinking of Gonzalo waiting and I do not respond, I am passive.

Gonzalo almost kneels when he sees me: "Anaïs!" Almost kneels, broken with anguish and jealousy. And I am in fragments. Oh, Gonzalo, make me whole. A part of me keeps crying for what was unfulfilled with Henry, for what Henry was not, which you are so divinely.

We could not be alone, we had to be with the others, and it was torture, our desire to touch each other, I felt him like a magnet, his eyes made me dizzy. I couldn't eat. I was sick with desire, and because I flashed my coral earrings, because I looked tenderly at Pita, at "Puck," as I call him, so as not to look at Gonzalo before Hugh and Helba, and because Pita, as we went out, grabbed my arm and made me dance through the streets so lightly, Gonzalo left us, dark and angry, and was drinking all night while I yearned and waited for him. Tortured himself for no reason, hated me, wanted me to be seen by no one, touched by no one.

Rushed to him this morning. Gonzalo, will you have the strength to make me whole for you? Rank failed, so many others failed.

In the heart of his pain he says, "Walk before me, let me see you walk."

"¡Que agonia, chiquita!" He talks of renunciation, of suffering. Is all passion suffering, possession, jealousy? He is shocked at my recklessness, my sacrilegiousness; on Joaquin's bed we lie, it is all love to me, love is all one, Joaquin, my Father, Henry, love, sex, purity, the dream, all one, the same fire, the same white heat, the same despair.

June and I both thought no one could take us away from Henry. If Henry had grasped, enclosed, if Henry had walked the streets crying, "Your voice envelops me, Anaïs, I drown in it; talk so that I may hear you, move your head, laugh, oh Anaïs, I fight against your voice and it breaks me." If Henry had fought off the other men, knelt, adored, defended—but Henry runs like sand and water: "Never cared enough, it made life painful, just didn't care a hang." Crying out with love only when we tortured him, and now I must torture Gonzalo. He is crying for it, he creates me, he invents for me what I must do.

Before I went to Henry he suffered, and so I was impelled to go to Henry and let him know at what time, and before his suffering I want to laugh, a sense of power of a demon driving me, of houses burning, flesh poisoned. He is tainted, he is tortuous—that is where I could not trust him, the joys, all our joys had to be twisted into acute pain, the waiting, the caresses, the desire denied, the labyrinth, clarity in flashes, Gonzalo and I walking over the bridge, the wind blowing my hair, Gonzalo in ecstasy, Gonzalo watching the whiteness of my face in the semidarkness, Gonzalo seeking all that I was before Henry came, the subtleties, leading to the sharp, simple, sensual fever world I fell into, with George Turner, before Gonzalo.

Yet the sensual fever is in me; I dream erotically, I dream the contrary of my life with Gonzalo. I dream of big men taking me, and I coming many times; I dream of bestiality and I awake with the taste of Gonzalo on my lips, wanting him; the world of flesh seems infinitely beautiful because I am leaving it so swiftly on the wings of Gonzalo's gold-brown flesh.

Life a dream, a nightmare, a dance, a fire, and a death, life and death, Gonzalo and I kissing in a frenzy of passion—"Anaïs, I've never been in love this way before, it's like a wound"—and Henry and I are lying in the dark without desire, and I am weeping hysterically, something has died between us. "I can't live without passion, Henry. Help me to separate myself from you. I will take care of you forever." Henry stunned and silent. Henry and I walking and Henry saying in a broken voice, "You are the only one. I thought you were the mother but it is more than that, life is without meaning since you told me about Gonzalo, I have lived through a nightmare, there is something so strong, something eternal."

Henry using the word *eternal,* I could laugh. Henry using the word *eternal,* Henry's love ring off my finger since the night Gonzalo and I sat by the river. Henry and I kissing without desire but with a love that poisons my joys, a dying love flashing through my dream with Gonzalo.

Gonzalo and I walking drunkenly, kissing, through the rue de la Gaîtée and I saw the hotel where I first went with Henry, and I walk alone crying over the death of our passion, and when I see Gonzalo my being trembles from how far we have come toward each other, how lost we were, Gonzalo drinking, destroyed by a woman he didn't love, drifting, and I denying my real self and living out of the dream, colliding with bodies, only bodies in a warm sensual world of utter loneliness.

How far we have come with mystery; caresses came before words, and now we wake from the drug of our kisses, we hear each other talk as we dreamed of the other's soul, and I cannot believe, I cannot believe in this collision of spirits, laughter and knowingness enclosed in the godlike body of Gonzalo, Gonzalo's half-finished phrases penetrating me so subtly, voluptuously. Gonzalo virtuoso of words, by all the multiple routes of sensibilities, nuances, senses, and music, his conception and understanding of me before the dissonances, his repudiation of the dissonances, reinstatement of the dream.

We are lying before Roger's door, Roger is out. We lie on the doorsteps, waiting, in the dark. He kisses me frenziedly and I fall back as I would when Henry asked me, and as Henry asked me, I slip my hand to unbutton him, but Gonzalo shrinks back, offended. Gonzalo in sex is a man, willful, proud, and leader; he will put my hand there when he wants it, and I remember the efforts I made, the violations, to please Henry. I had to be the lover. Now Gonzalo is the lover. Gonzalo gives to me, rules, ordains, creates, woos, worships; I have to be proud and receive. I *have to be*. He is giving, creating; he made the pauses, the detours, the subtle detours which increased our dream, created the legend, the night around it, the depths, the depths.

I am crying with joy. "Anaïs, your pride, I want your pride, the pride in you, you have aroused mine." I, too, desecrated myself, did violence to myself. His marvelous *pudeur* I had. I have not yet seen all of his body, and like his unfinished phrases, the mystery hovers, and the music swells us to ecstasy, nights of ecstasy, expansion into the infinite, flowers opening but no petals falling, silences, behind the beautiful ancient face, the face of centuries of poetry, lies a world, an immense world, like the one in me, of overtones. *"Quiero vivir, que impulso de vida me das, no sabes lo que eres para mi."* (I want to live, what a drive to live you give, you don't know what you mean to me.) He falls into wells of sadness, *"Porque te quiero demasiado, chiquita. I love you too much."*

Both of us feel the lovesickness, the pain, yes, the devouring fever, and the languor and the yearning, the unquenchable yearning, so deep the wound made of penetration, how he has enveloped me, tuned me—what a musician, waiting for the perfume, the hour, the song.

Fatigue. Bowed down with the marvelous. At moments I could not believe. Looking up at his face against the sky as we walked, listening to him, I could not believe. I am dreaming. I am dreaming this face, this body, and behind this face, this body, a knowingness, a subtlety, a dream of soul and spirit, a delicacy of texture, poetry, and music, and fervor.

An ardor greater than Henry's or my Father's, a passionate tenderness, sum of feeling, of deep love, of vibrancy, sensuality at one with love. "What magic, Anaïs. I lose myself in you, in your eyes, in your body so beautiful, so beautiful, your brow so pure, and eyes that are not pure, your face, the face of a Spanish woman of antiquity, the beautiful line of your shoulders, and the way you move your head. There are two Spanish ways of moving the head, one common, in the style of girls of Madrid which I don't like, the other, the way you move yours, with pride."*

JULY 21, 1936

BURNING LIKE TORCHES. WHITE NIGHTS. OUT OF sleep, voluptuous embraces. He only took me a few nights ago, Saturday, on Joaquin's bed, after arousing us both and denying the climax each time, all through the night.

Joys pierced with pain over Henry. Henry's faith and suffering. Henry still wearing his ring and saying, "I have no fear. Our relationship is beyond everything, it's eternal." And I had said in the dark, "Gonzalo and I love each other." But when Henry began to suffer, to be pale, his blue eyes worn, his mouth tortured, his voice breaking, I began to retract: I had not given myself. I was waiting. I thought the physical bond was dead between Henry and me. For days we

---

* In Spanish in the original.

suffered together at the thought of separation. Today, with breaking voice, Henry said he wanted to believe in this unbreakable bond between us, that we had tried to leave each other free, but it was hard. Oh, so hard. He too had been jealous, but he didn't want to destroy our love with jealousy, as I tried not to. At this moment he is suffering, whereas I have accepted what he honestly admitted as superficial infidelities.

Seeing Henry walk toward me moves me in the womb again, with an immense tenderness, but I don't desire him sexually. It was like a sensualized mother passion. I have not that feeling for Gonzalo. He is man to me, mate. I don't know. Twin perhaps. He leaves his phrases unfinished because I know. He is this dream which I express only in writing. He looks it, breathes, talks it, lives it. What a torture this burning which he will not allow to be sensual; every caress carries a meaning, every kiss is a communion, every possession comes out of the sparks of knowingness. *Quiero sublimar todo, subir!*

Ascension. My body is destroyed, on fire, no health or peace, but dizzy heights of emotion.

Last night, all night, honey flowing. The love and seriousness and depth in his eyes made me pause with awe. Gonzalo, I have never felt this I feel now for anyone. It's not the instinct burning but a kind of mystical passion; our bodies vibrate in its hold, vibrate, vibrate, burn, melt. Such an outpour of love, tender love, I have never seen. He burns my skin with his kisses. We lie for hours in a soft dream of kisses and mysterious introspection. He remembers every scene, every word, every mood of our meetings.

We parted at dawn, exhausted, hungry. Slept only one hour and a half, thinking I was too tired to feel anything, but when I left Henry at three-thirty (I have not been able to respond to his caresses, evading them) the hunger and pain filled me, my impatience rose. Gonzalo had begged me to see him. We rushed into each other's arms as if we had not seen each other for days. "I am crazy," he said, "I am crazy." He closes his eyes, melts into me. We are like a drug to each other. We get deeply sad when we awake.

All my life has stopped dead. Letters lie unanswered, my dresses are torn, *House of Incest* gathering dust, friends forgotten, analysis thrown overboard, life a lulling poison, the mind inactive. *"Yo persigo lo irreel,"* said Gonzalo. "I pursue the unreal." I am back in my original climate, the unreal but not the disease.

The mind in him, the subtleties, reveal themselves more and more behind the dreamy, brooding face. Aristocratic, bohemian. When his long hair is combed and he walks proudly, he looks like a king. Hair loose, kissing wildly, he looks like an Indian. Eyes burn with a sacred darkness. His skin, his strange sex, so dark. His *pudeur*—never shows his body naked, never lets me touch him, take him. Tenderness because I cut my toe; bandaged, washed. The same toe bleeding before a Henry helpless and inert.

I begged Henry today, "When you're so utterly passive, negative, you're not true to yourself."

"I have been disgusted with my inadequacy in life," said Henry. He talks of how June killed his faith and gave him such a terrible shock: "When I see pain again, I'm paralyzed, fatalistic. I can't act." When he thought he had lost me to Gonzalo he could only be silent in the dark.

I see that when I hurt him he loses his strength, his faith in himself, and that seems more imperative to re-create, so instinctively I do it and then I ask myself, What am I going to do? I have only three evenings, and I have promised Gonzalo not to go to the Villa Seurat, and I have promised Henry to come, and nobody will understand that compassion-love for me is as strong as my passion-love.

To Gonzalo I have not lied. He is too intuitive. I have told him, "My passion for Henry has died." I have told him whenever I have seen Henry.

My passion for Gonzalo at the same time arouses me so completely that it makes me hysterically sensitive and aware of all my loves, sensually in touch with everybody, and at the same time more isolated and proud in the dream (poor George, he fell out, he belonged to the ordinary world), but the well of love, sympathy, flows more deeply, overflows. I'm too rich. I must give. It isn't faithlessness to Gonzalo, God, I don't know; it's what flows out of my close, intimate, individual collisions, something beyond the personal and the two-ness which spills over the world; it's an abundance, the music and the love which brim over after Gonzalo and I meet and touch with burning bodies and burning minds, trailing after and around us haloes, and sparks falling over all the other ones, Hugh and Henry.

Gonzalo's face. Night is coming, in which I can bury myself with him, in sleep and secret connections. How I love his sadness, brooding, sudden humor. His sly and subtle way of calming Helba's jealousy. At one moment Helba wanted to kill me. Gonzalo was in a panic. His voice broke. "Anaïs, I'm so afraid for you, oh Anaïs, *mi chiquita.*"

He dreams of Spain, where walls, conventions, customs, laws would have made our meetings more difficult. He dreams of tortuous routes, renunciations; the direct route is criminal, he marvels that with the freedom I have had, I've kept that fervor of the Middle Ages, of secret, contained, inhibited lives, a fervor spilled and dispersed in modern life. These continuous chains of kisses with Gonzalo, his face against the stars or a café wall . . . Gonzalo. Hymns of love to the lover of lovers, the lover of women's dreams, possessed by his love, unable to sleep, to rest, tense with awareness, fear of loss, jealousy, worship. Writing for me as an act of love, a caress; the form of his body feminine in its softness of contour, his eyes when I walk toward him so piercing, visionary, and yet blind with emotion.

JULY 23, 1936

*T*HE FLOW BEARS ME ON, AND HE CRIES OUT IN agony because I have seen Henry: "I have to have you all to myself. I have lacked the strength to tear you clear out of your life; heavy chains hold you down, your charity and your humanness." Jealousy tortures him darkly, disproportionately; he twists sensuality, does not obey the desire which flares; lets it burn and die, returns by devious routes when I am quiet and feverless, does not stand naked with pride and naturalness, only out-of-sleep instinct burns pure, yet tense; and my own naturalness is shattered, I cannot respond, the honey is wasted, the night is full of thoughts; he seeks the night, out of pure sensuality rises the dream also, that he cannot see; so passion does not come as an explosion, a fusion, but as a struggle and a seeking, and it is bathed in dark, fierce jealousies; a blue mark on my thigh plunged him into despair. The evening I spent with Henry he was crazy with grief. I telephoned him: "Don't suffer, Gonzalo," and afterward he said, "Suffering was good, it makes me rise. Anaïs, what a thirst I have for sublimation."

All the sweetness of the earth calls me, invites me. Henry slips into the honey with such simplicity, takes the palpitation of live flesh; the womb beats with life and rhythm, as natural as breathing, the flesh lies still and full, the dream rises out of fulfillment, not out of Gonzalo's monk resistances, punishments and denials; the dream rises out of simplicity, and I see it all, tearing me, earth and sky.

Gonzalo with a thirst for danger, death, heroism. Out of our nights his energy is born, and he wants revolutions, Communism, action. Born king of the world, he wants not creation but the drama. Gonzalo, I'll go with you to Spain, then. I'll fulfill my early obsession with Joan of Arc. I'll die in blood and drama with you; but I am sad, and in the middle of the night, while I am talking about my Father, I say, "I want grandeur, yes," and Gonzalo says, "It was heroic; there is heroism in your life."

I close the shutters of the apartment. I hate the day. I lie in the opium den of Gonzalo's words, eyes, fever, and feelings. Into my dreams he throws Communism, and at first I didn't understand, and I was wounded, to be thrust back into the holocaust, the life to be burned out, to be thrust out of the sweetness of sensual life, to be enjoyed. Acrid joys again, sacrifice, communion, sin, confession, sacrilege.

Can I weigh him down?

I meet him dancing, with a joy that does not flame between the legs; the world is shedding blood, the faggots are piled high for Joan of Arc, for Gonzalo, god of terrible greatness, for whom life is not enough, ordinary life, who lives beyond caresses, beyond man and woman, who lives to deny life and reassert Christ. What a taste of Catholic distilled bread upon my lips; where is the heavy warm workman's bread Henry gave me? Lying at Henry's side, gentle, poisoned by my flight into the stars with Gonzalo, tossing, fever of great spaces, of other immeasurable ecstasies, rise and die in the flesh!

"*No mires a nadie.* Do not look at anyone but me," says Gonzalo. "Let no one open all the little buttons of your red jacket, be all mine." Yet it is the moment when I choose to be in love with the world, when the death of the revolutionaries in Spain wounds me like the death of the flesh I love, when I feel vibrations through all my senses at the bodies and faces I see on the streets; it is the moment when I am sensitive and open to every leaf, cloud, wind gust, the eyes around me, bodies, when I see most clearly the beauty of Pita, the delicacy of Henry's skin, the poetry in [Conrad] Moricand, the adolescent purity in Hugh, when I dissolve with passion and tenderness beyond Gonzalo.

Growing lighter and purer, walking dispossessed, as with June, walking without hat, underwear, stockings, walking poor to better feel reality, to be nearer, to be less enveloped, protected, to be purified, dropping people I do not genuinely like, falsities, forms, continuity.

Desire to be poor. Giving all I have, the dress I love, jewelry, money, because I am given, enriched, fecundated, hurt, and possessed, and I bless the God that permitted a man to come, to take, permitted me to live, to kiss, to be inundated, wooed, burned, destroyed, to be alive. I'm grateful, grateful.

To a friend: I have not, as you think, been unaware of the political drama going on, but I have not taken any political sides because politics to me, all of them, are rotten at the core and based on economics, not ideals. Suffering of the world is without remedy except individually. As I give all individually, I feel no need to take part in a movement. But now the drama is going on. Spain is tragically bleeding. I feel tempted to engage my allegiances. But I still remain outside, fiercely so, because I find no leader I trust or would die for, seeing only betrayal and ugliness, no ideals, no heroism, no giving of the self. If I saw a Communist who was a great man, a man, a human being, I could serve, fight, die. But meanwhile I help in a small circle, and wait. The people will do away with me because of my birth (shoot everybody with clean nails, they said in Spain) and with my individual personal giving too. And with the perfume, the clean nails, the cathedrals, the furs, and the castles will go poetry. It wasn't the king we valued but the symbol of a leader. Now we have no leaders, no ceremonies, no rituals, no incense, no poetry. Only a struggle for bread. We are very poor indeed.

JULY 25, 1936

THE OTHER NIGHT I FELL ASLEEP READING WHAT I had written about Gonzalo, to relive and re-taste it. I cannot wake from the dream. The opium. When we meet we start running toward each other. He comes all the way from Denfert-Rochereau just to kiss me for half an hour. I pass by the studio at rue Schoelcher where I was once so lonely, pass by with Gonzalo. We walk the streets embracing, kissing. It is the mystery. We talk so little.

I went out with Hugh last night and at eleven-thirty I said, "I must leave you now, must appear a little while at a party because of my book." Hugh accepts but insists on taking me there. I give Colette's address. I walk up the dark little street and hide in a doorway until Hugh is gone. I wait for a few minutes, heart beating. If he were waiting around the corner watching, if he were to follow me along the dark little street behind the Villa Seurat, follow me along the rue des Artistes, see me stop before Number Ten, see the light turned on in Roger's studio, see Gonzalo at the window?

I walk quickly. Gonzalo likes my recklessness, my audacities, the risks I take. He is waiting at the top of the stairs. Midnight. Fire in his eyes, and torture. Was I really with Hugh? Was it someone else who brought me? Did I come from the Villa Seurat? We threw the mattress on the floor, behind a curtain, "like an opium den," he said, and last night I weighed him down, the tiger was set free, I sensualized him. When I stood up at dawn, combing my hair, he took me back, three times during the night his passion poured into me. "What a difference, with you," he cried, "oh, what I feel with you, *chiquita*. Why do I so often think of you when you were twelve years old? Because of my love of creating human beings (he created Helba). I think of you beginning, of you before America. I would have been closer to you then. I believe in exclusive love, *chiquita*. I have to know you're all mine. I can't share you. I've never loved this way before. At twelve you were more Spanish."

He has seen the Catholics in Peru lashing themselves into fanatic frenzy. He calls for suffering. This makes me infinitely sad. He seeks torture. He has found it, in my full past, in my elusiveness, the feeling of insecurity I give. But I am sad. Because his love is steeped in pain, as mine was for Henry. He arouses me deeply. His body and face hold me spellbound. I look at him. I worship him with my eyes. His voice stirs me. His eyes. His *pudeur*. He says he is a Christian and I a pagan. "I drink red wine, like Christ's blood," said Gonzalo. "You like the white wine of Bacchus." He is surprised that I don't like to wash after making love. Doesn't it bother you, feeling all that inside of you? "It's beautiful," I said, "beautiful enough to drink." The night passes swiftly. He cannot sleep for his desire to kiss me.

He sees Henry at the Dôme surrounded by mediocre friends and he asks himself, How did Anaïs fit in there? I can't see Anaïs there. So I tell him how much I suffered from Henry's liking for white trash.

In the morning I was with Henry, eluding possession. Henry was saying, "I should have the courage to go off alone and write." But he won't. *Black Spring* is out, dedicated to me. I am the armature in Henry. What will happen now? Can I be the muse without love? My love is all compassion. No desire and no communion.

On top of a crumbling world. The more it crumbles the more I feel like asserting the possibility of personal love, personal relationships. We lie on a dreamer's opium mat, over volcanoes, *"Cómo sabes querer, chiquita."* How well you know how to love. *"Qué ternura,"* what tenderness. After taking me, he loves me more.

He did not leave for Spain with the others.

J U L Y   2 7 ,   1 9 3 6

F IRST LIE TO GONZALO. LAST NIGHT I WENT TO have dinner with Henry. We talked over the last pages, which are the most terrible descriptions ever written of dissolution and void. I talked about Henry's Gargantuanism, his seeking of quantity, his dramas and conflicts against the loss of the self, of the vitals, in quantity, and against the impersonal, symbolical of the American drama of the spirit to master too much material. I said the personal experience with June suddenly overshadowed the crowd experience, proved that everything else was worthless.

I have helped Henry to transform his material. I have breathed meaning into his streets, crowds. I have tried to put his vitals back inside of him. Even today.

Now, in this book, Henry's disease lies revealed, terrifying, all that I have suffered from, his dispersions, his atrophied emotions due to constant movement in the crowd, from his self so easily lost in the city ("shattered by the city," he writes), this self that I pursued, loved, clung to, that I finally reinstated into our personal relationships.

But what an interesting world, his world. How ever changing, how disquieting. I was walking through it, rediscovering his defects, his monstrosities, perversities, vulgarities. We were talking in the same direction again, creating together, simultaneously, and I was fired. I was talking ahead, Henry saying, "That's just what I was going to do . . ."

Creation.

No creation with Gonzalo. He is not a creator. He has eyes, ears, a nose, a palate, fingertips, marvelous seeingness, no creation.

Lover. He waits for me at Roger's studio at midnight. I say to Henry, "I can't stay the night because Hugh is at Helba's, and so insisted he could take me home, and there was no need for me to stay away all night."

Gonzalo is lying on the mattress we threw on the floor. He didn't see me with Henry. He is joyous, ardent. His brown body is alive, alive. And an hour later he is saying, *"Yo no soy creador."* (I am not a creator.) He analyzes, philosophizes. Not a creator. That is why he lives, why he took all the drugs, why he is a Communist, why he is so beautiful to love, to live with. He throws his whole self into the present. Into life. No split. In my life the perpetual struggle to piece the fragments. Creating and dead in life, Henry; man in life and not creating, Gonzalo; and I, both creating and living; and so I leave Henry, a shell, a shadow, for Gonzalo's live brown burning body. But sadness, bitterness. No change in my life. No one will understand. No one. No one. Sadness. A deep, deep abysmal lucidity. The abyss under a kiss. I fall.

What I think about the "world." When I write letters, telephone, seek people out, go to a café, to a party, I am looking for something, as when I returned from New York. When I find it (a deep experience, Gonzalo), I stop to taste, to deepen, to give myself wholly to it.

Henry goes on. More cafés, more movies, more people, mediocrity, a flux. No selection. No deepening. No evaluations.

J U L Y 3 0 , 1 9 3 6

*T*HE WORLD OF MAN IN FLAMES AND BLOOD. THE world of man disintegrating in war. The world of woman alive as it is in this book, as it shall be forever, woman giving life and man destroying himself, death, carnage all around me, death and hatred and division, and I so weary of lifting Henry, and Hugh, Eduardo, Rank, and now Gonzalo. The weakness in Gonzalo, so willing to die for me, seeking in me only the drunkenness and the dream, and when I am not there, Pernod. Gonzalo with a bottle in his pocket, rushing into death, with the Communists, and I weeping before the film of the sailors of Cronstadt; heroism: the heroism to die, but not the heroism to live, to love, to caress, and to defend the personal world, the soul.

My personal world unshattered, but it is hard to hear the music with guns in our ears, harder to hear the music with Mother and Joaquin in danger in Mallorca, Eduardo in danger, my Father in danger in Spain.

Henry writing, and I asking, "If we lose each other as people lost each other in the Russian revolution, what would you do?" He gets terrified. No strength to live, strength only with words.

Gonzalo's head on my breast, dreaming; all I want of you is the dream, you have the power to make me drunk, and our first dissonance comes when I say you believe that the dream comes out of the negation of desire. I believe the dream is born out of fulfilled desire; after fusion we rise stronger; out of sensuality we rise higher, flower mystically. "You're a pagan, and I'm a Christian. I want sublimation," says Gonzalo, and so he throws a blight on sensuality, and I feel myself dying, poisoned, blighted. No sensuality, now that it has died between Henry and me. No sensuality in the savage Gonzalo, who was fed on incense, and all my strength was in living in the flesh.

Tired of struggling against destruction.

AUGUST 1, 1936

*M*Y WARMTH IS WINNING OUT, MY NATURALNESS. Gonzalo last night freer, deepening his caresses; we fell asleep saturated with each other's flesh, bathed in it, he lying with his head between my knees, and I with his sex in my mouth, and slowly I am falling in love with his flesh, as it becomes more flesh; slowly we're possessing each other's flesh, in sleep and all night.

"I am a coward, Anaïs. I can't leave you. I can't surrender you and go out and fight in Spain. I should. You overpower me and drug me, Anaïs."

His beautiful flesh, his smell. Will I triumph over death?

"Because I love you, Anaïs, I want to die. Only death can come after this, only death is great enough after this."

He has not gone to Spain. Each day, I fear. Out of thirst for greatness, for the holocaust, he would die. Exaltation leading to dissolution. That Gonzalo is destroying life around him is apparent. People look at me with anguish. Charpentier, divinatory, offers me his strength: "You look in need, you look lost, trembling."

I look tired, nervous. No joy. I sing out of a world full of destruction. Where is my joy? A joy pierced with melancholy. What sadness in our love. Gonzalo saying, "I am ashamed of our happiness, when all the rest of the world is suffering."

At eight A.M. I rush home to Hugh in time to make his breakfast, to awaken him tenderly. At lunch I rush to Henry, and we read his horoscope, made by Moricand. At four I am at Helba's bedside, intending to stay; but Gonzalo begs me not to stay, to go with him to our nest. We're tired, we will sleep gently together. But once there, no sleep, but burning passion. Right after our night, an endless thirst and hunger.

AUGUST 2, 1936

NIGHT. GONZALO AND I WALKING IN PARC MONT-souris. Gonzalo is talking passionately for Trotsky against Lenin, and Communism. He moves his head vehemently, proudly, fiercely. He looks noble and heroic. He talks.

I have just come from an evening with Henry where I have read powerful pages, where we lay in bed and Henry said, "I am getting old. I have no more desires." And I have to console him, tell him it is temporary, that his work is draining him. His body is dead. And with it dies all my sensual happiness. An overwhelming tenderness for him makes me talk wisely. "It's all in your head now, you're writing about sex. When this is over you will come alive again." He says he desires no one. I feel his love and his anguish. He has anguish because his horoscope says seven feminine signs and only one masculine sign.

At midnight I am walking with Gonzalo and he is talking about the need to sacrifice and to die for the world. "I will die shot, Anaïs. How far will you come with me?" *All the way,* answers the woman, but my spirit remains aside, unconvinced. Out of the world, art, into death. I can only see it as death because I do not believe in it. Never so torn. Lack the strength to pull Gonzalo out of tragic fatality because if one pulls someone who is not an artist outside of the world of action and drama, you kill him. And action and drama pull me downward because I do not believe in politics. Art is my only religion. Politics to me are death and futile sacrifice.

And Henry's book grows immense, written with sperm and blood, and Henry grows each day more delicate, more frail, more soulful. And my body dies slowly because Gonzalo, with his lack of simplicity, directness and naturalness, poisons our sensuality. His tenseness, nervousness, mentalness act on my nerves, make me feel as I felt before Henry made me natural and easy. Gonzalo twitches beside me with exaltation and dreams and tensions and guilt, and paralyzes my own desires, and I can't sleep and I dream violent erotic dreams of big brutal men taking me. But the love for Gonzalo increases, sex is sacrificed, but, oh, the love—while he sleeps I look at his face, his shoulders, a feminine Gonzalo, made for love, beautiful to look at when aroused. What matters what arouses him? He is aroused and I desire to be lighted by the same fire but I can't be. A page of Henry's writing arouses me more than Trotsky's books. But Gonzalo wants to die.

Awakening out of a semislumber at dawn, I looked at him. Weakness and strength. The strength to die. I am sad and ready to die too, out of anguish and fatigue, ready to die because the strength I used to breathe life into Henry's work, and life into Hugh, Gonzalo, and Helba, is weakening me.

The honey ceases to flow. The weather is gray. No summer. No sun. Tragedy and death. Henry saying, "I am getting old." I hear Gonzalo in his sleep murmuring: *"Mi chiquita tan rica, tan rica tu boquita, tan linda . . ."* At twelve, I am riding through the Bois on a bicycle with Hugh. And I am singing. Singing with the joy of being alive, singing recklessly, defiantly, ironically. Singing, perspiring, bathing, making up my face, wondering when war is coming here and who will I save, where will I go, to whom, Henry or Gonzalo? Hugh I will abandon under cover of war and fire. I will let him think I have died. That life with him is dead. Hugh will not suffer if it is war and not betrayal.

AUGUST 2, 1936

*T*HE THOUGHTS BETWEEN THINGS THAT HAPPEN are almost always false. What one thinks while one is living: that alone is true. What I think in Gonzalo's presence (faith, emotion) is more exact than the process of separation and estrangement which takes place afterward, born out of my lack of confidence in love, in myself, and in life. Trust myself only to the felt, to the lived. The moment when thoughts and fears separate me from Gonzalo, as they separated me from Henry—annihilated by emotion, the presence of the loved one. These thoughts are the lucidity which destroys life and illusion, the lucidity which stopped Rank on the brink of dissolution. Nothing stops me, because dissolution is a part of life. Rank refused to live and suffer.

In Gonzalo's studio, with Hugh and Emil. Gonzalo and I, when we stand near each other, shiver with delight and try to inhale each other. A kiss stolen on the dark stairway is bliss. I feel he is slowly entering my body, possessing my body.

AUGUST 4, 1936

*L*AST NIGHT AT HENRY'S, LISTENING TO THE DAZ-
zling talk of Moricand. Whore, child, drug ad-
dict, schizophrenic. Moricand I have selected as the poet among
astrologers—clairvoyant. I feel him physically. I would like to be
touched by him. In his presence I feel what he calls the Neptunian
world, all I cannot express, all that lies behind my acts, my writing.

Having accepted Gonzalo as the lover but not as the man who
could have changed my entire life, I awakened to solitude again. Immense desolation. And so to work. Sober. Serious work. Hard to work
in a chaotic world. But with terrific will I have begun to write, to
make the apartment more of a paradise of peace, to live as if nothing
were crumbling. Gonzalo came with the grippe and fever. On Joaquin's bed we lay entangled. He slept on my breast and awakened
well, feverless.

AUGUST 10, 1936

*T*HE WORLD IN CHAOS. PANIC. HYSTERIA. CONTA-
gion. Mother and Joaquin home, safe, answer-
ing my passionate letters. Gonzalo sick, breaking down as I used to
break down before life and conflict, dragging himself to the art school.
Sick because he was starved for care, devotion, tenderness, great out-
pours of pure passion. A sensual afternoon with Henry after I carry
to him, as is my habit, new manna, Moricand's book *Le Miroir as-
trologique,* Blaise Cendrars's *L'Eubage* and *Transsibérien.*

A deep, inexorable need for a stoical order. So I work on the apartment, hanging curtains. I give my manuscripts to Deníse Clairouin. I correct diaries for her. I mail copies of *House of Incest* to the Gotham Book Mart in New York. I write letters tenaciously. Order. And when through order I rise above the turmoil, I feel strength. It's the synthesis I need for action, for the next move to act. I have to direct Gonzalo, Henry, Helba, Mother and Joaquin, and Hugh out of danger. I begin to brush up on my creator role by ruling and dominating in small ways, and then to fight the insecurities, indecisions, hesitations, and flabbiness all around me. Henry completely disintegrated, unable to work. All the artists quitting. I continue. It's true I can't write, but I can live. I can create life around me, give strength, stimulate, defend, love, save. I put all my manuscripts in the vault, and this diary too, which I shall finish tonight.

Last night in Roger's dim place, Gonzalo sitting cross-legged, talking: "I was brought up on the utmost cruelty. In my father's hacienda we had fifty families of Indians. Servants like one of the family, but if they committed a fault, if one were caught, there was a family court and judgment and punishment was meted out right there. When I was a child I saw many flagellations. I saw the Catholics in church lashing themselves. My first mistress, I took her with me to a small village they sent me to rule over. She was about sixteen and I seventeen. One day, insane with jealousy, the jealousy of a Moor, I tortured her. I hung her up by her hands with a weight hanging from her feet. I pulled the cord myself, left her there a few minutes. In ten minutes a man dies. I felt great joy, and yet it was all unjust. And when I brought her down she was dying of desire, *se moría de sensualidad.* All this was tamed in me later, first by the Jesuits, then by America, then even more in France."

I felt the great breath of savage life. I hungered for it. I was sorry that Gonzalo was tamed, that today his jealousy is masochistic instead of sadistic, that when he suspects me of being out with Henry he goes to the Dôme and gets drunk. Indefinably, I feel disappointed. I have felt disillusioned. Is the volcano burned out? Is the lion tamed? Spirit broken? A lion with the grippe, blood thinned by France, by America.

Seven years in New York. Seven years in France. The gorgeous vitality sapped. *Les rayons d'un feu amoindri.* His father was Scotch, his mother Incan. Perhaps the Indian in him grew ashamed, learned compassion. Even the Catholics in Peru practice Catholicism with savagery and violence. But we sit laughing in the little vegetable patch of France, *parmis les jardiniers.* What are we doing here, what in hell are we doing here? A war and a revolution may swallow up France.

AUGUST 10, 1936

GONZALO SAID, "WHEN I PUT YOU ON THE BALANCE on one side, and all the rest of the world on the other, you are worth more. I can't tear myself away from you. I must be a coward."

"You're not a coward, Gonzalo. It's just that you haven't sufficient faith in the others, in the Trotsky movement. If you had real faith, an absolute passion for the cause, no woman could stop you. Don't call yourself a coward. Look at me. I was open, ready to be drawn into politics. I let my instinct guide me. I felt no faith and no passion. And I trust what I feel. I don't say, 'I must be wrong and they right.' I say, 'I must be right for myself.' Your instinct has spoken. It takes more courage to stand by one's personal faiths than to adopt what everyone shares with you. It will take more courage for you to stay than to go to Spain."

Love increasing, deepening. The impetus tremendous. I think of him obsessively, even when I am with Henry. Henry so wan and pale.

Strange life. Henry and I lying down and making love so completely, as before. I lying quiet and satisfied. The physical world glowing again, flowering. A kind of peace. But that does not hold me. I leave Henry and I meet Gonzalo, like the night, like fire. We burn together in a kind of silence. I did not fight to keep him. I did not plead or talk. I lay waiting and loving. No direct influence. No words.

I waited. And he came out of his conflict. Today he is drawing all afternoon at the art school. He is slowly breaking with Montparnasse and with drinking. He wants his strength.

Turner came, and because I had not been with Henry for a whole week, because Gonzalo's kisses had aroused me, I liked his eroticism, pure sex. Lying down with him, and Gonzalo telephoning at that moment, and Turner caressing me between the legs while I am talking with Gonzalo. Turner, whose excitement is powerful, who gets an erection when he hears my voice over the telephone, the honey flowing but no orgasm because Gonzalo's face is before me, while Turner whispers obscenities, whispers hot words. And an hour later I meet Gonzalo, divinely beautiful Gonzalo, too nervous and too swift. Eroticism devours me, my sensual hunger is beating inside of me like a separate heart, a fire between the legs aroused by Henry—unquenchable. I cannot rise, I cannot rise out of the earth, even with Gonzalo. Gonzalo too much like a god, so I dream at night of orgasm at the very touch of Turner's sexual fire, and awake to images of Gonzalo's face. All in pieces. And yet . . . all in pieces, in pieces, body and soul pulling, creation pulling, fire calling me, water and air, on all planes. I flower, weep, kiss, love, desire. Why doesn't Gonzalo penetrate the sensual core of me and take possession of me there? Why? And Henry dying sexually, dying, diminished.

Mother and Joaquin saved by an eloquent letter I wrote them to leave Mallorca. Just in time.

My Father not heard from, but for me he is already dead.

Henry so panicky, so feeble in front of this disruption, that he went to bed. I found him in bed, and we floated like derelicts to a stupid movie. What feebleness in life!

On my letter to Hilaire Hiler, on top of my coat of arms on the back of the envelope, I wrote, "To the Communists: this does not mean capitalism, but poetry."

Ideas are a separating element. Sensuality a communicant. Mental worlds are isolators. Sensual days bring one nearer to embracing all things and everyone, all men, the world, creation.

Supervielle said he was always trying to catch up with the man he wanted to be.

Etat amoureux de l'artiste, continuous. State of vibrancy. On certain days I see so many mouths I would like to kiss. Being told that a certain formation of the lobe of the ear indicated cruelty, I walked around obsessively studying the people in the subway, the conductor, Gonzalo, Henry, looking at them intently and asking myself, Is he cruel? Is that a cruel ear? Seeing only ears. How ugly they are, ears. The ears of workmen, of drunk men, of hoboes, of taxi drivers, of butchers. How monstrous.

What gives doubt and suspicion are the falsities and treacheries in one's own self. If you act, pretend, deceive, then life itself becomes false, treacherous.

Gonzalo's first note to me came after a visit I made to his studio the first time, and I left my little engagement book. He brought it back to me with this note: "You forgot yesterday your little notebook and as I suppose you need it, I bring it back to you. Last night the ascetic atmosphere of my atelier was full of its perfume. It was so unreal and had such a magical power that I had to go deeper and deeper into myself. Gonzalo."

Making more notes on Fez. In the intricate streets of Fez I no longer tried to glimpse those parts of me which had died in order to prevent them from dying. I left no shreds of myself in Fez. Each moment being lived completely. I do not need to say in the diary, I am seeing. I am breathing. A twenty-year calvary of doubt. Doubts of everything. Of living itself. And here was Fez, shaped like the pages of my journal, only I can take the burnoose off, I can uncover my face to the world.

Relation between Henry's horoscope and mine. These two themes, says Moricand, are intimately related but particularly on an intellectual plane. There is a kind of spiritual foundation.

Strange . . . the fieriness. We were walking through the streets at night, kissing between short, unfinished phrases. Suddenly his very warm, very heavy hand was on my neck, his mouth on mine, and suddenly I was so infinitely aware, so completely, so devastatingly aware of the fire of love, that I almost fell on my knees to bless I-don't-know-who, for I can really say I have known the highest peaks of passion, of complete passion, sensual and mystical. That both Henry and Gonzalo, in different ways, have been the most marvelous of lovers, that I have received and given all the caresses possible to human beings, and that that is the maximum of joy to be known on earth. Love. Passion. Tenderness.

Gonzalo says my tenderness is terrific, that it is Spanish, and that no American woman has the warmth and the softness allied to passion.

Exploration with him, of his life in Peru, life in Lima, life with the Indians. When I exaggerate my diabolical sides, it is because when Gonzalo says, *"Bandida, qué bandida mi chiquita,"* he kisses me more fervently.

To Barthold Fles: If I had fully realized what an erratic, unreliable, temperamental person you were, I would have said: Fine, I like that in human beings, all my friends are erratic, they don't keep their word, they wander off and back, that's fine, only I don't work with them, I don't deliver into their hands my plans, hopes, or activities. My work I keep for myself. With the erratic ones I sit in cafés and talk. This means that I'm willing to sit around in cafés with you and talk. I know I'll enjoy it. But it also means I want you to return my book on Lawrence and my manuscript of my Father novel. I don't like the time that has elapsed since you took them, during which someone else would have done a hundred things for me. I don't like the fact that you don't answer letters, that you came and went without giving me any news. What I like in a friend doesn't go with my needs in an agent: order, continuity, and solidity. So please return both things to me as soon as possible. *Bonjour,* friend, and good-bye, literary agent.

A U G U S T   1 8 ,   1 9 3 6

O NE EVENING, WHEN GONZALO CAME WITH HELBA
and walked with Joaquin, we got desperate
looking at each other, not being able to kiss. After he left he went to
Roger's place, lay there, and thought of me. Picked up Roger's copy
of *Tropic of Cancer*. Leapt with pain and fury and disgust. So that
was the man at whose side I lay. The grossness, the realism, the
cheapness, the vulgarity. He would take a ship and never see me again.
What had my life been, what kind of world had I been living in, in
filth and dirt and vulgarity? Yet I, I was what I was, what he loved.
And this was the writer I said had value. Full of darkness and pain,
we met for only an hour. He wouldn't tell me what weighed on him
and I was far from divining it. "What a quarrel we'll have tonight,"
he said. I thought it would be over Communism. When he exploded,
when we lay together, I tried to explain how this was Henry before
I met him, how anyway this was not the Henry I knew; he showed
me the Real Henry (when women rush up to Henry today and say,
"Who's your latest cunt?" Henry blushes and moves brusquely away
from them).

"But all that ugliness is in his mind, in him . . ."

"But ugliness has character, Gonzalo, like [George] Grosz's caricatures, like Goya's."

But after a while I realized the storm was all jealousy and emotion
in Gonzalo, and all he said was irrational, contradictory, unwise, and
so all I could do was to seek to heal Gonzalo. And then it all overwhelmed me, the things in Henry that I had suffered from, his taste
for the vulgar, the cheap, the soulless. And I began to sob. "Today
the people I can live with are not his friends."

Then Gonzalo was moved. I said, "You've stirred up a past I had
forgotten."

"Not a past," said Gonzalo, with that same intuition Rank had, as if they could see the shadow of Henry still looming.

And the next day I saw Henry and all that I hate in Henry, and the contrast between him and Gonzalo is so violent that I can't help comparing. And I make Henry a scene about a puerile thing, a blind, bitter scene of disillusion, unfocused, inexplicable, which Henry takes with his head bowed, and I'm so sad I get sick, for Gonzalo doesn't make me happy with his obsession with politics. It's love and passion but not fulfillment or happiness. He is full of fissures, dualities, contradictions. Full of secrets. And when I press him into confessions I find flashes of understanding, flashes of lucidity, together with great blindness, and an absence of fundamental vision, always a core lacking. I have cured him of his attacks on the "ivory tower" and art, because I say, "Well, if you want me to take an attitude, then to me that means action. Your own conflict between individuality and collectivism is due to your hesitation about action . . ."

"I'll tell you honestly, Anaïs, I don't know what to do."

I can't help him, because, as I said, we're at the *envoûtement* (ensorcellment) period of our love. When we meet we're just hungry and get drunk on each other. I can't urge him to go to Spain to be massacred. I can't urge him to become a Trotskyist because he knows that I live out my ideas. He knows that. He knows once my faith is lighted I won't lie back and write books. If I don't catch fire then it's indifference. No *moyenne*. Extremes. And we lie there, burning with love, and wake up just as hungry, and decide nothing. At dawn we get up and walk, half-asleep, to the café at Denfert-Rochereau. We buy a newspaper. Blood. Massacres. Tortures. Cruelty. Fanaticism.

Gonzalo, at three in the afternoon, is sketching at Colarossis. I call for him. I watch him work, showing the serious, grave side of his nature. A minute later he may be drunk and laughing at the Dôme.

Henry is whining because with France lay his only hope of stability. He is dependent on cities, on externals, to hold himself together. I feel pity for him, yet I know now that in no man who seeks me out, loves me, worships me, in no man I will lie with, will I find strength.

August 20, 1936

*T*HIS STRENGTH THAT I GIVE TO OTHERS—YOU, MY diary, know where I draw it from. It is too bad that you always see me at my worst. You hear me groan and lament, but when I groan here, my effect on others has already been worked. When I see Henry the next day, he has been affected and is either working or struggling for cohesion. When I see Gonzalo he no longer goes to the Dôme but spends a few hours a day drawing and sings the praise of solitude and isolation. Things and people change. I rest my head here and weep, curse, and whine. But when I leave you, I leave you only to create and give life. I live in a period of dissolution and disintegration. Even creation and art today are not considered a vocation, a destiny, but a neurosis, a disease, a substitute. I named this diary "Drifting." I thought I too was dissolving. But my diary and I together seem to keep whole. I can only dissolve for a little while; then I must create and integrate again. At my first contact with Gonzalo I dissolved. Now I am becoming whole.

Henry's corruption is a *"fleur de peau,"* said Gonzalo. Mine is deeper. I am shattered not by a city but by a person. I now understand the anguish I feel in certain places where there is looseness, abandon, corruption. It is not my kind. I dissolve into love, desire, passion, sensuality, not loss of will but by failure, defeat, masochism, death. Henry is writing now, in *Tropic of Capricorn,* the very best description of void, disintegration, corruption. He symbolizes and represents the disease of the modern man. He is at one with the chaos of the world, of cities, of streets. His anonymity gives me the greatest anguish because it is collective, the loss of the self. I do not lose myself. His dispersion seems more deadly to me than mine. When I pass from one life with Henry to nights with Gonzalo and days with Hugh, that is a circuit, an expanded life, but not dissolution, though I skirt dissolution every instant.

My cruelty toward Henry for his passivity. How I torture him when he hurts me. By making him jealous, mentioning cafés where I have been, walks through the city. And then I wring from him some words or gestures of love which his Chinese attitude so often stifles. How he admires the Chinese lack of sympathy. After I have punished Henry for some small inertia, I love him more. So yesterday we were close again, with a profound, vital tenderness. I woke up after our caresses talking Spanish. He teased me and said, "You must have been sleeping with a Spaniard." All the elements of perversity, loving what I can't admire, Henry's life.

At ten I met Gonzalo and became more and more aware that he is the dream lover. *"L'amant esclave qui pourrait être bourreau,"* said Charpentier.

Singing in the dark: *"España que te mueres, No has sabido que te quiero."*

AUGUST 22, 1936

ROGER KLEIN CAME BACK FROM SPAIN, AT ONE IN the morning, and found Gonzalo and me in his bed. For the first time in a bed—we had been lying on a mattress on the floor without sheets, our "opium den," we called it. Gonzalo had stolen a little red lantern from one of the street construction signs, which gave off a dim little yellow glow. We had sunk that night into a kind of bottomless softness, a well of warmth and fusion, into that mingling of breath and yielding of the whole self which makes marriages, the dangerously profound loves. Step by step, like the steps going up to Roger's studio, we had walked deeper into each other, each being opened more and more. Roused out of sleep by Roger, we wandered out. Spent the rest of the night at the Hôtel Anjou; the fatal circle of sacrileges, remembering both Henry and Eduardo.

Clash the next night when Gonzalo and I have only one hour together. Gonzalo talks violently, extravagantly, unjustly, and the shock of argument is as painful to me as it was when Henry first attacked me in the garden of Louveciennes. I wake up suddenly to the first misunderstanding, to the first collision, the first separation.

The Chinese say the future is only the shadow of the past. There is a shadow of my past lying on my road, and a certain outline of it seen at a certain moment can make me leap as if a knife had pierced me. I felt such an anguish when Gonzalo attacked the world I live in, the Anglo-Saxon civilization, my absence of political attitude, a phrase in my book. Such an anguish and terror, a sense of discord and of struggle, a tiredness, and a feeling all my old wounds were reopened, that I jumped like an animal in a jungle. I became rigid, angry, inexorable, bitter, closed, and I struck back, and wounded him, and said I wouldn't see him the next day—who was he to attack me, what had he made of his life? I hurt him, because as I say this I realize he has begun again to draw, to fight off his alcoholic friends, to drink less.

We hurt each other.

And in this he found a voluptuous pleasure, in the vibrations, the pain, the wounds. I remembered his own words: "With cruelty you can make me create . . ."

But the hours of antagonism destroyed me. Was I to begin another struggle for my own existence, was this to be another duel as with the forces of destruction in Henry? I couldn't bear it. I am tired. I want unity. I wrote the usual Anaïs letter full of ferocities I could never say, read it with him, burned it, regretted my words, blamed the moonstorm, the monthly madness, the shadows of the past, the twistedness in me, the paralyzing fear of cruelty and destruction; went mad again for a few days, feeling the hatred of the workmen in the streets allied to Gonzalo's phrase "I want to make you class-conscious," and my reply: "I have an attitude now that is immovable. I shall remain outside of the world, beyond the temporal, beyond all the organizations of the world. I only believe in poetry."

"But the mysticism of Marx . . ."

"It's not my mysticism."

"You haven't the religious mysticism."

"Art is my religion."

That very night, after Gonzalo's visit in the afternoon, I left Henry at midnight, left a tender Henry, with a kind of pain and pleasure mingled, walked around the block, walked right around the café to another one, where Gonzalo was waiting. A few hours before, I had left Gonzalo in front of Colette's door and walked around and behind Colette's house to Henry's studio.

Gonzalo and I completely drunk on kisses. It is three in the morning and we're walking, stopping only to kiss with desperation. "How good our fight," he says. "How was the evening at Colette's?"

"Hablamos chino."

"Yes, yes, you talked Chinese," he laughed, "and you and I talked Chinese, and everything is Chinese and meaningless, except the kiss in which I feel you mine."

We were sitting on a bench and looking down at the shadow of the branches. I told him about the future being the shadow of the past. A huge gold-painted key hung before a shop. I said, "Gonzalo, take it to open a home for us somewhere. Now that Roger is back, *no tenemos casita,* we have no home."

And we can't bear hotel rooms. Both of us were sad in the hotel room.

Contrast: Gonzalo sneers at Cocteau's trip around the world, because no one should be writing about Greece, Egypt, India, and China while Spain is on fire; but when I meet Henry, Cocteau's writing about China is the only thing he has read in the newspaper, and the dream is immediately reinstated instead of violence, brutality, sadism, and the suicidal holocaust of the Spaniards.

AUGUST 23, 1936

Gonzalo, we can't go to a hotel room, and
no apartment will do either, nobody else's
house, nobody else's place. It will either have to be a *roulotte* (caravan)
or a houseboat."

"A *roulotte!*" Gonzalo caught fire. The idea transformed us, transported us. "A *roulotte*. A *roulotte*, a place out of the world that will
be ours, Anaïs. We can close the door on the whole world. It gives
me a feeling of possession. You'll come early and we'll cook our dinner
on a fire. We'll paint it your colors. I will have a refuge, a place to
run away to, to run away from the crowd, people. But keep it a secret.
I want nobody to know. Promise."

Walking and dreaming. I imagine a million scenes, bringing my
costumes, a few books. Gonzalo dreaming, inventing.

For a long time Gonzalo had wanted to sleep in my bed, in my
bedroom, which is covered with black velvet. Hugh went to London.
So I dressed up in my Maja costume, lit the candles from Fez, and
he came. Three times I have dressed in my Spanish costume for my
lovers. For Henry, and he didn't understand it at all and was merely
frightened by the strangeness; for Rank, who was admiring, exultant,
humble, but who didn't form a part of it, for whom it was exotic,
theatrical. But for Gonzalo. When Gonzalo came in with his luxuriant
black hair combed down flatly, with his air of grandeur, of nobility,
what an image my mirror reflected. What beauty, his tallness, darkness, intensity, the lover of dreams; and I so pale, eyes turned black,
mouth like the carnations, and all my racial memories surging. I who
lived beyond and outside of race, but race is a reality, it is a blood
reality. A night entranced, deeper and deeper into the layers of our
being. Gonzalo refusing possession, casting it aside, in order to find
new worlds of tenderness, new expressions, to extend the resonances,
seeking he-did-not-know-what; seeking to forget sex because, he says,

he and I had sunk into the realism of it; seeking new realms, new sensations we had not yet lived.

Finding love, the infinite.

Passion not sexualized flowing all around us. My arms hold him, the kisses multiply, expand, cover the body and resound, re-echo infinitely through a flesh made deep like a cathedral. What trances, what dreams, what waves and unfurlings of kisses. Kisses in sleep, souls touching. Sex throbbing but not answered, and so it is the soul that beats, beats on the temples and through the bodies. "The coldness of sex," he said, "of just sex." They have all complained. I have said this when Henry took me for the sex and so often gaily and without feeling, without emotion. I always with emotion. Gonzalo with endless emotions, with all the shades and qualities of feeling, with a thousand changes. At moments we feel grateful.

"At what a crucial moment you came, Anaïs."

"You came when I was most unhappy, Gonzalo."

How many rich and marvelous things we are unearthing, how much we buried away to live others' lives. Unearthing. Delicacies. A thousand delicacies. I curve my body, enwrap him. Creating all around me an atmosphere of warmth.

The fear of deep love is not in us, not in Gonzalo, because he gives his all to life, he is not neurotic and, thank God, is an aesthete but not an artist. I feared the depths of this love and defended myself against it with Henry and George. I feared to lose the earth I had so struggled to reach. And now the earth does not appear so precious, it seems heavy and prosaic, it has impeded my flights, there is too much of it.

I think of my life with Gonzalo as a dream and a passion. I am grateful. I am blessed. After the day when Hugh and Helba talked alone (Hugh is analyzing Helba) and Gonzalo and I went for a walk to kiss, under Hugh's eyes almost, under Joaquin's, I wanted to go to church, to thank someone, out of gratitude.

A day and a night of my life: Morning, I write letters to my human creations, my patients. Betty comes to read me her manuscript. She is blossoming. She says, "It's strange, everything seems to have become so real, so near, so vital." I put her pages in one of my folders, tack it for her, and send her off. At the dressmaker's I realize a dress out of the Hindu shawl, but I have nowhere to wear it. It does not matter, it's necessary, it's poetry, it is hanging there, it is symbolical, it is part of the ritual; perhaps if I wear this dress the world will cease to crumble and die. I may stem the scum of drabness, arrest the expansion of the prosaic. I wear the dress for Hugh, who is sad because he can no longer protect my dreams, as I am sad that I cannot keep Henry altogether free from the turmoil of the world. I kiss Hugh on the neck, gently, and he says, "You are looking so well, why are you looking so well?" I say, "It was the lovemaking last night,"—his lovemaking, which I endured with closed eyes. But Hugh is happy and we read the newspapers together.

At two-thirty I am with Henry, who says, "Let us take a siesta." The sun is shining on his bed, and Henry takes me with a simple, healthy naturalness which touches the surface of my skin, and the orgasm is strong yet it seems far from me, because it is an orgasm without the passion, the miracle has gone out of it, it is an orgasm but the miracle is no longer there, it is a physical pleasure without echoes, like food.

I read his pages, I seek to give him back his security so that he can work. I should ask him to give up the studio, to take a cheaper place, but I feel pity for him when he says, "It is the only place which really gave me serenity." So I yield again, and we talk whimsically about future trips while I wonder how I could bear one day's separation from Gonzalo.

Dinner with Henry. English surrealism. Cendrars. The *Minotaure*. "No sympathy," said Henry, "but defense against it began as a child. Can only and best understand the man who starves. Not the drama in Spain." I brought him a tablecloth and sheets. I tell him what I have been reading in the *Cabala*.

The *Cabala*. At ten in the evening I meet Gonzalo in a café and I say, "Your star is called Autare." We walk until my feet hurt me, we walk kissing, and Gonzalo is showing me his drawings of grotesque old women and drunkards. "Why am I drawing so feverishly for you, you haven't asked me to draw, you even said, 'I'm glad you're not writing or working, Gonzalo.' What a force there is in love, what a force in you, even when we are asleep together. I feel such strange things happening."

I am giving away more than half of what I have; that is why I could not turn toward the larger problems of the world: my individual world, my personal life, was perfect, in giving and receiving, full to overflowing. And such great needs near and around me. The drifting was a drifting amidst fullness and richness shared.

A U G U S T 3 1 , 1 9 3 6

*T*HIRTY, QUAI DE PASSY. IN PERU THEY CURE MAD-ness by placing the madman next to flowing water. The water flows, he throws stones into it, and his madness ceases.

So I look at the Seine, I hear the cries of the people: *"La Rocque au poteau!"* Gonzalo and I are kissing, but just the same, from the train window I suddenly saw all the trees with their *heads* in the ground and their roots gesticulating in space, I heard the words: *Roots, roots!* and a new *House of Incest* began while Hugh and I rolled to an insipid visit to the Turners and Gonzalo's head appeared everywhere I looked, like a mythological head.

In a world where everyone is sick with dispersion, where everyone scatters, enfeebles, splits, deludes, dissolves, Gonzalo can burn with a wholeness, an intensity which gives to his voice, even on the telephone, a quality which makes my hair stand on end, like the trees on the road. The Seine is flowing and I throw stones, my madness uncured, and *House of Incest* Number Two opens with roots and the page on fear, and so the revolution will find me insane with dreams, with passion for Gonzalo.

When does real love begin?

At first it was a fire, eclipses, short circuits, lightning and fireworks; then incense, hammocks, drugs, wines, perfumes; then spasm and honey, fever, fatigue, warmth, currents of liquid fire, feast and orgies; then dreams, visions, candlelight, flowers, pictures; then images out of the past, fairy tales, stories, then pages out of a book, a poem; then laughter, then chastity.

At what moment does the knife wound sink so deep that the flesh begins to weep with love?

At first power, power, then the wound, and love, and love and fears, and the loss of the self, and the gift, and slavery. At first I ruled, loved less; then more, then slavery. Slavery to his image, his odor, the craving, the hunger, the thirst, the obsession.

Hilaire Hiler writes, "*The House of Incest* is very sad, at the same time comforting in the way some drug which stimulated and calmed at the same time might be."

I say to people that I am not writing, but it keeps on wavering here, the tale, the writing that is not writing but breathing.

Breathing.

Loving. Caressing Gonzalo again.

"*La Rocque au poteau!*"

Rebecca West cables to reserve Monday night for her.

Moricand says, "You are in an *état de grâce*. The fairy tale is possible for you."

He understands me, he understands the larger wavelengths of my life, what he terms *les ondes*—like some divine and mysterious radio, all because of Neptune, he knows, and I like his way of living in a dream himself.

At night, in front of my window, workmen are laying the foundation for the 1937 Exposition, the Mosque of Timbuktu, Algerian palaces, Indo-Chinese pagodas, a Moroccan desert fortress; and around the piles will be moored Chinese junks, Malayan prois, sampans.

SEPTEMBER 3, 1936

I HAVE MOVED TO THE EDGE OF THE ARISTOCRATIC quarter, on the edge of it, next to a bridge which can carry me to the Left Bank, to Montparnasse, to Denfert-Rochereau, where Gonzalo lives, to Alesia and Montsouris, where Henry lives. The Metro carries us back and forth, the poor, the rich, back and forth, at all hours of the day. Gonzalo stands at night on that bridge after he has left me, and waits for my light to go out. Or he comes when he cannot see me and watches my window. The wide, wide window is open before me. I see the lights on the river, the illumined Tour Eiffel, the red moon, and across the river the Reds are holding a meeting to hear la Passionaria, the woman Communist. Gonzalo is there. In a little while he will come and get me. He wants me to see, to hear. My heart is tight, hard within me. I heard them singing an hour ago as they marched in. Taxicabs pass by, full of people singing, with red flags. What tightness and anger I feel, blindly, against them. Blind, unreasoning. The instinct has made a choice. I hate the workman. I hate collectivity, I hate the masses, and I hate revolutions.

Love of beauty has carried me here, to a Communist meeting. Love of a brown god with a body to worship, made for love and life and caresses.

But my whole being is set against it all—violently so—and the conflict tears me. I heard them singing while I was eating with Mother and Joaquin. It made my heart stand still.

S E P T E M B E R   1 0 ,   1 9 3 6

ONZALO CAME AND SAID, "WE WON'T GO TO THE
meeting. I'm glad to be out of it. I was getting
restless, thinking of you waiting for me. I saw your light all the time
I was crossing the bridge. What have you done to me? The meeting
didn't touch me. La Passionaria. Words. A lot of words and singing.
I fell apart. I hate the masses. *Chiquita mia,* you are more important
than everything else."

Kisses with infinitely changing flavors.

In this sea of strong flavors, Rebecca's visit was lost. No trace of
her passage. She couldn't live up to the drunkenness of Rouen, she is
weighed down by trivialities, she must know where my coat comes
from, and she says at the same moment, "You will be the greatest
writer, you are so much wiser than I, you have such an understanding
of people." She left me luminous flowers because "one feels like giving
you strange things," and in me a feeling of disillusion.

I was reading in the *Cabala* about crystal gazing; all forms of
trances, it did not matter which one, produced the same magical effect
of *unity.* The whole being drawn together, fused, entranced, and
capable then of ecstasy. Ecstasy is the moment of exaltation from
wholeness!

I am like the crystal in which people find their mystic unity. Because of my obsession with essentials, my dropping away of all details,
trivialities, interferences, appearances, gazing into me is like crystal
gazing. They see their fate, their potential self, secrets, their secret self.
Rebecca dropped her puerilities and became grave. It always happens.
It always happens too that she grows afraid of what she sees, and runs
away from it.

I never yield to small talk. I am silent. I skip so much. I turn away. I am always absorbed by this core of people, looking at it, interested only when it speaks. The miracle I await, the dropping of nothingness and of falsities, always happens.

When one conquers, one is even more wounded than when one loses. Because you experience the pang of responsibility. Has your influence been for the good of the other? Gonzalo, saved from Communism, was that right?

SEPTEMBER 11, 1936

A DAY AND A NIGHT. OPENED MY EYES WITH THE recurrent desire to sing or dance without ever knowing why, but there was already dancing in my room. It was the refracted sun on the Seine. How is it I am lying alone in my own bed? I have only been home since dawn. When I came home the ragpickers were searching the garbage cans and the *clochards* were still asleep on the doorsteps.

I am out of the dark forest of caresses, of smells, yearning to roll and bathe again in the smell of his black hair, to cover my face with it, to feel his skin, to drop into warmth, to float on worship, to swim and breathe in adoration, to put my hand around our kiss as if it is a little flame I am protecting from the wind; a mouth changing, so withdrawn at first, now flowering, filling, turning outward, hurt, melted, opened, wet. Changed the currents between the eyes, the currents between the mouths. Touched so many layers of the being, with fingers, mouths, and words. At first the eyes, lanterns and stars, candles, jungle and heaven, hell and desire.

The mouth alone touches the womb. Clouds of dreams, mists of diamond and sulfur from the eyes, but the mouth alone touches the womb, the mouth stirs, moves, flowers, the lips open, and there flows the breath of life and breathlessness of desire. The shape of the mouth shapes the currents of the blood, stirs, lifts, dissolves. To bathe, roll,

turn over dizzy in a bed of warmth—no warmth like two bodies—
this is the current of life.

Hugh has opened the door. "You're there, little cat—I never heard
you come in!" Janine comes softly with the breakfast, the newspapers,
mail. If it is mail from my patients it is always the same. My children.
It is always worship, imitation, identification, gratitude. It is always
awe, wonder, and thanks for the miracle. Thanks for resuscitating
me. "I am soon going to give a concert. I am writing my book. I have
written a story. I am writing about my childhood just as you wrote
about yours. I am still clinging to you. I am lonely. I have no friends.
I am getting married, thanks to you. I did not break down this time,
thanks to you. I wish I could be in your little room in the Barbizon
Plaza, talking to you. You have freed me. I feel stronger." Toward
them all I feel no love except for the moment of the miracle, for the
instant the Russian violinist sobbed on Fifth Avenue at the revelation
of the meaning of his life; for the breathless woman falling on her
knees as she left the hotel; for the girl weeping herself free of her
nightmare; for the blocked writer's first pages of writing and the first
flash of life in his eyes. Resuscitated from the dead. I have no *personal*
tie with them. I cannot return their love. I still spend myself writing
magical letters. They are not my friends. They deify me, separate me,
hold me as god and interpreter, and they make me feel lonely.

If it is a letter from Moricand, he thanks me in the name of
Neptune for my activity to save him from utter poverty. I show his
horoscopes, mail them to New York, translate them with Henry, talk
to Denise Clairouin. If it is a letter from Thurema, it is love, equality,
friendship, vital connection. If it is from Fraenkel, it is disease and
the static universe.

While I bathe, paint, powder, perfume, the telephone rings. I have
broken with Turner, who was my last defense against the complete
invasion of deep love. I abandon myself to Gonzalo, wholly. At first
I couldn't tame the sensuality in me, which he did not encompass,
but real love possessed me so completely that when he forced us both
into chastity, no possession, no spasm, just caresses, I was happy. *"Chiquita, eres el ideal mio, tu cara, tu cuerpo, todos tus movimientos, tu
manera de moverte—eres mi tipo."*

I am dreaming about Gonzalo again, always dreaming about Gonzalo, while I copy the 1922 diary volume for Clairouin, while I write letters, while I answer the telephone. Always dreaming about Gonzalo. His dark rusty voice over the telephone: "Can I come now?" "Come! Come!"

We are walking, looking for our *roulotte.*

We are walking through the village of ragpickers and gypsies who live on the outskirts of the city, at the Porte de Montreuil. Little villages of shacks with paths a yard wide, fences of black, rotted wood. Fumbling shacks open to cold and wind, men and women living in the mud, sleeping on rags, babies. All the leftovers of the city, the odds and ends, the rags, broken pipes, bottles, worn-out shoes, mangy clothes, things without shape or color anymore, detritus, broken objects without name, lying on the mud; and men bending over, bargaining and sorting. Women giving withered breasts. Children fetching water from a fountain.

Among the shacks, *roulottes,* small ones overflowing with big families. One bed for all of them. Among the *roulottes* and the shacks a pretty red-and-black house, a toy house with a miniature garden, enormous sunflowers, seashells, pigeons; sunk deep in the garden, a little house in red and black, provoking and unreal, like the houses out of fairy tales. Next to it is a shack, a friend of Django, a gypsy who plays the guitar, who is a friend of Emil. Emil told me how among the gypsies the men are made for music; the women work for the men, sell lace, and steal. The gypsy friend of Django shows us a *roulotte* we want. It is red outside; inside, orange ceiling and leather walls, leather walls like those of ancient frigates. A bed hung in midair like a berth. Little Arabian windows. Gonzalo cannot quite stand up in it. We want it. But it is only for sale. We cannot afford it. And they won't rent it because it is occupied by a *mutilé!*

On and on we searched, through other camps, other gates, saw the troupes which give the fair shows. *Roulotte à vendre. Pas à louer!* Kissing and desiring a little place, so tired of furtive meetings, of the little hotel room on the rue Vendôme. Searching. Searching along the Seine for a boat. Difficulties.

At dinnertime, I am at Henry's place, with dust on my feet.

Henry meets me with melting gentleness. It is one of his tender days. He has been writing so feverishly that he is afraid of going mad. He went so far and wide into new language and whirling, turning worlds to give the flavor of Broadway, of New York, that he is lost. He is dazed and lonely. He is grateful for his connection with me, for my being there. He puts his hand so tenderly on me, with a fatigue of visions, and we fall naturally into our world. Gonzalo—*Leoncito* runs through my veins, through my body, and chants inside of me continuously. His head lies in the foam of my ineradicable reverie. He does not vanish, pale. He is there, all evening, all the time I am with Henry—present, haunting.

Henry goes out marketing while I am sewing for him. We eat quietly and simply, the same words, the same glances, a gratitude in me for the past, for all that was, a gratitude for the strength he poured into me, for the gift of a self that belongs to itself. "Women," he says, "have not liked my books as you thought they would. You were wrong in that . . ."

It is true. They don't like to be de-poetized, naturalized, treated sexually, unromantically. I thought they would. I did for a time, because I had been too much idealized, and I was a real woman and I wanted to be lustily loved, and de-poetized, but all that, in the end, hurts woman, kills woman; and I felt the blight too, and today I was grateful for Leoncito's shower of illusion and the dream. At the thought of Gonzalo's ardent worship I feel myself reeling, as I felt myself reeling when he looked at me in the subway.

Lying in the dark with Henry. We feel no desire, but the diamond in our heads, the pineal eye, is flowing fantastically! Our voices roll and flow and ascend and murmur. Weaving together. Weaving in the dark luminous paths . . . *Voie Lactée.* Constellations of ideas . . .

Started on our journey from my conflict with the diary writing. While I write in the diary I cannot write a book. My books are not as good as the diary. Is it because I have not given myself to them; is it that I try to flow in a dual manner, to keep recording and to invent at the same time, to transform? The two activities, the transformed and the natural, are antithetical. If I were a real diarist, like Pepys or Amiel, I should be satisfied to record—but I am not. I want to fill in, transform, project, deepen; I want this ultimate flowering that comes of creation. As I read the diary I am aware of all I have left unsaid, which can only be said with creative work, by lingering, expanding.

Henry said I did not permit the *geological* change to take place—the transformation achieved by time, which turns the sands into a diamond.

"No, that is true. I think I like the untransformed material, I like the thing *before* it is transformed. I am afraid of transformation."

"But why?"

"Because it is going away from the truth. Yet I know it is attaining reality because I recognize there is a greater truth today in your fantastic description of Broadway than in my instantaneous sketches made on the spot in New York."

When I was a child I wanted to see how the plant grew. I used to stir the earth away from the growing pod, to see.

Fear of transformation has something to do with my fear of madness, the fear of madness which deforms all things. I fear change and alteration. I write to combat this fear. For example, I used to dread Henry's cruelty just as others dread the terrible life, the tragic. I used to find pleasure in describing our joys, the moments of serenity, understanding, tenderness, like something that could afterward conjure away the evil, the demoniac, the tragic. I was so aware of the insecurity. It is like this: A marvelous thing would appear to me, like the little flame of a lighted match to a primitive, a miracle. Like the primitive, I did not know it could be repeated, that other matches existed, that the power to produce a little flame lay within me. In this I have made no progress. This fear I confessed to Rank. Like the fear of a change in a face. Now it is beautiful, human, near. Now it becomes twisted, evil, cruel. But in the diary I have the two faces. As I write I dissipate the fear of alteration. My vision of the world is instantaneous and I believe in it. It is my reality. The transformation required by creation terrifies me. Change to me represents tragedy, a loss, an insanity.

Henry was surprised.

"Well, if it is my malady, Henry, I should express it to the utmost *through* the diary, make something of the diary, just as Proust made his work out of his disease, his malady for analyzing, his sickly pursuit of the past, his obsession with recapturing. I should give myself wholly to the diary, make it fuller, say more, live out my disease. Whereas until now I fought my disease; I tried to cure it. You tried to cure it. Rank tried to cure it."

"The problem," said Henry, "is one of arithmetic. You will never catch up with the days. And the record of a day will not satisfy you. A day is not everything. The record of the day goes on and on, and something bigger is left out, postponed, lost. It will be like a big web which will strangle you. Art requires an indifference. You're yielding to your primitive cult of life, to your adoration of it. And each day of record arrests the flow. The flow would amass in mystery, cause an explosion, a transmutation. You're also concerned with completeness. You say for instance you're worried about Eduardo's portrait. It isn't complete, as in one of Proust's characters. You talk as an artist."

"You see, I feel that Eduardo's portrait in my journal is only done at the moments when he becomes important to me, when he enters into relation to me. He rises and sinks, appears and vanishes only in relation to me. It's like a statue without an arm or leg, unearthed and having to be deciphered, divined. Whereas in truth Eduardo has a life of his own, an independent life which should be included."

Why am I not satisfied with a day—perhaps only because I did not make it full enough so that it could contain the infinite? One day of the diary should be complete, like a book; and all the spaces I skip, all the arms missing, all the layers not illumined because I did not touch them with my own warm fingers, love, or caress them, should be there in the dark, as the mystery of life itself.

What is this bigger thing I captured in my book on my Father that is not in the diary?

A day so full. Is it that the record prevents the supreme flights? Every day of record *counts against* this bigger thing, or can it be made so big and beautiful that it can become the whole thing, the infinite? Is the flowering possible only with forgetting, with time, with the rotting and the dust and the falsities? If I wrote in the diary for fear of madness, then it was for that same reason that the artist created, as Nietzsche said. For since the artist *is* his vision of life—of the tragic and the terrible—he would go mad and only art can save him.

At dawn Henry took me. It was like a secret between us as we ate our breakfast, something which happened in a dream, a dream which was in the past, for an hour. Later, I am walking along the Seine, asking the boatmen for a boat in which Gonzalo and I might live. As I stand looking over the parapet, the *"agent"* watches me. Does he think I am going to commit suicide? Do I look like someone who is going to commit suicide? He watches me. When I lean over the parapet to look at the *péniches* he watches me. When I walk down the stairs to talk to the owner of *Nenette,* a bright, lovely *péniche* with beaded curtains on the little windows, he watches me. I begin to think and feel I am about to commit suicide. And why? Because I can't go to Peru with Gonzalo, because he has said, "If I ever discover you are not mine and only mine, mine exclusively, if I ever discover someone else kisses you, takes you, I'll go away and you'll never see me again. It will kill me, *chiquita."* Because his scenes of jealousy hurt us both, lacerate us. But they leave me feeling innocent. Innocent. Always innocent. Innocent the Saturday night I could not go out with Leoncito because it was Hugh's night and I tried to dissolve Luminal, a sleeping drug, in Hugh's *tisane,* and he noticed the muddied color, and yet I was so lucky, so much protected by Ali Baba, the god of bandits, that he fell asleep at ten o'clock, and I lay waiting in my own room (after begging him to let me sleep alone) until I was sure he was asleep, then dressed in the dark and with infinite precautions slipped out of the apartment, leaving the front door ajar because it makes quite a noise when it closes, walking down two flights of stairs by the servant door to take the elevator there, leaving the house with a beating heart to meet Leoncito at the corner, wondering what would happen if Hugh woke up during the night, as he does so often, and came into my room.

Gonzalo, amazed and frightened that I should feel free to stay all night with him, thinking I would immediately slip back into bed. But we went to the little Peruvian hotel room and Leoncito was very passionate, after days and days of restrained desire. At five I awoke, feeling I must get home. At five-thirty I was back in my bed, and at six Hugh woke up! The luck of bandits. No guilt. Pity and fear, yes, concern at Hugh's possible anguish, fear Henry might know, or Gonzalo might discover my nights with Henry. But no guilt. Just love, a love that fills me, carries me, obsesses me; no time or place for regrets, hesitations, vacillation, or cowardices. Love running free and reckless day and night. For the next morning after this night I gave Hugh all he wanted, caresses, possession, a ride on our bicycles along the river. A gift to Hugh.

Letter to Eduardo: Ain't you got nothing to say but sun-worship, or boy-worship, or other worship—except that of Anahita, moon goddess analyzed by mortal men and on the way to her supreme mystical ascension? I'm not mad, just merry. So many comical things happening.

I should write a chant of thanksgiving to the taxi, which nourishes the dream, carries me everywhere, and permits isolation and reverie. The motion of it has given birth to so many fancies. The taxi is the nearest object to resemble the ancient seven-league boots. It answers to my need to leap, to my impatience, to my desire for reverie, continuous reverie. It is my vice and luxury. To sacrifice a taxi ride is the hardest trial I can inflict on myself. On days of madness it protects this madness, because I can talk freely to myself.

I think if I throw my cigarette out of the window it may light a tank of gasoline and cause an explosion.

When I vacillate I can vacillate further, deeper, wider, and longer than anyone. It is rare. I always know what I want so quickly. I choose things so quickly out of a hundred objects in a window. From the bus window, while passing a shop, I catch sight of a hat and can know it is the one I will buy. Instantly, I like or dislike someone. Instantly.

SEPTEMBER 17, 1936

GONZALO GOES THROUGH CHASTE DAYS WITHOUT possession. Then days of passion and sensuality. Then he has an attack of jealousy, as before, in which he writhes and tortures himself, is in agony, asks questions, doubts me, because he says he still *feels* Henry about. To console him, reassure him, I talk about the dead love for my Father, for Henry. I say to Gonzalo, laughing, "But your jealousy is necrophiliac, all these are dead loves!"

"But you're constantly visiting tombs with flowers! What a love you have for the dead."

I said to him, "Today I have not been to the cemetery."

Moments when the universe seems profoundly right for me, beautiful, complete. Henry is writing magnificently, Gonzalo and I are kissing, Hugh is exulting over some triumph in his work. Life, creation, protection, passion.

A deep conviction of Henry's genius, writing a crescendo to sheer madness. My novel on Henry prophetic. As I wrote about him, "an insanity produced by life."

Today he says his surrealism is born of life. That is real surrealism. Henry—juxtaposition of poetic and ugly. Henry is to me the only authentic and creative surrealist. The others are theoreticians. He is a surrealist in life, work, character. What I enjoyed in him was his surrealism. What I suffered from was his surrealism, for I am not a surrealist.

When I came the day before yesterday he had been writing intensely, and he said, "I've been working madly and I don't know whether it is good or not. Tell me. Am I utterly crazy or utterly right?"

I read the pages and told him he was utterly right.

After I wrote in here the other day (about art, etc.), I felt the danger of putting my art-need into the diary. Might kill its greatest quality: naturalness. I must split up and do something *apart*—it is a need. No consciousness of perfection must *enter* the diary. Good-bye, completeness. My plan of writing up a day and a night until I attained perfection.

While I was talking with Henry about his work I asked myself why it is people call wholeness *singleness* or exclusivity. I feel *whole* while I share myself between Henry and Gonzalo for such different reasons. I am again baffled by life. Is it that the artist never belongs to the One? Yet I feel whole within myself. Whole when I am with Henry, and whole with Gonzalo. They do not interfere with each other. Gonzalo is the dream. Henry can still await me with passion, take hold of me with his two hands, and possess me so sensually, physically, simply, and thoroughly, so humanly, so much like an animal. And I can go to Gonzalo and rise with him into great heights where possession is superfluous.

While I am dream to Gonzalo (unreality of night in Louveciennes, unreality of walks, of nights in Roger's place; reality of hotel room, of moments here in my place, unreal night in my own bedroom when I dressed as a Spanish woman) he does not suffer. When sensual connection flares, then he feels jealousy and terror.

"Are you all mine? Has anyone kissed you? It drives me crazy to think anyone might kiss you."

SEPTEMBER 20, 1936

FATHER'S LAST VISIT BEFORE LEAVING FOR SWITzerland. Salon talk. Twilight. Then, brusquely, taking my hands, face very close, he asks, "Tell me, have any of your lovers loved you as well, as passionately as I did? Just answer that."

Out of kindness, I lie: "No."

"That is all I want to know. For me those two weeks in Valescure were the heights, perfection."

We stood up. Kissed on the cheek. He sought my mouth lightly. I felt his desire. "What a strange way of loving you, Anaïs." I felt nothing. I said, "Papacito." He said, "Don't call me Papacito at such a moment."

He was drunk, drunk with desire. He said, "I don't want to see you again. Don't come to the station. I just want to keep this, keep this . . ."

He left. Downstairs he met my Mother. I saw it on her face. She was carrying a market bag full of things for me. She sat on the balcony and cried hysterically, *"Voleur, voleur!"* I consoled her with deep feeling. "No," I said, "he didn't steal your children, we love you more and more; the more I know him the more I love you." I felt her suffering so deeply. I felt nothing for him. Unreal. But her suffering I felt. I lulled her, caressed her, pleaded. "I never see him. He is always away. He means nothing to me. I don't love him." She was consoled. She was hurt because he had seen her carrying a market bag, like a servant.

At night I was with Gonzalo. He was walking home with me. I asked him to walk with me a little farther. I wanted to see if my Mother was asleep. I was tormented by pity, by the image of her carrying the market bag, by her hysterical crying. Her light was out. I went home. The next day I found she had gone peacefully to sleep, thinking that it was my Father who looked scared. Yes, he looked scared. "I am sure," I said, "he never noticed the market bag . . ."

The next day Mother left for Italy to join Joaquin. We spent the morning together, quietly. Had lunch together, then, while she was busy, I went to see Henry, who awaited me in bed and who pulled me on top of him, taking hold of me with his two hands, so lustily, and lustily possessed me. Then home to dinner for Mother, peace, domesticity, Mother and I working at a rug together, then the station, waving, tenderness and tears in the eyes, then asking Hugh to leave me off at a café where friends were waiting for me. "I will only spend an hour there." Making sure Hugh took the subway, following him deftly until I saw him being swallowed up by the dark Métro entrance.

Meeting Gonzalo then, arriving by a side street, my shadow very, very long, stretching out across the street; and when my shadow touched Gonzalo he turned and saw me.

At seventeen I wanted feverishly, yearningly, to receive red roses. *"Je voudrais des roses, des roses, des roses . . ."* In New York I was showered with the rarest flowers. At seventeen I also wrote, *"Je voudrais qu'il soit pauvre, très pauvre, et qu'il ait besoin de moi.* I wish he were poor, very poor, and needed me."

It was true of Henry, and it was true of Gonzalo, who thanks me for saving him from Montparnasse, orgies, drinking, and despair and bad taste in the mouth. "If I hadn't met you, Anaïs, out of disgust I would have gone to Spain and got myself killed there." Always the lazy man, the laughing debonair man with a love of the bottle, the tramp and bohemian. And I envy those who can drink, disintegrate, grow loose, slack, careless, ragged, sick, because I can't. Something pulls me up always. I go there only to find myself a lover, and then I come out, come out into ecstasies, trances, magic, but not disintegration. Away from death, and decadence, and corruption, away from the dying and the sick, but with regret and pain that I choose the tainted, weak ones who save themselves by their idealization of me, which does not permit me to descend, to be human, drunk, or obscene.

Image of virgin, of life and creation, predominates.

No one will believe the fits of eroticism which suddenly explode in me at the sight of a vulgar market woman leaning over her wares, exposing her legs to the thighs. No one will believe I took pleasure in the bestiality of Henry's writing, which sickens Gonzalo. No one will believe that I liked Henry's natural way of treating woman as nature. But to treat woman as nature leads to de-poetization and prosaic living, and I had to find poetry again in Gonzalo. When I see moving pictures of Meyerling, of Mary Stuart, of romantic love stories, I think of Gonzalo and not of Henry. Love stories. Romantic: Gonzalo. Human love: Henry; human, without illusion. Illusion in the worship I receive. There is no one around me who is not in love with me.

I see Gonzalo suffering the same jealousy I suffered with Henry. The day he knew I was going to see my Father at five he stopped in the middle of his drawing and began to suffer, to imagine, just as when I knew Henry was going to see the Ferrens, or Joyce, or go out with people from New York who considered him a good guide to whorehouses.

I don't suffer so with Gonzalo, I don't let myself. It was so infernal with Henry. I trust Gonzalo more because he is the type who hates sex for sex alone, who has to get out of the beds of the women he takes without love and go and take a bath, wash himself, feels dirty, does not enjoy orgies, needs illusion, and says, "Oh, God, *chiquita,* how much better, how wonderful it is with love, with love!"

Hugh is doing horoscopes at my desk. My eyes are tired from copying Volume Eighteen. I hope Hugh falls asleep, because at eleven I have promised to meet Gonzalo at my Mother's apartment.

Tremendous gaiety now because at first love is like a sickness; one sighs, is thirsty, hungry, feverish for the love; nearness makes one drunk, drugged, and profound and moody; and one is desperate when separated. Now we are used to our disease and out of the dream and caresses, we awake to laugh . . .

S E P T E M B E R   2 2 ,   1 9 3 6

*M*IDNIGHT. CANDLELIGHT. A ROOM THAT WAS Mother's—now our own. Gonzalo's cigarette butts and ashes stewn all over. Gonzalo's clothes on the floor, all but the white underdrawers which he never takes off except in the dark. The *pudeur* of Gonzalo. Body worship. He kisses my feet. Adores my feet. Kisses my legs. Adores my legs. The strength of them. Kisses one all over. Delights over the shadows, the curves. Raves about the space between my eyes. About my ears. "They are so small, so delicate, so lovely, so incredible. They are not ears. They do not look like *ears,*

Anaïs. I never saw such ears, such lovely ears. All my life I dreamed of ears like that."

"And looking for *ears,* you found me!"

Touching, touching the deeper layers of our being, gravity and depth.

"Anaïs, I feel you are mine. Oh, God, Anaïs, if I lost you now I would kill myself. You have enslaved me, enslaved me completely."

What is this? So many women passed through Gonzalo's life, as they passed through Henry's, leaving no traces; and I enslave, retain, hold, fix, for eternity.

"How we have changed, *chiquita.* When did you first love me?"

"I don't know, it was all so unconscious. At my party I felt a premonition."

"At your party I was already mad, and madly jealous. And with reason! Oh, *chiquita,* I want to lock you up!"

Dreamer. He wants the *roulotte,* he wants the *péniche,* but he lies there desiring, sighing. Surrenders before difficulties. It is I today who got the *péniche,* who pursued the quest, who walked along the Seine, saw Allendy, wrote to Maurice Sachs, persisted, discovered I could have half of Sachs's *péniche.* Isolation on the river. One big room and a bedroom. Walls of heavy wood beams covered with tar. Windows on the river. The ship's stern behind our bed. Our bed. Our place. Excitement. Seduced Sachs to get all I wanted. Charmed. Asked. Arranged. Paid. Planned to surprise Gonzalo. Fever. For a day or two I must keep a secret. Gonzalo. My lover. What racial, old, old blood past is stirred by his Spanishness, his jealousy—*"celos de Moro"*— *Celos!* the very word *celos! more* than jealousy!

Night of caresses, without possession . . . I do not understand this. Once he murmured, *"Soy débil.* I am weak." Another time: *"Te quiero demasiado.* I love you too much." The boy, eight years with the Jesuits. Not natural. He has never once urinated while with me. Never walks naked. After he sleeps, he is more natural. Then comes his desire, free. Never when fully awake. But at night, mysteriously, like a cat. But how often with his hand he pushes his penis down, controls himself; does not let me kiss it, or hold it. Timidity, shyness, *pudeur.* But the love so immense, sex unimportant. But today, today, after our night together I was coming back from the river, in a taxi, reading an erotic book given to me by Sachs, and I felt the most powerful orgasm, the whole city reeled, the taxi seemed to fly in the air, and once, twice, three times I palpitated in a long orgasm.

SEPTEMBER 26, 1936

*A*T NIGHT WE WENT TO SEE THE BOAT, CARRYING sheets and a fur. The wide, dark *péniche* lying there sunk among dancing lights of the bridge. We climbed the light *passerelle*. The boy René, asleep in one of the cabins, called out, "Hey there!" The old grandfather who lives there too, old grandfather of the river in his blue blouse and beret, peered through the glass of the little door. "Oh, it's you, Lady. Wait, I'll open." Doors opened. We entered the beamed rooms, smelled the tar. Dim light coming through the windows. Gonzalo said, "It is like a tale of Hoffman. It is like a tale of Andersen. It is a dream."

Our bedroom. Smell of tar. Grandfather and René gone back to sleep. We kiss, laugh, marvel, kiss, laugh, marvel. At last out of the world. At last we have stepped off the earth, out of Paris, cafés, away from friends, husbands, wives, from streets, houses, the Dôme, Villa Seurat. We stepped off the earth into water. We are on the ship of our dreams. Alone. Big shadows all around, beams of the Middle Ages, water slapping at the stern. The little dark room at the stern, like a torture chamber, with tiny barred windows—askew.

Gonzalo said, "I will lock you up in there and torture you if you ever deceive me." Kisses, laughter, passion, the dream. The water at the stern is not covered. I say, "We will raise fishes, we will bathe here. Poor Leoncito, you are from the mountains, you are out of your element here."

"You are taking me to the bottom of the sea, like a real mermaid."

In his eyes there is so often the look of a man who is drunk, reeling. In his eyes now there is the look of fever and reverie. "Where are we? Where are we?"

Lying on the bed, body to body.

Now and then a boat passes, stirs the river; the water heaves and our boat sways. The big wooden beams crack a bit; the tree that binds it to the shore with chains cracks, sighs, laments. And it is like being on the sea, like sailing. Gonzalo awoke during the night and murmured, "*Estamos navigando.*" We lay enchanted, *ensorcelled,* lulled, half-sleeping, drugged.

"I want to keep you here, *chiquita.*"

"I want to stay here . . ."

"The Incas, the aristocratic Incas, always had a little subterranean passage in their home which led to a secret garden. A garden which was called, in Kicho, *Nanankepichu,* which means 'Not a home.' "

"That's what we'll call our boat, Leoncito!"

"Nobody knows where we are. We are out of the world."

Every moment one of us would say, "*¡Qué felicidad! ¡Qué felicidad!*"

The river is alive, gay. The tar on the walls shines.

Next day, in the sun, Leoncito and I worked to fix the place. He remembered all he knew in his hacienda: carpentry, painting, making knots. I sewed curtains for the niche of the bed. Over the bed there is a balcony to which one ascends by a ladder to reach the middle window and get out on deck. Around this I hung curtains of sackcloth so that the bed is completely canopied, hidden underneath, as in ancient alcoves.

That evening I went to Henry, who is writing so deeply, so sincerely, so simply, about his childhood that it made me weep. He said, "You spurred me on the other day, to continue."

I read, weep, and spend the night with him. He is sober, thoughtful, swimming in creation and imagination. We talk about dreams, language, childhood. In the dark. In the dark he takes me slowly, lingeringly. Flesh and spirit touching, mysteriously. No fever. No orgasm, because I am thinking of Gonzalo. I feel the heaving of our ship, of our dream, the taste of his mouth. Thinking of Gonzalo tortured with jealousy of [Maurice Sachs] the man who shares the boat with us, and so relieved when he saw him (ugly and vulgar). Gonzalo tortured when he knew I was going to have a farewell dinner with Roger and that Henry would be there.

Three lives. Three homes. Three loves. Is it that I can let nothing die, that I cannot tear myself from the old, that I cannot bear separation, ends, deaths, the passing of love—or is it that my loves are eternal and profound, that the transformation of my feeling for Henry has brought us into a new world, a prolongation into the infinite of a tremendous passion, eternal reverberations, echoes into the vault of the skies? If a great sound wave were started at one end of the earth or the sea, how long would it take for it to die, traversing millions of miles? Look at the life of the planets, of the stars, the hours multiplied a thousand times, making so ridiculous and small our days, our months, our years. What is five years of my love for Henry? What is this love for Gonzalo, like a cloud I might see from the balcony of the Villa Seurat? In the sky and in the sea there is death of stars and fishes but not of the whole—no end to motion, evolution, shining, creation. Thus my loves go on, without boundaries.

I sit and sew buttons for Henry and as I sew his buttons I am aware all at once of his loneliness, that nobody understands him as a whole, of his greatness, of his genius, of his aging; of the world in his head, of the understanding between us; of the fact that as he gets deeper and deeper into his book and his sincerity, as the real Henry melts into Henry the creator, as his illumination spreads over and around the Henry of everyday, the prosaic Henry, touches his baldness, his hands, his housework—as all this happens it touches our love, his knowledge of me; he gets nearer to himself, to truth, and to me.

As I sit sewing the cover for Hugh's couch, I am aware of Hugh's bad health, of his anxieties, of his loneliness, of his lack of genius, but of his hunger for the extraordinary, aware of the beautiful humility in Hugh which made him weep when he read the diary of our first meetings, saying, "How I hate myself then, how inadequate I was, how one can see right through your idealization of me, my inadequacy! You depreciate yourself and exalt me, but one can see that you were the one who was marvelous!" As I sit sewing for Hugh I am aware of the ordinariness of his life and that I am his genius, I am his illumination, his gaiety, and his nonsense. The changeless world of early love.

When Henry and I awake, it is Henry who sings, utters nonsense, parodies, leaps, clowns, laughs around me. When Hugh and I awake it is I who sing, invent comedies, make Hugh laugh.

As I sit sewing for Gonzalo, his torn gray coat, I am aware of his thirst for the marvelous, of his hunger for love, of his loneliness, of his poverty.

How happy, how deeply happy I am, revolving—a wheel of infinites, of extremes, touching the vaults of creation and of passion!

If I did not move and dance between them the three would turn to stone, for they are passive. Yearning, suffering. Jealousy, reaching out, is the maximum of their activity. They would fall asleep if I lay still somewhere. Henry, Gonzalo, Hugh. A kind of death hovers around them, a kind of stillness. It is only my dancing, my dancing which animates them. I slide out of Gonzalo's bed like a snake. I slide out of Henry's bed. I slide out of Hugh's bed.

Alone with Hugh, I died. Henry killed June. Gonzalo killed Helba. Killed her life instincts, her creation, by his Oriental fatality, his yielding.

I dance untrammeled—return to each full of that space in between, that change of air. Dancing, I find my flame and my joy, because I dance, slide, run, to the boat, to quai de Passy, to Villa Seurat; I keep the wind in the folds of my dress, the rain on my hair, and light in my eyes.

"Look, Gonzalo, when we kiss each other the boat rocks! We make the boat rock!"

A kiss which makes our legs weak, a kiss which suspends us between earth and sky, like our boat in the night, when the cracking and heaving of the heavy rotted wood rocks us with a heaviness and strangeness of midocean. Departure from the present, downfall when I come home to Passy and Hugh talks to me about the devaluation of the franc, the Standard Oil Company; no downfall at Villa Seurat when Henry is writing: "And as the train stops I put my foot down and my foot has put a deep hole in the dream . . ."

While I am sewing buttons for Henry I am sewing not buttons but all of Henry's world. I am sewing together the things he wants, nourishing his dream and his writing; it is the care I give to what he feels, laughs, wants, to his tears, his desires, his loneliness, his words. It is that I am listening to all he writes, it is that I lie under his reverie, making down for it. I lie under his reverie sewing magic buttons on the spiderweb of his world, giving the brightness by loving his words, seeking always to put my finger on his soul so that he himself can feel it there and feel what he feels and then write so he can make himself weep with feeling, because I took the poison and the bitterness, I took the *banderillas* out of his bleeding, enraged body, which the world tainted and made so hopeless that all he could do was to hurl insults, to spit. And now he can wander, wander and write. We can lie in the dark and talk about the language of the nightlife which he found. He found it in this craziness which I cannot find because I am too human, because I am the mother of the dream, because I could never dream violently, and altogether because I was the mother of the dream. I am sewing buttons, torn coats, because it is I who give to Hugh the father, to Hugh, who plays the father of care of all of us—while Henry writes, while Gonzalo and I dream on our boat. It is I who *know* what the father is doing, who thank him for it with a share of my own life, who am aware, and when I leave the father to enter my magic worlds with Henry and Gonzalo, I am still the mother who drugs with life and not poison, who gives to Henry not the poison June gave, which made Henry lie in the gutter and drink and curse (*Tropic of Cancer*), not to Gonzalo the heroin that intoxicated him until he fell dead in the street and was taken to a hospital, his heart breaking, exploding inside of him. I have a kind of pity for those fathers and mothers who can only give birth to us, feed us, take care of us when sick, and who give us death at the same time because that is all they can do. They put us in the *wrong* world, from which we have to escape.

SEPTEMBER 29, 1936

*T*HE LARGE WHEEL TURNING, THE WHEEL OF three-days-within-one, three-nights-within-one. At ten-thirty in the evening I am sitting in Colette Robert's studio, with her husband and Henry. Henry is in one of the moods I don't like. He is common, red faced, false, talking about Fred and reproaching me for not liking him, for not being amused by his *veulerie,* his squirming, his clownishness. I am not happy. Colette babbles with her French suavity and puerility; Robert is like a dog who shakes with dreams when asleep by the fire. Awake, he is just a good dog, a domestic dog. I look at the clock on the mantelpiece. Gonzalo is waiting, waiting in the boat. At the end of a sad day there is Gonzalo waiting in the boat.

OCTOBER 4, 1936

*P*ROBLEM OF NIGHTS, MORE AND MORE INTRICATE. Hugh so good. He lets me leave him at ten-thirty or eleven to go to the café with "Colette." Lets me spend the night at "Colette's" so as not to risk coming home late at night. But Gonzalo never has enough. If I say we have visitors, he says, "Come after they leave." I often risk a catastrophe by leaving when Hugh is asleep. The nights I spend with Henry so dangerous. I tell Gonzalo I am with Hugh. The other day I had told Gonzalo that Hugh was not very well, which was true. Gonzalo said he would telephone at nine-thirty to see how Hugh's foot was. I had to say to Hugh, "Gonzalo invited me to dinner. You know their dinner does me harm, it is always so late and so heavy—so I said I was dining with you and would join them later. But I have accepted dinner at Colette's, so please don't tell Gonzalo I am out or he will be hurt. Say I just went down for cigarettes."

Hugh promised. I left to go to Henry's for dinner. At ten minutes to nine Henry and I were taking coffee at Zeyer's. I said I had to go to the toilet. I telephoned Gonzalo. My fantastic luck would have it that he had just called Hugo, so I said, "I went out just to telephone you, Leoncito."

Luck is with me. Half of it is luck.

But Friday evening, after I had left him at six, saying I was going home, he *felt* I was not going home, and he was right. I got into a taxi and rushed to Henry's. At seven-thirty Gonzalo telephoned to give a message from Helba and I was not home, which confirmed his feeling that I was at the Villa Seurat. He was tortured all night, could not sleep, was crazy with pain and visions—suffered exactly as I suffered during those nights at the Barbizon Plaza from jealousy of Henry's daughter, of his past, and of his love of Broadway and dance halls. Gonzalo went several times to the Café Zeyer, unconsciously hoping to see me there. It just happened that this night Henry had not wanted to go out. He had bought the food, we had quietly made dinner and gone to bed early. I felt no desire, no desire whatever; I just let Henry take me.

But if we had gone to Zeyer's—

Last night after going to the movies with Hugh I begged him to let me go to Colette to hear some music—said I could not sleep, and as Hugh had seen me very excited, stimulated and keyed up by my writing of a story about the ragpickers (which I sat down and wrote at ten-thirty, when I returned from the Villa Seurat, worked on through lunch, and spasmodically all afternoon), he let me go. When I met Gonzalo he was dark and angry: "Where were you last night?"

I only admitted to having seen Henry with Kahane for an hour after I left him, to explain my not being home at seven-thirty, but the rest I denied.

When he is with me he believes again, as I believe when I am with Henry, as Rank believed me when I was there.

I am terrified by his suffering because I ask myself, Am I wholly his?

"There are dualities I don't understand," said Gonzalo. "We both have too much intuition to lie to each other."

Just as Rank had too much intuition, too.

Am I going to lose Gonzalo again to Henry—is it to be always Henry?

I dance on top of a volcano.

On Saturday afternoons, in the winter, Hugh and I like to pretend we are rich. He likes to take me shopping. He likes shops, has a fetish for underwear. I go out with him all dressed up in my black velvet suit, with mutton sleeves like those of 1900, with my velvet hat with a feather, red velvet scarf, and gloves. Everybody turns in the street to look at me. We take a taxi. We have tea. Hugh's care, patience, generosity are divine. On weekends I do all to give him pleasure. I act desire, love. I act to amuse him.

Henry said, "Whenever you are about to describe something in your diary, sit down and write about it outside of the diary, write as much as you can about it."

The result was a fantastic story about the ragpickers' village.

One night, on the boat, Gonzalo read my old "boat story," which now seemed prophetic to us.*

Is it prophetic, or is it that I carried those fantasies inside of me and they had to materialize?

The boat story has materialized. Let us invent some more.

"The imagination is nothing," I said, "I was not able to invent *you*."

---

* Anaïs Nin's story "Rag Time" appeared in the August 1938 issue of *Seven,* a short-lived literary magazine in London which also published her story "Mischa and the Analyst." The "boat story," apparently, refers to the manuscript of "Waste of Timelessness," a story written by Nin in the late 1920s in which a female protagonist discovers an old boat beached mysteriously in an overgrown garden. She enters the boat and embarks on an imaginary voyage which takes her away from her conventional life.

OCTOBER 5, 1936

*G*ONZALO AND I ARE SITTING IN A CAFÉ AND HE IS reading the ragpickers' story with delight. "How fantastic, Anaïs; I find one of my own feelings in it, about the love of fragments, of the unfinished."

Henry and I are sitting on his bed, and he is reading the ragpickers' story. "Strange and whimsical, very strange and wonderful."

With Gonzalo, as with Henry, I descend again into a kind of underworld, the caves of Pluto, among *clochards,* ragpickers, scamps, rogues, vagabonds, anarchists.

Talking to Henry, I said I didn't like clowns. I liked madmen. Henry said, "Madmen are too serious. I like clowns."

On the same day I can have sweet moments with Hugh, Henry, and Gonzalo. Whimsical talk with Hugh about my jealousy of the cat because he can take him into his coat. With Hugh I feel small, defenseless, hurt by the world, dependent. I would like to lie like Mickey inside of his coat. To be with me a little longer, Hugh takes a three-quarter-of-an-hour ride in a bus, on our way back from a visit to Elsa at the hospital. He is late to the office.

With Henry I am mature and must do the protecting.

With Gonzalo I feel physically protected. He would knock a man down. He takes care of me romantically, lights the fire in the boat. *Serves.* But he is a *tzigane,* made to play the guitar and to love.

Artistically, he has infallible taste. He knew the flaws in the ragpicker story. He pushes me out into the fantastic, which my life with Henry had destroyed.

OCTOBER 8, 1936

*M*OMENTS WITH GONZALO WHEN WE ARE SPANISH. Moments when I am aware of my Spanishness, when I feel at once sensual and pure; when I feel the crucifix I used to wear at my throat, the medals, the incense in my nostrils; when I remember the balcony in Barcelona, the little altar next to my bed, the candles and the artificial flowers, the face of the Virgin and the sense of death and sin; when I remember all I was before I landed in America. I feel like a girl of nineteen who has been sheltered by her father and mother, who has lived with a fear and respect of father and God, a virgin. I feel my small breasts in my modest dress, my legs closed, the hymns I knew, and the first awe before the drip of honey. I feel that Gonzalo has come from the Jesuits' school, on his horse, having traveled all night to catch a glimpse of me, and he sees my face as the face of the Madonna, and he will marry me and keep me jealously to himself, like an Arab woman, and the world remains unknown, and the tremors of innocence are lovely.

I feel that Gonzalo could kill the man who dared to approach me, to love me. I feel that he can never forget I have been a woman with legs open, and that I have shouted with voluptuous joys.

At moments when he is taking me, when my legs open to him, an image comes before him. He stops dead, he closes my legs. I see the cloud in his eyes. They roll with a kind of madness. He murmurs unfinished phrases. At first, I did not know. Then I heard the words: "Exclusive, it must be exclusive. I can't bear . . ." And I know he remembers Henry. Lines out of my Father novel (I never showed him the novel about Henry).

What he suffers from, too, is my pagan statements. When I am with him I remember my old *pudeur*. I remember my girlhood, when I had no thoughts of sex and no sensuality, but passion. Have I done violence to my real self to gain liberation? Am I so pagan, do I like my body naked under a dress? I associated *pudeur* with inhibition and hated it. Today, now that I am free, I can return to my natural *pudeur.* But there are things I cannot recapture. I have become so natural in sensuality that Gonzalo's *pudeur* touches me and yet instinctively I try to free him. I have not yet seen him naked; I have never seen his sex. There is almost a furtive quality to his lovemaking. It is I who laugh and tease and am pagan.

All the while I am grateful to him for loving my real self, for coming closer to my soul than Henry. But all evil, corruption, and deceit are out of our mystic marriage. No darkness between Gonzalo and me. No perversities.

He is winning back his vitality, his strength, and his potency. He is grateful to me. He is more sensual, vigorous, but he inhibits me. I cannot feel the orgasm with him.

Gonzalo saying, "Get closer to me, get closer. *Pégate a mi. Pégate a mi.*"

O C T O B E R   1 1 ,   1 9 3 6

WHEN I GAVE MYSELF TO HENRY, TO HIS WORK AND his life, I gave up and denied part of my real self: that is, the subtleties, the refinements of feeling, the delicacy in relationship. I went to Henry *knowing* about his grossness, his lack of understanding, his brutality, and enjoyed the lustiness, and thought I would get strengthened as one does by real life, troubles, struggles. But in all this I lost my happiness. Henry found happiness in the way I treated him.

OCTOBER 12, 1936

*T*WO DREAMLIKE NIGHTS WITH GONZALO. I SEE
him as a child. Vital. Overflowing with vitality.

After being with him, to go to Henry is like going into a Nordic
climate. The hard blue eyes, the lack of emotion. When the sex is
over in Henry, then nothing takes its place. It was all sex, sex. All the
emotion he was capable of, he spent.

The first thing Henry says when I rush over to him this morning
because he is sick is "Do you like this nursing business? I don't. If
you were sick I guess I'd run out of the house. When people are sick
I think they ought to be left to die, that's what I think."

I know he's boasting, and I go right on. He takes the hot rum,
the medicines, the electric radiator. He begins to revel in feeling better
or warmer. But I feel harder toward him, toward his selfishness. I
leave him asleep, without remorse, to meet Gonzalo, who is insane
with jealousy, who felt I would see Henry today, who suffers, suffers,
suffers. And we sit in the café while I say passionate things to him.
"If I were asked to, Gonzalo, if I were given a chance, if anything
happened such that I could make a choice, I'd choose you out of the
whole world, I would give up everybody and everything for you. I'd
let the whole world die. It is only pity, only pity which made me go
there today. I feel the absolute with you, completeness."

My voice, my feeling, touch Gonzalo. He believes me. And I give
him a proof of love. First today I had planned to spend the night with
Henry, but I felt so drawn, such yearning to be with Gonzalo, such
discouragement at the lack of *union* with Henry, of nearness, of
warmth, that after taking care of Henry all day, I left him, pretending
not to be well myself and promising to return early tomorrow morning. Then I told Gonzalo that Hugh had not come back and that he
could come. What joy, to await him in my warm perfumed room.

O CTOBER 1 3 , 1 9 3 6

*L*AST NIGHT GONZALO SO SENSUAL, POUNDING, pounding and saying, "I have never come off so violently, so strongly. Why am I so slow to come? I am very slow." He does not seem to know that it is good, good for the woman. He seems to have little confidence in himself, in what he is, in all he does, feels. The Indian slowness. So good.

His kisses taste to me as no other kisses I have ever known. At the bottom of Henry's kisses I always felt a blindness, a wetness, an instinct, a blind animal feeling, impersonal; the body aroused, the instinct.

With Gonzalo I am terribly aware of love, of the taste of his flesh, of the *noblesse* of his flesh, of desire permeated with feeling, less bestiality, so much knowingness of *each other*. I taste Gonzalo all at once, the quality of his deepest being with the quality of his flesh, a flesh made of dreams, of humanity, of sensuousness. Flesh and soul intermarried, no evil, no baseness, no deceit, no grossness, no cowardice. The expression of his eyes is dazzlingly beautiful at moments—never saw the burning of spirit with life in one—eyes of coal, animal eyes and soul eyes—all at once—softening one, stirring I-don't-know-what layers of idealism.

No need to keep my eyes half closed, as I had with Henry because at times I could see what Henry was to me, and the other Henry who revealed his unconscious in his work and toward others, the Henry *unheroic,* the beggar, hard, calculating, cynical, with a love of dirt and grossness, the false, the buffoon. I knew *my* Henry was sometimes an effort for Henry to maintain, and when we went out together my Henry exploded.

GONZALO ATTRACTED BY BLOOD, BY MY THREE DAYS of bloodshedding. A night of orgiastic love-making. A new Gonzalo. Sexual, sensual, erotic, and extravagant. Blood madness. Exhaustion.

He lies there wondering over our month of chastity. "What did you think? At first I couldn't understand it myself, then I did. I saw there was a psychological reason. I couldn't take you as I would another woman. You meant too much to me. You overwhelmed me."

"You had to find a more devious route, make large circles around me, and thus you found a new way to me, touched new layers."

Through the soft layers of passion and reverie, I feel the steel blade of danger.

Destruction.

Everything around Gonzalo becomes inert and fatalistic. Even in the smallest detail, he blocks himself.

Helba confided in Hugh, "Gonzalo and his fatalism, Gonzalo always saying *mañana,* killed my career." It finally paralyzed her. Gonzalo's fear of success, of commercialization. "He is a bohemian." Helba, like all real workers, is not.

So, again, I get the bohemian, the destroyer, and the weight.

But today Henry is creating, living creatively. I won. He did not kill me, as he killed June. Gonzalo won't make me sick and weak, as he made Helba; frustrated. Creation which cannot express itself becomes madness.

I am certain of my strength. I can leave my serious, orderly work, my gravity, my unbohemian world, and go with Gonzalo, for reverie and passion.

He is the man I want. My *tzigane.* Let him fill his slave and lover's role. I'll do the rest! On love and worship I can build a million worlds, and create infinitely. With his voice, his laughter, his gaze on me, I can create! With his arm around my shoulder, his black curl behind his ear, his heavy-shoed feet, his humor, his love of wine, and his sensitiveness, I can create! With his adoration and his eagerness, his passion, his jealousy, I can create!

OCTOBER 21, 1936

IL S'AGÎT DE MIEUX MENTIR, DE DÉJOUER L'IN-tuition même des autres. For that I prepare myself like an actress. I study my role. I ask myself what mistake I made the last time. Found first that I must not *think* that I am going to see Henry while I am with Gonzalo. I must not live ahead of the present, because Gonzalo feels it. I must put myself in the mood of being absolutely and wholly with Gonzalo, and at six o'clock I must leave him for an obscure reason I have forgotten. I must put myself in the mood of the story I am telling. If I have said I am going home to Hugh I must keep myself in the mood I would be in if I were going home to Hugh—that is, resigned and regretful. Here the role begins. I imagine I am going home to Hugh and how I would feel. I get into the mood. Sad eyes. Regret. Clinging to Gonzalo and the present moment. No eagerness or hurry. Anyway, not to arouse doubts, I must never hurry away. Above all I must put myself wholly *in* the present.

If I were acting the role of Mélisande I would equally have to be wholly in the role. I could not let my thoughts wander to Ophelia's feelings, or I would not be conscious that after the show I would spend the night with my lover. Wholeness. While I am with Gonzalo my passion for him makes it easy for me to throw myself into our world. *Pas de distractions!* To the jealous temperament the distraction is fatal. It is that wholeness maintained till the end which is convincing. I can easily concentrate this way, lose and abandon myself to whatever I am doing. And as I do so I get more and more exalted by the present—the moment with Henry, Gonzalo, or Hugh. And it is this wholeness which they feel which gives them the perfect illusion of a complete love. I set out to make my night with Gonzalo *absolute,* my nights with Henry, or a Saturday afternoon with Hugh. *Pas de distractions!* It is rare when I think of Henry while I am with Gonzalo. It is with Hugh I have the greatest difficulty to keep attentive. Our life together is the palest of all, the most unreal. Then comes Henry, who is transposed to cooler regions and pales before the fiery hours with Gonzalo.

Having been wholly with Gonzalo yesterday afternoon, and having kept all thought of Henry out of my head throughout, I could leave him at the Gare Montparnasse Métro station and ask him in a hazy way, "Where do I change for Passy?" And he felt nothing, no pang of doubt, no fear. In fact I had succeeded in hypnotizing myself into thinking I was going home so completely that once in the Métro I came to with a jerk, just as an actress does when the curtain falls, and only then did I look at the signs and took the opposite direction.

Sincerity in acting comes from feeling the part. The acting of deceptions on the stage does not impair at all my sincerity of feeling, of love. It would be like saying that an actress could not really fall in love in her private life because she did so much pretending on the stage. The sincerity of the love, on the contrary, helps and impels me to lie better and more artistically for the sake of not causing pain. It is a game in which I always risk the loss of one man, perhaps the three, my whole life and happiness. In the movies I always like the spy stories, the need to act, to deceive, to pretend, even love. Counter-spying, cleverness, astuteness.

The drunken grandfather of the river began to resent our presence. He had been alone on the boat for a long time. Gonzalo's darkness frightened him. When Gonzalo lit the stove he came out to curse the noise we made.

OCTOBER 22, 1936

*H*ELBA ALWAYS TELLS THE STORY OF WHEN HER mother first saw Gonzalo: *"¡Ay, qué negrito! Dios mío, qué negrito sus pecados."*

The color of his sins!

The mattress on the floor. The tarred beams over our heads. The stove snoring. The boat creaking. The water lapping the flanks of the boat. Semidarkness. Shadows. Street lamp twinkling through the windows. Gonzalo and I blinded with sensuality—mouths, penis, vulva, caresses, wet kisses.

Old man shouting, throwing things against the wall at the moment when we are most intoxicated.

Gonzalo leaping up, furious, eyes blazing, hair wild, big body tense, snorting fire. Throwing himself on the old man's door, kicking it with his feet, demolishing it. Old man terrified. Lying half-naked in his smelly pile of rags, with his beret on, holding a stick. Gonzalo in his obscure, muddled French shouting, "You're a bad old man. Get out of here. Now you're going to get out of here or I'll fetch the police."

Old man hazy with drunkenness. Frightened. Refuses to move.

Gonzalo sends René to fetch the police. He forces me to hide so I won't be mixed up if there is an investigation.

The police come. Gonzalo holds the oil lamp. René talks and shouts, "Get dressed. The proprietor has told you to get out. I have the papers here. Get dressed."

"Who demolished the door, I ask you, who? It isn't I who should be taken to the police station."

He lay there. Could not find his pants. Talked. Policeman talked. They could not dress him. He kept muttering.

"Well, what do I care? Suppose you do throw me in the river.

It's all the same to me. I don't care if I die. I'm not bad. I run errands for you, don't I?"

"You make a big noise every time we come, you raise hell."

"I was sound asleep, sound asleep, wasn't I? He knocked the door down, then you come for me. I'll not get out. I'm too old. I can't find my pants."

For an hour, thus, innocence, haziness, drunken logic, until finally the humor overwhelmed everybody and he was told he could stay if he lay quiet.

"*Je ferais le mort,* I'll play dead," he said. He was thoroughly docile, bewildered, too drunk and too frightened. I stood hiding in the other room, where I could hear everything, and laughing at the old man's remarks. The policeman left. René went to bed. Gonzalo and I laughed together, still resentful that the old man was puncturing our dream, breaking our intimacy. Gonzalo said he would go mad if he thought the old man could have seen us through a crack in the wall. His whole *pudeur* was outraged at the presence of another, so near to our caresses. The *pudeur* of jungle animals, of cats. This *pudeur* in me which Henry's way of living outraged. Yet I liked the humiliation of my secrecies, my prides. I thought it was good for me, the openness, the absence of delicacy, Fred in the next room.

But now I liked Gonzalo's fury—his strength.

The rage had awakened us. Somehow we came to talk about Rank's philosophy, Helba's neurosis. Gonzalo eludes the life of the head. He understands, he asks questions, he says, "I want to read those books"—then suddenly he turns against it, plunges into kissing, curses the intellectual worlds, the literary worlds, pleads for life. And now I realized what a marvelous fit he was to my present mood. After Rank, Fraenkel, and Henry, a great intellectual laziness overpowered me. When I came back from New York this time I wanted only poetry and emotion and the night. Then came Gonzalo. The night. The dream. Made for life and passion. Quickly, I too close my eyes, plunge into kissing. We don't need ideas. Gonzalo and I have reached the marvelous point where we are impregnated with *meaning;* what we have thought, studied, intellectually sought, has melted, fused, disappeared, merely to color a passionate life with significance, but subconsciously. We meet in darker regions. Strange alchemy. The head is clouded. Bodies alive, but not just sexually alive, not alive as I was with George Turner, but alive with the soul within mystery and darkness.

This darkness I want to keep. I would like to see him only at night. I would like never to awake again to a life of thought, to forget it all for sensation.

This flare of emotion, with subtle accords of nature, of instinctive and spiritual elements, satisfies me.

When the incident with the old man was over Gonzalo commented on its mellow ending. He said a Spanish *clochard* in the same circumstances would have already set fire to the boat, or poisoned the water we drink, or murdered one of us in the dark. These are the very things I imagined the old man would do. These are the fears which Rank would have termed neurotic and which arise from my blood ancestry, my heritage of violence and revenge. Gonzalo said he could easily kill a man in a moment of anger. I know what plans I made at night to kill the women I was jealous of, to poison them, throw them from a window. This violence is in me and is equally tamed and powerfully held in by Western civilization. I like to see Gonzalo's great primitive force break through Western restraint. I enjoyed that shattered door.

But the enemy today is not jealousy but fatigue. This life on three floors, three levels, in three languages, three climates, three tones, three rhythms, is wearing me out. I am deeply tired. I crave solitude, isolation.

OCTOBER 25, 1936

GONZALO IS A SENSUAL VOLCANO, AFIRE, NEVER enough. I am ready to ask for mercy! I did not believe, after all the idealism, the chastity, the emotionalism, that we could descend into this furnace of animal desire. Now it is several times in one moment, until we lie dead with exhaustion. He smears his face with honey and sperm, we kiss in this odor and wetness, and we possess each other over and over again madly. Yet I cannot have an orgasm. Why, why, why?

I left Gonzalo yesterday, after an hour with him, and went to Henry; and he can rouse me to hatred, anger, despair almost, so aroused am I sexually, not by a difference in vigor, but by something undefinable, slower, wetter, mellower, more purely animal than Gonzalo—or is it by Henry? Am I giving Henry the *whore* faithfulness, the orgasm faithfulness, the ultimate surrender? Gonzalo has not yet reached the deepest layer of my instinctual being. I can't understand. Yet I rush to him and not to Henry when I have a choice, and I leap with joy and hunger when he comes for only an hour Sunday afternoons. His desire is savage enough, full of jealousies and exclusivities. He was tortured by jealousy of Eduardo. And I seem to remain loyal to each relationship. I think only pain keeps me away from Henry.

Loyal to my relationship with Eduardo, I receive him with great joy. Get drunk on talk with him, find my head, which I lost with Gonzalo: daylight, analysis, clarifying, complete confidences, unending. Eduardo struggling to part from Feri, who has deceived, cheated, and betrayed him.

With Eduardo, this life which buffets us, loses us, hurts us, makes us dizzy, gets orchestrated. The river ceases its tumult; we empty our boats of surplus water so as not to sink! We call upon the stars and philosophy to cry why, and how, and to rebel, curse, accept, forgive! Wherever life baffles or hurts us.

Gonzalo wants to live in opium and under the sea, where I love to live best of all. *Mais je suis un poisson volant* (But I am a flying fish).

Henry starved for me. Met me at five in the afternoon, already in bed, waiting for me to get in with him.

Gaiety. Do I seek only the high moments?

I don't know—I don't want to know. I want to live until I crack, crack with too-muchness, until all my harem turns jealously against me, rebels, divorces me, until they all cry out with pain and joy, anger and murder, until they murder me for my betrayals. Yet I have been the most tragically loyal woman in the world, loyal to the past, to my early loves, to *my man Henry,* to my lovers, my victims, my games, my illusions, past, present, to my own Father and brothers! Too much love! Never enough!

I wish, I wish Gonzalo could penetrate into the deepest, deepest womb in me, stir my womb as Henry did, lie there, obscurely, inside my flesh. He says I make him leap several times a day—at the very thought of me! I am in love, but I am not branded, burned, scarred by him. Is this the love that makes one happy? Can I lie back and let him suffer? Watching his suffering sometimes does strange things to me. When Eduardo came I thought with *pleasure,* Gonzalo will be jealous. He will imagine Eduardo and me alone—Eduardo in my room.

And I took pleasure in seeing him suffer. He asked me the question I expected: "Where does he sleep?"

I remembered my desperate torment over Henry, the pictures which kept me awake. I thought, How foolish, all this pain. It makes me cynical, just as Rank's suffering did—to see the other suffer. Is there always a scale? Must one always suffer, and the other not, a difference?

Instinctive love is like a wound in the body. Primitive love is torture. And does it only happen once?

Pandora's box. I want to live with my eyes closed. I don't want to *know,* I want to live.

Knowing stops you from living.

Closed eyes always and the honey flowing . . .

But I ask myself this: When I tortured Henry, his instinctive love was aroused. Will mine for Gonzalo only awaken then? Is this only a rest from pain, such as I gave Henry after June? For the moment Gonzalo is suffering. I am at rest. Then it will change. Or am I free forever?

NOVEMBER 2, 1936

SOMBER DAYS. EVERYONE WEIGHED DOWN, OP-
pressed. Eduardo obsessed with his Feri.
Hugh suddenly jealous of Henry and trying to find in the reading of
Black Spring a trace of me. Helba like a wounded deer—always weeping. Gonzalo dark and tormented by a new conflict. If he goes to Peru
he can get his inheritance from his mother and solve their economic
troubles. He suffers at taking help from us. He says he has been living
blindly, that now his pride is aroused, that he questions the value of
the things he lived for, that he has come to the end of his self-
effacement. (Repetition of Henry's very early phrase: "I have been
living blindly.") But what are we to do? He can't bear to leave me
for three or four months. I can't bear to let him go.

Until now Gonzalo had not entered my being deeply, physically,
had not touched the cords of instinct. But yesterday the thought of
parting was so intolerable that it awakened me to a full realization of
the bond. When he stood there talking in the middle of the room I
had a yearning and pain all through my body, a tearing feeling which
I know well. I have come slowly to this feeling for Gonzalo, but I
have it now, and it is overwhelming. There is certainly a long resistance to love, to being possessed, out of the fear of pain. I am beginning to suffer from jealousy too, but I will never suffer as I did with
Henry, because Gonzalo is faithful. How amazing that I can feel this
love for Gonzalo when he does not possess me sexually. I cannot feel
the orgasm with him.

The diabolical undercurrents are Helba's confessions to Hugh,
who is analyzing her with all he learned from me. So that through
him I discover that Helba never loved Gonzalo with passion, that they
are brother and sister, that his fatalism destroyed her. Helba yesterday
kissed me passionately with the same drowning-woman eyes as June
did, and just as with June, I try not to displace her, though she has

had crises of jealousy. Underneath we admire each other, and because we admire each other we realize how much right each one has to Gonzalo's worship; and just as with June, she does not altogether let go of him, *only* because she fears abandon, *not* because of love of Gonzalo; and *again* I combat my own jealousy of her through love, loving. I want Gonzalo for myself but I see his devotion is like mine to Hugh, to the past, to Henry, even when I do not desire him.

But all this time I feel I am fighting against a dark force, a weight. I feel restricted. I feel that within a thousand walls I manage to take flight, to soar, to create a fictitious and illusory heaven for myself by taking only the intense moments, the beauty of my talks with Henry, and not the life or people around him; solitude with Gonzalo on a boat and *not* the cavelike blackness, dampness, poverty, and sadness around him, not the apartment with a sick Helba, an unbalanced Elsa shouting, quarreling, or touching her neck where she was operated, touching it as a pianist touches a keyboard; not a mad Dostoyevskian violinist, Prague, who eats excrements and washes his face with urine, who married his manic-depressive wife while they were both in an insane asylum; not the food served on the table with wine stains, cigarette ashes, bread crumbs.

Was my ragpicker story a humorous, fantastic acceptance of futility? Is my life, when it seems to culminate in a heaven of passion, most illusory, most dangerously balanced over a precipice? The further I soar into the dream, the essence, the maximum, touching the vault of the sky and the center of the earth, the tighter does the cord of reality press my neck; the more I move within this magic pattern, the more I suffocate under a nameless terror and anxiety. Expansion, so wide, like the full opened compass. Break? Or fatigue. Fatigue of soul and body and sex . . . seeking an absolute only by multiplicity, an absolute in abstraction, a synthesis of dispersed elements, not one man, one home, one love, one bed: one, the absolute in fragments! An absolute that does not flow serenely but that I have to grasp by sheer wakefulness, as if I had to grab a constantly shooting star out of a capricious sky. There! In flight always, and the madness of being too awake, passing from one bed to another, lurking, waiting.

As I come out of Henry's studio—Henry, who was waiting for me in bed, a starved Henry, eager to possess me—I see a man standing at the end of the Villa Seurat. It is Gonzalo, waiting to confront me—Gonzalo, whom I left at the Colarossi [art academy].

This force in me, which did not twinkle into an orgasm, did not catch the ultimate fire in Henry's arms, because I did not desire him, this force I now carry like unexploded dynamite. It is dynamite that has not exploded, but the cord is lit, the little flame runs up and down the cord with a kind of Dionysian joyousness, a dancing, the little flames run around the heart of the dynamite and do not touch it, and the little flame keeps me breathless, nerves bristling with their heads up, necks stretched, eager, hungry, thirsty, eyes open, ears peaked, all the little nerves waiting for the orgasm that will send the blood running through them and make them sleep.

The nerves awake, clairvoyant, on the brink of hysteria, the myriad little nerves on the brink of hysteria wait for the pause of sleep and death, for the dynamite to explode, for the walls to fall, for the past to crumble, for the absolute that does not shoot through the sky, always fugitive, a fugitive absolute, uncapturable, *tête de Méduse,* legs of a centipede, of an octopus. Do all burning fires have a hundred flames pointing in all directions, was there never a round flame with one tongue? Why does this force, which did not erupt in quicksilver through the veins, why does it rush out in typhoon shapes and round up each monster walking through the street—to question its intentions, to imagine its perversities, to slide between the lovers, the darkest desires, the blackest eroticisms, the most twisted appetites.

This man with his little girl, why are his eyes so wet, his mouth so wet, why are her eyes so tired, why is her dress so short, his glance so oblique, why this malaise I feel as I pass them; why is this young man so white, his eyes haggard, why is there scum on his lips, the scum of veronal; why does that woman wait under the lamplight with a hand in her muff—a revolver—why did the two sisters murder their crazy brother, living many years with him alone in a big house? . . . Prague's wife sits absolutely silent, with a wrinkle between her eyes . . . Elsa touches her neck with the fine scar around it, Helba puts on her coat made of two coats sewn together, Helba puts on a brooch with all the stones missing. We ate oysters in a room all glued with seashells, as I wanted my room covered with seashells, furs, and colored stones, because I am still seeking the fairy tale, while the man who sells us stockings and cigarettes at half price carries cocaine in his pocket. I did not guess it. I never guess these things. That is my innocence. I do not invent or decipher evil or danger except at moments when this force in me, which did not explode, poisons me, overflows, spills out in the street, runs into the gutter, perceives the twists, the old grandfather hidden in the prow of the ship waiting to stab Gonzalo; perceives the rust on the coal *coffre,* the leak in the roof, the rain falling on the floor in puddles, the fire that has gone out, sour wine in a cup, cigarette butts on the floor, and the lover's snoring; perceives, is saddened, closes her eyes, brushing against ugliness, destruction, descending trapdoors without falling into a trap, passing through as if invisible, untouchable, the one the automobiles cannot crush though she crosses without looking right and left, desiring always the jaws of the whale, the dismembering in the jaw, meeting always with wings, with eyes opening on my passing, eyes opening to the heavens, heavenward, angels dancing on the cord of the dynamite, flames turning blue like the mystic watch lights of hospitals, convents, I am still listening to those who are weeping, it is right that the seed should not burst in me, that the body should leave the earth pulled by the string of nerves and spill its pollen only in space, for the fairy tale wears a gown that makes a breeze, a space between the feet and earth or wood, the footsteps must not be heard, the blood must remain quicksilver shining up and down blue veins, blue like the pious lights of hospitals, to hear, to catch the rhythm of wings.

What I call heaven: when no one is *suffering*—when I know Mother is happy, Joaquin fulfilling his desire, Henry able to work in peace, Gonzalo satisfied, Hugh contented, Eduardo relieved of his pain, Helba consoled. If *one* of them suffers I suffer too—my joy is spoiled. If Gonzalo is tortured I cannot enjoy Henry. I cannot enjoy myself while the other suffers. That is the real secret of my life. That is why I cannot explode, take my choice, sacrifice several people to my happiness—it would not be my happiness.

The night we had dinner at Helba's, Gonzalo was counting the people to set the table and he did not count himself.

Gonzalo has a marvelous intuitive mind which he refuses to use. He calls astrology "dry." He seldom reads.

He says he loves in me my warmth, aliveness, and that I am not "literary."

Suddenly he will say the most intuitive thing—clairvoyant. At other times he is all mixed up and he raves. I have learned, with Henry, to accept the wisdom and overlook the errors, because that is primitive!

NOVEMBER 8, 1936

WHEN I HAVE TO WAIT FOR GONZALO I PLAY WITH fire. I try to get the lanterns working. The lanterns I stole won't work. I try alcohol, oil, petrol. I let the lantern fall. The flames spill on the floor. The glass breaks. There are little explosions. I watch everything without fear, with delight. Fire fascinates me.

I would like to be a spy and live closer to danger.

When Turner danced with me, more desirous than ever, I felt nothing. I feel nothing with Henry— nothing. I hate Hugh's caresses more desperately. I only feel Gonzalo. Now it happens that talking with Eduardo I have made several discoveries about sex: Some men have what corresponds to frigidity in women. They have an erection, they even come off, but they don't feel satisfied. Unsatisfied women or men, all behave alike: I *before* I met Henry, June, Louise, Gonzalo. Tenseness. Search for other sensations. Fever. Nervousness. Sleeplessness. Much activity without pausing. Nerves tense.

Satisfaction brings relaxation.

Gonzalo's sensuality was difficult—from all he told me. Much in the imagination. Before, or after. But realization, satisfaction rare. Feeling of disgust when having been with a woman not loved. When loving someone, it took him time. Now he has said repeatedly, "I have never come off so powerfully. It's so strong, Anaïs—so strong." He pours his whole being into me. I remember my Father saying the same thing: *"Nunca he venido tan fuerte."* Eduardo says it means he is satisfied, has found his type. He will get less restless, less tense, less nervous. And I, I am getting nervous, keyed up, my imagination is in a fever, no more feeling of *"apaisement,"* no more connection with nature, with earth.

I can't tell whether it has come out of fidelity to Henry, or because I have to be passive and with Henry I had to be active, or because Henry communicated to me his slowness and *"détente,"* which is marvelous for sensuality. I don't know. But I am not satisfied. Yet I love so much I would go anywhere with Gonzalo. I don't care about the sex. There is plenty of passion outside of the orgasm.

Perhaps I just need time, just as Gonzalo did. Or perhaps I have to feel wholly, absolutely possessed by one—as I felt for a few weeks, when I went to Rank in N.Y. believing I loved him.

I don't know. But I am happy that Gonzalo is satisfied. Happy to feel his vigorous desire.

Dream: Sitting on the roof of a house in China, waiting for the darkness. Sitting among the roof tiles made of broken Chinese cups and saucers, with the last of the tea leaves still in the hollows of the cups. Sitting among the cups and saucers and waiting for the darkness, when I would slip down and enter the city secretly. Sliding down the sandalwood beams, finding that the walls were made of sliding panels. A Chinese woman with a porcelain face slid open the panel and showed me the way in. I was kneeling before a meal, an immense round plate at my knees, filled with pearl-studded slippers, a sauce of angel hair, *foligrane,* icicles, and melted gold. I looked intently and caressingly because I knew that each room I would be in, I would be in only once, and all I saw I would see only once, so I looked caressingly at the carved panel, at the dish at my feet. I smelled the odor of this room, I saw the light filtered through parchment paper. Each panel I moved led me through the Chinese house but also out of it, and once I was out it would be for good, and so I pushed the panels lingeringly and passed through each room with regret, looking caressingly at the light filtering softly yellow. The carving on the wood was so fine that I thought I could read it like a book. I began to decipher the carving, but the meaning eluded me; it reminded me of many things, none of which I could remember entirely; and the last panel, which I pushed gently, found me out in the streets of China with doorless houses, windowless, with lanterns swinging all alike and dolls sitting on the sidewalk.

NOVEMBER 12, 1936

*L*YING DOWN WITH ME, GONZALO SAYS, "THIS IS the infinite." Lying down with me, Henry says, "A good fuck will fix you fine!" Lying down with me, Hugh says, "Take care of yourself, little cat. You look tired."

Gonzalo gets mad with jealousy. Hugh gets dark and somber and silent. Henry barks, rants, raves at something else *surrounding* the affect of the jealousy.

What I call making a heaven for myself is making a harmony. I am always trying to compose a heaven, picking the best moments out of all relationships—like finding Henry starving, Hugh eager for Sunday, Gonzalo thirsty! I, ready to cry for mercy, have all the intensity I wanted. Spending three-quarters of my life in bed. Glad when I am taken only once in a day. Trying to avoid lying with Henry and Gonzalo the same day but sometimes it happens and their sperm mingles in my womb.

I know only one recipe for happiness: Take the sperm of three different men (as different as possible!), let it mix in your womb. If the transfusion can take place the same day the alchemy will produce perfection.

When Gonzalo and I are lying close, he says, "This is the only thing that counts in this world." Like a woman—born the lover of woman's dreams. Henry says playfully, "There go twenty pages!"

At two o'clock I am in *Nanankepichu*. Gonzalo whispers: *"¡Qué linda hora!"* At five o'clock I am in a taxi which follows the boulevard Raspail and catches up with the bus. Gonzalo is standing on the platform. Did he see me?

The pleasurable *frisson* of the gambler. He did not see me. He is dreaming. He is sad. If he had seen me he would know I was on my way to Villa Seurat.

At Villa Seurat Henry is in a blaze of activity. People. Letters. Hopes. Reviews. New friends. Ideas. Ideas.

N O V E M B E R   1 8 ,   1 9 3 6

ONVINCED NOW THAT UNDER A BALANCED EXTE-
rior I am hysterical. The hysteria reaches its maximum during the moonstorm. I am always on the verge of explosion. I want to cry, laugh, sing, or dance, or scream. I cannot easily fall asleep. I hate tranquility. I am tranquil only when tired. I hate the recuperative processes—sleep, and repose, and pauses!

I get very tired because *everything* touches and moves me. I am never indifferent. Each person I see touches my feelings, sympathy, pity; or arouses my creativity. I have to meddle with broken lives— repair, blow life into the drowned, pick up the fallen. I am bitterly tired of suffering, but there seems to be no way out of suffering but cruelty. Indifference, passivity, is impossible to me. I have to be either a masochist or a sadist. When I am a sadist I suffer *with* my victim.

No way out of slavery but that of becoming the slavedriver.

I do not deny the occasional pleasure I got from maltreating Hoffman, Turner, and other men. But when Gonzalo is lying in my arms and is telling me how much he loves the places where he has suffered, my heart stands still with a kind of horror. An abyss under my feet. I feel then the one who *can* be the tyrant. I feel the man who can be tortured. I feel the slave yielding. Domination is aroused. I see how I softly dominate Hugh, delicately dominate Henry, and invisibly dominate Gonzalo. But each time I hurt them I feel all they feel. And I have struggled to free them from their need of pain. Gonzalo is begging for suffering. The more passion I pour over him, the more tortured he is by jealousy.

Since it is my strength they love, it is hard not to use this strength cruelly. I don't. I rule by seduction, charm, devotion, and by returning with interest all that is given me. If many women think they can make three men's lives marvelous, let them try. It takes superhuman agility, thoughtfulness, the gift of enveloping, of pouring so much into one hour that it seems like a complete day and night to the man.

NOVEMBER 20, 1936

ANANKEPICHU: NOW THERE IS A BLACK RUG. THE Byzantine lamp which glowed in my bedroom in Louveciennes hangs over our head. There is a black lacquer table. I brought food, which we heated. We ate on a box, by candlelight. I lie on the rug next to the stove. Gonzalo is kissing me, warming my feet, warming my kimono, enveloping me in adoration. Most of what happens between us happens in silence. Very little is brought to light, to the surface.

After taking me in the afternoon Gonzalo took me again at night, but boldly, facing me, all nervousness and hesitancy gone. He looked at the lamp and said, *"Lamparita aphrodisiaca."* He talked about our month of chastity. Said he had felt anxiety—had asked a doctor friend, who had only said: *"Eres un anxioso."* Now he knew it had been my fault. He wanted to punish me for my sensual life, wanted something else. I came very near fulfillment that night. The little lamp, the shining blackness, the water lapping—all this takes us far away. When we heard a sound of something falling in water, I said, "It's a little fish leaping."

The next day, in the café, we have a scene. "You were at Villa Seurat." I say it is no different than his care of a sick, deaf Helba. Emotion. Chaos. Blindness.

I leave him to go to Villa Seurat! *That* he could never imagine.

There Henry and I lie on the couch quietly, talking. He is tired. We are talking about the clippings from newspapers. Henry has been cutting out humorous and fantastic items. I, the horrors. I say, "Let's make a scenario of them." I have some notes already. I have been noting some in my diary. Henry thinks it is a fine idea. I have begun.

One night Hugh was listening to the radio. After a piece of music there was a silence and then we heard clearly the ticking of a clock. Hugh said, "That's my watch at the pawnshop calling me!"

The other day, when we were doing the accounts, he said, "I know you're cheating me, but that it is for others."

He said it with a twinkle, a divine indulgence. He has been wearing paperclips in place of his gold cufflinks—the *sous-directeur* of the National City Bank!

He is happy. I am out every night now, home only Saturday and Sunday. He talks with astrologers, he goes to the movies with his friends, or he falls asleep very early. This is better, he said, than if I were in New York!

Louveciennes is dead. It was dismantled, the furniture was put out in the garden and sold at auction. I kept the Arabian bed and a few other things for *Nanankepichu*. It was a feverish day, tragic and comical. I felt little pain, tried not to remember. But each object auctioned off contained a fragment of my past. I had no regrets, except for the passing of time and the death of homes, objects, and the passing and changing of love. I remembered mostly my passion for Henry, our caresses, the furnace of our talks.

When it was dark and the sale was still going on, the empty house, lit up by bare bulbs, shone out like a mosque once more, in gorgeous warm colors, shone vividly in that colorless gray and petty French village—and died. Everybody carried off furniture and ornaments, mirrors, curtains, pots and pans; and all the traces of our life there were scattered all around in different homes.

I came home hysterically gay, saying I wanted to go on selling, a fever of *dépouillement* and sacrifice devouring me. Often these days I have wanted to be poor because I can't bear the envy and jealousy of others. I can't bear to have more than the others.

Surrealism bothers and irritates me. I am near them but not one of them. I like their theory but not what they write.

NOVEMBER 22, 1936

*L*AST NIGHT: THE ORANGE ROOM AGLOW. HUGH talking astrology with an American woman. Moricand saying, *"Il y a des grandes ondes et des petites ondes, il y a des ondes courte."* He talks in terms of the sea, heavings, and waves. He has the language of the invisible and the rhythms of poetry. Evreinoff the Russian actor is gesticulating: *"Le moi séparé de mon moi—le moi archaïque, qui parle, et le moi . . ."* One can see the mirrors and candles and faces repeated to infinity, as when the Russians stand between two mirrors with a candle. Colonel Cheremtieff, the *entremetteur* who delights in mixing people, murmurs dates of history while history is being made across the river. We hear the shouts, the fermentation, the songs, and the loudspeakers. Gonzalo is there, but his faith is separate from all other theories; he has an ideal Communism, a pure mysticism, he defends the downtrodden. How can I push him to fulfill his destiny and live out his strength without sacrificing our human happiness?

Nunankepichu so marvelous, so much like a fairy tale.

I rush all the way to Montparnasse just for one kiss, yesterday, yet he still says at times, savagely, "I love you more than you love me! I feel you are mine when I hold you to me—but afterward . . ."

I tell Evreinoff my idea for the play on analysis and he likes it. I begin a film of horrors but it is all invented and I throw the clippings in the scrap basket.

Gonzalo says he would be happy if only he could lock me up.

He introspects obscurely, waywardly, without wisdom, with madness. If I say Hugh is happy, he broods on this and interprets it that

Hugh is happy because he feels that this time I am not as much in love as I was with Henry: not so much danger.

I have never written out all my torments from jealousy, because I was ashamed and I tried not to notice.

I have a whole world, intellectually, which Gonzalo cannot penetrate—or rather, which he is too lazy to penetrate. But it is a world I am done with. I feel a great laziness myself. I like my poetic, floating, soft, sonorous, mysterious present. Trying to write the play on Rank today, I felt a lethargy, an indifference; I wanted to close my eyes again. Why should I strain and struggle? If you lived in a fairy tale, if you were swimming in caresses, if you lived among the stars and clouds and felt the warm sperm pouring into you, would you write?

NOVEMBER 24, 1936

NANANKEPICHU IS ALMOST COMPLETELY CREATED, piece by piece, effort after effort, care, thought, energy, desire. Magic requires labor. In each house I seek a maximum of perfection, but on different levels. According to the taste of the man. Hugh likes order, luxury. I add to this home warmth, softness, beauty. Henry likes simplicity. Without falsifying the background he needs, I have made it as comfortable and satisfying as possible. With Gonzalo I could be fantastic, yet I made the room warm, soft to the ear and to the eyes. Three creations, three backgrounds which I have made for the *other*.

Nanankepichu is like an opium den, like no place on this earth— it might be anywhere and nowhere, *Tales of Hoffman*.

The clock of the Gare d'Orsay looms immensely in my eyes. Immense *cadran* of light, with enormous black hands pointing to all the hours. The hour when we meet, the hour when we part. The gongs toll. Gonzalo is taking me while the hours ring. Gonzalo is talking emotionally, hotly, about Communism. I am awake and he is now asleep. The little lamp lights a face where the hair and eyelashes are drawn with charcoal. Gonzalo, asleep, is kissing me still.

Midnight, as we descend the little stairs. One o'clock, when Gonzalo is undressing me. Long quarters of an hour dimmed with floating reveries. Silk in our eyes, music in our ears. Two o'clock, when we are saying, *How hard we tried to make ourselves realists, and we did not succeed.* Two-fifteen, when we lie silent, drunk on kisses. At dawn, I feel cold. At nine, the morning light makes me want to run away from the reality of making coffee in a cold room, of my face crumpled from too many kisses!

I always want to run away when the music stops. Daylight. The stove grown cold. Ashes. Wine in the coffee cups. The water far away. A stale croissant from the night before. That stillness in the ears. The pauses and the descents. I am always looking for the music. Always looking for the music, for the dance. Reality is a constant source of pain. Always a collision.

I wish that, like Henry, I would not mind.

NOVEMBER 25, 1936

A TENT OF GREASY FOG. A PENETRATING REVIEW OF *The House of Incest* by Stuart Gilbert. A jeweled night with Gonzalo, except when he says, "Eduardo is a victim of capitalism. Artaud is a victim of capitalism."

My attitude modified. I am in sympathy with his Communism (a hatred of injustice) because it is idealistic and pure. I could have died for the Russian Revolution when it was pure and idealistic. But now it is split, impure, false.

The organization of the world is a task for realists. The poet and the workman will always be victims of power and interest. No world will ever be run by a mystic idea, because by the time it begins to *function* it ceases to be mystical. When the Catholic Church became a force, an organization, it ceased to be mystic! The realist always conquers the poetic as the human. Interest wins out. The world will always be ruled by soulless people and power.

So in the fairy tale there is a stain of daylight. Gonzalo has a thirst for sacrifice which he has satisfied in his life with Helba. Now he has a thirst for sacrifice and heroism on a grander scale. He talks about Spain, but he is lying on the black rug with me, the *péniche* is heaving gently.

The fog weighs on me. Sunday, in a fever, I wrote three pages of my "horror" film. Began with newspaper clippings and then transformed them beyond recognition. Could not continue to copy the diary of 1922—it hurt me so much. The present alone seems bearable. The present alone seems beautiful, except when I have returns of the old clutching at Henry, who belongs to the public, like a movie star! At the same time, with Henry I can share an electric activity which I must conceal from Gonzalo. Henry does not sleep anymore! He works, writes, corresponds, visits. He works for my book. He got Stuart Gilbert to write the review. He talks about me. We have a lot of work together. And Gonzalo blocks me. Gonzalo's rhythm is loose and vague, with much waste and inertia (as Henry's was!). So I rush away from *Nanankepichu* and plunge into activity at home! Letters and visits and relationships. A life like a stained-glass window.

NOVEMBER 26, 1936

ONZALO GETS EXALTED TALKING TO ME ABOUT MY work, my value, and how he wants me to give myself to my writing, cease giving to others, live for myself—just as I used to get exalted talking to Henry. I see on Gonzalo's face the same fever for sacrifice that I had, the same desire to abandon oneself, to offer oneself in sacrifice to someone's creation. He is following his pattern faithfully. There are so many analogies between Helba and me—the dancing, the love of form, the grace of body, the intensity, her way of writing about her childhood, her poems, her early sufferings, her father's abandon of her, her hypocritical sweetness covering a violent nature, her lies, her control of a dark nature.

Gonzalo saw in Helba's creation the "line," the form, the plastic quality. He sees the same in my motions, in my decors, in my costume, and in my writing. He perceived her rhythms as he perceives the rhythm in my work. He is sensitive to her dancing and to mine.

My need to give has been a vice—and yet not altogether destructive. Perhaps I find myself by dissolution. No matter how much I give, I don't lose myself. But I have wasted myself.

Yet to give *is* to love—it is a necessity.

I find myself, with Gonzalo, in an ironic situation. I cannot give him anything except myself. I cannot give him to himself as I gave Henry to himself. He *lives* on the gift of himself. His drawing is not sufficiently essential to be lived for. I have no sacrifice to make for Gonzalo, except to his Communism, or to give him *up*. That I can't do. And I see that he wants as much to be needed and used as I wanted it. That perhaps he is made more for love and life than for war. He says I hold him here, but perhaps it will all be taken out of our hands—our fate. He waits.

To go or not to go and fight in Spain is a current conflict now. I threaten Gonzalo with "If you go, I'll go too—and I'll fight. I won't wrap bandages, I assure you." The wounded are coming back. Roger is wounded.

I do not have the faith, but I would die with Gonzalo. I could not live without him.

Gonzalo only reveals his secrets at the end of the night, after consuming caresses.

"You don't know, *chiquita*. I never told you what a torture it was for me to read your book on your father."

He is tortured with jealousy of my past. "I could forget it, *chiquita*, but it is all written down." He is haunted by my pages on the hotel room in Avignon with Henry.

I remember my tortures while reading Henry's careful descriptions of women he enjoyed—of June.

I was overwhelmed with pity for Gonzalo. At that moment I could have thrown all my diaries into the river, to save Gonzalo from pain—something Henry would never think of doing for me. Nothing can stop Henry. He is the artist. Everything stops me: thoughts of Hugh and Henry and Gonzalo and my Father.

Sacrificed appearing in the magazine *Confessions* for that reason. Innumerable sacrifices to my human loves—all but *silence*.

Objectivity of artist: Henry felt pain at reading my Father manuscript [*Winter of Artifice*] but subjected it to his interest in my works, as I used to do at the beginning. Now it is harder for me to be objective. I used to say to myself, I will leave Henry when he writes his book on June. Sometimes I felt it was this obscure sense which inhibited Henry—I don't know.

D E C E M B E R 8 , 1 9 3 6

*A*DAY AND NIGHT. HENRY AWAITS ME IN BED AT three in the afternoon, takes me, caresses me; and then we cannot sleep or rest afterward, because his head is like a fast-moving picture. I have written something about his new book: "*Black Spring* represents life on all levels. It is an orchestra. Henry Miller seizes upon visible life, human life, the life of impulses, appetites, lusts, hatreds, instincts, and is grasping at the same instant the dream that obsesses the poet. . . ."

Henry leapt, shouted, said it made him feel like sitting at the typewriter immediately and writing!

At seven o'clock Gonzalo and I are in *Nanankepichu,* which looks as if it's lying at the bottom of the Seine, with all the reflections of candlelight and lanterns on the watery, shimmering black-tarred walls. The mirror has a depth and dimness other mirrors don't have. We are eating dinner, sitting like Arabs on the rug by the stove.

Insomnia. We cannot sleep. Two o'clock. Three o'clock. Four o'clock. Gonzalo is talking about his childhood. It is much like mine in its goodness—devotion to others. When he says one of the secrets of his attachment to Helba is all he had to do for her, the struggle and creation for her life, of her life, I say it is the same [for me] with Henry. When his devotion to Helba hurts me in my possessiveness, I hurt him by mentioning Henry. Gonzalo said, "If we drew a triangle of you, Henry, Helba, and me, you would be much nearer to Henry than I am to Helba, because Helba is a sexless being—but you are extremely sensual, you sink yourself in love, yield, abandon yourself . . ."

"I see you as more than other men," I said. "I see you sometimes as a mythological figure."

We do not find a place for each other's devotion. I am surrounded by Hugh's care and not helpless in any manner. He is not helpless, and denies himself all I might give him, wears his old suit in preference to the new.

So, with my clairvoyance, my impatience, and my *fears,* I try to see ahead, to prevent dangers. He says quietly, "Do not force anything . . ."

His caresses arouse me so completely I cannot understand why ultimately I can't respond.

Turner pleads, entreats, pants, begs. Moricand subtly waits. I can give Gonzalo all the feeling in me, while Henry says I am sometimes overdemonstrative.

In 1921 I wrote that I would specialize in fantasy.

I rule by seduction.

DECEMBER 13, 1936

WITH GONZALO I DO NOT SUFFER. I CAN BE FAITH-
ful to myself. To be happy with Henry I would have to be more callous, debonair, equally egotistic; tougher.

Strange, the strong, violent malaise which warns me when I enter a milieu, a roomful of people where I cannot stay—a real anxiety. Places, people I am not made to be with because I cannot stop *feeling*, roués, *débauchés*, hard-boiled, erotic people, callous, cynical. I suffer too much. I lack the brutality to live that way. I become a victim.

To permit Henry to be natural, I endured all his confessions. But I could not be natural. Now, not to torture Gonzalo, I refrain from confessions. With him I have to curb expression, analysis. It is hard discipline, after spilling out with Henry. He does not want things said—brought to light. I needed this. There was too much clarity with Rank, a supernatural clarity, a death. I sink with Gonzalo.

The demon in us, the other, working secretly, insidiously. My demon is unmasking itself. I can see it better. I can see myself walking into a room full of people with a certainty that I am going to charm someone—a smooth certainty which amuses me.

More than love, men need the annihilation of their solitude—that *is* the function of love. It is through the crevice of this solitude that the magic fluid seeps in and enslaves.

And everywhere I walk I seduce.

Artaud is telling Gonzalo that I am a green-eyed monster, a criminal. He is back from Mexico—old, drugged.

Cela m'amuse. I have committed crimes without enjoying the *frisson* of evil. The *frisson* I feel now is power—power to enslave and to torture. *Je m'amuse des crimes que je pourrais comettre,* by the scandals I could cause. *Je m'amuse de mes mystères.* I can never say where I come from. But it is not necessary to say it. Does Henry know I draw my happiness from Gonzalo? Do I know that he draws his happiness now from power, not from love; from his ascension, recognition?

Lying down, I am suffocated by my anxieties, those no one sees, the fear of loss and all my life like a mirage. Always a little breathlessness as I try to touch my mirages. I fix my eyes on the sapphire blue ring, on the sapphire blue necklace with silver stars, on the sapphire blue glass ashtray. I say to myself: Beauty, pleasure. A room that stands still, in which I lie among black velvet pillows—here the *simoun* does not blow, the revolution does not cut the flesh, men and women do not torture each other. It is blue. A bath of blue. A symphony of blue. Blue. Cosmic peace and magnanimity.

It was true what Mrs. Gilbert said: I did wrong to seek to find my mystic trance by religious routes, in church. It was a cosmic mystic trance. I suffered so much, expanded so much, gave so much, enlarged myself to the limit, melted in cosmic ecstasy, there on the hospital bed. A little further, and I would have died. A little greater the loss and dissolution of the self, and I would have died. So great is this feeling I have of immensity, of pity on a large scale, of sympathy reaching to my sick people in New York and in eternity, of a love to all those who are alone, of a deviltry which laughs in unison with all nature tricks, with all the monkeylike humorous and tragic pranks of nature.

With all extreme points of the compass, with love, passion, sensuality, creation, pity, one touches the greater cosmic consciousness, or dissolution.

I began with a passionless, selfless, all-comprehensive will. Then primitive passion and the personal with Henry.

Pisces, says astrology, has the power of abstracting oneself totally from the immediate surroundings and throwing oneself into an imaginary life at will.

It is a sign of self-denial and of withdrawal. I wanted always to write anonymously.

Sign of the Messiah or the outcast.

The final solution of problems, and some of them must be solved by meekness and humbleness. Christ!! Jesus! I say this cursingly.

[Charles E.] Carter [*Principles of Astrology*] calls Pisces "cosmic grace."

There is something so soft, so smooth and so nonresisting about this sign that it often gives a wrong impression.

Pisces do not believe that the truth is the best thing to tell, and consequently, since they hate to hurt, they substitute what they believe to be a cosmic truth for lesser truths. The connection of this sign with enchanters and with enchantments is very plain.

Unworldliness, self-sacrifice, romantic ideals, inspiration, and glimpses of a larger consciousness.

I dropped into astrology out of laziness . . . !

December 18, 1936

I ALWAYS WRITE THE TITLE ON THE DIARY BEFORE it is filled. I never realized myself, when I wrote *"Nanankepichu"* and *"Vive la dynamite,"* how contrasting they were, how opposed. Why did I include them together? Prophetically. One the dream, unreality, passion—the other reality, the world drama, revolution, anarchy, war.

I kept Gonzalo from going to fight in Spain. He made a dozen drawings. He lay quiet—infinitely satisfied. We reached deeper and deeper layers of sensuality—until one night he knelt before my opened legs, raised them, pounded into me with tremendous violence—Gonzalo the savage, aroused—and this picture of him, this feeling of his strength aroused me so much I felt I was about to reach the spasm I have not yet felt with him. The night left me shaking, with a stirred womb. I kept seeing him kneeling before me, naked, brown, hair wild, groaning with joy.

Out of this night he sprang like a real lion, and definitely entered into his activity as an agitator, writer, leader of eighty South American intellectuals. Out of *Nanankepichu* was born a visionary Communist leader. Out of dreams and caresses. He himself says, "It was you—and how strange that you, who are so far from all this, should have aroused this need of action in me. Your love has given me the strength . . ."

My first reaction was pain, shock that something I could not believe in should have been born out of our love—this leadership, this revolutionary force. And the shock was that I lay in warmth, that Gonzalo seemed soldered to me, that with him I forgot my loneliness, that our dream would be sacrificed, our personal life. Again I had to give myself to the creation of man—first Henry's work, and then Gonzalo's Communism.

I suffered as a woman. I lay at his side and sobbed. I felt no desire, but a tearing, a deep anguish, surrender. Surrender. He needed my faith. Helba was against him. My love had given him the impetus. Would I hold him back now, when I had ignited him? I sobbed.

But Gonzalo's passion about politics, his vehement speeches, his sincerity had not been without effect. I was not won over to Communism—but to Gonzalo's communism. Above all, I understood that *because* he was so vital, so rich in blood, in passion, he had a need of action and drama. He cannot be kept in a studio, drawing. He is too full of fire. *Because* our relationship was so vital, as he said, so alive, so devoid of literature, of art, of intellectuality, I gave him a life-impulse, not an art-impulse.

What I love in him is precisely what drives him into plotting, anarchy, and risk. After the pain of releasing the clutch, the first fear of losing our dream, the destruction of *Nanankepichu,* the feeling that I was being sacrificed—*my* need to his need—I rallied my strength, for love, realizing I had urged him to fulfill *his* destiny, not to be the slave of another woman, as he had been the slave of Helba's career, and that this was the result, and I was the one who urged each one to fulfill himself, and this could never fulfill me. For love of Gonzalo, of a strong Gonzalo, for love of seeing his eyes shining with life, his head held high, his hands eager, I gave up my selfish desire to keep him enclosed in my arms, inside of me, and inside of a dream.

I awoke quite broken with fatigue, eyes swollen. Gonzalo had been very tender about my suffering but not quite understanding it.

I rushed home. I sat down at the typewriter and typed twenty-four envelopes for his "declarations to my Communist friends." I took the envelopes to him. At moments I felt broken. My heart hurt me. I felt weak and I wanted to sob. At others I whipped myself into will. Again. Woman *always* has to act a role, for the sake of the love. A woman can never be wholly true to herself, for the sake of the love. Subtly, I always have to *act* this Amazon which my real strength creates the illusion of in others. Now I have to be a woman in action, firing Gonzalo to a visible and (to me) *unmetaphysical* anarchy. Henry's anarchy was literary. He was the satirist. I must secretly like the bomb throwers, the destroyers. I like nature. I like power. Power is dangerous, blind. I turn this power into creation. Henry has become *effective,* not just explosive, *potent.* Gonzalo will not throw bombs. There *is* destruction in him—but I shall make creation of it.

So I am typing envelopes, to Communists. And I think about Communism. I am in sympathy now with its aims. But I cannot get *fired.* That drama is, to me, a naïve European one. But *all* drama is unwise. We do not live by wisdom. We live by the *drama*—tragic loves, misplaced energies, errors, prejudices. Errors. I believe in making human errors, in having illusions. Gonzalo has the illusion of rearrangement of the world. I respect his illusion. I will help him. I am already outside and beyond capitalism and Fascism. I have been a spiritual anarchist. In politics I have no illusions. But I have illusions about love.

Heavy, surcharged with my conflict, I spent a humorous, gentle, whimsical, harmonious evening with Henry, the integral artist, who is becoming paler each day. The blood boils less—the blood is running through the channels of the imagination and remembrance. In the dark he lies passive, like a woman, and gently leads me to caressing him. When he is inside of me, he gets wild with my moisture. He arouses me to bestial frenzy—pleasure—pleasure—pleasure—and I awake strong and joyous.

I awake strong and joyous. Overflowing with energy, courage. The sacrifice is made. Now I am full of activity. I will not look back. I urge Gonzalo to use the big room in *Nanankepichu* for the meetings. I like to think of them plotting there. Risk. Danger. I say, "Lock our bedroom."

I like danger. I like those who are willing to turn the world upside down, to dynamite it for the sake of an illusion, maybe for the sake of seeing the fire and hearing the shouts of the murdered! No matter. Nature is at work. There has to be hail, tornadoes, earthquakes. They are necessary. War is necessary. Death is necessary. Glory to the drama, always unwise, always unjust, always an expression of our human Dionysian need.

My masculine soul must be a satirist, a warrior, a hero—for such are the men I choose.

My feminine flesh is too tender. Fortunately, my tears often turn into steel and fire. Amazing the anguish I felt, the pains of childbearing—part of my flesh demanded, torn away to expose the dangers of the world. Man lies in my arms, crawls and rests in my womb. Sex for me is not only the joy of the orgasm, it is this holding of man inside the womb. Man can never know the loneliness a woman knows—a woman whose womb is empty. Man lies in the womb only to gather strength. He nourishes himself from the woman. Woman always continues to give milk and his blood. And then he rises, he rushes either into battle or into creation. He *leaves* her. He is not lonely. He has the world he makes. Woman is lonely because she has only the man—his presence, his body.

I am woman.

I cry out when he rises and acts.

I ask myself: Where is Thurema? Will I now need the beautiful, strong Hurtado woman I met the other night?

I take my diary and walk the streets. I plot with Gonzalo. I fall into a reverie. The time to act has come, and man awakes first. I have to catch up.

I could love Thurema if she were here. I am affectionate with Eduardo, who is staying in Paris now.

The first *break* in the fairy tale—at Maxim's—a place of luxury, a fairy tale for me, decorative, glamorous. I never saw the people—I lived in a world of my own. Lately—because of Gonzalo—my eyes opened and I *saw* the faces—really—the faces of the rich, the aristocrats and the nouveau riche. And they were *pigs!* And, outside of Katrine Perkins, I do not know one rich man or woman of any value.

Poor Hugh. He is growing steadier and steadier, entrenched because of his responsible father role in the defense of capitalism. And I, who have fought only for real values, for my independence, who have used my money only for those who needed it, and little for myself, I would like to give up *all* comforts and give more. Poor

Hugh, because deep down all I do is a constant menace to his happiness, yet nothing can stop me.

To him I owe the greatest debt of all—he permitted me to be true to myself.

Let us see if I can carry out the role of mistress of a hero, plotter, anarchist as gaily and magnificently as I carried out that of Henry's muse.

Meanwhile, let us make it as dramatic as possible. The room on the *péniche* very dramatic. Gonzalo in one room delivering speeches, in another lying intoxicated with caresses, saying, "You kept me absolutely drugged for two months."

Perhaps I do carry dynamite in myself which is not to explode on paper alone. Perhaps it is not my diary I will throw out sometime, ignited, among people terrified of truth.

When Gonzalo came today for an hour and I met him dancing and alive and on fire, he stayed all afternoon. It was a springlike day. We walked, unconsciously, to *Nanankepichu*—lay there.

I know now some mystery holds me back from the orgasm with him, some spell of Henry's. When I left him, aroused, stirred, I picked up two erotic magazines on the stalls and looked at the pictures in the taxi on my way home and felt the orgasm with such intensity, just sitting there, that I nearly fainted.

Having violent dreams at night. And the night before Gonzalo became definitely active in the Party I dreamt that a crowd of people, masses of people, were preventing me from reaching him. I fought them desperately. Last night I dreamt that criminals were forced to have an erection just before they were murdered and that they struggled violently to arouse themselves and couldn't.

I cannot lie down without being haunted by erotic pictures, violent desires.

I am so terribly aroused by life—mentally, physically—I am living so intensely, that I am at once aware of my sex, of being hot there, of being wet, of the beating of the blood, and at the same time of being in a reverie. Gonzalo says, "My relationship to you is so vital, so vital. I have found my sexual rhythm with you." To watch his enjoyment stirs me deeply.

He says he has a Christian concept of sex—the *love* concept, like the feminine concept. He believes I write about sex like a pagan, and certainly I am a pagan compared to him. But the only real pagan is Henry, who can take any woman, not out of love, but merely *pour satisfaire ses instincts.*

Eroticism troubles me. No one I know is erotic, except Hugh, whom I don't desire, and George Turner, whom I don't desire. I am erotic and perverse, and that is left out of my healthy animal life with Henry, and out of my emotional one with Gonzalo. Maybe it's repressed. Gonzalo has plenty of eroticism. He worships my feet, he loves to kiss me with his mouth. Henry has none. He is simple.

D E C E M B E R   2 1 ,   1 9 3 6

O H, GOD, THIS IS TOO GREAT A WAVE OF STRENGTH! I swing from such extremes of weakness to a mood so powerful that it is almost unbearable. It is like Vesuvius, as I tell my Father in a riotously humorous letter. One night I sob in Gonzalo's arms because the cotton of our caresses, the mists and the drug, are threatened by creation again. The next day I awake, made of steel and fire—an Amazon.

I write my Father a letter, to get a [duplicating] machine we need to print propaganda. I write him a fantastic letter, saying I need it to work for Spain. Naturally, he thinks it is for the Fascists. I laugh at the diabolical idea. Please, Father, give me your printing machine to work for Spain. I want to give my strength to Spain—I am rallying a group of intellectuals—I am breathing strength into them.

And it is for Communism. I laugh because the interchange is a sort of cosmic joke, I don't really care whose side I take, they are all wrong, who think they live and die for ideas. What a marvelous error and divine joke. They are living and dying for emotional errors. So I am working for Republican Spain because I am in love and that is all that counts. I like to see a radiant Gonzalo arrive breathless from his plotting, and he can lay his head on my breast and tell me all he is doing, and we can prepare the big room in *Nanankepichu* for the eighty plotters, and my woman's soul is laughing at all men's categories and names because I see through and beyond them. It is their game which they take seriously and I take laughingly, and they laugh at *our* tears and tragedies—which are real! So I say, Fascism or Communism, I take the side of love; and I laugh at men's ideas, secretly. I write Father a letter. I gather chairs together. I am wide awake and gay and writing virile letters right and left, laughing! Gonzalo is won over and laughs too, saying we will publish one pamphlet for the Fascists, just one copy for my Father!

So my strength explodes within me. I dance for Hugh, farcically. I write humorous letters. I am aware that it is the fairy tale I am creating to keep everything eternal and marvelous. No illusion ever broken; nothing changes in the map of my world, no war or growth disturbs the illusory fixity: Mother is there; Joaquin is there—where they were when I was sixteen—Hugh is there; Eduardo is there; love is eternal, and I pass through, everywhere preventing earthquakes and fighting death. *I will let nothing die.* The monster I kill every day is the monster of realism. The monster who attacks me every day is destruction. Out of the duel comes the transformation. I turn destruction into creation over and over again.

I feel as if I were bursting with power.

As if the world were again an orchestra. I feel lifted, carried, pushed by tremendous forces. Music and fire.

Next to our dream corner—a large room will contain Gonzalo's creation. And I will incite him, sustain and push him. What drunkenness, my God! No need of wine. The whole world reeling! Music everywhere. Chairs for the plotters, a stove, and coal from our own supply. Man awakes first from beds of down and sperm.

Bursting with power.

I sing, I dance, keep everything alive. Henry says to Eduardo, "It is all due to Anaïs, what I have been able to do. In Louveciennes she gave me my integrity."

Letter from a patient in New York: It has been lovely knowing you, and my one wish is that we will meet again in the not-too-distant future. Thank you over and over again for the sense of release you gave me, for the ability to face the world more bravely and scornfully, so that I may stand naked before myself and say, "This is what I am and what I feel and I am not ashamed of myself." For despite all griefs and cares I have a constant sense of renewal, of growth and expansion. What ecstasies are wrought from mingled joys and sorrows, what maturities!

To Henry: When you leave on the bicycle I am concerned over you all evening—conscious of you with a feeling which would give you joy to realize . . .

My imagination is all aflame with that *real* journal for Hugh. You don't know how I would love to write it all at once. I began it tonight. Five pages, all craft. It may turn out a marvelous piece of mystification, the two sides of an attitude, and it becomes so real to me while I write it, like the determination (for Hugh's journal) never to be possessed by you because men remember longest the women they have not had, that I believe if you read this journal I could almost persuade *you* you have never had me at all! To confront the two could easily drive a man insane. I would love to die and watch Hugh read them both. I will in it explain the origin of every *invention* relating to our story. How I got to know the aspect of a certain hotel room from your talk about it. Will reconstruct the séances with Allendy: He telling me to distinguish carefully between my *literary* adventures (you) and my truly human one (Hugh!). Ironies. Reversals of situations. When you read it you will regret *not* having had me. You won't know after a while whether you did or not. Depends on which journal you read. You will be offered a choice! To begin with, try and remember that the *real* journal is the *unreal* one. Wonderful. *This* is the journal of my true feelings. Which one? The *tone,* you say, but when a man is a real actor, you can't tell about the tone. I suppose I am sublimating a situation which, deep down, I feel too tragically. Enjoying it intellectually. Making it bearable. As you said. I was also able today to see all the humor in the Lowenfels–Constad legend. It is the men who take the women to the circus, and the women go to hear the men laugh!—Anaïs.

Delicacy of 1921 journal like Chinese life. Flowers. Nature. Dream quality. Fragility. Perfect *form.*

Je suis facilement éblouie. I'm easily dazzled. But that is necessary to the sense of wonder, and ecstasy. *Éblouissement* is one of my most frequent moods. I fall easily into a trance.

My way of seeing people is to absorb them. I feel myself inside them, lose myself in them, feel how their skin feels, the features, the hands, the voice. I get impregnated. My mystical trances are cosmic and not religious. Expansion always brings me that ecstasy: sacrifice of the self. (I work for Gonzalo. I do not believe in Communism. I only believe in individual salvation.)

*Letter to Father (who has rented a house in Madrid):** I am sending you a few pages of the beginning [of *The House of Incest*], translated by Moricand, but they don't give you an idea of its musical quality, since French doesn't lend itself to song. The characters are three different women who blend into one and are represented by one woman. Watery birth, symbolism, the imprisoned inner life, then deliverance into the light of day. I describe the night of solitary anguish, dreams that precede real, human, healthy life. *The depth of things.* Our mysterious underwater life which slides over what we are and what we do during the day.

* In French in the original.

Well, enough literature. I simply wanted to make you feel that you had read the book.

I'm so happy to know that you two are not too isolated, that you feel alive, that you play music and that there is enough to keep Maruca entertained.

About ourselves, I have only good things to tell you. The atmosphere in Paris also stinks and suffocates in politics, but we are not yet reduced to living in the Métro, as are the poor people of Madrid. We don't have to sleep there. We only ride in it to go to see friends, so we can't complain. Also we don't have to spend New Year's Eve with the same gentleman as last year but instead will be with the most aristocratic of White Russians.

I've discovered a way to perfume the apartment with something that costs almost nothing (what a miracle!) and smells good. Are you acquainted with patchouli? It was in fashion at the time I finally decided to show my face in that extraordinary society. Your nose would recognize it.

Just now I was thinking of all the trouble I must take to protect my fairy tale from attacks of realism. I kill one realistic dragon a day, and unfortunately the meat is too tough to eat or we could save money on steak. Dragon meat is impossible—gelatinous and at the same time stringy, sinewy, and drooling.

Well, Culmell and I have just danced a takeoff on a Spanish dance with a fast rhythm, and I am so out of breath I can't finish my letter!

So write me. I hug you with all my strength.

DECEMBER 23, 1936

THE SYMBOLISM OF SMALL TRAITS: I HAVE NEVER lit a fire that has gone out. When Hugh and I first went to the beach together, when I was nineteen, we wanted to heat the food. We started preparing the fire and found we had no matches. I went with a newspaper to the fire made by other people quite some distance away. I lit the newspaper, which I had shaped like a torch, and then I began to run back with it. Naturally, with the wind my torch burned quickly, almost to the end. Hugh kept shouting, "Drop it! drop it! You will get burned!" The flames were nearly touching my hand. I continued to run, and I lit our fire.

When we light a fire at Villa Seurat, Henry says, "You do it. Mine always goes out." And I light a marvelous fire. I am fearless before fire. I touch it almost without fear. When I have to light the stove in *Nanankepichu* it is the same. It never goes out once I have started it. I never have to begin again, as people so often do.

Curiously symbolical.

The tragedy is that it takes so little to kill my joy. If Gonzalo is late, if Henry teases me, if Colette's husband says I am too serious, if Helba shows her jealousy, if Henry raves about a new movie star, if Gonzalo goes to a party and gets drunk and then sick for two days, if Henry gets an admiring letter from a woman, if a magazine returns my review of Henry's *Black Spring* because it is not an analysis of its content.

DECEMBER 27, 1936

CHRISTMAS NIGHT. POISSON D'OR. CAVIAR AND vodka. Sad and delicate Ponisowsky, his sister, and her husband. Elena Hurtado like some ancient Roman goddess. Hugh, Elena, and I talking across the desert of others' talks with elation. The elation of strength. Immediate understanding. *Tzigane* songs. Caviar and vodka. Vodka is my drink. I had written a page about it once, before tasting it. And Christmas night this page came true. I drank fire. A white fire which did not hurt me, which set my head on fire. All night, music and fire. Sparks between Elena and me. I want to get up and dance. I want to get up and dance alone. No one has the rhythm I want to dance. Russian music. My feet are dancing. My head is dancing. My hands are dancing. Five in the morning. A Russian breaking glasses against his head. Five-thirty, and we are out on the boulevard, wide awake. Elena wants to walk. Ponisowsky, sad and delicate, bowing to all our wishes. The other lady wan and listless. We will go and have breakfast. Where? Elena wants to walk. I would like to walk with her all over the city. I say to her I am grateful for her presence, she made the evening beautiful for me. The pleasure of looking at her lovely face, of feeling the power in her. We are sitting in Melody's bar. The orchestra of Argentines, a few Negresses, two or three men left. It is six-thirty in the morning. I want to dance. I want to dance my joy and the fire in me. The orchestra plays a *paso doble*. I get up and dance, stamp and turn and walk and stamp. The musicians incite me with shouts. The Negresses shout. The joy of it, the joy of it.

It is seven in the morning. Dawn is blue. Elena's eyes are blue. The halo of the sun is around her.

I fall asleep. I fall in a crevice, in an abyss. But at ten-thirty I am still full of joy and fire . . . dancing around the Christmas dinner. At the last moment I beg Gonzalo to come. I'm drunk. I wear my Persian dress with the wide skirt; I am drunk, drunk. Gonzalo comes. We eat and drink joyously. I am laughing, laughing. Eduardo is quiet.

Gonzalo leaves and I fall into another deep sleep. I lie in the bowels of the earth. Joy.

When Gonzalo and I met yesterday afternoon the passion exploded. "Oh, I desired you so much yesterday, *chiquita*. How beautiful you were! How alive! I never saw you so clearly—so wholly. What a contrast with Hugh and Eduardo. You were so sensually alive, you were enjoying everything, radiant, magnificent. I wanted you so!"

If I could poetize analysis and wring out of it the elements of magic, why can't I do the same with Gonzalo's Communism? It is the life-motive of the moment. It is the drama.

I am again in *Nanankepichu*. Gonzalo has brought the smallest and the most mysterious lamp: all blue.

I say to him, "My conflict is not between Communism and

Fascism or anarchy, but between the dream and realism. When the struggle was to achieve religious liberation, I could have died for it. When the struggle is one for economic independence, I cannot feel the mystic or metaphysical drama in it. But I am with you. Only you make the dream so perfect. With you I could dream so perfectly that action in the world seemed at first a death, a disillusion."

The fire burns again. His climax is violent and lasts a long moment. He kisses me with a frenzied gratitude for the perfection of the rhythm. His joy gives me a tremendous joy. The little blue lamp seems no longer blue. Marvelous smells rise from our caresses, make us drunk over and over again. Desire does not die with the orgasm.

My talk with Henry an hour before was closer to my soul than Gonzalo's passionate plea against capitalism. Henry and I talked about the poem. Soon he said he would write only in the form of the poem, like Dante. Soon he would become altogether the poet.

Gonzalo's drama—in terms of Communism or capitalism—I must see beyond the appearance of it. I must keep seeing Gonzalo living. His body in motion, talking vehemently, trembling with passion, desperate to create in the visible now. Above all, I want to see the rhythm underneath—the heat of blood which alone is life—the blood rhythm beneath the dance, fighting; wherever this rhythm beats, I go.

I want to dance and laugh. I want to dance. Nothing will shatter my individual world. No storm on sea or earth. The earth turns. It is Communism, they call it. The poem and the rhythm, I say. Vodka. Fire. Man struggling. Rhythm of illusion.

December 28, 1936

*T*HIRTY, QUAI DE PASSY, PARIS.
      In my sleep I was bitten by a small snake,
bitten on the tip of my head, hard, until it hurt. Without terror, I
tore at my hair, shook it. I saw two small snakes on the floor. I crushed
them slowly and completely. I wondered whether I should take an
antipoison.

The night before, I saw small birds fly out of a little Negro boy's
mouth in Fez. These birds covered my face. I was afraid they would
pick into my eyes with their beaks. I got lost in Fez.

My breasts hurt. Am I pregnant?

I see Elena sitting on my couch. The head of a Greek goddess.
Strong head. Elena saying she would like to be a man because a man
can look at all things objectively; he can be a philosopher. When she
found herself married and the mother of two little girls, she was
terrified, almost insane. She did not know it then but she did not
want to be the mother—the mother of children. She wanted to be
what I am, the mother of creations and dreams. She suffered from
terrors—terrors of nature, of being swallowed by mountains, stifled
by the forest, absorbed by the sea. She has a horror of the actor and
of metamorphosis. When she talked about her dream of being carried
by a centaur I could see the centaur and her head, the head of a
woman in a myth.

I think of the Olympians and the mythics as *large* people, larger
than human beings. Elena is big, as June was. Gonzalo seems of the
myth. Perhaps my own exaltation enlarges, magnifies, deifies them.
Perhaps I enlarge people. I call them *myth* people because they have
a symbolic significance. I separate those who are ordinary from those
whose lives are significant, symbolic, who have grandeur. In this world
I breathe freely. I am always dropping the mediocre, creating a world.

Enter Elena and her many dreams, her strength and positivism. She belongs with June and Louise and Thurema. Henry and I represent two opposite attitudes. I embellish, romanticize, and idealize—*but* from a basis of honesty, of truth. I mean: Henry *is* a genius, June *was* a character, Thurema *is* a force, Louise *was* a personality, Elena *is* a value, Gonzalo *is* supernatural. Henry disillusions, satirizes, minimizes, caricatures, also from a basis of honesty and truth. The characters he chooses *are* unheroic, mediocre, stupid, obscene rogues. We understand each other and live together on a basis of sincerity. I mean, I knew the poet in Henry, and he knew the realist in me, the woman who knew that miracles are creation, creation rises out of labor, desire, intelligence, work.

Henry helped me to accept life; I helped him to accept the power of illusion, which he had ceased to believe in because June's illusions were on air, not creative, false. My illusions are creative and real. I am not the illusionist of the fair, with only cardboard around me and behind me, playing tricks. I am an illusionist with real power, the power to make things come true. I promised Henry he would not be a failure, that I would make the world listen to him, and I kept my promise. Much of what I wanted for myself did not come true. When I wanted to live with Henry I could not—for the *sake* of our creation, his creation. For magic, for the vision, I work day and night, with my hands, my head, my body, my will, my soul, my prayers—every moment. When I open my eyes in the morning it is to proceed not only with my incantations but with my labor, labor, labor, and with sacrifices.

I suppose the day the creator wants something *for himself* his magic ends. I cannot write now because I am inside of everything, inside of life, inside of love, inside of creation. *I am on fire.* If I were to touch paper I would shrivel it.

It is a question, not of being happy or fulfilled, but of being on fire.

I dream that Elsa and Helba hang themselves. I would like to see Helba dead.

Passion is over between Henry and me. I do not desire him. Yet the world we live in and created I cannot find with Gonzalo. There is no creation in Gonzalo. There was creation between Gonzalo and Helba. He could contribute to her work, play the piano for her, find names for her dances, blow life into her. Between us now there is his action in the political world, which does not stir me. I do not want to dwell on my fears. I suffer from too much clairvoyance, from seeing too far ahead! I have to think that, having passion with Gonzalo, I can create alone. Why alone? Because I fear that Henry and I will be separated when we separate physically. Our bodies are separating.

JANUARY 1, 1937

*A*BIG BED. SOFT WHITE WOOL RUG FROM MOROCCO. The black cat lying on a newspaper. Hugh lying at the other end of the bed, unshaved, sick, reading a book on palm reading. The radio mooning.

Red wax fell on the floor last night. Red wax from the candles on the tables and from the lanterns. Red wax on the table. Empty bottles of champagne and of vodka. Last night around the table: Gonzalo, Helba, Elsa, Eduardo, Grey and a Javanese girl, Carpentier, his wife, and Mother. Not I. I am lying in the dark, in my room. All afternoon I prepared the banquet, the candles, the lanterns, the red paper table-cloth, the setting of the table, but I was sick. I was sick as I was in N.Y., in Louveciennes, Avignon. Head turning and fits of vomiting. But I dressed myself, painted my face. Lay down. Paced up and down. Blamed it on a glass of vodka I had the day before with Eduardo at the Dôme. Sought a deeper reason and could not find it. Did not seek it very long. Gonzalo came to see me, adoring. Hugh came to see me, saying, "I love you. You arranged everything and it is going beautifully."

I believe that one should touch the furniture thinking, Enjoy this chair; lay a table thinking, Enjoy this meal; light a candle thinking, Enjoy this candle. Enjoy this food, this wine, this glow, the orange walls. Enjoy each other, enjoy Gonzalo's beauty, Eduardo's green eyes and marvelous teeth, enjoy Helba's heavy black hair even if she is sad, Elsa's long eyes, Grey's dancer figure, the Javanese girl's high cheekbones, enjoy the pig, the *turron,* the place.

I lie in the dark, thinking of Gonzalo saying, "About Christmas I don't care. That means nothing to an Inca. But about New Year's I have a superstition. I want to be with you."

We are under the same roof. I hear his voice. Why am I sick? I was too happy. Happiness, too, breaks me. I hate so to be sick. Gonzalo does not like sickness. He likes health and life and vigor. He has taken care of Helba, but he has gone out elsewhere seeking life. Loving life. He likes the life in me. I don't want to be sick. I want to dance. I have nothing to be sick about. Henry's and my hunger for each other ended at the same moment. No tragedy.

It is midnight. They are drinking champagne, saying, each in his own language: Happy New Year. Gonzalo said, *"Nanankepichu."* I did not hear it. But I got up. I got up and found I did not reel anymore. I came out of the room. Having slept, I looked fresh and beautiful at that moment. My appearance caused a tremendous effect. The Javanese girl and Grey, who had never seen me, seemed thunderstruck. I wore my coral lamé dress. My face was very white. I felt beautiful. Let one go about and feel beautiful and everyone will think so. I go about feeling beautiful and feeling powerful. We drank champagne again. Helba looked immensely sad, and I know now she is sad because I make her feel unbeautiful. For three years she has been sick and has not cared. She has never loved passionately, with desire. She is completely shut inside of herself, thinks sensual love is repugnant. Poor Helba. And so she is tortured with hatred of life, pleasure, and love. Perhaps now she will be saved. But meanwhile she hates and loves me, hates me and loves me as life itself.

When Gonzalo has to take her home, he leaves her and Elsa downstairs and comes up again to see me. We shut ourselves in the dark kitchen and kiss.

Today I run to *Nanankepichu* and we get into bed. An hour before, I lay alone on my bed and desired him, desired him. Saw his body kneeling before me and savagely pounding me. Saw his whole body, his dark penis, his ever-hungry mouth, and desired the fire in him.

Three hours together, floating in happiness. But I tell him my first lie. I don't know why. He did not believe the vodka could make me so ill. He said he felt there was something else. Was there something else? Yes, there was something else. It was gas—gas intoxication. I had breathed gas at Henry's place. Henry had turned on the gas. I had come away in time. Nothing had happened. Eduardo had smelled it when bringing him a note from me in which I said I could not come during the holidays.

So the sickness became a drama. At the end all I wanted was to convince Gonzalo of my absolutism, because I ended by telling him Elena Hurtado was in love with Henry. And Gonzalo said, "You are not jealous?" And I said, "Why should I be?"

I got the idea that Elena might love Henry because she said he resembled a young Argentine poet she had loved and I could not see any resemblance. Now, the strange thing is that I do not suffer at the idea of Elena loving Henry; or perhaps I run fast ahead of the present in order not to receive a shock or a surprise. Henry told me he had met a marvelous woman. At first I was jealous, but the minute I saw her I liked her, and I charmed her. Did I want to find out if I had to fear her? Was it fear? I liked her, found her intelligent and imaginative. We understood each other. When she told me about the poet and his resemblance to Henry I felt a shock of fatality. But now it has become possible for me to distinguish between my fears, which made me imagine the whole of a tragedy based on Lillian Lowenfels's feeling for Henry. I imagined them together because she was vulgar and tough and I thought she could live Henry's life so well with him, could like all I didn't like, because she had no sense of beauty, was disordered and lazy, but intelligent and lustily humorous. Remembering all these fancies which never came true, how can I believe in my fancies about Elena? What is the difference between fears and clairvoyance?

I live too fast. I imagine too much. I imagine a million things, a million things happening each day which never happen. My instinct says no to Elena—yet I tell Gonzalo yes. Just as June left Henry in my care the first time she came. Perhaps it is I who would choose Elena, because Elena, so beautiful, yet with too heavy and masculine and maternal a body, does not arouse passion but a kind of intellectual admiration. Perhaps because I have betrayed Henry with Gonzalo, I feel I ought to be betrayed, yet I feel strangely innocent.

I feel that Henry, when he began to create, ceased to represent life for me—creation, yes, but not life. With Gonzalo, everything is life. That is all he cares for. He reads very little. He has a friendship with Artaud, for example, based on talks, on what they did together in the theater, yet he has not read his books.

Gonzalo gets up saying, "Now I am happy. That is a beautiful beginning to the year."

All I feel is gratitude. And Henry showers a quiet, deep gratitude over me. He makes me feel that he knows all he enjoys today came from me, and we feel tenderness. Wistfully I regret not having had all I wanted—a life with Henry—but sometimes I say, If I had had a life with Henry, I would only have suffered. I got objectivity from the space between us, and life in that time between my visits to him.

To Lawrence Durrell: Had such a strong impression reading your "Christmas Carol"* that I find it hard to write about it. Yet I want you to know that you have done something amazing, reached a world so subtle, almost evanescent, caught a climate so fugitive, the fairy tale, the dream, the life directly through the senses, the odor of pure fantasy, the clairvoyant phrase, beyond the might of words, music, and rhythm. Beyond the law of gravity, chaos, and the sounds of invisible accidents. A language which is shadowy and full of reverberations. Magical phrases like those used in incantations. The *mystery.* You wrote from *inside* the mystery, not from outside. You wrote with closed eyes, stuffed ears, inside the very shell. Caught the essence, this thing which we pursue in the night dream, and which eludes us, the incident which evaporates as we awake—this you caught.

---

* Manuscript of a prose poem, eventually printed under the title "Asylum in the Snow." A friend of the Guilers, Barclay Hudson, while on the island of Corfu, had given Durrell a copy of *Tropic of Cancer,* which triggered the extensive correspondence between Henry Miller and the young British author, who had asked in one of his first letters, in December 1935, "Who is Anaïs Nin?"

You will see when you get *The House of Incest* that I tried to get there. You'll see that some of the same sensations disturbed us. I am going to sit quietly sometime, after the first chaos which was produced by your rhythm, and tell you about those phrases that I consider so deep in meaning.

I have a confession to make. I have read your letter to Henry and so I know you. Reading "Christmas Carol" made me want to throw my *House of Incest* into the Seine. Too heavy—too heavy. Durrell traveled faster and lighter. He danced on an echo.

JANUARY 3, 1937

*T*HE SECRET OF MY SEDUCTION IS THE DEVILTRY in me which none of my acts betray and which men sense—the mystery is my intelligence and acting and what I do with them. The enigma is the lie. The lie I told Gonzalo, intended to reassure him ("See, I give up Henry altogether"), turned into a drama because all he could think of was that Henry's attempt at suicide had made me ill, broken me down. All he could think of was how affected I was by what had happened. Then he heard, accidentally, that the day after the suicide Henry was eating heartily, and he deduced that Henry was playing on my feelings to win me back. He sensed all the time something false and twisted but could not tell what it was. From the time he was told about Henry's appetite to last night at eleven, when I met him, he was tortured by jealousy. He knocked his head against the wall, blind with fury and baffled by this dark corner in me, which he never could penetrate. Now, all afternoon I had been with Henry, who had received me with passion and tenderness. I had not responded to Henry, but I yielded to him. So Gonzalo's fears and doubts that Henry still has a hold on me are true—but not sexually, *creatively*. With Henry I enter a magic world of creation. We are still working together. We want to publish each other's works. When I meet Gonzalo and he talks to me about politics I feel cold. It is poetry I live with Henry.

What irony. Gonzalo pleads and entreats, "Oh, *chiquita,* I love you too much. I want you all to myself." The strange thing is that I feel such deep despair at the doubts of Gonzalo, despair that he should suffer, despair at seeing him withdrawn and tortured, that I really suffer with him deeply, and we get all entangled in useless words and chaotic emotions, all foggy and mad, and then suddenly, with tremendous vehemence, I say, "Oh, Gonzalo, how can such little things affect your faith in our love!"

"What little things?"

"A few vertigoes!" I say quickly, and we burst out laughing, irrepressibly, at what he calls my diabolical humor.

But deep down I am sad; I am as sad as if I were faithful to Gonzalo and he doubted me. Deep down I feel innocent. It seems to me that I can be faithful not to people but to cosmic life—to loves that are beyond men and individuals. I live in a mysterious world that faithfulness cannot encompass. I am alive, that is all I know—alive and feeling Gonzalo—alive in a different dream with Henry.

I couldn't sleep. I thought of our publication plans with Henry, our enjoyment of Durrell's writing, our banquet of ideas and inventions. And I thought of Gonzalo's politics and hated it.

"Don't you feel me all your own when I am with you . . ."

"Yes, *chiquita,* but as soon as you climb the little stairs out of the boat you enter another world."

Passing from world to world, giving to each my fullness, why is that treachery? You can only betray what *exists.* What there is in Gonzalo or between Gonzalo and me I do not betray. I do not give Henry the feelings I give Gonzalo—not even the same caresses. I do not take anything away from Henry, because I am still loyal to his creation, his life, and full of love and care.

It is I who could knock my head against the walls while composing this *absolute in space* not found in one man.

I am quite broken, quite broken now. No one would believe or understand.

Evening: I testify to the wonder of life, which surpasses all I have ever read.

Rising haggard from the chaos of Gonzalo's jealousy, feeling in myself a conflict, or rather two. One: How can I prevent Gonzalo from suffering? Two: How can I poetize politics? For there lies the problem. *Life for me is a dream.* I mastered the mechanism of it, bending it to the will of the dream. I conquered details to make the dream more possible. With hammer and nails, paint, soap, money, typewriter, cookbooks, douchebags, I made a dream. That is why I renounce violence and tragedy. Reality. So, I made poetry out of science. I took psychoanalysis and made a myth of it. I mastered poverty and restrictions for the sake of the dream. I lived adroitly, intelligently, critically, for the sake of the dream. I lied for the sake of the dream. I sewed and mended for the sake of the dream, served the dream. I took all the elements of modern life and used them for the dream. I subjected New York to the service of the dream. And now it is all again a question of dream versus reality. In the dream nobody dies, in the dream no one suffers, no one is sick, nobody separates.

Now politics. Shall Gonzalo put my name down on the list? It gives him pride to do so. I am with him. He won me from my world. He tore me from tradition. He awakened me. Illusion. The dream. Let him put my name down, I say. Veils. Illusion. I shall make the poem. I can make the poem out of ragpickers. But neither Hugh nor my Father must know. Of course, Elena is a "Fascist." Elena, supremely intelligent, believes what I believe—beyond politics. The dream. Elena's friend is Delia del Carril. Delia is a friend of my Father and Maruca. Delia is "red." Delia is among the plotters.

Gonzalo asked me if I would come Wednesday evening. I said yes. I do not believe. I believe in love, illusion, and the dream. I entered the world of psychoanalysts, didn't I? With my seven veils. The men who reduced all things—all but Rank—the great tearers of illusions, the great realists, the men who look at the phallus as you look at a lambchop. I entered their world, saw their files, read their books, found Rank the mystic among them, lived a poem, came out unscathed—free, a poet. Not all the stones tied around my analyzed neck can drown the poet. I laugh. Life is a dance to me, a profound, sacred, joyous, mysterious, symbolic, soulful dance. But it is a dance.

Through the marketplaces, the whorehouses, the abattoirs, the butcher shops, the scientific laboratories, hospitals, Montparnasse, I walk with my dream unfurled and lose myself in my own labyrinths, and the dream unfurled carries me. Illusion. Politics. Here too I must dance my own rhythm. I will bring my white face, my faith (the immensity of my faith), my breath and passion. I am unbearably, profoundly, incredibly alone, alone, alone right in the furnace of love, right in the center of brilliant friends, glamorous excitement, continuous riches. Individual in my vision, I alone see and hear this way. It is my dream I hang on to. Is this the crime, to love, to love, to love and follow man in his mad ventures, touching mouths and bodies, mouths and hair, loving, adoring, laughing as I laughed last night, saying, "A few vertigoes"?

I have so much. And I must not hold on to everything. It is in my insistence on the dream that I am alone, when I take up my opium pipe and lie down and say, Politics, psychoanalysis—they never meant to me what they mean to others. Nor New York. Nor nightclubs. Nor anyone around me. Nor Montparnasse. Rank alone *knew*. He knows. It is like a secret. It is my mystery. They always want me to become serious. I am passionate and fervent only for the dream, the poem. Whether I ally myself to the analysts to find I am not an analyst, or to Communists to find out I am not of the world, does not matter. I feel my solitude at the same instant as I make my greatest connection with human beings, the world, when I have a husband, two lovers, children, brothers, parents, friends, a stream of people passing around me; when I am in full motion, life and warmth; when I have reached the maximum of love!

Quand on danse on danse seule. When one practices witchcraft, one does so alone. One interviews the devil alone. One is Machiavellian alone. One is the lover alone. The loved one alone. And when you are attached profoundly, by blood, sex, soul, to human beings, you feel alone. *Ce qui m'amuse, ce sont les complications.* It's complications that amuse me. I laugh alone. Something is happening here of which I am not afraid. It is not insanity, but it is creating in space and loneliness. It is not schizophrenia, it is a vision, a city suspended in the sky, a rhythm which demands solitude. Creation issues only in separateness. The clay is sliced, the painting is begun with separate spots. Vision means separateness. Love means unity, wholeness. Music swells my sails. *Nanankepichu* is afloat with a flag of fire, stained with the blood Gonzalo loves so much.

I feel hysterical, on the verge of ecstasy and madness. My body trembles with delight and despair.

JANUARY 4, 1937

*L*AST NIGHT AFTER I WROTE THIS, I LET HUGH FALL asleep and I slipped out to *Nanankepichu*. Gonzalo, too, was worn out. We wanted softness and serenity after our orgy of emotions. Strange to watch a suffering you do not share. I see Gonzalo suffering all I suffered with Henry. Because I am all his happiness, his fear of losing me is tremendous. His joys, too, when after his sensual satisfaction he lies back and says, "You can't imagine what plenitude I feel! Everything is marvelous!"

I seem to be living over again all the joys and anguish I lived with Henry, their depth, the terror, and the ecstasy.

I am happy. After the fusion, which is always incomplete for me, I feel happiness. The joy Gonzalo feels goes through my body. I live inside of his body.

Rhythm requires this—just as in the sexual bout. *One* can be active and it forces the other into passivity. It is not a tragedy, but it makes one the lover and one the beloved. I was Henry's lover. June was his lover, too. And it is in my active role sexually that I found the orgasm. In passivity I experience happiness, but no orgasm. But I am happy, happy, and I desire Gonzalo. I want him. When I see him with others and I cannot kiss him I get desperate.

I see Henry, who, when not sensually hungry, is cool and inexpressive. But today he is hungry. We get into bed. In spite of myself, I get aroused, so aroused—then I feel the sweetness and *éblouissement* Gonzalo felt last night. I smoke my cigarette voluptuously. I lie in a dream, and I dream of Gonzalo, Gonzalo. When I came in, I came in breezily, glowing, talking. I was telling Henry I was happy. I had received a letter from Rebecca West, who had shown my Father manuscript to a London publisher. The first reader got sick. It affected him like something lethal. The second one too! The publisher said it was a masterpiece, and the other partner too. But it remains uncertain—for puritanical reasons.

Henry, I know now definitely what I must do. In the diary I am natural, sincere. I must stay in the diary. In the novel I am artificial. I must take each volume separately and make it flower, fill it, complete it. That I must do.

Eduardo tells me over the telephone, "After seeing Gonzalo, Elena, you cannot rise any higher, you have the best. I am behind you in my friends."

I feel power. Power to seduce, to work, to love, and to be loved! Power. Power.

Sitting before Henry, thinking that I had only relinquished him imaginatively the night before, and seeing how we could talk and have sex, I was perplexed. Creation. Sex. No jealousy. Is it my *feelings* I have taken out of my life with Henry, my soul, my emotions which made our relationship intolerable? Is it my soul and feelings I have poured over Gonzalo, like a fire, which he takes for love? Is it love? I don't know. I will not question. All my feelings rush out toward Gonzalo, respond to his. A naked sexual exchange, a creative harmony, a bond with Henry—these persist.

Who has the best share? If I were Gonzalo I would prefer the feelings. It is, as he says, with time. I feel now that only the day I relinquish Henry will I experience the orgasm with Gonzalo which will make our rhythm complete. Mystery—how right his jealousy, his instinct. What a hold Henry has on me! How many men have tried to break it! How I have tried to break it myself! I have sometimes the feeling that my other loves are like anaesthetics to make my life with Henry bearable, because I could not bear the pain.

Accepting the mystery and trying *not to live too fast* with my terrible intelligence, losing myself in the moment, spending all I have each day, emptying myself, and sleeping profoundly at night: thus I live without anxiety or nerves, with less terror of this life which wounded me too deeply, with a greater faith. A day of assurance, of certainties, won by such great struggles. Marvelous to feel not one cell in one asleep, all of one's self burning. I feel my intelligence dancing. Gonzalo talks sometimes as if I were the one moving all the strings of our destinies. Because I *see,* sense, so far? Or because I like to play God, or because to create my own life, an *active* life, I stir so much blood around me?

I deny all calculation, all Machiavellian premeditation. But I have this strange pride and feeling that, yes, I have made all this. I have conquered the friends. I have won by love, devotion, and vision. I have truly constructed, with clairvoyance, mine and others' lives around me. Yes, a power to enslave, but not to make a slave; to make others fulfill themselves.

Why do I see so clearly, see so well the mischief, the trickery, and the play-acting with which I enact the most sincere and passionate of all destinies? When I leave the apartment, Hugh and Eduardo sitting there, to meet Gonzalo. When I see that Eduardo can see me go out from where he is sitting, and I not only wave at him but I show him the bottle of wine I am taking for Gonzalo, which makes Eduardo blush and call me perhaps a cynic! I feel not cynical but humorous.

JANUARY 10, 1937

*M*Y LIFE IS TRAGIC ONLY IN RELATION TO MY UN-real conception, my desire for a paradise—an artificial paradise. Henry taught me a great deal of acceptance of human life as it is—passivity. I learned to be happy, to enjoy. But I continued to create what I call an absolute in space, a paradise suspended in midair, made up of various elements, one composite heaven, disregarding faithfulness. I took Henry's elements, creation and sensuality, Gonzalo's soul and emotion, passion, love. For this reason I never talk about unfaithfulness. I gave Henry a whole love, but I suffered while I was having human life with its limitations, imperfections, tragedies. Then I grasped my dream with Gonzalo. Then human life demands choices—absolutes again. If Gonzalo suffers at my infidelity, I am baffled. I don't wish to cause suffering. Terrible, unanswerable aspirations, desires, push me out of human life. Terribly real anguish, real thirst and hunger. Then human life interferes. I may lose one of them, according to human laws, because I desire happiness, and all absolute is tragic.

Suffering horribly now at the possibility of separation from Henry, feeling probably I deserve it, seeing Elena's warm enthusiasm for him, hearing Elena saying, "He is so good, so winning. He resembles this man I loved so much."

Strange talk. Henry has just awakened from sleep. I am telling him that I have willed all the diary to him because we had been talking about who I would will it to, and Henry has been thinking I could not leave it to him because of my treacheries, but I said to Henry: "I am leaving it to you." I have nothing to be ashamed of. I have loved Henry even while I lay with other men. I have never been untrue to Henry. I would not mind if he read all my diary.

Then he told me again he thought I should stop writing in the diary and write a novel.

I am not natural outside of the diary. The diary is my form. I have no objectivity. I can only write while things are *warm* and happening. When I write later I become artificial. I stylize. I become unnatural. I have struggled enough against my neurosis. I am no longer neurotic. I know what I am. I am like the Chinese. I will write slender little books—outside of the diary. Live greatly and produce only a poem. I feel right with myself. I must perfect what is natural.

"When you look at it from such a superior aspect I have nothing to say. The diary is a drug, a narcotic," said Henry.

"Do you object to the Chinaman's opium? Is it not right in him?"

"Yes, there is nothing to say to that. But are you satisfied? Why do you seem to prefer what *I* do?"

"I prefer what you do—dynamic, objective, artistic, creative work—yes, of course. But the very fact of my devotion to it may prove I have not got that in myself. I accept what I have in myself. I am far beyond neurosis. I have lived reality, faced reality; I know reality—I am not cut off, I have no fears, no anxieties—but I prefer the dream. *La vida es sueño.* I repudiate violence, because I chose the dream. My nature, my temperament."

As I say this with quiet assurance, I move my hands with soft fatalism. Henry can no longer reproach me for not making sufficient *effort* in writing. I make all my efforts in life; all my dynamism is in life. In writing I am passive, flowing, drugged, yes, not because I cannot connect with reality, but because of my voluntary hatred of it.

My last night with Gonzalo, after I had imaginatively yielded up Henry, I responded to him sexually for the first time—but it is all in wanting not to love Henry. It is all with or against Henry. Just as I served Henry to escape from June! How ironic!

Let Henry read all this. As it is June's story, too.

I wanted to get inside of life. I got so deep inside that I cannot get out. Working on the old diaries is harrowing because I have made the past so warm and alive that it still hurts! No objectivity anywhere. No power to transform! Henry is at peace, transposing his life with June—*how* to tell it is his obsession. I am inside, with Gonzalo, who is inside. I cannot talk about creation with Gonzalo because he is personal, emotional. That is why we can have together a world of feelings which makes me happy.

Funny. When I met Henry I was objective. I became personal and emotional. Elena is now objective and detached. I know what is coming to her!

Gonzalo suffers because he reads a manuscript of mine and doesn't care how it is written—all he cares about is that *I*, his love, was kissed or taken, or that I kissed and loved. For that Gonzalo gives me the feeling of the you-and-I—alone and isolated right in the midst of life, crowds, wars, friends, popularity; and Henry rarely gave me that feeling—in fact only in Louveciennes, and in New York when he lost me for a while.

Working on the diary is too much like living. I touch real flesh, real tears; I hear real words. It is intolerable. Can people read it? It is warm, wet, it writhes, it exhales odors like flesh itself. Too near, too near. That is why I find Henry's world cold, Gonzalo's *warm!* No sensuality, no creation can create the same warmth as the feeling, a soul loving, a flesh loving in immediacy. Henry loves in space, in time, in imagination. Henry, contrary to all appearances, is not *in* life, not inside. *Il subit la vie.* He endures life. Passive. Never acts, but afterward spills out in writing.

Pas si vite! I am tearing through the skies of my inventions, disheveled! Nothing has happened. Under the calm surface of life I am always sensing demons! Underneath the fog and perfumes of the dream I sense the inexorable destruction and separation of life which I rebel against—against the evolution of time, when I evolved quicker than all the rest, when I projected myself out of Henry's life—and yet I can't accept definiteness—what a wrench! So it is the exactness I keep here, the breath and the odor, to keep everything alive! But we cannot bear to keep everything alive; that is why death was given us, because we cannot feel so much; we crack. Parts of us must die, must die to free us, to lighten us. How well parts of Henry die in him, because he possesses the gift of destruction. I can only gather life together until it becomes unbearable, the too-muchness of it, the intensity; and I explode in hysteria, into a million fragments, too much life! Too much feeling about life. Inside. It is torture to be *inside,* to hear and see so much, to know so much, to have no detachment or protection or refuge from being alive! Someone ought to make me unconscious! Kill me. Render me insensible, lethargic. Parts of me ought to die, but how well I have prevented them from dying. The diary swarms with live things, cracks with reality, bursts with warmth!

Art. Where is the art that keeps us from insanity?

———

When Gonzalo thinks he will get money from his mother he says, "The first thing I will do is buy *Nanankepichu.*" When we talk about his magazine, the printing press he wants, the publication of my work and the group's work, he is afraid of invasion and the loss of our intimacy. He wants to get a smaller boat, where he can be all alone with me and only water around us. He even resents René's presence on the *péniche.* I suggest we take refuge in the prow, a small painted room with two tiny square windows. We could cut it off from the room we now have, and enter it by a trapdoor on the top. Absolute secrecy. He preserves the two-ness.

JANUARY 12, 1937

AFTER THE TALK WITH ELENA I BEGAN TO suffer—inside of my body. A physical, fleshly pain at the fear of parting from Henry, as if he were being torn from my body. Two days of pain during which I rushed out to see Gonzalo for an hour, throwing myself inside of his immense protective goodness, a strength of love I feel in him even when he is my child too—a different kind of child. Gonzalo, hold me. I am going mad again. I create an artificial paradise, an unreal happiness, and human life destroys it, is against it.

I respond for the second time to his caress. What a joy in me when I felt the orgasm for the first time in his arms, when I abandoned myself wholly. I do not doubt his love. His body is always there, his mouth, his caresses.

But the pain, the pain of separating from Henry. Guilt makes me feel that I will lose Henry because of the happiness I seek outside of Henry.

Monday I get up. I rush to Henry. He greets me with a warm kiss. He is cheerful, soft, like a pot of honey. We have lunch together.

After lunch he is eager to get into bed. He takes me with appetite, lingeringly. I respond bestially. He utters bestial words. We sleep. Everything seems the same. I have brought work with me. He works too, until I leave.

I leave to meet Gonzalo at *Nanankepichu* for the first political meeting. *Comité Ibérien pour la Défense de la République Espagnole.* The big room is lit by one lamp. The men arrive—Mexicans with long black hair, gold rings, colored shirts; Chileans, Nicaraguans, pasty Cubans, poets, medical students, law students. They like the place. It is romantic, frightening. Too frightening. It terrorizes those who have not got their papers in order. The policeman always on guard at the top of the stairs which lead to the quay frightens [Pablo] Neruda, the inert and sickly poet. He runs back to tell Gonzalo, who is waiting for other comrades at the quay d'Orsay station. Gonzalo gets a shock: "My God, Anaïs is in trouble, I have got her in a mess." He runs back and finds us all quietly smoking. I have been introduced: "A new *camarade*, Anaïs Nin." We have to leave *Nanankepichu*. They are all afraid. We all go to a café. Gonzalo stands apart, physically bigger and of an altogether different quality. He is the only active, fiery, *whole* one there. The others pale, vague, prosaic. The main theme is how to utilize, exploit the death of a Mexican poet who died in Spain for the cause. A pamphlet should be written. Some of his poems should be published. How much money is there in the *caisse*? Forty francs. Stop. How to get the money? Neruda rubs the soft white hands of the politician. Gonzalo looks like a man from another planet. The way his hair waves back suggests idealism and heroism. The height of his brow throws off a glow of mysticism. His mouth is that of a child. It is ready to tremble. The look in his eyes is warm, caressing, magnetic. His chin is strong. His hands are thick and made for action. He is nervous, like a racehorse. He should not be doing politics. He is an idealist, a fighter. How can he use this ardent, vital body?

I look at his neck, his magnificent neck, like that of a statue, solid, boneless. An animal bothered with a soul. The dark Indian in him, cursed with a soul.

I give him my eyes, insight, wisdom afterward, inciting him somehow to act alone. I say he is wasting his strength pulling others along. But politics *is* carrying others along. It is work with the masses.

I felt the beauty in the politics last night. I knew I did not belong there. But I want to stand by Gonzalo, be loyal to him. *Malaise* among those people, as I always feel in certain milieus—as a kangaroo might feel being suddenly placed among a herd of elephants.

When he talks about the artist's role in the transformation of the world, I answer with great sweetness and gentleness: "I thought that when I was sixteen. Afterward, I realized the futility of it and I worked obstinately to build an *individually perfect world.* This I have done outside, abstracted from reality."

"Yes, but there has come a moment when this perfect individual world is blocked by the outer world. Now you cannot go any further. You are blocked. Your work cannot be published, because it outrages the bourgeois ideals. You cannot lead your own life, because so many are dependent on you."

This is true. Somewhere, at a certain point, my individual world touches the walls of reality. I am faced by outer catastrophes—wars, revolutions, economic disasters, decadence, putrid society.

Henry destroys what is rotten and stops there.

And I? I have built, regardless of the rottenness, a world. But deep down, deep down, I know no outer change can alter the inner mechanism of man. I know too well that it is psychology, guilt, fear which motivate or block us.

Gonzalo is so sincere I respect him. The best moment is when we kiss, when our bodies mingle. When he lies back panting and says, "Oh, God, how happy you make me . . ."

A printer, brooding on the loss of a woman he loved, set her name in type and swallowed it.

A gangster who attacked a man to rob him, put a nail through his hands to tie him to a bench.

A man violated his fourteen-year-old daughter in front of the mother.

In Spain—a bullfight, but instead of the bull a man—sticking explosive *banderillas* into him.

Dynamite in the wombs of women.

Bed in *Nanankepichu* floating.

Honesty with Elena. Urging her not to marry a man she does not love. Thinking sincerely of her happiness as we talk, pitying her for her empty, lonely life. Yet hoping that by talking about my harmony with Henry she will feel we are close and not think of him. Eduardo reassures me by saying, "Elena has too strong a personality. Henry would not want that struggle again. He wants either you or a sexual diversion now and then."

Elena strong, emphatic, positive, unyielding. She could only give him the same intelligence and understanding I gave him. No more. With all this, I was working on the old diaries for Clairouin, which did much to revive my dream happiness with Henry—the perfection of our relationship alone, out of the world. It is the Henry in the world which hurts me, because he is so feminine, yielding, impressionable. Yet even behind this *appearance* of easy connection with many people I realize Henry connects profoundly with very few. Only, he knows how to connect lightly, whereas I can only connect deeply or not at all.

Elena said something so true: She said to live *within* meaning, and not outside. Which has been my experience this year, to move away from analysis, to live inside, knowingly, and formulated simultaneously in the *act*.

Seeing for the first time my Father as a *child*—absolutely a child—who naturally lacks all protective instinct.

No memories left of Donald Friede. Evaporated. Such must be the feeling of men about women they did not love.

JANUARY 16, 1937

FATIGUE AND DISCOURAGEMENT. I HAVE TO FIGHT Gonzalo's masochism. He is another perfect animal spoiled and twisted by Catholicism. He has a cult of suffering. And he comes when I am through with suffering. Why must I always drag weights behind me? Will no man ever run ahead of me and carry me?

I fight to keep him from lighting the fire, to make René do it. But he does it, and our last night together he was all wet from the rain, and getting up finished him. He gets a terrible grippe. I rush over to him the next morning and find him trembling with fever and chopping wood for the fire in his home, while Helba and Elsa sleep. I offer to go and buy wood. He refuses. He creates endless complications for himself, useless tasks, does things in the most difficult way, harms himself, hurts himself. I bring him cigarettes and rum. He works all day at his political work. I spend the day with Henry, working on my diaries. At six o'clock I get restless to see Gonzalo. I bring him more rum and cigarettes, but sick as he is he will go out and attend a meeting with Gide, Malraux, and his *camarades*. I leave him, feeling very tired and sad. Henry and I go to the movies.

Since the first I have been gnawed and weakened by intestinal grippe to which I paid no attention. Reeling every morning. Staying in bed only one day. Hugh brings a stray cat home.

JANUARY 17, 1937

*T*HAT IS HOW ONE CHANGES, NOT LIVING BUT *watching* life (sometimes not living after a shock, after a tragic experience, divorce, detachment, my girlhood), living *for* others, *through* others, or *like* others.

I deny calculation. I say it is instinct. I have several violently impulsive instincts: desire and protection. I desire, love, get on fire— simultaneously, I protect. I protect Gonzalo from the pain of my past. Knowing so well what I would like to hear, what helped me to live, to believe, to abandon myself, I can say to Gonzalo what he needs to hear: I imitate perfectly the words and actions of whole love (as I did for Rank). I understand others, their fears, desires, pains; I know *exactly* what to say and do. A natural gift for giving helps me. Gonzalo's instinct tells him I am not wholly his. I have to reassure this instinct. This desire inspires me to the most subtle words and acts. Today, lying together, I said to Gonzalo, "If I didn't have you, I would go to Spain now, not to America. America, Anglo-Saxon life is finished for me."

"Are countries mixed up with people for you?"

"Yes. I suppose they are."

I knew he was thinking that America was tied up with Henry, so I expanded on this spiritual divorce from America, from which only two things have entered my blood: the language (not the spirit) and jazz (rhythm). I said, "It must be because of you, Gonzalo."

This is not a lie. I was starting to tell lies and struck a truth! Very often I tell lies which are deeply true.

Gonzalo says he has a feeling that great changes will take place this year for all of us.

My belief in unconscious mimicry, in the assuming of roles preceding real living, is so strong that I have not shown my novel to Elena, for fear she might see in the June–Anaïs story a possibility of the same thing happening to her. A *tougher* woman (and Elena *is* Valkyrian) could be happy with Henry!

I say I hate analysis, and then I use it as a philosophic order. To stop the pain. The diary is a lazy act. I ought to tell more. How I talk in the dark to Gonzalo, fighting his masochism, about equilibrium between sacrifice and living for one's self—due to guilt, Christian remorse. I tell him how he makes greater sacrifices than he needs to in proportion to what happiness he takes. I say it humorously, tenderly. I say, "Gonzalo, think, when you cut your finger you are cutting *my* finger; when you burn yourself, when you drive yourself, even when you are sick, you are hurting my body. Would you maltreat me?"

"I am improving. I am the happiest man on this earth, today."

Inside life, one goes mad.

Sexual response to Gonzalo complete now.

Hell. Either analysis or life is maddening. Both lead you to impasses, walls, with a sky perpetually mocking you overhead, and a pair of wings hung on the ramparts, like the circular lifesavers on a boat, with directions! But the sky that is laughing is all the *unlived and the unknown*—whispering, breathing, oscillating, like a serpentine open road away from equations and emotions. New York is a *pantin,* marionettes dancing. The music is outside, the music is marvelous. But the *pantins* are agitated and the wind whistles through the straw and stuffings, and I can't save them. I discovered that when I analyzed them. One can save a *soul.* One cannot *create* a soul, inject it. In Spain the blood is running. The beast in Spain, the cruel animal, the sensualist, the suicidal maniac—living only in the flesh and dying of flesh wounds. I do not see a vision there, I see blood dancing and blood spilled, either sperm or fury, the African animal, dancing and dying. In New York I danced, stainless, sexual and yet not sensual, perfumed, rhythmic. In Spain I would like to die, to feel how alive flesh is when it is torn, or burned. I lie in *Nanankepichu,* where flesh is tasted like the wafer of communion, marriage of heaven and hell. But the talk is about what is passing in the streets, too near, too real; the talk is about this drama of Spain, which the blood yearns to participate in, and the sacrifice. I am really fighting death again, always fighting death, and my own vertigo, my own vertigo toward death. Stronger is ascension and the living instinct, but stronger, too, the bitterness that all heavens require war and struggle.

Less and less. Less struggle. I am far less loaded. This year perhaps I shall carry no cross, the cross tattooed on me by pious Christian hands.

Even jealousy, even jealousy I defeat with love. With love of Elena I defeat this poison and this putrid corruption caused by jealousy. To give Henry my diary would be like giving him all he wanted to know about June. Here the mystery is revealed!

The effect of disillusion in the Chinese theater applies to Henry's writing.

He gets congested with unselected enthusiasms and ideas.

JANUARY 19, 1937

*D*AY AND NIGHT: CLOSE AND LOCK MY CLOSET FULL of perfumed dresses and diaries. Out in the street, with Volumes Thirty-five to Thirty-seven under my arm, to fill out the names for Stuart Gilbert. Arrive at Henry's, who meets me with warmth and gaiety: "You have your nice skull cap on" (The same one he did not like a week before). Lunch and humming and purring. Henry enjoying the admiration he is getting, from schoolgirls too! Henry wanting to go to Denmark. Henry cutting out a picture of Mae West because she was born in Brooklyn. Henry waiting for the plumber. Henry saying, "Everything is fine. The stove is hot. I got a fine letter from Denmark, a stupid letter from England" (the role of art as *sterilizer,* says an Englishman). He suggests a nap and takes me so completely and absolutely, in every nook and corner of my body, that I have the joyous feeling of a world swept of ghosts, on its axis, moving with solidity, with a round grinning face; a carnival, a dance. We laugh while we make love, tease and joke, and I say, "Now your stove and your wife are both well stoked." Laughing. Sleeping. Here is the plumber. Henry has some work to finish. I walk a block away to the Cité Universitaire and see Eduardo, who has not been feeling well. He walks out with me. We have tea at the Dôme, where everyone looks soiled, putrid, haggard, derelict. I return to Henry, who is still purring. I tell him about the "black sun" Moricand said I was, shining inwardly and secretly. He says he envies me my madness when I write such things as my "film"—that I can get so detached from reality, whereas he remains rooted to it.

At seven-thirty I am at Elena's because she wrote me about a dream of death she had, ending her letter, *"Te quiero tanto."* I love you so much—like a cry of distress. No matter how fast I run I always hear the voice of those who are behind me. Elena is behind me in life, choked by fears and scruples and conventionalities. I thought she was ahead. And so it is I who am pulling Elena out of darkness, liberating her. She says someone introduced Henry to her thinking he would fall in love with her.

"Do you think he is the type of man you need?"

"No, I don't want an intellectual. I'm too selfish for that. I don't want to be sacrificed to a work."

I tell her a little about our life. I feel like putting my head on her ample breast and saying, "Do not take Henry from me."

How we talk! She too enjoys *awareness*—she cannot sink, become unconscious. She too is masculine in her sense of form and synthesis. She too lives quickly—clairvoyantly. We talk with eyes blazing, inundated in clarity. I promise I will help her to reconcile herself to herself. I feel that she is full of anxieties and fears. We laugh about the times we tried to sink, *déchoir,* fall away; and how, like lifebuoys, we kept afloat. Like sisters. I see her as *atlantide,* too. I like her quickness, sharpness and honesty. We talk lustily, ardently.

At ten-thirty I am at *Nanankepichu.* Gonzalo tells me the Spanish *legacion* is with them, delighted to be able to connect with South America. They will supply money, stamps, paper, printing facilities. Gonzalo has written the first manifesto. He is glad. I ask questions, I listen. I try to remain near. It is not so very different from Hugh telling me about the stocks, the bank, or politics from an economic point of view. I struggle desperately not to get cold. Where is all the keen life I lived all day, where is the current of marvelous inventions, discoveries, discussions, voyages, the interplay I felt with Henry and with Elena?

When he says with hatred, "The capitalistic world killed the artist in me," I realize the artist was not very strong; nor is Gonzalo's vision of the world very profound. He sees outside all that comes from the inside. Limitations and restrictions are inner, not outer. I know I am responsible for my own restrictions: pity, weakness. Gonzalo is equally full of feeling—that is what has destroyed the artist in him, made him the selfless helper of another artist. But I cannot enlarge Gonzalo's vision yet. We cannot talk. As soon as I mention Elena he leaps with fury and demolishes her, out of jealousy. I do not defend her, I see

385

the jealousy. He ends by saying, "I don't want you to love anyone, man or woman, but me!"

This kind of jealousy—the one that kills the other because he is guilty of living or enjoying outside the beloved—I have never let myself express, even if I felt it. My desire to *give* life was stronger. I was sad.

Only our caresses were sweet.

I could not sleep—I was so awake—yet feared to awake completely and *talk* to Gonzalo. Morning. Exhaustion and discouragement.

JANUARY 20, 1937

ELENA BECAME VERY SICK—INTOXICATED, CHOKED with *angoisse*. Went there for a moment and stayed four hours, pulling her out of the darkness, illuminating the darkness, chasing away the evil spirits, poetically, humorously, affectionately. I, the sage, reading the hieroglyphs of her obsessions. No matter how fast I run, the tail ends of others' ghosts pursue me and I am fated to hear the same words: "I never found anyone I could lean on, anyone who understood me—until you. What strength you give me. I am well."

Elena sitting among her horoscopes with dark stars shining on her, dark stars digging their points into her flesh, her sun-colored flesh. Elena dreaming of a big man without a head, breathing like a flower, his stomach swelling at the intake of breath.

Elena saying she will paint me as Daphne in the act of becoming a plant.

Elena says exactly as I say: "There are so many people who say things I never hear or remember."

She says so much that is exactly what I say that at one moment I wanted to laugh, to laugh and say to her, "You know, it's very funny, but if Henry heard you he would have to say, 'I have already heard all this . . .'"

*H*ENRY HAS READ THE VOLUMES CONCERNING HIM and June. Clairouin has read from thirty-one to forty-one (leaving out "Incest"), and now the only one reading them patiently and completely is Stuart Gilbert, and he is overwhelmed:

"I have never read anything like it. The *lucidity* is amazing. You let yourself go, and at the same time you are seeing yourself. It is *dédoublement*. You are at once the warmest-blooded person I know, and the coldest! At times you are absolutely ruthless!"

The veritable demon in me is this aware self which feels as if *she holds all the strings.*

Rarely have I lost my bearings. In the most chaotic life, I feel like a demon that holds the strings. At times I feel like a creator, a god, acting on others, on Henry, June, Elena, Hugh, Eduardo, like a Fate. It is I who make the motions, the things happen. A me which *plots* without plotting, a driving impulse in me of which I am aware, which makes me instinctively live my life and create it. There is a will. I feel it. There is a demon. I feel it. I am not always aware of what the demon is plotting. But the obscure work goes on: my life. This demon has green eyes and *great desires* and great fears and great defenses, great illusions and great ruthlessness. I would like to be in closer touch with the demon. It chides me. I look at myself, quietly writing. Innocent face. An instinct like nature, which accomplishes its needs, satisfies its appetites, is human, pitiable, ruthless, like nature. But a spirit which *rules* the nature, so as to dominate the chaos . . .

Stuart Gilbert is right.

Such innocence and love last night, in *Nanankepichu*. Gonzalo is talking about his childhood. I can see him. The beautiful Jesuit school in the gardens and woods, in a necklace of volcanoes. Gonzalo at fourteen, sexually unawakened when his comrades were already sleeping with maids and prostitutes. Timid before woman. At sixteen a girl sends him a note to come and see her at the park while she takes a walk. He goes but at the first sight of her he runs like a wild doe. As he talks I see in his face the same expression of the gentlest animals—doe, fawn, cat—soft and animal, an animal with an old soul, so pure. I feel so pure. I too awakened late, sexually. At nineteen only. The demon and the angel sleep side by side.

I listen gently to Gonzalo. When he talks about Communism he trembles with passion. When he talks about the Indians—leading them to rebel against the white tyranny—something leaps in my breast, and I tell him. The Indian—*pure.* Injustice to the pure. But the rottenness of the European—the putrid Europe—my heart can't beat for. I would rather burn Europe than save it. Fire. The purifier. I would rather see Europe burn, because it smells. I would rather save the Indians.

JANUARY 22, 1937

*E*LENA AND I TALKING. ELENA AND I WALKING. Elena saying, "I get drunk with you. *¡Que borachera!*" And I, later: "With you, I want to be above jealousy."

"Anaïs, because I look so strong nobody ever thinks I need help. You are the only one who knew . . ."

Today she will come and watch the hairdresser fix my hair differently. I was drunk too, talking about our lives, lies and truth.

I can't get drunk on politics. But I can get drunk on Gonzalo's body, on his love. After walking half across Paris with Elena, I meet Gonzalo, and I let myself sink into sensuality looking at his sensual nose, seeking my pleasure blindly.

Henry brings two people he has been seeing and likes: [Abraham] Rattner the Jewish painter and his wife. Incredibly mediocre, absolutely without interest, and common, ugly. I tried hard to keep my gaiety, but slowly I got sad, sad, sad.

What made me happy is discovering that Henry is afraid to lose me, that he clings to me, that he is jealous and says, "While I go to Denmark I want you to sit here quietly and wait for me." But meanwhile he had expected me to cook dinner for these impossible Rattners!

I seek drunkenness!

JANUARY 24, 1937

NIGHT OF NIGHTMARES AND INSOMNIA, TORTURED by imagining Henry and Elena together—because, to end the doubts and fears, I questioned Moricand, and he wrote that there was an attraction between the two horoscopes, but illusory and not profound. Like a superstitious medieval woman, I questioned the stars. I said to myself, Well, if I have Gonzalo, I should let Henry have Elena. During all this Henry has made no move to see Elena. But the difference is Henry knows nothing and does not suffer, whereas I would *know*.

When I reached the bottom of suffering I swam up again, clinging to my happiness with Gonzalo, his love and soulfulness and feeling, clinging and calling to him. And only the day before, I had seen Helba and had found her tortured with jealousy of me. After I left her she had a scene with Gonzalo. Bitter life. I fought my way out of my bitterness, overpowered it so well that I saw Elena today and my admiration for her was intact. She says people are violently attracted to her, but never for long.

What slaves of pain we are! Helba, too, loves me.

It all enrages me. And Gonzalo's suffering, and all the chaos and pain, and the fire and bitterness of it all! I hated it.

Saw Gonzalo today a little while. Bit his lip until I marked him. The gasoline stove caught fire. I kept him, with violence, from approaching it, for fear of the explosion. He said he felt like setting fire to things, as he already did once with a cigarette. Moment of passion, of life. He said, "You are my life. My affection for Helba is like that of a brother, but you are my life, everything to me." And I know it is true.

What sadness and poison! I fight. I fight upward. I work on Volume Forty-one, about the first meeting with my Father, and find it good, powerful. I read Carlo Suares's *Procession enchaînée,* the only truly mad, truly schizophrenic book I have read.

Face my own coldness. Entice it, court it. I seek cold thoughts, cruel thoughts. I have a desire to torture others rather than myself. I feel like an enraged lioness, no longer a Christian lamb willing to be sacrificed or enslaved! I say to hell, to hell with loving so deeply, roots, sex, soul, and all!

Riding in the taxi, I think of what Elena says about the soul. *It is always there,* but separated from the body sometimes, unable to manifest itself, disconnected. I like this because it explains my faith, my search of the soul, my labyrinthian pursuits of my Father's soul, its elusiveness, schizophrenia, and death, all I wrote about the frail Japanese bridge I was trying to cross. Elena is right. She says, as I say, "I never know the real age of people." She runs behind me, a few steps behind me. She sees in me, as June did, the quintessence of her being (in her, clothed in a more solid body). I am the perfume. And I envy her her Renoir body, her big hands and feet and ears, her bullish neck. She says, "I look like the moon."

Letter to Durrell: I thank you for seeing Henry as a *whole.* Few people do. They nibble at him. Your letter to him and about him was the only one I ever really liked. It was strong in its vision.

All you say about *House of Incest* is true, but only for *H. of I.* I don't always write with that detachment. That is the black poison culled from the *greatest attachment*—to people, truth, reality as seen without vision (we have days without vision even when one lives inside the meaning), and this other face, the opposite of *H. of I.,* is a diary of fifty volumes! The roots, the peaty soil, the water, the blood and flesh, the stutterings, and the purely human growls exceed the quintessence, without conquering. Thus I believe in the common reality transformed. I believe as you believe. But what you got in *H. of I.* was the smoke (Henry says "the neurotic fulguration").

Yes, I want to change the title too. Facing a title, for me, is facing the impossible. I feel life and creation as an orchestra, a constellation. A title is an absolute. It terrifies me because I worship the absolute. I hold many strings, but I have a fear of signatures. It has something to do with magic. To conjure or not to conjure. I live, feel, write music. A title is a word— *the* word. It may dispel the evil spirits and it may also make them too real. My titles will always be bad, maybe because I'm not a writer. Henry is the real writer. I am just breathing. I breathe with fins, antennae. How I use words—so definite— when my element is fluid, I don't know. A title, the ultimate catalyzer, is an event. It reminds me that my communication with past, present, and future is so vivid I can never begin or end. I can never remember dates, ages. They are the titles. As soon as I am or write something, I see the metamorphosis so quickly that the title disappears. This *is* a sea. Or a dream. A title is an act of violence and positivism. Do you know Calderon's *Life Is a Dream?*

Perhaps someday you might take sides on a problem unsolved, the only one Henry and I differ on—continuously. I pass from the human, soft, truthful improvised diary to the stratosphere or the asylum—from the least artificial to the artificial. I use a pair of rusty scissors. I clip the painted mandragores. Duality. Henry says, Close the diary, the transformation will happen inside—but I say my untransformed work is better. They hamper each other. The immediate destroys the other—and you get the smoke. Why I ask you this I don't know. Maybe because I felt that the scissors had given you a fragment.

From the very first I liked your "heraldic" world. Behind it I sensed faith, symbol, the meaning. The opposite of narcissism, since each one must be himself plus the symbol—a greater himself. The opposite of neurosis, since each one must see his part in a whole, with faith. Nobility, which aureoles the word, I take as an integrated quality. A lion all lion, as Lawrence would say. Not hermaphrodism. Quality. Intactness. Gift. Heraldic (I am only analyzing its flavors—I never read your definition) seems to have a law of spiritual gravity. Its convolutions in space are cosmic not in the circus. Am I right? Anyway, it is a word with a magic, a secret glow to it.

As I work on the diaries I have a feeling that I am traversing a long dark tunnel, that I was struggling out of death and suffocation. It is only when June left Henry that I began to breathe. More and more air. Meeting my Father was no salvation but a test, an ordeal. More and more light and air, freedom of motion and feeling, up to this year, which was a dance.

Yet even today I hate the Métro!

JANUARY 29, 1937

*H*ENRY TOOK ME TO SEE HANS REICHEL. HIS PAINT-ings are beautiful, delicate, and full of mystery. Walking back, Henry said to me, "Now you will quietly write in your diary the whole thing. Then you must read it to me so I can get inspiration. Give me some of those finite phrases."

I said, "You are too humble. You know no one can write like you."

But I never saw so clearly my fecundation of Henry, like a sexual act. He first went to Reichel like a woman in rut, laughing, groaning, purring, stuttering, raving. Then he took me there, and it was I who saw the eyes, who talked of metamorphosis, communion, marriage, who said all Reichel wanted to hear, who spoke of the womb. Back in Villa Seurat we both sat down to write. I wrote a little, and then as Henry read me what he'd done, which was tremendous, I let myself be engulfed in the large, sonorous, expanded, enriched impact. But I have sown the *seed*—I had penetrated into his chaotic enthusiasm—and *he* gives the birth! "You give me ideas," he says.

A strangely perfect night. It seems when I stick my powerful vision into him like a fiery phallus, move it around in him, stir his blood, plant the sperm of my solid creative unity, Henry is stirred and then he, in turn, wants to take me physically, wants to stick his penis inside of me and stir my blood. The cycle is complete; we awake renewed, fecundated, enriched.

We are so divinely happy together when we can *share* an enthusiasm, heighten it in each other, open each other's eyes, get excited together. The thermometer rises to maximum heat.

Unhappy together when, through his everlasting curiosity and love of life, he loves too far outside of me and I get jealous or lonely. Or when he feels the same about me, since I have this curiosity, enthusiasm, and expansion.

Gonzalo kills all my enthusiasms because he cannot share them. I can't share them. I can't share his passion for politics. Gonzalo and I are only happy together in *darkness*.

In Reichel there was a bell that laughed, a flower petal with an ear—and a man in despair. He possesses a tiger-eye stone, a piece of sandalwood, seashells, old clothes; and is hungry. Henry shows all his pity and generosity now, toward other writers, painters. He helps, stimulates, encourages.

What I feel is such an overflow of love that it has encompassed Gonzalo—but Henry remains at the center. I write a love letter to Thurema. I kiss Elena good-bye and send her off to [C. G.] Jung.

After Henry has taken me there are still a hundred caresses not given, words to say—the fire still burns.

I have to live my life by mysterious laws, but I want to give to each man the illusion he needs, of loyalty, exclusivity. I work quietly to give Gonzalo confidence—he who has so many doubts. I say and do all the things which resemble absolute love. The need to give the illusion is greater than the need to be true to myself, openly. For instance, Gonzalo entreats me so fervently and desperately not to yield to Hugh's caresses that I tell him I do not. I invent the scene and the progression of the break. I pretend I no longer sleep in the same bed. This gives Gonzalo a great proof of love. As a matter of fact I dislike intensely Hugh's caresses and therefore, although I yield to them to give Hugh happiness, I do not consider that I have given anything of myself. I always have the feeling that I am leading a life no one could understand, or that if they *knew,* I would cause deep suffering. When Henry and Gonzalo both want to come to my place at almost the same hour I give one of them an excuse and say to Eduardo, laughing, "What a son of a bitch I am!" Eduardo says one could forgive me everything because of the way I do it. At moments I laugh (causing no one pain, I can laugh) at my tricks. I enjoy carrying this diary around like dynamite—within reach of Hugh, Henry, or Gonzalo.

Reaching always for the fairy tale causes great havoc with human laws.

FEBRUARY 2, 1937

AFTER THE NIGHT WITH HENRY AND SEEING REI-chel's painting I finally wrote the childbirth story which had been preying on me—fifteen pages of naked, savage truth to be inserted in the diary, as part of the diary.

All day the story possessed me. Full moon and fever.

Evening. *Nanankepichu.* Gonzalo passionate, but then he yields to what he calls my hypnotic kisses and falls asleep, like a child, exhausted from the night before, when drunken Neruda and his friends had dragged him out of his bed at four in the morning to finish the night with them. I slipped out of bed and sat on the rug by the stove. Full moon. Everything in the room clearly outlined, but in lunar tones, blacks, grays, silvers, elephant color, pearl, lead, and charcoal. Gonzalo sleeping heavily, snoring. I thinking humorously of a prayer to the gods: "I am supremely happy, blessed in all ways, but please, could I have a lover who would not snore?"

But the night, the full moon, and my overfulness hurt me. Too full. Too awake. Hurt and tormented by the ferocity of what I wrote during the day, uneasy with the feeling there was something lacking—a meaning not yet revealed. Hurt that Gonzalo should have so many drunken friends, hurt by nothing, angry with Gonzalo's friends and his easy yielding to them. The full moon and the anxiety of aloneness. Could not sleep. Could not read. Could not write. Decided to leave, to go home, just to hurt Gonzalo. Leaned over him before leaving and he awoke, so surprised by my cruelty, opening his eyes to caress me; but with his head on my breast, falling asleep again in great and utter trustingness and peace. I tried to sleep. Dreamt of *Nanankepichu* in three pieces. I at the prow fighting enormous waves. Feverish restless night. Black-sour morning. Came home and added the pages that were missing, about not wanting to push the child out—like a poison. Went to see Maggy and saw a little girl, a lovely little girl, which hurt me, the living picture of what I had killed. Went to the Dôme and met Dr. Endler! Like one of Breton's coincidences which are not coincidences but the powerful magnetic attractions of what we think about. Exhaustion. Depression. Gonzalo's fervor over the telephone: "I have waited all afternoon for your call, *chiquita!*" and meeting him for a half hour in the rain gave me warmth and life again. Creation is the act of the devil. God frowns upon it—as we frown upon those who initiate us!

Debauch of movies Sunday with Hugh and Eduardo. Communist meeting with Gonzalo. And his passion last night, a vigorous desire, after a lovely afternoon with Henry, complete. No more sexual completion with Gonzalo, but a mystical joy, a personified personal sensuality. It is *you,* Gonzalo, *you* pounding into me. What ecstasy! It is you, your darkness, your revolutionary demon, your fervor, and your goodness. It is you, with your courage, your legs made of steel, your odor of sandalwood, your unfinished thoughts, your disorder.

One can never be really unfaithful, no matter what detours we take! I left Spain. I found Anglo-Saxon and Germanic thought. I found Spain again, and I am separated from it by the *intellect*—the inner world. I find Spain, Spanish literature, and Spaniards full of emotion, eloquence, and color—but no meaning. Religious and soulful, but not transcendental. Gonzalo is that to me. Like June, there are moments when he understands everything, but it is an animal understanding and it is not a world. It is a flash. I have discovered I tried to lose my head and could not. What I discovered in America was not only English, it was the contents of my Danish head. I find Spanish poetry now with a taste of fruit or blood, but no meaning. From Gonzalo, in daylight, in the conscious world, I can separate. The phrases which make him vibrate ([Rafael] Alberti's poems) are just color to me. A stained-glass window, grandiloquence, romanticism, not the little wise flame of the Holy Ghost.

When I step on the light *passerelle* of *Nanankepichu* to get on *land,* I enter a daylight world of such depth with Henry that the deep animal soul, the unformulated soul, of Gonzalo seems like the knowingness of a woman. I have a world. He has not a world. He has a body—a body so beautiful that it takes my breath away. He has a soul, a soul so deep it is like a hymn. But under the brow, the noble brow, with its temples built massive like some Grecian monument, under the brow shines desire, intuition, delicacy, but no world, no world with a sky of its own, columns, windows, lights, storms, erected, created, composed. The mystery shines like the Host in its golden *ciboire,* with silk incense around it, the soul, the self, but like the mystery of the Host, it is always the same. Here is bread and here is the wine. My flesh and my blood. Every day it is flesh and blood. Communion.

Eduardo still gets himself into knots, like a rosary or a twisted tree root. I like the unknotted ones!

About politics: All these words I hear, lyric speeches, romantic flourishes, sentimental wreaths, prayers, and poetic lamentations (all bad art, of course), irritate me. In revolution I see a vital life-and-death matter, a struggle one must enter directly and violently. In this I cannot bear intellect or unreality. A revolution is a vital life-and-death matter. Why do they talk so much, recite poetry, these Spaniards? Gonzalo tells me a great deal of Spanish poetry was heroic, war-incited, revolutionary. Too bad Gonzalo has the glamorous physical attributes of the hero, the passion and the courage. What touches me is that he is himself disillusioned with the men he has to work with. He gets bitter at their vanity and vagueness. He gets sad and talks about going to Spain to fight, while they read each other's mediocre poems.

FEBRUARY 4, 1937

*T*HE *DÉDOUBLEMENT*, THE DUALITY, COMES AT THE moment when *I watch myself live*. It takes the form of a fantasy. I imagine someone else watching me. I play at the someone else who, like God, can see me everywhere, and must therefore be the face of my guilt—not in relation to myself, only in relation to the one I am betraying at the moment. When I first stayed at Villa Seurat I imagined Hugh listening at the door to all my scenes of tenderness with Henry. Now it is Gonzalo whom I imagine hiding behind some window of Villa Seurat, seeing me marketing, walking into Henry's place. Gonzalo entering de Maigret's place. (Once I did the reverse with a friend: When de Maigret had just moved in and I was curious to see him, I went on the terrace of Henry's studio, which communicates with de Maigret's. It was a summer day. De Maigret's window was open. We looked in. He was not there but we laughed to see his bed unmade.) Gonzalo could see de Maigret, whom he knows, step on the terrace and look into Henry's studio, which de Maigret's friends have often done during a party. He would see me dancing to the "Firebird" with hands folded as for a prayer and body moving as in Balinese dances, or on Egyptian reliefs—a dislocation. Gonzalo would see me setting the table and Henry lying on the couch, reading to me about Reichel. While I stir the soup Henry comes up behind me and puts his hands on my hips. We lean over a letter from Durrell, laughing and talking. Do I imagine Gonzalo's pain? Does it give me pleasure? I pass from this long fantasy to another: Henry is following me when I walk along the quays, sees me going down the stairs to *Nanankepichu*. Henry sees me in the restaurant with Gonzalo. Gonzalo has his arm around my shoulder.

I fear Gonzalo is so sensitive to relationship that he remembers every *étape*, every scene and word. A few times he has shocked me by his sudden transition from a kiss to an idea. He has the same scatteriness as Henry, eyes turned on the external world, the difficulty in concentrating (like Henry's description of a schizophrenic mood, of all that goes through his head when he is kissing a woman). But Gonzalo has the power to sink into love like a woman, with few exceptions, these usually happening in daylight—as if his conscious and unconscious worlds were deeply separate. He said delicately, "There are times when I can't shut out the daylight. This has happened three times."

The precision of this was amazing. He is aware that three times it happened. Henry is unaware and would never notice it. This never happens to me. I can sink completely, blindly. I can cut myself from reality, easily. Both Gonzalo and Henry are great realists—Henry as a German, Gonzalo as a Spaniard. I love this in them, even though at times it leaves me alone in my communion and ecstasy.

All of them, after passion, fall asleep with great trustingness. It is at this moment, lying at man's side, that I dream and ponder man. Passion awakens me. I cannot sleep. I lie there, with Henry asleep, or Gonzalo asleep, and marvel at my happiness, at this woman's need to have man inside of her. The most ecstatic moments of my life are with my loved one's penis inside of me, or his head on my breast. *In my arms*—awake, passionate, or tender and trusting and asleep—*but in my arms*. Then I feel fulfilled. The orgasm is not necessary. My joy is in the communion.

FEBRUARY 6, 1937

*I*T WAS ALWAYS MY LOVE FOR HENRY WHICH I associated to all my experiences, my other relationships. My love for Henry lay over the whole of my life like the very sky itself. It looked down on me; it was the background, the destiny, the *voûte* one forever watches and feels watched by, the all-encompassing arch throwing down the colors and rays of its moods, its changes, as the sky throws down lights and shadows on us. Between each breath, between each twinkling of the eyelid, it was Henry I saw. When Rank loved me, what I lived deeply was seeing him re-enact my love for Henry. All my tortures did not come from the relationship with Rank but from identification and comparisons, from questioning and doubts. Did Henry love me, or not love me, in the way Rank did? Being June to Rank meant to me *becoming* June for Henry, throwing into the current of our love this new self which alone the passion of Rank had made possible. In Gonzalo's love I see also reflections of my love for Henry. When I see Gonzalo suffer at what I write, I see my suffering at what Henry writes. When Gonzalo struggles to realize how much is dramatization and how much reality, when he separates the skeins to find the real me, I inwardly say to myself, That is how Henry is dramatizing his love for June, which never really exploded or manifested itself as vividly, was never lived out in such a tone or with such intensity. Instantly, the association is Henry. Henry. Everywhere I pursue a relief from my love for him, a relief from obsession, which is *death*. All obsession is death. There is life only in the currents, and currents mean changes. So I have learned to flow around and away from Henry, but still he is the sky that casts all its colors upon my steps, words, kisses. Henry, *his* moods, his eclipses, his storms, his indifferences, his softnesses. The relationships with others pour like tributaries into this all-engulfing sky. It is always the sky, and Henry in the sky, no matter what country I travel through, what flights I take, what voyages, and what amnesias, what intoxicants, what sedatives, what drugs. Moments of respite, of renewal, flowing back to this eternal sky without end, without horizon.

FEBRUARY 7, 1937

LES PLUS GRANDES CAUSES DE MES SOUFFRANCES are my too-quick rhythm and vision. I *see* too quickly. If Henry is expanding too much, wasting time, thinning out, I see it. Long afterward Henry sees it. If Fraenkel is bad for Henry I know it. Much later Henry breaks away from him. Usually I say nothing, but I suffer. This knowledge of error, this advance and impatience makes me grow spiritually fast, but it is painful and lonely. I am *forced* into the leader role.

Sitting at the Dôme with Eduardo I am desperately aware that I want something else, and I *go after something else*, desperately. Other people are just content to want, passive. I saw a sensually attractive man who looked Hindu, a friend of Gonzalo. As I passed he shouted: *¡Alli va una española!"* I turned quickly, smiled, nodded. Wanted to torture Gonzalo. Why? Feel disillusioned, feel the drunkenness dispelling. Was anything durable created? Just like June, he slides down, runs out. Can fall into the most ordinary world, and when he is ordinary I don't love him, because the only one I love humanly is Henry. The others must be *marvelous*—or else what are they, since they enter neither my creation nor my sensual being? Cold thoughts. Anger and bitterness. So I smile at Gonzalo's friend. Revenge against disillusionment.

In the subway I correct what I wrote about Henry and the sky, which I typed hurriedly just before leaving for the hairdresser.

One night I read the childbirth story to Gonzalo, who was gripped by the vitality of it against his will because at first the realism shocked him. Forced to bow before an all-powerful document.

Just before this reading I was holding Gonzalo in my arms and was moved to dissolution—almost breathless with dissolution—and wondered if this were love deepening.

Afraid of mirages. Working on diaries reveals terribly the mirage of Rank, the mirages of Allendy, Father, Artaud. Afraid. Each day for me is so full of terrifying metamorphosis I can awake loving no one. I can awake strong, fulfilled, feeling I could write superbly about anything. I can awake, like Alice in Wonderland, in a world of music and miracles. I can awake, like Alice, feeling diminutive in a huge world, or immense in a miniature world. Feeling a demon, a woman without illusions, or overflowing with faith and illusions and ecstasies. My ecstasies carry me far away.

Gonzalo gave me, more than anyone, the dream. Yet he lets me down so, with the politics, the people he sees, his human interests, his lack of creativeness. He hides what he writes. His drawings lie in a drawer (I begged him to let me see, have, enjoy) He begins translations and drops them. Talks. Drops everything. June. June. June. Gonzalo, you are my June—with all your drugs and drinks and the talking. Shh! Shh! Shh! Rain. Rivers overflowing. You aroused my illusions, awakened wild hopes, wild illusions.

I began a sketch of Moricand complaining of his great miseries, and dropped it. I was baffled that I mocked his tragic statements, felt no pity. Now I know. He is a *voyant*. His eyes look beyond one. He smells the essence. He is nonhuman. His body cannot be warm. He is in a trance. He only shivers at perverse memories. He remembers. He transcends. He talks. But he does not touch the present. He is the *voyant*. No walls. No doors. No conversation. Monologues.

The *mirages*—for me—turn out to be vital and human needs in the others: Rank, Artaud. They were humanly caught.

Nobody is satisfied with his envelope. If I look like the moon and feel in me a savagery, a sensuality, a force which is not expressed in my body, Gonzalo looks like a primitive and is a Catholic. Elena and June look like Vikings and yearn to look like me because the delicacy in them is not apparent.

I owe Rank the *déchets,* the superfluities vanished from the diary.

FEBRUARY 8, 1937

*M*ONDAY I ARRIVED AT HENRY'S AND HE IMMEDIately leaned over me and began kissing me and caressing me, locking me in his arms with an intensity rare in him, holding firmly and pouring his whole being into me. I felt the full force of his subterranean love. Fell asleep. Awoke. Talked about "horror film." Smoked.

At *Nanankepichu* at seven I met Gonzalo. I had planned a lie. Because he always says "If I see you with Henry I will go to Spain," and dreading that he might see me, I thought of telling him I was married to Henry—to explain my not being able to break off brutally and absolutely. We have to make arrangements to separate. I still have to *take care* of him. I can't throw out my *old* husband. It is not love but respect for the past. Hugh let me divorce him when I went to New York (spiritually true). I married Henry there (spiritually true—he bought the Indian love rings). I tried to live with him (I did) and was not happy. I could not live with Henry happily (spiritually true). When Hugh came back, sick, I returned to him (spiritually true).

Gonzalo was shocked and hurt. He talked wildly about going to Spain.

"Henry has been the greatest love of your life."

"Not the greatest."

His talk about Spain completely unnerved me. We could hardly eat our dinner. Rushed back to *Nanankepichu,* threw ourselves into each other's arms, burned with caresses. He was violently desirous; we kissed and caressed for hours. He said, "Who is your husband?"

"You, Gonzalo."

Later in the night we talked so gently, softly, deeply. He could even see the humor—the way I did things to make the others happy. "Curious temperament," he said. He talked romantically, said he wanted to have me before any man and often thought of how I looked like a little girl. I said all the past served to make me love him more. A deeper, richer love. He told me how he was like a woman in that he could only enjoy sex fully when he loved.

We talked almost until dawn. At such moments, in the night, Gonzalo seems to understand everything—which gets confused later with the chaos in him. He always reverts to his youth.

With his fiery love and Henry's subterranean love I was in bliss. It is true that because of my doubts and anxieties *I only believe in fire.* It is true that when I wrote the word "Fire" on this volume I did not know what I know today, that all I have written about June, who only believed in the fire, is true about me. That this is the story of my incendiary neurosis! *I only believe in fire.* My entire torture with Henry was due to doubt. It is doubt I am running away from.

But now this mirage of Gonzalo takes on a warmer, lovelier body than other mirages. His body and his seductiveness are greater. His charm. His child-and-animal gestures. The cat-pawing way he rubs his face. The way his eyes close like a cat's, top and bottom lids closing together. His immense tenderness, his hunger for love. I love to see him suffer because I know I can make him divinely happy.

Elena comes back and reawakens my anxiety.

FEBRUARY 11, 1937

*E*VENING WITH HENRY, WHO TAKES ME TO SOME friends of his because "we will get a good dinner." The minute I enter I am stifled by the atmosphere—disconsolate. I cannot leap out of myself and talk and laugh. I feel rebellious. I look at these ordinary people and I say, "Why, why, why?" He yields. He accepts. He eats and drinks and attains beatitude. I am angry not at the people but at Henry, for his acceptance and his enjoyment. I get restless, nervous, absent. I tremble with revolt at his passivity. Rather be alone. I say, "Why can't you ever be alone, why this *vice* for people, like for bad movies?"

Up in his studio I burst out. Chaos. Henry emotional. Suddenly he bursts out, "I don't want to go mad. I don't want to be like Nietzsche. I want to accept and enjoy myself. I demanded even more than you. I am not really happy, but I want to be happy, so I take what I find and I enjoy myself. You demand too much. I don't care."

"It's like a bad movie."

"Yes."

We raise our antagonism to a higher plane—a contrary attitude. He is Chinese. He says, "If things go bad in France I go away. I go to Holland. *Finito*. Escape. Above all, I don't believe in struggle."

Talking about friends, he makes this statement: "The truth is, the real truth is that I have a lot of friends who love me but I love no one. If only they knew how little I care."

He appears to care. He gets soft, melting, sentimental. Everybody is taken in. He creates an illusion of warmth. But if any of them came with a real need, they would find out.

I appear not to care. I create an impression of distance. But if anyone has a real need, they discover I love.

That very afternoon Elena had said, "Henry was an accident—

created for me to know you. You gave me the life I needed. I know Henry couldn't have given me what you have."

Even last night, bored and restless and at war with Henry because he seems to embrace, to love everybody, it was I who felt pity for our hostess, Betty, withdrawn and sad. Henry, whom she believes a friend, said, "If she stepped right out of the window and killed herself, I would not care."

Because he does not care, he can be in the world all the time. Because I care, I can't.

He himself said, "Like a mollusk. I want to live like a mollusk."

All our pain comes from passive-active rhythm. This mollusk irritates me as soon as we are out in the world together. The Henry-in-the-world, I hate: his sentimentality, his spilling, his stupid enthusiasm for everything, his dissolution, his passive, stupefied, *abruti* mood, his digestive beatitudes, his falsities, his vanities, his callousness and rapaciousness, his using of others. In the world he is false and whorish.

I yearned for Gonzalo so desperately.

Jean Carteret: tall, with electric eyes. When I opened the door his eyes flashed, transcending. He *saw* me immediately, transparently. I saw a man with eyes. It was I who was unveiled. His vision was even quicker than mine. He saw, and he said, "You are a personage out of a myth; you live in the myth. I see you as a fine, impeccable mirror. A pure, pure mirror. The mirror is important for you. The day a large mirror is delivered to you, given you, will be fortunate. If a mirror breaks, you will be unfortunate. You wear your bracelet on the left arm: You are dependent on your affections. But doors and walls do not exist for you. You are ultimately independent."

Full of electricity. Trying to fit his gift into the mold of astrology or psychology. Dynamic. Sensual mouth. Vulgar lower half of the face. Upper half illumined. The chin and lower cheek pockmarked. Not inhuman, as is Moricand, who depersonalizes. No.

FEBRUARY 12, 1937

*I*N THE MORNING I WORK ON VOLUME FORTY-four, expanding the child story, the events following it, the taking of Villa Seurat with Henry, my enjoyment of Rank's passion, the wonderful mystical experience resuming all, flesh and blood bringing me to God, like the communion symbol.

Elena comes and tells me about her conversation with my Father. He is tearing his hair over the title *House of Incest*. More so because he cannot read what it contains. I wrote him about its meaning. Elena explains it to him. He says, "Anaïs lives in unreality. I like logic and order."

"Anaïs," says Elena, "lives in another reality. She can do without logic and order because she has her own core. *You* are the romantic and possibly chaotic one, and you cling to the outer order. Her life is a kind of play."

To me it is intensely humorous, my giving the *Incest* title, knowing it will give my Father chills of fear, in defiance of his great hypocrisies, and for some mysterious punishment for his closed nature. For I have now a cult of open natures—those who do not cover their doings with shame, as cats cover their dung. If I could do so without hurting anyone I would expose all this. My Father does not even expose himself to himself. So I wrote on the cover of a book in large characters: *House of Incest*. And I laugh. Just as I laughed when I wrote my preface for *Tropic of Cancer*. I love to throw bombs.

With Elena I live out a perverse relationship full of exquisite torture and love. I loved her enough to save her life, to restore her enthusiasm, her appetite, her faith in herself. Yet there are times when I listen to her and watch her as if I were *living* her possible relationship with Henry. I look at her as Henry might look at her. When she says, "I have a strong sense of the comic," I feel a little stab, for I say to myself that she and Henry would have much in common. He would like her love of food, her lustiness, the fact that she, like him, has more enthusiasms than love, lives more on the surface and more on the earth.

When I help her out of sickness, I then see the demon, the mocking, sensual, selfish woman in her.

Henry, the mollusk, does not move. He loves his tranquility. When she left for Switzerland I told him. I did not tell him when she returned. I told her Henry was planning to go to Denmark (he is leaving in a week). I have a feeling that I must gain time, that meanwhile she may find *the* man and her sexual hunt will be over. I feel my power over her, her need of me, and my own enjoyment of her spirit and imagination. We act like electricity on each other. It is what I admire in her, with my spiritual honesty, what my vision sees in her—*that* makes me fear her. Strange undercurrents of love, envy, jealousy. She envies me my body desperately, as June did.

As I live this imaginary relationship to its culmination, I arrive at the revelation of her selfishness, as upon the end of a journey, and I say, Henry will arrive there too; and stop.

FEBRUARY 14, 1937

*A*FTER SAVAGE CARESSES IN *NANANKEPICHU*, GONzalo falls asleep; then, at three in the morning, he awakens and we lie in the dark, talking. He loves to talk about his childhood. His adventures. The Catholic discipline. The Jesuit discipline. A sixteenth-century Spain.

He gets so soft, talking so gently. It is the primitive in him I love, the body, the blood, the emotions. I told him my love for him was a sixteenth-century Spanish love.

After a night of him I am left hungry. Desire a real hunger in me. I ache all over, dissolve with want. If I have to choose, I choose to be with Gonzalo because I am happier.

Seeing Tarzan today in the movies, I identified him with Gonzalo. The beauty of the body, the *pudeur* and *sauvagerie* mingled with tenderness. Nature. He is nature to me, good and wild and cruel. But he is loyal to the one who tames him, loves him. I feel truly as if I had captured a lion. The demon in him is a revolutionary demon. How can I help him to live out this demon!

We laugh so together—whimsical fantasies. We have our own humor, he and I. What we have in common is our old race. It is the old race in us which makes us both hate the movies, while Henry and Hugh love them. We need more subtle, more perverse amusements. We are not simple. I see Henry more and more as a simple man in his everyday life.

I tolerate the movies. I enjoy one out of ten. It is, to me, the lowest of all drugs. Any drug but the movies. Or no drug.

FEBRUARY 18, 1937

NANANKEPICHU. THE SECOND TIME I BRING YOU here. Once, the lonely night after I wrote the child story, I wrote here while Gonzalo slept. Today, because I am in a desperate mood and no one can help me. I'm a drunken sailor inside of a Greek vase. I'm a rebel. I do not have the gift of resignation.

The key words to inspirations spring out of the most ordinary talks.

I want to write a story from what I have seen in mirrors. Scenes on the mirrors only. *Mirages.*

I owe people four thousand francs. I have only one pair of shoes to wear. Not one pair of good stockings.

FEBRUARY 20, 1937

*H*ENRY WRITES ABOUT THE INCIDENT OF HIS TRIP to London after the break with June and gives it a completely different twist. Instead of being a victim of June's rage he and June sit drinking merrily, and in a fit of drunken sentimentalism he gives her the money. It is all written in a hard, brassy manner. This preyed on me, as well as the phrase "If I had said one word she would have come back and stayed with me forever," which was utterly false. It suddenly seemed to me that it was his letter to me at the time which was a lie, and that this was the truth. It seemed to me that all Henry's tenderness was a lie, and that his hard, cynical writing was really himself. My world trembled with the old anxiety. I was again inside of cruelty and of lies.

Henry said, "This is just to make a story." But this sounds so much like things I tell Hugh that I almost laughed hysterically. I was to spend the evening with Henry, and suddenly, after reading the story, I couldn't. I felt hysterical. I craved Gonzalo desperately, and his humanness. I was in a labyrinth of doubts and lies. Henry said gently, "You pay the penalty for your lies. It makes everything unreal." His attitude was gentle but I craved Gonzalo's deep humanness. I left Henry and called up Gonzalo.

I had dinner with Henry, during which I conjured up a gaiety from a kind of drunkenness on pain. Always that picture of a hard Henry superimposing itself over the tender Henry, and a terror of the cruel Henry, the brutal Henry. Drunk and hysterical with doubt and pain, I am telling Henry about my new story of the mirrors—a story of all I have seen in mirrors, life refracted, the pictures which run parallel to life, a parallel of reflections, dissociation, *dédoublement*. Henry admires the idea. We go back to his place. He tells me about Reichel's stories, laughing. Henry does not want to come too near to what I feel. It would disturb his tranquility, his health.

At ten-thirty I leave him. I am half an hour late for Gonzalo because he is always late—as Spaniards are. I allowed half an hour. But when I met him he was in a tumult. "I was here at ten, *chiquita,* and for half an hour I have been desperately jealous, wondering where you were, who was courting you. I was jumping around with jealousy."

He had left his friends to come. We got into bed, caressed wildly, deeply. I lost myself in his body, blinded myself with his hair, his mouth, his bigness. "What a battle, what a battle to have you all to myself," he said. "A battle which you won."

He is my happiness. We woke up at dawn in a mood of twinkling humor, half-asleep, laughing, caressing, laughing softly. No demons. No ghosts. But he suffers. What irony, what a bitter comedy. He suffers because he is so human, so full of feeling, so sentimental. *My past hurts him.*

My whole being turned toward him, gave itself to him, detached itself from the nonhumanness of my life with Henry. I had said to Henry, "It is not your past which hurts but the doubts of the present which this past evokes." I am too human to go on living with Henry. He needs a cold, hard woman. Gonzalo and I are alike in tenderness. I love him. I love him. Slowly I am becoming obsessed with him instead of with Henry. *L'image de Henry s'efface.*

I am weary of pain.

FEBRUARY 28, 1937

*A*FTER WRITING THIS ON SUNDAY, I ARRIVED MONDAY at Villa Seurat and found Henry sick with a grippe, and he had been two days without care. I melted and set out to heal him, feed, care for him—enveloped him in tenderness.

When I see Gonzalo at night he is desperate because it is René and not he who handles the little boat we have to take to reach

Nanankepichu because the Seine has inundated the quay. He is irritated because it is René who lights the fire for me, and not he.

It is Gonzalo's way of loving. When I left at dawn, in his half-sleep he was anxious about my climbing the long ladder from the quay to the street level. It is the language of his love. Irony.

Back to Villa Seurat. Errands for Henry. Dinner with him. This evening is his. We talk about surrealism, which he is writing about. I say the chaos artificially produced by the mind, by geometrical absurdity, merely placing an umbrella on an operating table (Breton), is not fecund. The only fecund chaos is that of the emotions, feelings, nature. Henry is a true surrealist because his *chaos* does not come from the unconscious. Absurdity does not produce poetry or fantasy. We talk about psychoanalysis and I say, "It had to be a Jew who invented a *system* of integration—we could not be integrated by life." But this system only heals those who have *faith*. Those who have no faith cannot get cured. We have not yet found a way to give *faith*.

The fact that my feelings oscillate between Henry and Gonzalo, and that I cannot separate myself from Henry, is reflected in my sexual drama. I cannot have an orgasm with Gonzalo, in spite of the fact that he is a perfect lover. When I have been very close to Gonzalo, I can't have it with Henry because Gonzalo fills me too much.

But this makes Gonzalo only more tantalizing to me. I feel him sensually, or more voluptuously than I do Henry. Our caresses are so voluptuous, so lasting, so subtle, so stirring and enveloping, they arouse me all over, from toes to hair tips. I think of his neck, of his tongue, of the very very black hair over his sex, and desire him savagely. The very mouth I did not like at first because it was small in proportion to the rest of the face, and it betrayed his weakness—this mouth has become infinitely moving. I see how sensitive it is, how trembling, how uncertain. I see the feminine delicacy of it, and the child. I feel its caressingness. He can kiss by the hour. It arouses me to frenzy. His long hair, his emotionalism, his voluptuousness such as woman dreams of and usually finds only in woman. When he shows his tongue I say, *"C'est le chant pour appeler la pluie."* It's the song to bring the rain, because he teases me about my wetness. Henry has an appetite, a voracious appetite, but Gonzalo has a palate, an amorous, worshipful, adoring, ardent palate.

Sitting in a café, he kisses me impulsively because I am talking about Betty's writing. He says, "I love your enthusiasm." He has no confidence in himself. When we gamble with twenty-five centimes in the slot machines of the café, he turns his back to the machine before awaiting the results. When he wins he can hardly believe it. I point this out to him and thus I humorously create a new faith. It makes me desperately sad when jealousy of Henry hurts this faith.

Elena's magic wears off. I don't know why. My "court" is already tired of her—Hugh, Eduardo, Allendy, Carteret, Moricand. They feel the vampire in her.

MARCH 3, 1937

*D*AWN. *NANANKEPICHU*. THE LIGHT, REFLECTING on the turbulent swollen Seine, shines too brightly. So it is dawn and I am half awake. I look at Gonzalo's hair, coal black, wild, covering the pillow. I have poured into his ragged pockets the money for his rent, for their food, and for Helba's medicines. Three days ago Hugh gave me all he could give me, and it is all gone. The day before, I paid Henry's dentist. I have seven francs in my pockets. I have two pairs of stockings, mended, which Betty gave me, two pairs of shoes worn out, two pair of pants worn out. I owe money to my Mother, Eduardo, our doctor, our dentist, the cleaner and the telephone company. I still have to pay the three hundred francs for *Nanankepichu*, Henry's rent, and live until March 15. I have no more cold cream, no more face powder; I owe the hairdresser, I have my jewels in the pawnshop. I owe Thurema for medicines she sent. There is no wine for Gonzalo in the little barrel, no more crackers to eat at night. Henry needs underwear and shirts and socks. Gonzalo's shirts are full of holes. They need coal because it is cold. Henry has no rug.

Un tourbillon. A whirlpool.

The light and the money theme awakened me fully. I have been like an ostrich. Yet I feel so gay, so irrepressibly gay; a little nervous, but gay. The room is inundated in cold sunlight, which makes the black rugs and the black tarred walls look smoke colored.

I must get up.

Gonzalo sighs. I kiss him.

At nine o'clock René is taking me to the ladder on the little boat. I jump over the wall and run because the idle pedestrians are leaning over the parapet, observing the Seine, René's antics with the little boat, and me climbing the ladder and leaping over the top of the wall. So I run in the cold winter sunlight with ten francs I took back out of Gonzalo's pocket. I take the subway to the avenue des Champs-Elysées, where I have a *café* and a *croissant.* I steal the sugar that is left in the saucer for Gonzalo, because he never finds French coffee sweet enough, and he carries sugar in his pockets. Every café I go to I take the sugar wrapped in small bands for Gonzalo: "So you can follow my traces and know where I have been," I say, laughing. The coffee is marvelous, and the *croissant* delicate and warm. Champs-Elysées looks forever festive and ornate and golden. At nine-thirty Hugh will be at the bank. I go to his office. Nobody sees me come in. I sit down at his desk and steal a blotter and a few paper clips. I telephone Hugh: "Here I am at your desk. I have pressed all the buttons and have nothing else to do. When are you going to start work? I am already at my office."

While waiting for Hugh I write a letter to Henry Mann the Communist, on the bank paper, telling him about Gonzalo's group work and asking him to send me a little of what he owes me for my analysis of him.

Hugh arrives. With great charm, seduction, sincerity, and earnestness, I extort from him the hundred francs for Helba's rent, which he had refused me before and which I had already given to Gonzalo! Very cheered by this solution to the immediate emptiness of my pocketbook, I left to meet Betty, whom I had promised to help with her shopping. Betty and I walked for two hours, chose a velvet suit, planned her wardrobe.

At one o'clock I was home for lunch with Hugh. After lunch I slept deeply for half an hour and went to see Allendy, who begged me to visit him, to renew his request that I should sleep with him. Entertained Allendy for an hour and went to Elena's because her concierge had telephoned me that she was anxious because Elena had not come home the night before. Gonzalo said over the telephone, "Don't bother about Elena, she probably slept with somebody."

"I do worry, precisely because she has no one to sleep with. If she did I would not worry."

I find Elena unbalanced, after two nights of insomnia, of walks, saying, "I have a feeling that I repulse people, that they regard me as a monster. All but you and Hugh. I feel unwanted everywhere."

Gonzalo had asked me to telephone about five. But at this time I was talking to Elena about her anxieties and I could not call up Gonzalo in front of her, because already my Father's question to her in Switzerland—"Who is Gonzalo?"—may have awakened her own suspicions, and if she is unconsciously interested in Henry she would like very much to know that I am betraying Henry; whereas, on the contrary, I try very subtly to create in her the image of a great unity between Henry and myself, which diverts her thoughts from him.

When I leave Elena and call Gonzalo, he has gone out. And Henry is expecting me for dinner. If Gonzalo calls me up the maid will tell him, *"Madame est sortie pour la soirée. Téléphonez demain matin."* And I am supposed to be with Hugh, because Hugh is leaving for London the next day.

While I market for Henry I call up Gonzalo again. I feel uneasy. Is all our happiness of the night before to vanish again? I feel so gay, so inexpressibly, irresistibly gay, it can't be. The day cannot turn into a tragedy.

I cook dinner for Henry but I am uneasy. Henry arrives from the dentist, glad of a dinner cooked at home. At eight I pretend to have a message to give Hugh. I go to de Maigret's apartment and call up Gonzalo. He had telephoned quai de Passy. Janine had told him to call up next morning! And, still worse, Hugh had told him, "I don't know where Anaïs is. I have to let her know I am leaving tomorrow at eight in the morning, earlier than I thought. If you see her, tell her to call me up." Still worse, Hugh telephoned *chez Colette,* where I am supposed to be, and the maid answered she did not know who I was.

Colette was in the American Hospital and had a baby Sunday. Monday night, which I spent with Gonzalo, I was supposed to be at Colette's. I telephone Hugh. He is not uneasy but surprised. So I promise to be home at midnight. I tell Henry about Hugh leaving early. I can't explain the Monday-night problem because I stayed with Henry Friday night and then Colette had no baby. To explain my obvious uneasiness I talk fully to Henry about the effect on Hugh of Colette's maid not knowing my name. I am terribly uneasy, thinking Gonzalo's doubts will awaken again as to where I really was. From the café I call up Gonzalo and tell him so. "If you want to, I'll meet you at eleven-thirty at our usual café." "Yes, *chiquita.*"

Henry and I go to the movies and see a tortuous, elliptical, and mad Pirandello play: *L'Homme de nulle part.* I say he is the man who tantalizes us by coming nearest to real profundity without entering it, skirting it as the madman or the neurotic does. Enjoyed it. Talked with Henry warmly and excitedly. Left him. Met Gonzalo. Drank with him. He had not been tortured. We walked toward quai de Passy. I was dropping with fatigue. To nourish the happiness of three men in one day was really a task! At one o'clock, when I meowed at Hugh's door so as to send him off to London contented, I was exhausted. Fell into bed.

Slipping like an eel through barriers.

But I give life. I can rarely wield death. Yet I have the power to destroy.

Life. Fire. Being myself on fire, I set others on fire. Never death. Fire and life. *Le jeu.*

ALBERTI, RAFAEL: Spanish poet, born in 1902, who joined the Communist Party in 1931 and renounced his earlier "bourgeois" work. During the Spanish Civil War he composed political romances for those fighting on the Republican side. Upon General Franco's victory in 1939, he and his wife, Maria Teresa Leon, went into exile in South America.

ALLENDY, DR. RENÉ FÉLIX *(1889–1942)*:   French psychoanalyst, author, and co-founder, with Sigmund Freud's protégée Princess Marie Bonaparte, of the Paris Psychoanalytic Society in 1926. In 1932 Anaïs Nin became his patient and romantic interest and, to pay for her sessions, she did research for him in alchemy and mysticism. He introduced the Guilers to his patient Antonin Artaud, the drug-addicted poet and theatrical innovator, in March 1933. He also analyzed Anaïs Nin's cousin Eduardo Sanchez and her husband, Hugh Guiler, and stimulated the latter's growing interest in astrology.

BEL GEDDES, NORMAN *(1893–1958)*:   Stage and industrial designer, author. Born in Adrian, Michigan, he became known in the 1920s as the *enfant terrible* of the American theater. After an early involvement with silent films, he designed numerous theatrical productions, including Max Reinhardt's *The Miracle* in 1923 and the *Ziegfeld Follies* in 1925. In the same year he startled Paris with a massive production of Mercedes de Acosta's *Jean d'Arc*, starring Eva Le Gallienne. One of his daughters, Barbara, born in 1922 while he was married to Helen Bell Sneider, became a film and television actress. Remarried in 1933 to Frances Resor Waite, he maintained an apartment on East 37th Street in Manhattan during most of the 1930s. In 1935 he designed and produced the play *Dead End*, and in 1936, *The Eternal Road*.

BRANCUSI, CONSTANTIN *(1876–1957)*:   Romanian-born French sculptor. He briefly worked with Auguste Rodin in 1907 and developed his own distinctive and controversial "organic" style, which sought to reveal the essence contained in his materials, as in his famous *The Kiss* and *Bird in Space*. A small, gregarious man, he loved to talk and entertain in his almost completely white studio in Paris. "He cooked shish-kebab in his open fireplace," Anaïs Nin recalled, "and served this with big bottles of red wine." Among his numerous visitors were June Miller and her friend Jean Kronski on their visit to Paris in 1928.

CARPENTIER, ALEJO *(1904–1980)*:   Novelist, musicologist, and journalist born in Cuba to French and Russian parents. After having been imprisoned for his opposition to the dictatorial regime in Havana, he left for France in 1927, where he became associated with the surrealists and various musical circles.

CLAIROUIN, DENÍSE: Brittany-born French literary agent who tried to interest New York and Paris publishers in Anaïs Nin's early diaries, written in French, and in transcripts of later volumes in which names and places had been thinly disguised. Anaïs Nin described her appearance as that of "a Greek head placed upon the body of a pudgy child," with "an expression of innocence and lucidity. There is something mystical, or fanatical about her."

DELTEIL, JOSEPH: French author, born 1894, biographer of Joan of Arc and Francis of Assisi, whose work was much admired by Henry Miller. Married to Dorothy Dudley's daughter, Caroline.

DE MAIGRET, ARNAUD: A young French photographer who lived across the landing from Henry Miller's studio and Anaïs Nin's "office" at 18, villa Seurat.

DE VILMORIN, LOUISE (1902–1970): French author, member of an old aristocratic family, who met Anaïs Nin in 1931. Married several times, she remained closely attached to her two brothers, André and Roger, and served as the inspiration for "Jeanne" in Anaïs Nin's House of Incest and the story "Under a Glass Bell." After she and Henri Hunt divorced in 1935, the Guilers briefly sublet the couple's Paris apartment. Although she was praised for her wit, sophistication, and "genius for language," Louise de Vilmorin's work gained wider acceptance only in the 1950s and 1960s.

DUDLEY, DOROTHY (MRS. HARRY HARVEY): American journalist and critic. Born in 1884, she covered the French literary and artistic scene during the 1930s for a number of American publications, including The Nation and the American Magazine of Art. Her biography of Theodore Dreiser appeared in 1932.

ELSA: Gonzale Moré's niece, who lived with him and his wife, Helba, in their Paris studio.

ERSKINE, JOHN (1879–1951): American educator, pianist, and best-selling author (The Private Life of Helen of Troy). He was Hugh Guiler's much-admired English professor at Columbia University in the late 1910s. He befriended Guiler and his young wife, Anaïs Nin, and visited them in Paris in 1928. Married, with two children, he apparently was involved with a number of mistresses. Anaïs Nin became infatuated with him, which precipitated the first major crisis of her idealistic marriage, though the relationship never developed and ended in disillusionment. She tried to deal with the experience in her eventually abandoned "John" novel. (See The Early Diary of Anaïs Nin, 1927–1931.)

"FERI": A young Hungarian homosexual who solicited clients in various Parisian cafés and with whom Eduardo Sanchez tried to establish a relationship.

FLES, BARTHOLD: Austrian-born New York literary agent who refused to take on Henry Miller's writings but briefly represented Anaïs Nin's work without success.

FRAENKEL, MICHAEL (*1896–1957*): Lithuanian-born American bookseller, writer, and publisher who settled in France in the 1920s to pursue a literary life. Living off his investments, he published some of his own work—*Werther's Young Brother, Bastard Death*, et al.—and that of his friend, the American poet Walter Lowenfels, as well as other titles, under the Carrefour Imprint at the Saint Catherine Press in Bruges, Belgium. In 1930, Fraenkel helped out the destitute Henry Miller (who turned him into the "Boris" of *Tropic of Cancer*) when he briefly sheltered Miller at the house he owned at 18, villa Seurat. Anaïs Nin eventually rented the studio in the building that served as Miller's first permanent address in Paris between 1934 and 1939. For a short time Fraenkel was involved in the publishing activities of the Villa Seurat circle, the Siana Press, and he arranged for the printing of Anaïs Nin's *House of Incest* in 1936. His brief involvement with Joyce, a chorus girl from New York, prompted his essay "The Day Face and the Night Face," which eventually appeared in *The Booster* as "an autobiographical fragment."

FRANK, WALDO DAVID (*1889–1969*): American author, best known for his books on Spain and Latin America, especially *Virgin Spain* (1926). He attended DeWitt Clinton High School in New York, a private *internat* in Lausanne, Switzerland, and graduated from Yale University in 1911. After a stay in Paris in 1913, he married Margaret Naumberg, the founder of the Walden School in 1916. His first novel, a psychological study of an outsider, *The Unwelcome Man*, appeared in 1917, but it was his curious story of a fallen woman who is mysteriously relieved of any sense of guilt, *Rahab* (1922), that established him as a fiction writer. In 1936 he was at work on *The Bridegroom Cometh*, one in a series of lyrical novels that dwelled on his second marriage, in 1927, to Alma Magoon, and, allegedly, he substantially revised the novel after meeting Anaïs Nin. Active in left-wing politics, he attended the Communist controlled "International Writers Congress for the Defense of Culture" in Paris in June 1935 as head of the League of American Writers.

FRIEDE, DONALD: American publisher, born 1901, who joined Chicago bookseller Pascal Covici in the 1930s to form the New York publishing firm Covici-Friede. In the early 1940s, he gave up publishing and joined the Myron Selznick Agency in Hollywood, where Henry Miller met him and described him as "a feeble Cagliostro, rather suave and pleasant at first sight. Completely egocentric, too." Friede recalled his adventures in the 1920s in an autobiography, *The Mechanical Angel*, published in 1948.

GILBERT, STUART: American essayist and translator who spent most of his life in Paris and survived part of World War II in Vichy France. A friend and champion of James Joyce, whose *Ulysses* he explicated and translated into French, he also wrote introductions to many works by other writers and translated a number of major French writers into English, among them Roger Martin du Gard, who won the Nobel Prize for Literature in 1937.

GUILER, HUGH ("HUGO") PARKER *(1898–1985):* Born in Boston, his Scottish parents sent him and his younger brother to a boarding school in Scotland when he was six years old. After a childhood spent in the tropical paradise of a sugar farm in Puerto Rico (where his father worked as a design engineer), the dour, restrictive world of Ayr, in Halloway, and later the Edinburgh Academy, proved to be traumatic. In 1920, he graduated from Columbia University with degrees in literature and economics and eventually signed up as a trainee with the National City Bank. He met the eighteen-year-old Anaïs Nin at a dance in his parents' home in Forest Hills, New York, in 1921. After a protracted courtship they were married in Havana, Cuba, in March 1923, against the objections of his family, who did not approve of the Catholic daughter of a musician father. In December 1924 the Guilers moved to France, where Hugh had been assigned to the bank's Paris branch, and for the next fifteen years they remained there until the outbreak of war in 1939 forced their return to the United States. Encouraged by his wife, who called him the "poet-banker," Hugh Guiler pursued his interests in music, dance, the graphic arts, and astrology, but his business life, which involved a great deal of travel and long periods in London, where he developed the bank's trust department, curtailed his artistic impulses. "The dissatisfactions of my life were a result of a good deal of internal strain, of being pulled in two directions," he wrote, looking back on the conflict between his artistic ambitions and the economic needs of survival. In the early 1930s, he became a patient first of Dr. Allendy and later of Dr. Otto Rank. The story of his courtship and marriage to Anaïs Nin, and their early years in Paris, is covered in great detail in the three volumes of *The Early Diary of Anaïs Nin*, spanning the period from 1920 to 1931.

HILER, HILAIRE *(1889–1974):* American artist, color theorist, musician, raconteur, and briefly manager/co-owner of the Jockey Bar in Paris. He met Anaïs Nin in the summer of 1934 at Dr. Rank's special seminar for American psychiatric social workers at the "Psychological Center" of the Cité Universitaire, which he attended after having read *Art and Artist.* At his studio in the rue Broca, he gave art lessons to Henry Miller.

HUARA, HELBA: Peruvian-born dancer who met Gonzalo Moré in Lima when he came to interview her, after a performance, for his brother's newspaper.

Though she had been married at the age of fourteen, she followed Gonzalo to New York, and the couple eventually settled in Paris. In the late 1920s, she appeared on Broadway in *A Night in Spain* and other exotic shows at the Guild and Schubert Theaters. In Paris she became known as "the dancing Inca," and Anaïs Nin saw her perform the "Dance of the Woman without Arms" at the Theatré de la Gaièté in the early 1930s. With Gonzalo as her piano accompanist, she toured Germany in 1933, but illness soon forced her to give up professional dancing. A columnist described her elaborately costumed performances as a mixture of "savage and soul."

HUDSON, BARCLAY: English writer and friend of the Guilers. While on the Island of Corfu in 1935, he presented Lawrence Durrell with a copy of *Tropic of Cancer*, which triggered the correspondence and subsequent friendship of Durrell with Henry Miller and Anaïs Nin.

HUNT, HENRI: French businessman married to Louise de Vilmorin. After the breakup of their marriage, he remained a friend of the Guilers, who briefly shared his Paris apartment.

HURTADO, ELENA: Aspiring painter from South America and mother of two children. She befriended Henry Miller at Villa Seurat, and he introduced her to Anaïs Nin.

KAHANE, JACK *(1887–1939)*:   English-born writer and publisher. He left the family textile business in Manchester in the 1920s to settle in Paris. Married to an affluent Frenchwoman, he set up the Obelisk Press in 1930 to publish his own "naughty" novels under a pseudonym as well as other titles that, due to the existing censorship, could not be published in Great Britain or the United States. His autobiography, *Memoirs of a Booklegger*, which embellishes his relationships with writers such as Frank Harris, Cyril Connolly, Lawrence Durrell, and Henry Miller, appeared in London a few months before his sudden death in September 1939.

KLEIN, ROGER: French left-wing intellectual who volunteered to fight with the Republican forces during the Spanish Civil War. Together with his Greek girlfriend, Maggy, and his brother Jacques, he befriended Anaïs Nin, who occasionally used his studio in the 14th Arrondissement, near Villa Seurat, to meet Gonzalo Moré, whom she had seen there for the first time during one of Roger's parties. Wounded during the civil war, he returned to Paris, where, in early 1936, he worked a night job at the weekly *Paris-Paris*.

LOWENFELS, WALTER *(1897–1980)*:   American poet and writer. He spent most of the 1920s and early 1930s in Paris before returning to the United States, where he became an editor of the Communist *Daily Worker*. He, and his wife, Lillian, often entertained Henry Miller at their home, and he appears as

"Jabberwhorl Cronstadt" in Miller's *Tropic of Cancer*. Some of his writing, such as an *Elegy for D. H. Lawrence* (1932) and *The Suicide* (1934), appeared in small editions under Michael Fraenkel's Carrefour imprint.

MILLER, HENRY *(1891–1980):* Brooklyn-born American writer. In 1924, after a checkered career of odd jobs and a lengthy stint in the personnel office of the Western Union Telegraph Company in New York, he quit his last paying job to take up writing "seriously." He was encouraged by his second wife, the former taxi dancer June Smith, who, for the next six years provided their often precarious livelihood as a "hostess" and through other schemes. At her urging, Miller left for Europe in 1930. His struggle to survive in Paris, homeless, penniless, and often near starvation, provided the raw material for his first breakthrough book, *Tropic of Cancer*, which finally appeared in 1934 under the Obelisk imprint when Anaïs Nin underwrote its publication with borrowed money. Miller met the Guilers in December 1931, and after a brief teaching interlude in Dijon which Hugh Guiler had helped to arrange, Miller returned to Paris. The literary friendship with Anaïs Nin, which had unleashed an avalanche of correspondence (See his *Letters to Anaïs Nin*), in March 1932 turned into a fiery love affair that was to last for many years. Its details came to light only in recent years, with the publication of *Henry and June: The Unexpurgated Diary of Anaïs Nin, 1931–1932*. June, who had made two brief visits to Paris in 1932, divorced Miller in Mexico in 1934.

MORÉ, GONZALO *(1897–1966):* Peruvian artist, revolutionary, born in the provincial capital of Punto, on the shores of Lake Titicaca. Of mixed Scottish, Spanish, and Indian parentage, he was educated at the local Jesuit school. His father, a well-to-do landowner, eventually sent him to the university of Lima, where he also worked for his brother's newspaper, covering sports and the theater. He briefly tried his hand as an amateur boxer. When he fell in love with the young, married dancer Helba Huara, the couple fled to the United States. After a spell in South America, they settled in Paris, where two of his brothers—the writer Ernesto and the artist Carlos—had lived at various times during the 1920s. A champion of the Andean-Indian cause, Gonzalo Moré joined the newly established Peruvian Communist Party and in December 1928, with his closest friend, the part-Indian poet Cesar Vallejo (1892–1938), established a *"cellula marxista-leninista-peruana"* in Paris. For a time Vallejo, his French wife, Georgette, and ocasionally Gonzalo's brother Ernesto lived together with the Morés in the three corners of a large studio space in the rue Froidevaux. In 1933, on one of the last *tournées* with his dancer wife, Gonzalo found himself and Helba stranded in Berlin when her Jewish manager ran afoul of the new Nazi policies, but they managed to return to Paris.

An occasional art student, Gonzalo exhibited some of his work in Paris, but with the outbreak of the Spanish Civil War, he became deeply involved in the anti-fascist struggle. With Pablo Neruda, Vallejo, and the Cuban poet Nicolas Guillen, among others, he founded a number of committees for the defense of the Spanish Republic. In the generally poverty-stricken, hard-drinking South American artist colony in Paris, Gonzalo "enjoyed a popularity unequaled in Montparnasse," his brother Ernesto remembered, "due, no doubt, to his uniquely generous spirit, which manifested itself every day in a thousand ways."

MORICAND, CONRAD *(1887–1954):* French astrologer, occultist, who wrote under the pseudonym "Claude Valence." His *Mirroir d'astrologie* (1928) became a favorite of the Guilers, and since he was living in abject poverty after having lost a family fortune, Anaïs Nin tried to help him by having her friends commission horoscopes from him. Henry Miller described Moricand as "an incurable dandy living the life of a beggar."

NIN-CULMELL, JOAQUIN: Pianist and composer born in Berlin in 1908. A brother of Anaïs Nin, he went with her, his brother Thorvald, and their mother into "exile" in New York in 1914 after their father deserted the family. He returned to France during the 1920s, and with his mother lived for a while with the Guilers in Louveciennes. A student at the Schola Cantorum and the Paris Conservatory, and a pupil of Alfred Cortot, Richard Viñez, and Manuel de Falla, he gave his debut recital in New York in 1936.

NIN Y CASTELLANOS, JOAQUIN J. *(1879–1949):* Cuban-born Spanish pianist, composer, musicologist. In 1902 he married Rosa Culmell, the daughter of the Danish consul in Havana, and moved with her to Paris. Their daughter, Anaïs, was born in 1903, followed by two sons, Thorvald and Joaquin, born in 1905 and 1908, respectively. He left his wife and three children in 1913 and eventually married one of his pupils, Maria Luisa Rodriguez, a Cuban tobacco heiress. When he met his daughter again, after some twenty years of separation, an incestuous drama ensued, which is recorded in Anaïs Nin's unexpurgated diary *Incest: From "A Journal of Love,"* published in 1992.

PERLÈS, ALFRED *(1897–1991):* Austrian writer and journalist who worked for the Paris edition of the Chicago *Tribune* until the paper folded in 1934. A friend of Henry Miller, whom he had first met in 1928 when Miller and his wife, June, briefly visited Paris, he shared an apartment with Miller at 4 avenue Anatole France in Clichy from March 1932 to late 1933, as well as many aspects of their always financially precarious lives. In one of his books, the "novel-souvenirs" *Sentiments limitrophes,* he portrayed Anaïs Nin as

"Pietà." After he lost his newspaper job, he worked for a while as a freelance researcher and ghostwriter for a French politician.

RANK, DR. OTTO *(1884–1939):* Austrian psychoanalyst and author (born Otto Rosenfeld). He belonged to the inner circle of the nascent psychoanalytic movement in Vienna for almost twenty years until the publication of his study, *The Trauma of Birth*, in 1924, provoked a break with Sigmund Freud and his more orthodox followers. With his wife and young daughter, Rank moved to Paris in 1926 and, eventually, to the United States, late in 1934, when his economic situation in France had deteriorated. His books *Art and Artist* and *Don Juan et son double*, and his writings on incest had a great influence on Anaïs Nin. She became his patient in 1933 and followed him to New York in November 1934, after they had become romantically involved.

SANCHEZ, EDUARDO *(1904–1990):* Cuban-born amateur scholar, astrologer, one-time actor. He came to Paris in 1930 and at various times, lived with the Guilers in their rented house in Louveciennes. As Anaïs Nin's beloved cousin (see *The Early Diary of Anaïs Nin, 1920–1923; 1927–1931*), he played an important role in her life. Having been analyzed to deal with his homosexuality by a pupil of Dr. Rank, in New York in 1928, he stimulated Anaïs's growing interest in psychoanalysis and encouraged her writing, especially her study of D. H. Lawrence. (See, also, *Anaïs: An International Journal*, Volume 9, 1991.)

SCHNELLOCK, EMIL *(1891–1959):* American graphic artist and teacher. Henry Miller called him his "oldest friend," since they had graduated together in 1905 from Brooklyn's P.S. 85. During Miller's stay in Europe, Schnellock served as his major link to his past in the United States and as the last remaining contact with Miller's estranged wife, June. (See Henry Miller, *Letters to Emil.*)

SOKOL, THUREMA: South American musician. A graduate of the Music Conservatory in Mexico City, she appeared as a solo harpist and a member of various musical groups. At the time of her friendship with Anaïs Nin, she lived with her husband, Andrew, and her son John, on Long Island, New York.

SUPERVIELLE, JULES *(1884–1960):* French author, born in Uruguay, best known for his poetry and fables, and his novel *Le Voleur d'enfants* (1926), which appeared in English in 1967 as *The Man Who Stole Children*. Among his poetry volumes are *Gravitations, Le Forçat innocent, Les Amis inconnus,* and *La Fable du monde.*

TURNER, GEORGE: American businessman, associate of Hugh Guiler, who pursued Anaïs Nin for many years, in Paris and New York.

WEST, REBBECA, PEN NAME OF CICILY ISABEL FAIRFIELD *(1892–1983):* British writer and journalist. After briefly attending the Academy of Dramatic Arts in Edinburgh, she gave up acting and became an early advocate of feminist causes (her pen name derives from Henrik Ibsen's heroine in the play *Rosmersholm*). In 1930, after a ten-year affair with the married writer H. G. Wells, to whom she bore a son Anthony, in 1914, she married banker Henry Maxwell Andrews. Her biography, *St. Augustine*, appeared in 1933, and one of her novels, which tend to be psychoanalytical studies, *The Thinking Reed*, in 1936.

Nin, Anaïs (*continued*)
and drinking, 56, 58, 128, 130, 142, 193–95,
207, 212, 215, 228, 305, 358–60, 363–65
and drugs, 130, 161, 174, 175–76, 181, 193, 228
feelings about June Miller, 9, 11, 13, 19, 20, 25,
45, 60, 61, 70, 93, 110, 142, 143, 150, 157,
210, 213, 220, 221, 228, 230
fire imagery, x, 135, 178, 238, 258, 259, 261, 262,
268, 273, 278, 279–80, 290, 333, 357–60,
362, 364, 371, 388, 389–90, 393, 403, 415
on France, 187, 188–89, 277
in Henry Miller's writings, 110, 112–13
and houseboat ("*Nanankepichu*"), 287, 308–9,
311, 312, 315, 316, 323–26, 335, 337,
340–41, 344, 348–50, 354, 359, 371, 377,
378–79, 385, 387, 394–95, 398, 402–3,
407, 408, 410–13
on homosexuals, 163, 183, 217
illnesses of, 12, 24, 25–26, 72, 75, 105, 144, 147,
151, 168, 178, 179, 218, 241, 363–65, 367,
381
on illusions *vs.* reality, 40–41, 50, 54, 72, 75,
77–78, 82–83, 85, 86, 90, 110, 117, 248,
341, 362, 369–70
jealousy, 97, 98, 100–101, 106, 108, 110,
112–14, 137, 167, 168, 170, 174, 175, 178,
243, 244, 306, 314, 326, 330, 340, 343,
365–66, 377, 380, 383, 385, 388, 389, 393
on lies, 11–32, 35–36, 39, 41, 43, 45, 49, 52–53,
57, 58–59, 70, 73, 77–78, 83, 133–34, 190,
209, 215, 220, 223, 226, 238, 303, 322–23,
347, 367–68, 382, 409
loneliness of, 33, 65, 73, 89, 90, 93, 97, 100, 103,
109, 152, 160, 164, 167, 170, 178, 189,
200–202, 231, 275, 351
and madness, 290, 298, 299, 301, 316
on men's talk, 214
on menstruation ("moonstorm"), 101, 122,
145–47, 161–63, 174–75, 179, 202, 222,
285, 321, 336
as model, 143, 144, 186
as mother of creators, 14, 114, 131–33, 136,
149–53, 157, 179–80, 183, 187, 191, 259,
262, 271, 310–12, 319, 336, 349, 351,
361–62
name variations of, 7, 13n, 108
on Paris, 101, 107, 147, 151
politics, 78–79, 266–67, 269, 270–73, 277,
278, 281–82, 285, 292–93, 339, 341–42,
348–51, 353–54, 357, 396–97
and pornography, 229, 308, 352

possible pregnancies of, 37–38, 46, 53, 56, 57,
61, 63, 127, 361
printing press, 96, 97–100, 108, 122
search for perfect love
["absolute"], ix, x, 78, 86, 88, 90, 95, 101–2,
105, 111, 115–16, 127, 143, 150–51, 160,
167, 177, 208–9, 220, 222, 230, 243, 258,
270, 282, 400
on seduction, 168, 345, 346, 367–68, 372–73
on shipboard, 1–2, 43, 93–94, 103–4
as supporter of writers (*see also* Miller, Henry),
96, 161, 175
on surrealism, 177, 255, 302, 338, 411
on war, 215
wifely identity of, 6, 79
writing, 125, 128, 141, 152, 275, 279, 290, 291,
315, 409. *See also* Nin, Anaïs: diary-
keeping by; *titles of works by*
anonymous, 347
childbirth story, 394–95, 401, 406
on D. H. Lawrence, 56, 57, 92, 121, 167,
197, 280
on films, 342, 384, 402
about Henry Miller, 128–29, 135
preface to *Tropic of Cancer* by, 131, 406
quality of, ix, xi, 62, 104, 106, 111, 112, 127
"Ragpickers" (story), 314–16
sensitivity about, 122, 137
Nin, Rosa Culmell de (mother), 11, 37, 45, 48, 58,
67, 93, 181, 204, 220, 306, 412
Anaïs Nin's concerns about, 38, 41, 102, 140,
271, 278, 332
Anaïs Nin's emotional support of, 99, 276, 304
letters from Anaïs Nin, 77, 91, 185, 255–56,
275, 278
letters to Anaïs Nin, 185, 204
trips to New York by, 161, 173
visits with, 92, 163–64, 193, 292, 363
Nin, Thorvald (brother), 185
Nin-Culmell, Joaquin (brother), 15, 40n, 48, 220,
251, 261
Anaïs Nin's concerns about, 38, 41, 102, 132,
140, 271, 276, 278, 332, 344
Anaïs Nin's love for, 75, 85, 109, 258
letters from Anaïs Nin, 11, 91, 275, 278
letters to Anaïs Nin, 204
and mother, 52, 205, 304
as musician, 95, 136, 183, 185, 192, 304
on Rank, 50
trips to New York by, 161, 173
visits with, 92, 193, 281, 288, 292

Reichel, Hans, 392, 393, 397, 409
Reinhardt, Max, 195, 211
Roberts, Colette, 155, 167, 168, 170, 171, 174, 190, 267, 313–14, 415
Roberts, Robert, 190, 313, 358

Sachs, Hanns, Dr., 205, 206
Sachs, Maurice, 307–9
Saint Catherine Press (Bruges, Belgium), 117n
Salmi, Sylvia, 26
Sánchez, Eduardo (cousin), 48, 127, 145, 207, 213, 243, 328, 355, 365, 396, 412
  Anaïs Nin's emotional connection with, 100, 108–10, 132–33, 146, 157, 166, 176, 185, 187, 188, 225, 271, 284, 327, 332, 372–73, 380, 394
  on Anaïs Nin's writing, 112
  astrology of, 92, 99, 102, 139
  in diary, 299
  and Fraenkel, 133, 137, 139
  letters from Anaïs Nin, 21–22, 91, 225, 252, 301
  letters to Anaïs Nin, 56, 205
  at Louveciennes, 93, 96, 124, 155
  loves of, 139, 142, 143, 149, 174, 327, 329
  in Paris, 163, 351
  on sex, 333–34
  socializing with, 105, 116, 128, 130, 131, 134, 137, 140, 151, 160, 181, 359, 363, 384, 395, 400
Scenario (Miller), 117, 117n, 136, 161
Schiff, Frances, 48, 53, 92
Schnellock, Emil, 15, 22, 62, 70, 78, 117
Seurat, Denis, 127
Siana Press, 108, 117, 139
Sokol, Thurema, 205–7, 210, 213, 216–22, 224–29, 231, 233, 237–38, 241, 295, 351, 362, 393, 412
Soler, Señor, 48
Spain, 143, 266–67, 269, 272, 277, 282, 286, 289, 305, 342, 343, 353–54, 378, 383, 395–96, 402
Spengler, Oswald, 106, 114, 171

Suares, Carlo, 390
Supervielle, Jules, 176–77, 190, 279
Svalberg, Marguerite, 242, 247

Thoma, Mrs., 195–96
Thoma, Richard, 114, 139
Thurema. *See* Sokol, Thurema
"Tommy" (Rebecca West's lover), 119, 130, 131
Transsibérien (Cendrars), 275
Tropic of Cancer (Miller), 51, 76, 116, 133, 178–80, 223, 281, 312
  Anaïs Nin's investment in, 185, 190
  Anaïs Nin's preface to, 131, 406
  reactions to, 366n
Tropic of Capricorn (Miller), 109, 193, 194, 283
Truth and Reality (Rank), 51, 62
Turner, George, 15, 20, 24, 94, 129, 222, 241, 244–47, 249, 259, 263, 278, 288, 290, 295, 326, 333, 336, 345, 353
Twain, Mark, 2, 172, 177

Villa Seurat, Nr. 18, 98, 105–6, 113–15, 118n, 125–27, 133, 136, 139, 140, 142, 145–46, 153, 154, 170, 187–89, 237, 241, 251, 263, 267–68, 336
Virgin Spain (Frank), 197
Vogue (magazine), 155
"The Voice" (Nin), 44n, 116n

"Waste of Timelessness" (Nin), 116–17n, 315n
Wells, H. G., 119
Werther's Younger Brother (Fraenkel), 97, 140
West, Rebecca, 89, 92, 126, 128, 129, 132–34, 146, 197, 213, 225
  in analysis, 131
  on Fraenkel and Miller, 136
  letters from Anaïs Nin, 121
  visits, 89, 118–19, 130–32, 293
"What Are You Going to Do About Alf?" (Miller), 146n, 149–50, 167
Williams, William Carlos, 86
The Winter of Artifice (Nin), 23n, 28n, 44n, 116n

Zadkine, Ossip, 174, 190